$30 Film School

$30 Film School

Michael Wareham Dean

Premier Press™

A Division of Premier Press

Premier

The Premier Press logo and related trade dress are trademarks of Premier Press and may not be used without written permission.

Press ™

Final Cut Pro is a registered trademark of Apple Computer, Inc.

Final Draft is a registered trademark of Final Draft, Inc.

Sound Forge is a registered trademark of Freedom Scientific®

Acid, Vegas, and Vegas DVD are registered trademarks of Sonic Foundry, Inc.®

CineStream and cleaner are registered trademarks of Discreet.™

Premiere is a registered trademark of Adobe.®

Hoodman is a product of Birns & Sawyer, Inc.

All other trademarks are the property of their respective owners.

Important: Premier Press cannot provide software support. Please contact the appropriate software manufacturer's technical support line or Web site for assistance.

Premier Press and the author have attempted throughout this book to distinguish proprietary trademarks from descriptive terms by following the capitalization style used by the manufacturer.

Information contained in this book has been obtained by Premier Press from sources believed to be reliable. However, because of the possibility of human or mechanical error by our sources, Premier Press, or others, the Publisher does not guarantee the accuracy, adequacy, or completeness of any information and is not responsible for any errors or omissions or the results obtained from use of such information. Readers should be particularly aware of the fact that the Internet is an ever-changing entity. Some facts may have changed since this book went to press.

ISBN: 1-59200-067-3

Library of Congress Catalog Card Number: 2003101204

Printed in the United States of America

03 04 05 06 07 BH 10 9 8 7 6 5 4 3 2

Premier Press, a division of Course Technology
25 Thomson Place
Boston, MA 02210

Publisher:
Stacy L. Hiquet

Senior Marketing Manager:
Martine Edwards

Marketing Manager:
Heather Hurley

Associate Marketing Manager:
Kristin Eisenzopf

Manager of Editorial Services:
Heather Talbot

Senior Acquisitions Editor:
Kevin Harreld

Project Editor:
Sandy Doell

Technical Reviewer:
Michael Prager

Retail Market Coordinator:
Sarah Dubois

Interior Layout:
William Hartman

Cover Designer:
Mike Tanamachi

CD-ROM Producer:
Brandon Penticuff

Indexer:
Sharon Shock

Proofreader:
Jenny Davidson

To my father, Jack Earnest Dean.
He taught me the value and honor of being self-employed.

Acknowledgments

Mike Kelley, London May, and Jo Moskow for spiritual handholding.

Amelia Worth. J.P. Kelly, Bink, Newt. My agent and editors who "get it"—Kimberly Valentini, Kevin Harreld, and Sandy Doell. P. Kimé Lê, Li'l Mike Martzke, Mike Nudge, Mark Garvey, Steve Weiss. Noah Harald for letting us use his camera as a prop for the Jen/Adra Lydia photo shoot. Lydia Lunch for being such a swell, smart doll. And my Uncle Rod Mason for inspiring me as a child to like photography, which later led me to filmmaking.

And especially to Tiffany Couser, my sweet Texas kitty. Having her suddenly dropped into my life is the bonus reward from the Universe for working 18 months straight full-time on art at 50 cents an hour.

MEOW!~

About the Author

Michael Wareham Dean is a scruffy little man who lives in Los Angeles' Silver Lake district.

He was the singer in the rock group *Bomb*.

His first novel, *Starving In The Company Of Beautiful Women*, was published in 2000.

Michael's first feature-length film was the critically acclaimed *D.I.Y. or DIE: How to Survive as an Independent Artist*. Of this movie, Dean says, "I wanted to interview my heroes and my unknown buddies, and put them side by side with no star system separation. Our little video is all about finding the common thread in artists who make cool stuff regardless of a paycheck." He did a self-booked North American tour with the film in 2002 and 2003.

Michael didn't go to film school. He does have some sort of certificate in Microcomputer Business Applications from *The City College of San Francisco*. He loves computers and rarely leaves his block unless it's to be flown thousands of miles away to show a film and lecture, which he does often.

He writes, directs, and produces films and occasionally acts; he writes screenplays; does Web design; graphic art; oil paints; sings; plays guitar, bass, and keyboards; produces and engineers music; programs computers; and doesn't sleep enough.

His next film will probably be an adaptation of *Starving in the Company of Beautiful Women*.

Michael has been featured in *Film Threat Magazine*, interviewed in the *San Francisco Examiner*, on radio and TV, and has been a guest lecturer at *Cal Arts College*, San Francisco's *Yerba Buena Museum* and at the *Los Angeles Museum of Contemporary Art*.

Michael likes cats and sings in a band called *Kittyfeet*.

Contents

Introduction

Tough love from the cranky little guy who wrote this book:

I can't make your movie. Please don't send me your script. I'm too busy with mine. *Do it yourself.* That's the whole point. And please do your research before you ask me a question that is already answered in this book. I don't want to be mean; it's simple logistics. As of this moment, before this book reaches the stores, I already get about 150 e-mails a day. Half are Spam. The remainder are actionable. Also, please keep this in mind if I take a while to write back, or more likely, don't write much.

And please don't send suggestions of people I should have interviewed for *D.I.Y. or DIE*. I get those all the time, and that film's done. I loved it, but I'm so over interviewing artists. My next movie is probably going to star my cat. Or maybe just objects.

Please do not add me to any mailing lists without asking.

If you want on my mailing list send an e-mail to kittyfeet69-subscribe@topica.com

Okay, now that we got the rules out of the way, here's my personal e-mail:

CatToy@30DollarFilmSchool.com

Want to send presents that are not e-mailable?

My current snail mailing address is listed on my Web site.

Books kill trees. I need trees to live. Please plant a tree after you read this book.

Filmography for Michael Dean

Every film I've made as of this writing

(1980) Made a 10-minute super 8 film in high school with one other kid named Peter Conlin. (We're still friends).

(1991) Helped make an eight-minute SVHS promo video for my band, Bomb, with Charles Cohen and Li'l Mike. (Li'l Mike is in *D.I.Y. or DIE*—he's the guy interviewed in the gas station parking lot at night.)

(2001) Made a three-minute trailer for a film I am working on, *Starving in the Company Of Beautiful Women.* (This will probably be my next feature film.) You can download it here: www.CathodeRayMission.com.

(2001) Made a five-minute film of my dad's 80th birthday as a tribute to my dad. Gave copies to everyone in the family for Christmas.

(2002) D.I.Y. or DIE: How to Survive as an Independent Artist.

(2002) Promotional reel for actress Amber Taylor (edited only—didn't shoot).

(2002) Ten shorts for Extras section on D.I.Y. or DIE: Burn This DVD.

(2002) "I Left My Pants In San Diego" (the little training film on the CD that comes with this book).

Completed Screenplays

Starving In The Company Of Beautiful Women: based on my novel. As of this writing unproduced. Trailer completed. It's all about the greatest rock star you never heard of.

Hollywood: The Last American City. Unproduced. About two kids who sneak scripts into Hollywood production companies and mess up "the system" via computer hacking. (No, it isn't based on the Sean Connery Golf Project; I wrote this script before I ever heard of that film.)

Published Novel

Starving In The Company Of Beautiful Women, 2000, Kittyfeet Press, Library of Congress Card Number: 00-108701, ISBN 0-9705392-0-7.

Published Non-Fiction

$30 Film School, 2003, Muska & Lipman

Praise for Michael W. Dean and $30 Film School

"Michael Dean is a Hollywood-hating, just-let-me-make-my-damn-movie kind of guy. For the nine-zillion hungry souls who fall into the same category, *$30 Film School* is the perfect book. The ultimate guide for the ambitious, artistic, alterna and penniless."

—Jerry Stahl

"Read this excellent book and learn how to produce profitable independent films while sticking your finger in the eyes of the devil-worshiping media conglomerates who are sucking us dry of our spiritual and economic capital."

—Lloyd Kaufman
President of Troma Entertainment
and creator of the Toxic Avenger

"In *$30 Film School*, Michael Dean and his crew give great insight on how to avoid the tired conventions of commercial filmmaking and etch the subversive onto the screen for the greater good of cinema and mankind alike."

—Joshua Leonard, Actor/Cameraman, *Blair Witch Project*

"Read this book, do it yourself, and rebel against the outrageous amounts of money Hollywood wastes to justify its lack of vision."

—Lydia Lunch

Chapter 1

Writing

You don't need big bucks to make great stuff. Computers have made it possible to make great films on very little money. They say that whatever effects the big studios have are four years away from the desktop, that is, four years away from *your* computer desktop. Big effects at low prices are here now.

But great effects aren't what make a great movie. Neither is money. There are some great Hollywood movies that wouldn't have been nearly as good on an indie (independent) budget. *The Player* and *Fight Club* come to mind. But they also had great stories. Great movies *come* from great stories. So you have to train yourself to think in terms of story. And you don't have to fall into the Hollywood three-act format, though it's not a bad place to start. It is a cliché because, like most clichés—12-Bar Blues, the 3-minute pop song, or Internet sex as a business plan—it works.

In Hollywood, scripts (screenplays) almost always contain:

- **Three acts**. 30 pages, 60 pages, 30 pages (give or take).
- **A strong hero.** We have to love him/her. Introduced in first five minutes.
- **A problem** hero is trying to solve. Introduced in first ten minutes. Without the problem, there is no story.
- **Obstacles** to solving this problem.
- Often this **quest** involves travel.
- An unsuccessful **struggle** to solve the problem.
- At the end of act one, hero is failing miserably.
- At the end of act two, hero is failing miserably and is usually in danger of dying.
- Beginning of act three: **a trial by fire** that gives the hero the strength and purity to finally solve the problem.
- A **speech** in act three that sums up story. Speech must contain **catchy phrases** that sum up the movie: "You want the truth? You can't handle the truth." "I'm out of order? This whole god damned courtroom is out of order." And so on.
- Then, after the hero solves the problem, there are a few minutes of **anti-climax** to tie up loose ends, and get you set up for a sequel.

Now that you've heard this formula, you'll never watch films the same way. They **all have it**. Well, 95 percent do. The rest have concurrent stories going on in parallel that sometimes intersect (*Pulp Fiction, Magnolia*) and often have a cyclical format; the beginning meets the end somehow.

And then there are Woody Allen movies, which are therapy sessions with funny clarinet music.

The Hollywood three-act format is old. It's in Shakespeare. It's in the *Bible*. Oral tradition that predates written language includes it. Today, it exists not only in dramas, but even in the news, documentaries, and commercials. *Especially* commercials. (I hate a lot of commercials, by the way, but some of these "little movies" are the best things on TV.)

We are so accustomed to seeing this, that even if we don't know that this format exists, a movie feels incomplete if it doesn't have it. We feel "wrong" if certain types of things do not happen at approximately the same time in a story. This is why so many people are resistant to new and interesting films: They are addicted to this contrived, boring setup/knockdown, and need it.

I have three words for most Hollywood films: *stunningly photographed crap.*

"The Formula" is even seen in mockumentaries: In *This is Spinal Tap* (one of the best and most convincing films ever made; every rock band in the world *still* quotes it all the time in the practice room) when Nigel throws his guitar and storms off stage, I almost cry, even after 20 or so viewings. When he rejoins the band two scenes later, my spirit soars and I feel absolutely uplifted (**redemption** in the third act).

Even a huge nationwide liberal ultra-PC cable network wanted this format. They turned down my film because it didn't follow the formula. They forgot the first rule of filmmaking...if the final product is compelling to watch, it doesn't matter what rules you break. Good examples of compelling movies that really have no plot and definitely don't follow this format are *Clerks* and *Timecode*. Timecode breaks some other rules, and some ground. And it's shot on DV. And when I first heard the premise of this flick, I groaned and thought "art school BS," but the end result is actually pretty undeniably amazing.

The *only* reasons I can see to learn The Formula is as a jumping off point, or to make fun of it. Sometimes cartoons do this best. *The Simpsons* do it well, though they are often parodying particular films when they do it. *South Park* does it extremely well, especially the part about speeches in the third act. (And even parodying the script convention of the third-act ticking clock by putting the words "Third Act—the Ticking Clock" on the watch that they keep looking at in *Bigger, Longer and Uncut*.)

Working with an Outline

I wrote this book without an outline. That's like swimming without a map. My original chapter titles followed the chapter titles in my movie. (Purpose, Integrity, Commerce, Self-Definition, Overcoming Adversity, and Giving Back.) Once I turned in this book, the editor said it was too random, and that the chapter headings didn't reflect what was in each chapter. He was right.

He had me go through and write a word or two next to each paragraph to describe what it was about. Then I constructed an outline based on that. Then I cut and pasted each damned paragraph into separate documents for each chapter, then moved them around and wrote transitions to make them work. Then I had to print it out and start all over.

I could have avoided this by writing a two-page outline. I've learned my lesson now. This was a bass-ackwards way to work.

I guess they tried to teach me how to write an outline in high school, when they were having me write term papers. But I said, "How's this going to help me in later life? I'm going to be a punk rocker when I grow up!"

Here's the outline I composed *after* I wrote my damn book:

Intro: I Get My Own Coffee

I. Film Crew (wearing many hats in indie)

    A. Director

    B. Assistant Director

    C. Lighting

    D. Sound

    E. Actors

II. Directing and Producing

    A. Directing

        1. Process

    2. Study Films

    3. Shooting

        a. Shots

        b. Angles

        c. Low High

        d. Framing

    4. Directing Actors

    5. Dealing with Camera People

  B. Producing

    1. Process

        a. Getting People to Do What You Want

        b. Release Forms

        c. Interns

        d. Making the Most of the Least

        e. Fundraising

III. Writing

  A. Outlines (include this one)

  B. Revision

  C. Software

  D. Standard Story Structure

    1. Avoiding Standard Structure

  E. Writer's Block

IV. Technology and Process of Indie Filmmaking

  A. Computers

    1. Mac vs. PC

    2. How Much Computer Do I Need?

    3. Software

  B. Medium

    1. DV

    2. Real Film

C. Cameras

D. Lighting

E. Sound

    1. Recording on Location

    2. Dialog Replacement

    3. Music & Soundtrack

    4. Audio Editing

F. Editing Images

    1. History

    2. Linear vs. Nonlinear

    3. Stacking, etc.

    4. How to Edit

    5. Making Mistakes Work

    6. Titles and Credits

    7. DVD Subtitles

V. Manufacturing

A. VHS Production and Replication

B. DVD Production and Replication

VI. Promotion and Touring

A. Promotion

    1. Interweb, Phone Calls, etc.

B. Touring

    1. Advancing Shows

    2. Border Crossings

    3. Doing Radio Interviews

VII. Selling Your Movie

A. Selling Copies

B. Licensing Rights

    1. Theatrical Rights

    2. Home Rights

C. Negotiation Skills

VIII. Hollywood: Ignoring the Call
  A. Bucking Trends
  B. Being Self-Sufficient
  C. D.I.Y. Is Good.
IX. Rights
  A. Copy Protection
  B. Copyright and Trademark
  C. Ratings
X. Art Karma (and Green Karma—Money)
XI. You
  A. Integrity, Spirituality, Motivation, Persistence, and Drive
  B. Dealing with Criticism
  C. Dealing with Resentments
  D. Overcoming Adversity
  E. Overcoming the Desire to Give Up
  F. The Secrets to Eternal Happiness
  G. Wrap Up
XII. Interviews with Other Filmmakers
XIII. Appendices
  A. Author Film Tour Dates
  B. What's on the CD
  C. Contact Info

So basically, what I'm saying is: Outline, good.

Your outline also more or less becomes your table of contents in a book, so you save time later on that.

Compare this to the final table of contents and note that the layout of the book went through several more drafts before becoming the actual book. My editor and I worked on a few permutations, finally settling on basically taking the above outline and moving it around to reflect three sections: Pre-Production, Production, and Post-Production.

The Argument for Three-Act Format in Screenwriting

On the other hand, here is the flipside of my "three-act-storytelling-is-overrated" slant:

I recently had a meeting with Joshua Leonard. I had approached him about possibly playing Cash Newman in my next film, *Starving in the Company of Beautiful Women*.

The meeting basically turned into him giving me a mellow, free crash course in three-act script structure and why *Starving* could use some, and how I might rewrite it so it does. (It was amazingly similar to the advice from my editor for this book. Basically, "You wrote it without an outline, so what you have to do is study it, write an outline, and reconstruct it.")

He quoted his friend, writer Arty Nelson, saying that good screenwriting is "poetry over math." And if you do it right, the math is totally hidden, but the poetry is made to work by the underlying math. I was all obsessed with the idea of a rewrite after the conversation, thinking I had to jump right into doing it now. That's how I am. Then I saw a billboard, an ad for a bank that said "GIVE CASH TIME OFF." So I will.

Here's the crux of what he told me about rewriting and three-act structure:

That characters not only have to be interesting, but we want to see them grow or change.

He said he's all in favor of Beatnik-style (read: unedited) writing in *literature*, but that filmmakers are storytellers, and a good story usually has a flow, and is rewritten with the audience in mind. Not in the sense of "appealing to everyone" (it could be a very selective audience), but that whoever is going to see it, we want to entertain them, and take them somewhere.

Several people have noted that my script for *Starving,* as it stands, is interesting in any given place, but monotonous overall. I said that was intentional to show the monotony of what it's like to be a junkie. (In retrospect, that might just be an excuse.) Joshua said there are better ways to show that without boring the audience, and cited *Requiem for a Dream,* which shows the same thing in six-second high-speed montages that come up repeatedly throughout the movie.

Funny, my friend had just told me the day before that the most important thing in art is to learn the basics before you break the rules. This is a lesson I'm just learning now, at 38.

It's like how I'm into punk rock and think it's the best thing ever to happen to music. It tore down the doors and gave life to rock music, which was dying before punk helped it out. But the best punk songs, as rough as they are, still usually follow standard pop format: three chords, three parts: Verse, chorus, verse, chorus, break, chorus. They are basically the same as an Elvis Presley song, just half as long, twice as fast, and no guitar solo.

Joshua said that to rewrite a script, some people make index cards, one for each scene in the script, and then write three things on each card. (The popular screenwriting computer program Final Draft has a utility called Scene Reports to help with this. See Chapter 7, "Computers." You can export this list and then write on 3" × 5" index cards based on the scene report):

> What the scene is
>
> What it means
>
> What it does for the story

The first part, what the scene is, would be like "Cash and Melody meet Jillian in bed," i.e., what the camera sees. The second would be, "Cash and Melody overcome loneliness for a moment," i.e., what the underlying crux of the scene would be. The third would be, "This sets up Cash and Melody knowing Jillian, to make the speed scene in the third act make sense," i.e., why this scene matters to the movie.

Then you go through the cards, and put them in order on your floor, and look at the big picture, without having to wade thought the script itself. You keep the scenes that work and advance the story, and cut the scenes that don't. It will also help with rearranging the order of the scenes you keep, which is easy to do in Final Draft with Scene Navigator. You just hold down the mouse and move scenes like tiles and they rearrange perfectly, without tedious cutting and pasting.

Johnny Cash said of songwriting, "If you can take a line of lyrics out of a song without changing the meaning, take the line out."

Joshua suggested making the 130-page script into a streamlined 100-page version and letting the camera show the rest. He suggested reading through and deleting some lines. I mostly cut and pasted it from my book, and what works in a novel is overkill in a script. In a novel, you can't see it, so it's good to be very descriptive. In a movie, a shot can show with no words what pages of a novel can't touch. He pointed out that I had several places where I say something very well, but then say it again.

Later I went out for coffee with my friend Duke (Daryl Haney), a professional screenwriter who wrote *Friday the 13th, Part 7*, and about 30 other horrible cult classics (including some Rodger Corman stuff) and says he's never used three-act structure. We go to a Denny's in Echo Park so we won't run into any other screenwriters. (I can't stand those people.) We sit chatting up a storm from midnight until 4 a.m.

He's gonna look at the script and give me a second opinion.

Today I also watched William S. Burroughs' "Commissioner of Sewers" video, in which Wild Bill speaks repeatedly of the "cutup" technique of writing as a valid form of expression…of throwing much more randomness into art. This was quite contrary to the discussion with Joshua. (But to Structure's credit, I'm much more into hearing Bill Burroughs talk than reading his books!)

So it was a well-rounded day in *$30 Film School* for me.

Storytelling

Even though three-act format is the standard place most people start, it's not the be all and end all of script writing. The rule that breaks all the rules is if something is interesting, it doesn't have to follow the formula. You should invent new formulas. Look at *Memento* and *Requiem for a Dream*. *Memento* has a story, but a very nonlinear structure that had even really smart people scratching their noodles. *Requiem* had absolutely no redemption in the third act, yet came from the Hollywood system and was both artistically beautiful and commercially successful.

Just tell your tale, keep it interesting and be willing to cut what works. Even the best writers don't produce gold in every sentence. (Just look at TV!) Be willing to cut the stuff that doesn't work. That's a very important part of writing. Again, table readings can be helpful (covered in depth in Chapter 5, "Directing"). So can letting a few friends read your script. Let them write notes in the margins. They don't have to be filmmakers, and it's probably better if they aren't. They just have to love movies and be smart. Be objective though, and try to gauge their ability to be impartial. It's common for friends to love everything you do because they aren't doing anything. They're just impressed because you're actually doing something, or they just wanna give you an "A" for effort because they love you. Conversely, some people will tell you to cut too much because they feel they aren't doing their job for you if they don't. (This is also a problem of a lot of studio executives and editors.)

Editing in the story phase cannot be emphasized enough. Writing is free. Even the cheapest digital film shoot costs something. If not money, at least the investment of other people's time. Do them a favor and work out the bugs before they show up.

Action and Dialogue

Action and dialogue make up a movie. They are the meat. Action makes us feel. It imitates life. Look how it's used in movies you like, and how it's used in ones you don't.

Dialogue should be believable, more so than action. We are used to insane situations and actions in films, but dialogue has to really fly. Read it out loud to see if it works.

Exposition is action or dialogue or voiceover that gives us information we need in order to understand the motivations of a particular character. Sometimes it's given as *back story*, a jump back in time to explain the present.

They say, "Show them, don't tell them." In other words, it's usually better to show your characters going to the graveyard than to have them say, "We went to the graveyard." This is part of the difference between a novel and a screenplay. In a screenplay (script), you show action.

You don't have to show everything. Sometimes what you don't show is more important than what you do show. Sometimes you want to skip action. Go from "Wanna go to my apartment?" to the characters in the apartment. You don't need to show them driving there, unless you want to have a chance for more dialogue. Skipping action is necessary sometimes to work a year of a character's life into an 80-minute movie.

You can skip dialogue also. A good example would be in the movie *Office Space*, when Peter asks Michael Bolton if he would still program the virus if he didn't have a good job. In the next scene, Peter and Michael are in a bar and Michael is screaming, "Those bastards are firing me!!!???" You know by logic that in between the two scenes Peter told Michael that he was getting fired. They don't have to show it and it's cooler that they didn't.

Action is indicated in the "slug line" in a script—the header before the conversation that shows what's going on, as in Figure 1.1.

Many first-time screenwriters make the mistake of writing too flowery in the "action" line, as in Figure 1.2.

This type of writing is more at place in a novel. Remember that a script is for the director to fill in with her direction. You don't want to give her the direction. Even if the director is you—make it simple. Remember that a script is a totally stripped down writing format. It has none of the extra description that a novel would have. That's to be filled in later with direction, acting, camera work, set design, and so on.

```
INT. A GRAVEYARD - DAY

MICHAEL and DEBBI walk into the graveyard. They are afraid,
and keep looking over their shoulders. A MARMOT looks at
them. We see a close up of the marmot sniffing the air as
they pass.
                        MICHAEL
              Gosh Debbi, what are we gonna do
              about the witch's curse?

                        DEBBI
              I think the wizard said that if we
              make out in the graveyard, the
              spell will be broken.

They start making out.
```

Figure 1.1 *Action indicated in a script.*

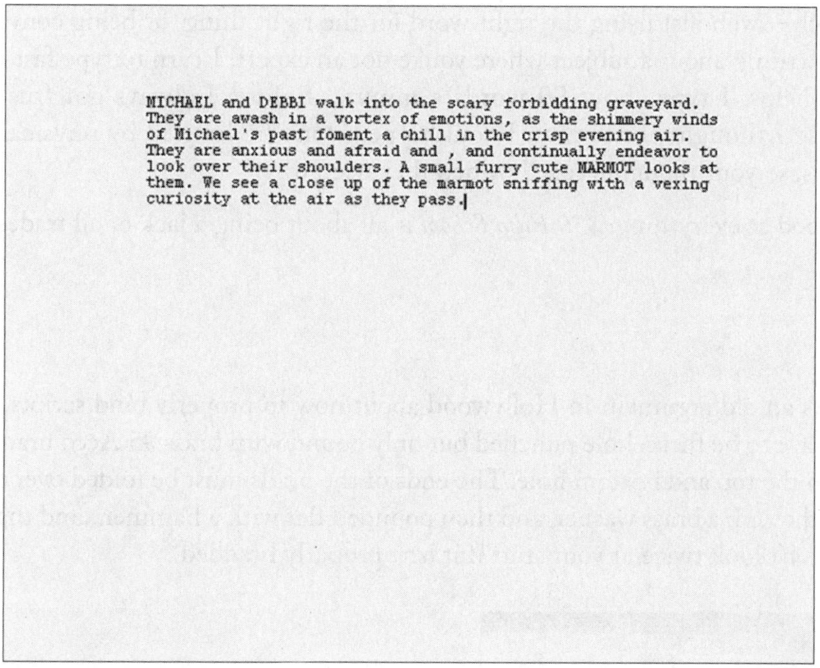

```
MICHAEL and DEBBI walk into the scary forbidding graveyard.
They are awash in a vortex of emotions, as the shimmery winds
of Michael's past foment a chill in the crisp evening air.
They are anxious and afraid and , and continually endeavor to
look over their shoulders. A small furry cute MARMOT looks at
them. We see a close up of the marmot sniffing with a vexing
curiosity at the air as they pass.
```

Figure 1.2 *Avoid a flowery script.*

Editing Your Script

Editing is the most important part of writing. The reason many writers aren't good is that they don't edit. They buy the Beatnik Lie that first drafts are pure and that revision is a sellout.

I always see folks in coffee shops writing on laptops (in San Francisco it's poetry, in New York it's novels, in Los Angeles it's screenplays), but I never see people editing. I spend more time editing than writing, and it's still an evolving process.

I usually yammer and hammer something into a rough draft, print it out, and go through it with a red pen. Then I enter all the changes into the computer file, back it up, and hammer away for a bit more on the printout with the pen, make the changes on the computer, back it up, then print it out again. I did that 10 times with my novel, and it's still a jumble, but a readable and enjoyable jumble. I only did that three times with this book, and it's much more coherent.

Learn your word processing program inside and out. Learn the keyboard short-cuts and how to do advanced searches. Same on the Internet. It's invaluable for research—even just using the right word for the right thing, or being convincing when writing about a subject where you're not an expert. Learn to type fast too. It really helps. I type about 90 words a minute. Before, I always got frustrated because I thought faster than I could type. Don't be limited by physical constraints, so your thoughts can fly when they need to.

Get good at everything. *$30 Film School* is all about being a jack of all trades.

Brads

There's an old argument in Hollywood about how to properly bind scripts...that they have to be three-hole punched but only bound with brass #5 Acco brads, and only in the top and bottom hole. The ends of the brads must be folded over on the back, through a brass washer, and then pounded flat with a hammer...and that studios won't look twice at your stuff if it isn't properly bradded.

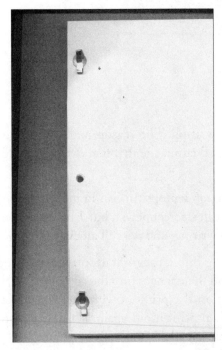

Figure 1.3 *Back of script.*

Then there is the counter argument that says "What's between the brads is more important than how you use the brads."

We $30 Film Schoolers aren't really concerned with impressing the studios. Basically, if you care too much about this stuff, you're reading the wrong book. But a properly bound script is a noble thing. It looks and feels good, and your actors and crew will thank you because it won't fall apart.

You are binding a book that has to be read and handled and folded and written in a lot. (See "I Left My Pants in San Diego," the movie on the CD-ROM for a step-by-step walkthrough of the bradding process.)

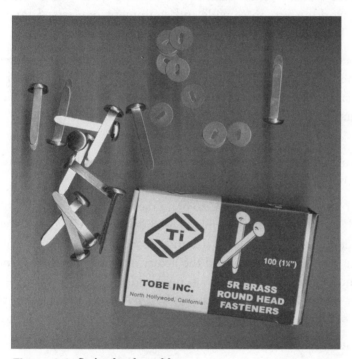

Figure 1.4 *Script brads and box.*

Writer's Block

I heard somewhere that when you find yourself unable to write, you should write letters to the editor of a magazine, or a letter to a corporation telling them what you like or don't like about a particular product. (Telling them what you like might get you free stuff...I know starving artists who get food this way. Telling them what you don't like can be a whole dada art exercise unto itself. See "Dear Mr. Mackin" in Appendix A, "Recommended Viewing, Reading, Surfing, and Listening.")

When I have writer's block, which is rare, I write funding letters, fill out funding applications, and work on promo e-mails and equipment requests. Sometimes cleaning my room helps. But I never get blocked for more than a day.

One thing some people say works is to sit down at the same table at the same time each day, with paper and a clear head. I guess the idea is "If you show up each day, and the muse doesn't make it, it's not your fault, it's hers." It doesn't work for me, and I don't like blaming God for my shortcomings, but it may be the way for some artists.

People move to Hollywood to sit in cafés and write screenplays. People go to Paris to write novels. Screw that. I can write anywhere.

I have a friend who kept going from NYC to San Francisco every year or so trying to write her novel. In 10 years, during which she didn't finish her novel, I wrote two books, two screenplays, made a movie, and recorded four albums. We $30 Film Schoolers are poor and cannot afford the luxury of going somewhere cool to write. I write at home, on the train, and on my hand. I edit in line at the post office, on the bus, at temp jobs. I carry a shoulder bag and always bring some printed out pages of whatever I'm working on and edit when I have a minute.

We aren't on this world for long—39,420,000 minutes if we're lucky. Don't waste any of them. I want to get a *lot* done before I get deleted from the org chart of life.

Deadlines

It's better to avoid cramming for the exams of life. I will say it frequently: "Slow and steady wins the race."

But sometimes life presents deadlines. Meeting them can be fun, and sort of a macho exercise in sleep deprivation, workaholism, and poisoning one's self with too much caffeine and nicotine. Unplug the phone. Exit your Internet connection. Lock your door. Finish.

I actually got a lot of writing done a few years back while temping. I got so good at the temp crap that I could do an eight-hour day in three hours. I would spend the rest of the time working on my novel. *Starving* was mostly written while wearing a tie and sitting behind desks at various law firms in San Francisco.

You just have to get really good at the Alt+Tab keyboard trick, which you do as one fluid motion to leave your work and return to their work when you hear them coming. Make sure you back up your work often to a floppy that you keep in your pocket. Temp jobs can end at any moment, especially when you do what I just told you to do.

Carpal Tunnel Syndrome

I have it. I've had it for about five years. Constant art did it: writing and playing bass mainly.

You can see me stretching my wrists from pain in *D.I.Y. or DIE* on the left side of the frame in the J Mascis interview while he's saying, "I'm all consumed by music…"

You don't want it. It burns and makes it hard to not only create, but live life. Learn about ergonomics and make sure your desk and chair are set up correctly. Use an ergonomic keyboard. Get up from the computer, stretch. (Watch what your cat does and imitate that for starters. Cats have stretching *down*.) Also check out http://www.carpal-tunnel-questions-and-answers.com/html/stretches_to_do_at_home.html.

Learn keyboard shortcuts for all the applications you frequent. (Keyboard commands are less stressful on the wrists usually than mouse clicks.) Use my program MouseCount (included on the CD-ROM) to help monitor and moderate your computer use (see Figures 1.5 and 1.6). It will tell you how many times you've clicked and how long you've been on the computer.

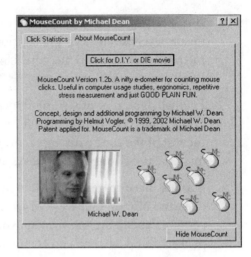

Figures 1.5 and 1.6 *Monitor and moderate your computer use with MouseCount.*

Get a massage once in a while. Get a strong vibrating massaging unit and use it on your hands, wrists, arms, and back (and other places—might help with writer's block). You really don't want to take this to the point of surgery. You don't have to. A little prevention now avoids the surgeon's knife later. Stay out of the carpal tunnel.

Summary

Writing is the first step in making this great. Without planning and writing, you don't really have a movie. Too many people get caught up in the glitz of filmmaking, and forget that filmmaking is storytelling. Make sure you have a good story.

Your actors and audience will thank you.

Chapter 2

Fundraising

This aspect of producing a film is making sure you and your crew have the money for the art supplies you need to make your art. This includes cameras, video tape, food, transportation, computers to edit on, software, tapes to make dubs, postage to send tapes out to festivals, and so on. You don't have to buy all this. You can borrow, beg, trade, Dumpster-dive, and more. Anything for art. It beats working!

There is something cool about desktop filmmaking: the idea that with limited resources, we are making something good that has the potential to be seen by a lot of people. It's huge. There's some magic to the whole thing somehow.

Movies done on 35 mm film are the second-most expensive artistic medium in the world. I can understand why studios go with scripts that pander to the Lowest Common Denominator of human emotion. I kind of feel sorry for rich people in Hollywood. They are locked in. We're not. We are lucky. I don't have a mortgage. I am totally free. I don't have to make a movie this year. Or any year.

I think I will though, but because I want to, not because I have to.

A friend who manages one of the biggest rock bands in the world told me, "Michael, the entertainment industry is just like working in a bank, but with better lighting."

D.I.Y. filmmaking on DV (digital video) is way cheaper than making films on film, but it still costs money. It's not much to shoot, but to get it looking and sounding great, and get the final product out of your bedroom and into the world, takes some money. Not much, but some. Here, you will learn how to get it.

This is the most important phase, in my mind, of getting a film out to the world. I'm going to show you how to pull money and materials out of thin air, and have people thank you for the opportunity to help out.

A car doesn't change the world for the better; it changes the air for the worse.[1] It is said that a movie can be made quite well and promoted worldwide for the price

---

1. *Ever notice how the air in Los Angeles is brown? Aside from that, L.A. would be one of the most physically beautiful regions in the country. Brown, dead air...what a fitting quality for the home of Hollywood.*

of a new car (or in the case of *$30 Film School*, a used car), and can change the world.

We will show how to do this, and more importantly, why to do this.

Ask and Ye Shall Get

First of all, ask around. Don't be afraid to ask anyone and everyone for money for your art. You aren't being greedy, especially if the art isn't all about you. A few people will get mad, but a lot will give you $20 or $100 or $1,000.

Don't expect anything though. Ever. With anything. As we know, expectations are appointments with resentments. And resentments get in the way of life. But you really can get people to help out a lot if you just ask.

Excerpt from a letter I sent to an airline trying to get tickets. (It didn't work, but it could have…)

Dear Airline:

The project has fiscal sponsorship in the form of 501(c)(3) nonprofit status from San Francisco's *Intersection for the Arts*, who have consistently sponsored select, cutting-edge projects that expand the definition of community for over 35 years. The contacts for the project at Intersection for the Arts are _____ and _____. (415) xxx-xxxx.

Given your history of helping media projects with an emphasis on community, we feel the documentary would be a good fit for funding.

Enclosed is an overview of the project. We are seeking specifically three round-trip tickets from San Francisco to New York and three round-trip tickets from San Francisco to Los Angeles at the end of this summer.

Respectfully,
Michael Dean
Project Director

If you ask nicely, sometimes local merchants will give you free stuff if you mention them in the credits of even the smallest film. If they aren't chains, I see nothing wrong (and everything right) with this kind of product placement.

Try to get local bars, stores, camera shops, and other businesses to be sponsors. Charge them $35 and put them in the credits and on the Web site and in any promo flyers. It will lend credence to your project and bring in more people too. *People help people who people help*. Getting the first one is the hardest.

Helping the local economy and letting it help you is the American way, the way it used to be when America was started. It's totally righteous, and it's the opposite of getting corporate piggy backing like the idiots do. And when you're traveling, tip the motel maid and all waiters and waitresses, even if you think you can't afford to. It will come back a hundred-fold.

NOTE

I will never do paid product placement, but I will do free endorsements for products, services, organizations, and software that works well and does what it should. There's nothing wrong with this at all. It's just passing on information to others.

Nonprofit Status

Believe it or don't, but originally my movie *D.I.Y. or DIE: How to Survive as an Independent Artist,* was going to be about me and me only. In April of 2001, I submitted a proposal and treatment (short outline) to San Francisco's *Intersection for the Arts* to get nonprofit status to help make a film of that name about me. They approved it, and I got umbrella 501(c)3 nonprofit status through them. This enabled me to seek grants from sponsors who do not give them to individuals, only to nonprofit organizations.

501(c)3 nonprofit status through fiscal sponsors is the rare case of a huge cranky bureaucracy actually doing something cool. America is not nearly as friendly to artists as many European governments, and is getting even less so. So get on it while these programs still exist.

It is possible to get this status from the IRS by yourself without having to go through (and pay a percentage to) an umbrella group. But it's a huge hassle: tons of paperwork, audits, and it takes a long time. I recommend finding local arts organizations you can go through as your fiscal sponsor (see the section later in this chapter, "Getting Fiscal Sponsorship"). It's worth that 10 to 15 percent.

So, I had this outline written for a movie just about me. My Friend, "L'il" Mike Martzke, suggested that I add a couple more people and expand the film a bit. He suggested a few likely candidates. I contacted these people, and they agreed to do it. This sort of snowballed until I had so many people that I took myself out of the equation. This was one of the smartest things I've ever done, and it happened organically. I'm very glad I did. I don't think I would have gotten the amazing out-pouring of support I did with this film if it had been about me and no one else.

One reason people really got behind *D.I.Y. or DIE* is because it wasn't about me; it was about community.

I couldn't have strategized a better plan for a first movie…though I didn't set out to. I ended up getting attention from the star power of the candidates, and also had use of their resources: They linked me on their Web sites, gave me their press contacts, and more.

Making a doc (documentary) with lots of people in it was a logistical nightmare, but it helped make a very clear case for the thesis by featuring a diverse group of viewpoints.[2] And it helped sell the thing, because most people are fans of at least one person in it. Also, everyone in it talked it up, so effectively I had many high-profile people pushing my first film.

And putting unknowns in equal light in the movie, initially not a very conscious decision, became the main selling point, and the thing that made the film unique. This had been done before in fanzines, but rarely in film. I did it with unknowns that I felt were peers with the well-knowns. The few times I'd seen it done (for instance *URG! A Music War!* and a few other films), it seemed like blank nepo-tism…like somebody's father worked for the studio; you know: "Soundtrack fea-turing The Clash, Dead Kennedys, Men Without Hats, and introducing Harry and the Houston Houserockers!"

Also, most of the places I was showing it were D.I.Y. places, so the idea of the movie instantly appealed to them. "Wow, someone made a film about what we do!" It made people want to help, and this made money come our way.

2. My next film is probably going to be about ONE PERSON. (Unless I have a support staff.)

Mission Statements

When you're going for fundraising ideas, it helps to write a mission statement. I have to write one a year to keep my nonprofit status with Intersection for the Arts. But it wouldn't have hurt to have written one before to help solidify my ideas. And they are good to show to perspective people you're asking for money from. They can also help with the thesis of a documentary, which helps you edit better.

2002 Mission Statement for Michael Dean's project:

D.I.Y. or DIE: How to Survive as an Independent Artist

Requested by *Intersection for the Arts*

These are, in no particular order, my goals for this project for the coming year:

1. To finish the film *D.I.Y. or DIE: How to Survive as an Independent Artist*. (ETA April 10, 2002, less than one year after it was begun.)

2. To promote this film. (Get it shown on TV, PBS, cable, at theaters, youth centers, high schools, universities, and film festivals; and to travel to, and personally present it, at same.)

3. To recoup costs incurred by the filmmaker in producing and promoting so far* and any incurred in the future.

4. To help *Intersection for the Arts* keep going through administrative percentage.

5. To pay the editor, who did work mostly on deferred payment.

6. To promote digital filmmaking as "the new folk music" i.e. the new medium accessible for everyone to tell his story. To do this through lecture, Internet, CD-ROM, books, articles, and DVDs. To teach others how to make a quality film on a limited budget.

7. To make the world a better place by encouraging more people to make more art.

*As of March 18, 2002, it was somewhere between $15,000 and $20,000 (I have not yet tallied up the big box of receipts) not including artist fee (that I've yet to make back) written into the original budget submitted to *Intersection for the Arts* last year. We feel that documentaries are news. They are history in the making. We are writing our own history.

Someone called our movie "the punk rock *Artist's Way.*" I liked that. Movies can change people.

The more art there is in the world, the fewer guns and bombs there are in the world. And this movie is not only art, it is art that will encourage other art. So yeah, I'm on a mission.

The way things have been going for a while now, I think that the world may be bombed back to the Paleozoic era any day now, and it's important that people see this movie. That's why I'm not discouraging people from copying it for noncommercial personal use.

Every aspect of filmmaking is all fun and it's all work. And it all makes a difference. To me, all this is part of production, and funding, and money karma, and getting things done. I look at everything as one interconnected multitask, broken into individual acts. You can become more successful at making art, producing, fundraising, and all if you train yourself to think like this. It's a synergistic act, and it's a lifelong process. I'm almost 39, and I'm still figuring it out.

I had a nail-biting time the last week of putting *D.I.Y. or DIE* together. Pulling cats out of hats and herding them…like being on the front page of the San Francisco *Examiner* but not having my rent…having to borrow as much as possible from a bunch of friends. Then my friend Kevin Wengler cosigned for me to get a credit card and said "Go nuts, make art, just pay the minimum balance and pay the rest someday."

Getting People to Work on Spec (Speculation)

Miles Montalbano did an amazing job editing *D.I.Y. or DIE.* I helped by giving guidance. (My joke is that I stood over his shoulder and yelled.) I paid him 800 bucks out of pocket with a promise of 15 percent of any profit. And I put that in writing. (It started as 10 percent, but I liked what he did so much that I grabbed a pen and his contract and gave him a virtual raise as we were working.)

I got all the camera people to work for free. I just had a cool thing that they wanted to be a part of, and I was nice to them. You can get your films made very cheap if you live like this.

But "How do you pay the rent? How do you get your movies made?" I hear you asking. Well…

◆ I work out of pocket. Every cent I make goes to art. Always has and always will.

◆ Donations from crew. I have a sort of Ed Wood philosophy: You want to be in my movie, I'm going to ask you for money. If someone says "No," I'll still have them in my film, but I feel no shame in asking the subjects, actors, and crew for money. Because we have nonprofit status, they get a tax write-off. (Unfortunately, you can't give tax write-offs for their time, only for goods and money.)

◆ Donations from strangers. When I need something, I search it on eBay, and cut and paste this e-mail to everyone selling one:

> Hi. Did you sell it yet? We are working on an arts documentary with nonprofit status and can get you a tax write-off if you want to donate it. If you want, I can send you information.
>
> Love,
> Michael Dean
> Project Director

◆ Donations from friends. I have a lot of friends with good jobs. I hit them up once a year for a donation. They get a tax write-off.

NOTE

There is no shame in asking for donations. I'm not begging for me, I'm asking on behalf of the art. Believe me, there is a difference.

◆ Licensing use of the film to television. (This comes later, after you've finished, but once you get one project, it can fund the next one. It's a cycle.) Not very much so far. $750 offered for six months nonexclusive use by a national satellite TV service. Free for cable affiliates. If anyone writes and asks to show it on their local nonprofit show, I ask them to at least purchase a copy, to offset costs of sending lots of free stuff out. If they are humble but broke, I send it to them anyway.

◆ Selling copies of the film (again, this is later, or one project funding the next). Online and in person. And I always keep a couple copies in my car.

◆ Paid showings of film in bars and microcinemas.

◆ Do anything for your art as long as you can sleep at night. If you have a mind-numbing job at a multinational conglomerate that's destroying the environment, quit. But before you do, run all your tapes going to film festivals through their postage meter.

◆ Go through Dumpsters to get props, old computer monitors, paint, anything you need. Just know what you want, target the company, be slick, and go for it.

◆ Apply for everything. Here's a sample letter to apply for an all-expense-paid artist's retreat:

Dear:

I am applying for your New Zealand Writer's Getaway because I would love to leave the hustle and screech of Los Angeles to work on my new book, *$30 Film School* (proposal attached).

$30 Film School is a how-to book on very low-budget filmmaking. There are several quality books out there on how to make independent films on little money, but this one would be different. I have yet to see one on how to make quality films on almost **no** money, and how to promote and tour with same. This will make a difference in society because it will show anyone how to tell their story without being impeded by conventional economic and cultural blockades to filmmaking.[3] This will encourage more storytelling by people who currently feel marginalized and cut out of the filmmaking process.

I have published one book, *Starving in the Company of Beautiful Women*.

---

3. Their mission statement said, "All projects must better society in a clear way."

In April of 2002, I finished a documentary called *D.I.Y. or DIE: How to Survive as an Independent Artist*. This film shows how 30 uniquely American artists operate outside of any studio system and make compelling, heartfelt statements with no funding. A main thesis of the film is showing well-known and unknown people in an equal light, based on what they say, not on who they are.

I was turned down for many other grants and film festivals, primarily because I was a novice. This is not unusual for up-and-coming auteurs. The thing of note is that I **completed my film anyway, without this help.** Similarly, I will complete *$30 Film School* whether I do it in bucolic New Zealand or smoggy Los Angeles.

I make art regardless of outside circumstances. I feel that this is, by definition, the only way to survive as an independent artist: One must be independent of relying on outside help. Otherwise, nothing would ever get done!

In the last four months, I not only completed my film, I took it on tour, amassing a compelling press kit (attached), including an interview on the front page of the *San Francisco Examiner*, and I did an interview for NPR. My film has been shown on cable TV in San Francisco, Los Angeles, Seattle, Philadelphia, and Maui. 800 copies have been sold to the public, and copies for educational use have been purchased by Drexel University, Hampshire College, and The Whitney Museum.

I am currently working on a DVD of the film, which will be called D.I.Y or DIE: Burn This DVD. It is being released without copy protection. People are encouraged to replicate it, as I feel that the message is more important than my making a big profit.

I work at home, so I can leave any time. Sooner rather than later (March of 2003) would be better, however, because I could really use a (working) vacation! Life in Los Angeles really wears me down, from the self-involved people to the poor quality of the air.

Since I am constantly driven to work regardless of external forces, there is a good chance I will have actually completed *$30 Film School* by March of 2003. In this case, I would love to go anyway, and will certainly be working on the next treatment, outline, book, or script. Or perhaps I would just use it as a much-needed sabbatical to catch up on correspondence, charge my psychic batteries, and commune with my creator in a calm setting. This is as important to my writing process as the writing itself.

I have a valid passport, and I just renewed it. I traveled extensively in Europe with a rock band in 1991: Germany, Austria, Switzerland, and France for three months. I've also been to Mexico and to Canada many times. (I recently took my film on tour to the Blinding Light Cinema in Vancouver, and spent a week up there writing.)

Carole has a copy of my documentary. She waived my entrance fee for this, via e-mail, 8/11/2002.

Thank you,
Michael Dean

◆ Be creative. I got a trip to another country partially by stapling to the application a fortune cookie fortune that said, "Your present plans are going to succeed."

◆ Ask everyone for everything (or get interns to help). Here's a letter I faxed out. It didn't work. But it could have:

Hello.

We are a nonprofit arts organization with 501(c)3 status looking for a company willing to give us billboard space as an n-kind donation in exchange for a tax write-off. Anywhere would be good, but Los Angeles would be best. An overview is attached.

◆ Putting charges on your credit cards and using other credit cards to pay off the first card. I call this Credit Card Poker or Russian Roulette. This is how a lot of independent films get made. It's not recommended, unless you have a movie that's really going to make some money. And even then….ah hell, you'll probably do it anyway

Here's a tip. If you actually have a credit card, **leave it at home**. Only take it out when you have a purchase planned. This is inconvenient, but that's the point; it keeps you from making impulse buys.

A good thing to know about credit cards is that if you need cash and have one with credit left on it but no cash advance left on it, about the only way I know of to get some cash is to order traveler's checks online. Gotta do it online and have them sent to you.

◆ Asking friends to put charges on their credit cards (recommended even less, even though I did it). It helps if you have a movie that's not just about you. Here's a letter I wrote to successfully get a friend to do this:

So, check it out...can you help with this?

_____ sent me money to *Intersection*, but it didn't get in to them in time for me to get it for this week's processing cycle. But I will have it in two weeks. I will have 300 of that to put into VHS tapes.

Can you put the whole thing and a cheap plane ticket on your card? (about 900 bucks total). I will send you 300 when I get it from *Intersection*. Also will give you most of what I make from the ATA show (I will get 200 bucks there if it sells out) and the Berkeley show (we may do two shows over there). And pay the rest within a month or two, or at least pay the minimum balance and get it all paid off quickly after that.

I'm waiting to hear back on a number of funding sources. One of them is bound to come through.

I can also give you a CRAPload of tapes, some to give away, some you can sell and keep the money from, as interest.

The 500 VHS thing is $781.18 with tax, and has to be paid like this Monday or Tuesday, before they start. You could call George at Nu-Media West, Tel:(714) *XXX-XXXX*, (Anaheim) and make the payment and set up the account.

If you can get me a plane ticket on Priceline (it will be about $120), I could come up April 11-16 (out of Burbank is best, easiest, and cheapest. And I couldn't leave before April 11, as the tapes won't be done until the 9th or 10th). I could get there and do a little promotin'. Maybe a radio interview or two.

I know this is a lot, 900 bucks total on ye olde carde, but I'm good for it, and I think people are really wanting to help this project, so I foresee some cash coming in soon.

md

He let me use his credit card. And I paid it all back within six weeks. The key to borrowing is to pay people back, even a little bit, without being asked, whenever you get some money. Keep track so they don't have to. And send them a thank-you note each time. And free art.

◆ Getting student loans but spending them on making films. Like credit cards, with better terms. Better off is starting film school, getting the loans, staying long enough to learn the basics, get more loans, and then drop out.

◆ Paying things late. Bills. Debts. Rent. It helps a lot if you have an understanding landlord. Mine is an artist and believes I'm changing the world, so it's cool. Main thing about paying people and companies late is they mind less if you tell them well ahead of time. Or better yet, *ask* them if it's okay, well ahead of time.

◆ Money from people who fancy you. I let a girl or two that I was sleeping with give me money to help me make the film. But I wish I hadn't.

◆ Sending out fundraising postcards to everyone you know. Helps if you have nonprofit status. A lot of people, not just Christians, tithe ten percent of everything they make to nonprofits. They're probably more likely to give to a *Save the Children* thing than your transgressive sexy druggy art flick, but hey…it can't hurt to try.

◆ Adding donation information to the sig-line of all outgoing e-mail (including the URL for your PayPal page).

◆ Adding the PayPal icon to your Web page. Again, you ain't begging, you're sticking up for your art. Your art is an underdog. People like it when people stick up for an underdog. How you ask determines whether it's beautiful or pathetic.

◆ I have other friends who did a traveling film fest for years. Before they finally bought a DV projector (very cheap, from a junkie filmmaker who needed money quickly for some reason), they would simply buy a big screen TV in each town on a credit card and return it for a full refund with the chain store's no-questions asked policy. Of course, they had to use different credit cards after a while…

NOTE

The Vancouver arts weekly *The Westender* wrote, "On the promotional Web page for his documentary *D.I.Y. or DIE: How to Survive as an Independent Artist*, director Mike (sic) Dean gives a plea in bold font: 'The filmmaker is over $10,000 in the hole out of his own pocket. Support the Arts: Make a tax-deductible donation.' Below the plea, a Visa credit card icon. For most movie makers, the admission of being out of pocket would amount to a public-relations nightmare. Given that *D.I.Y. or DIE* has everything to do with pursuing creative passion—money and audience demands be damned—Dean comes across as remarkably cool."

◆ Donations from businesses. I asked a lot of local small businesses to donate goods and services. One company donated a really bitchin' computer. They got a tax write-off.

NOTE

Use my queries and letters—for funding, getting gigs, asking for interns, and so forth—as examples only. Don't just cut and paste them. First of all, letters to friends have to be personal. You can write your own and then cut and paste it to different friends, but it has to come from your heart. Second, with letters to organizations, you'll be writing the same organizations I did. If you and everyone else reading this book send the exact same letter, they're gonna think you're all lazy and reject outright any that look exactly the same.

Here's a letter I wrote (from a file I have on my hard drive called Gimmie_Stuff.doc):

DOCUMENTARY SEEKING TAX-DEDUCTIBLE GOODS AND MONEY

Dear _____

We are producing a one-hour documentary on the do-it-yourself art ethic called

D.I.Y. or DIE: How to Survive as an Independent Artist.

The project has 501(c)(3) fiscally sponsored through San Francisco's *Intersection for the Arts*.

We are seeking in-kind donations of goods and services from vendors to defer the cost of producing this worthwhile exploration of community and the triumph of the human spirit over adversity.

Almost any imaginable donation useful in the filming arts (as well as supporting considerations, i.e. transportation, food, editing, lighting, duplication, equipment or studio time, rental cars, airplane tickets, etc.) would be useful. Any donation of goods or cash will be tax deductible as well as acknowledged in the credits. Cash is always welcome also and would receive the same status and thanks.

Letter of 501(c)(3) IRS determination available upon request.

Thank you.
MICHAEL W. DEAN
Project Director
415-_____
md@_____

Here's a letter I sent to an artist's emergency fund in New York City. (It's on my hard drive as "Begging.doc.")

Hello...I would like to apply for a one-time grant of $755. $555 to pay my rent, and $200 for my overdue phone and electric bill.

I am currently finishing editing on a documentary on independent artists called *D.I.Y. or DIE: How to Survive as an Independent Artist*. The project has 501(c)3 status through San Francisco's *Intersection for the Arts*. I basically spent all my money making the film.

It is showing in NYC at The Knitting Factory, 74 Leonard Street, New York, NY 10013 (AlterKnit Theater) Sunday, May 19th, two shows: 7 P.M. and 9 P.M.

Attached is info and letter from fiscal sponsor.

Thank you for your consideration,
Michael Dean

They turned me down and said, "You shouldn't have spent ALL your money." I say screw them. I had to spend *all* my money. It's in my blood to do that. And it all worked out okay in the end.

Again, don't forget to thank people. And if carefully timed and worded, a thank you can actually be a follow up to a pledge, to enumerate the specifics of what you need.

Here's a follow-up letter I wrote to a woman who donated the fast (for the time…2001) computer that I used for everything from inputting and pre-editing the footage, to editing this book.

I really appreciate your offer to donate a computer to edit our documentary. You will receive a tax deduction for the retail price, as well as you folks getting mention in the credits of the documentary.

Our fiscal sponsor, *Intersection for the Arts*, will fax you our 501(c)(3) IRS determination letter today.

Since we will be editing a feature-length film on it, the computer will have to be fast. Here is the minimum criteria my editor says we would require:

Pentium IV or equivalent	700 megs RAM
1 Ghz processor	Must have FireWire to input video
80 gig hard drive	DSL network card
DVD player	Dial-up modem
CD burner	21" monitor
Fast CD reader	Good speakers

Let us know and we will come pick it up.

Respectfully,
Michael Dean
415-_____
Project director

Here's a posting (Give_us_money.doc) I cut and pasted to post on several film Web boards. Also, a more personal sounding variation was snail mailed to several friends and acquaintances. Much of it was cut and pasted directly from our original fiscal sponsorship query. That is another reason it's important to write those well—you end up using the information over and over.

Completed documentary with 501(c)3 status needs help with distribution money.

Broke production with great film, drowning in debt. Unable to get steady outside work since 9/11. If you're doing O.K. this month, please help us out with a tax-deductible donation.

D.I.Y. OR DIE: How to Survive as an Independent Artist

An arts documentary by Michael W. Dean

Project has 501(c)3 status through San Francisco's _Intersection for the Arts._

OVERVIEW:

A 60-minute film on the methods and motivations of independent American artists in different genres and mediums[4]

A celebration of the Underdog. The film profiles a fascinating group of icons and unknowns working in various media including print, film, graphic art, performance art, and music. The three-dozen interviewees are mavericks who operate outside of any "studio system," are beholden to no one, and produce influential, quality art regardless of a continuous paycheck.

A main difference between this and other arts documentaries is that the people included are given face time based on what they say rather than who they are: The unknowns are given equal weight with the famous interviewees.

Thank you,
Michael W. Dean
Project director

---

4. _This was an estimate. The film actually went through several permutations in the timeline, including a snore-inducing 75-minute version. We finally decided the film wanted to be 55 minutes...it seemed to get its point across at that length without boring._

- Donations from foundations. They get a tax write-off.

- When asking for money, it's always helpful to say "us" and "we" and "our" rather than "me" and "I" and "my"…movie, project, and so forth. People are more into promoting community than supporting individuals. Don't do it if you are absolutely working alone. But chances are someone is helping you in some way, so it's honest. (It goes without saying, but brush your teeth and wear deodorant when you go to talk with normal people to ask them for money in person.)

- It is good to put something in a grant request that implies you are not dependent on this one source. People who donate money are wary of getting people dependent on them, as this can lead to resentments. I wrote this paragraph for my friend Tiffany to use, concluding her letter requesting a residency for a dance performance:

> My artistic drive is such that this performance and the associated workshops will happen in some capacity, at some time, no matter what. But help from _____ would make sure it happens right, and would help bring in people who might benefit from it and enjoy it the most.
>
> I would be honored if our piece is chosen for residency.

- Also, people don't want to be your *only* source of money. Once one funding source is secured, others are more likely to fall into place. It is to your advantage to mention, not hide, secured offers to other potential contributors.

Getting Fiscal Sponsorship

It's hard to get 501(c)3 nonprofit status from the IRS. It is not as hard, however, to get umbrella status through a *fiscal sponsor*. This means that they grant you the use of their nonprofit status to seek donations. The donations are paid directly to them and they take between 10 and 20 percent for administrative fees. They have to then demand receipts from you and quarterly reports and yearly mission statements to make sure you're really spending the money on the project.

Our fiscal sponsor takes 10 percent. It's best to not go with ones that charge 20 percent, for two reasons. One is that it's obviously more money. The other is that a lower fee means you are with a sponsor that actually cares about your art. Some sponsors just rubber stamp these things to have a cash flow. Also make sure that you get a sponsor who does not insist in their contract on owning the final project. Some do. Ours doesn't.

On the following page is the original query and budget written for *D.I.Y. or DIE* film when seeking fiscal sponsorship. This is pretty much the one I wrote to get fiscal sponsorship. We got it easily. (The footnotes are my comments and were not in the original document).

The original one obviously didn't have the "501(c)(3) fiscally sponsored through *Intersection for the Arts*" heading and such. Once we got it approved, I added the text about having fiscal sponsorship, and submitted it to foundations. Out of 300 foundations queried (names culled from The Foundation Center: www.foundationcenter.org), we got one donation of $2,500.

Writing these things is also very useful to hone your mission statement and plans. Writing one not only helps you to be able to describe your project easily (and "pitch" it to people), but actually helps you formulate and hone your vision in order to execute the art. In the end, it was done for waaaay less than this. More like $5,000 or $10,000 rather than $158,836.

Always ask for the most you need, not the least. People are afraid to ask for too much, and often get turned down because the donor can tell they don't know what it will cost to do it in the "real" world. Ask high, not low. You'll be taken seriously. Also, if you are a nonprofit, you can eventually get all this paid back before you have to give up your nonprofit status.

501(c)(3) fiscally sponsored through
Intersection for the Arts:

Grant Request for

D.I.Y. OR DIE:

HOW TO SURVIVE AS AN INDEPENDENT ARTIST

An arts documentary by MICHAEL W. DEAN

OVERVIEW:

A 60-minute film on the motivations and modes
of
independent American artists in different genres and mediums

MICHAEL DEAN
___ Bush Street,
San Francisco, CA 94104
Email.: ___@___.com

We are seeking $153,836 in funding (cash and/or goods and/or services) for the production and distribution of a documentary *D.I.Y. or DIE: How to Survive as an Independent Artist*, on the subject of the D.I.Y. (Do-It-Yourself) movement in art production and distribution.

INTRODUCTION/BACKGROUND

San Francisco multimedia artist Michael Dean and director of photography Peter Spicer are producing a documentary on artists who exemplify and embody the D.I.Y. ethic. The film will profile a unique group of icons and unknowns working in various media including print, film, graphic art, performance art, and music. The two-dozen interviewees are mavericks who operate outside of any "studio system," are beholden to none, and produce influential, quality art regardless of a continuous paycheck. Unlikely to sit around waiting for their next assignment, these are American artists who are uniquely compelled to create and share their vision. Several of our subjects have found an enthusiastic audience and even financial success despite overwhelming odds and marketplace indifference.

Most of these people are able to make a somewhat comfortable wage at their art. Some are just scraping by. A couple are millionaires. A few have been major influences on modern culture. However, they all have a common denominator: The need to make art is their biggest reason to get up each morning. They all feel driven to express the complexities of how they relate to the world, and to do so in a useful form for other people. The documentary will examine the personal as well as the economic forces compelling them.

We will learn why some turn down a huge record contract to maintain the artistic control of running their own small label for far less money. We will learn how others manage to survive on $100 a week and live to create powerful portrayals that move people and have the ability to change lives and unite communities.

In short, we will be asking all of these virtuosos, *"What's it like to be you?"*

We will also touch on the importance of the digital revolution, which has aided independent artists by taking the means of production and dissemination out of the hands of a select few corporations and bringing it within the reach of anyone with a job.

Another point of view to be covered is the lone wolf aspect of operating as an indie artist: living alone with the struggles of the job, and conversely, having no one to share in the triumphs.

PROJECT DESCRIPTION

The project has fiscal sponsorship in the form of 501(c)(3) nonprofit status from San Francisco's *Intersection for the Arts*, who have consistently sponsored select, cutting-edge projects that expand the definition of community for over 35 years. The contacts for the project are:

> Deborah Cullinan or Rebecca Koppelman
> Intersection for the Arts
> 446 Valencia Street
> San Francisco, CA 94103
> (415)-626-xxxx

Michael Dean has long been inspired by independent artists in every genre and medium. While producing his own multidisciplinary art in the form of writing, music, and filmmaking, he has been inspired by many of these same people. He has planned for years to create a documentary that could capture the essence and spirit of his many influences and contemporaries.

The mixture of covered mediums, genres, and artist lifestyles will be woven together by narration and Q&A segments featuring Dean's disarming interview style (honed as a fanzine writer and college radio DJ).

The wide choice of subjects runs the range of filmmakers, writers, musicians, Web designers, dancers, publishers, cartoonists, and more. Also interviewed are a few people responsible for administering fiscal sponsorship, and one catalyst who helps match artists and resources to facilitate other peoples' art. (This is an important facet often overlooked in presentations of the art process.)

The list of interviewees includes men and women; several gay artists, lesbians, and people of color. This will bring a cross-section of the vibrant independent arts scene to many people who would not experience this world otherwise.

Through a juxtaposition of mediums and genres we will show independent art as a whole, and encapsulate it in a bold and unique one-hour presentation.

The following people have agreed to be interviewed:[5]

Beth Lisick (performer/poet)

Cintra Wilson (social essayist)

ck0 (open-source computer programmer)

Craig Newmark (founder *Craig's List*)

Curtis White (author/first amendment congressional cross-examinee)

Cynthia Connolly (Photographer/ *Dischord Records*)

Dana Schechter (graphic artist/musician *Bee and Flower)*

Danny Plotnick (filmmaker)

Dave Brockie (singer in *Gwar*/filmmaker/novelist)

Debra DeSalvo (musician/writer)

Denise DeLaCerda (tattoo artist)

Doug Wolens (documentary filmmaker *Butterfly)*

Eric McFadden (songwriter/singer/entertainer)

Ian MacKaye (/musician-*Fugazi*/label owner-Dischord Records)

Indra Lowenstein (*Choreographer)*

5. *Some of the people proposed ended not being filmed, or not being used after being filmed, for various reasons.*

Intersection for the Arts and *Film Arts Foundation* staffers

J Mascis (musician *Dinosaur jr.*)

Jenny Toomey (musician/indie label owner/Internet activist)

Jim Rose (Pageant of the Transmundane director/*Jim Rose Sideshow*)

Jim Thirlwell (musician *Foetus*)

Keith Knight (cartoonist *Fear of a Black Marker*)

Killian MacGeraghty (singer *Gun and Doll Show*)

Liza Matlack (dancer)

Lydia Lunch (singer/writer)

Lynn Breedlove (singer in *Tribe 8*/activist)

Madigan Shive (cellist/*Bonfire Madigan*)

Maggie McEleney (painter/graphic artist)

Maggot and Nikki (zine editors/*Bacchanalia*)

Matt and Mark Enger (painters and installation artists)

Mike Watt (musician *Black Gang/Firehose/Minutemen*)

Mr. X (painter sponsored by The Healing of the Nations)[6]

Noah Herald (filmmaker *Life Ends Merge Left*)

Pamela Z (electronic composer)

Richard Kern (filmmaker/photographer)

Ron Ashton (musician *The Stooges*)

Simon Clifton (painter/actor/musician)

Stephen Elliott (writer/activist)

Storm Large (chanteuse)

Suki (actor)

Vale (writer/publisher *ReSearch Magazine*)

Our basic criteria, with few exceptions, is that all subjects

1. Make a living at art

6. *A painter who grows pot for a living. I was gonna interview him with a hood on in his basement full of pot. He later blew it by going insane and posting slanderous things about me on the Internet for no reason. Needless to say, he is not in the film.*

2. Influence many people in their respective medium

3. Do something very unique

4. Impress the heck out of us

HISTORY AND IMPORTANCE OF TITLE

The first half of the documentary's title, *D.I.Y. or DIE* is an old battle cry of the early punk rock movement, circa 1977. It was a response against the prevailing belief that the way to be accepted as an artist was through conventional channels: schooling, nepotism, and being one of the lucky few to gain distribution through established corporate media outlets.

Many inspired youngsters began working *around* the "culture industry" to create new channels of creative dissemination. They put on their own concerts, made their own films and videos, started tiny but influential record labels out of their basements and used their bedrooms to do the paste-up for hand-Xeroxed "fanzines" to review and promote each other.

The world sat up and took notice, and a movement was spawned. The D.I.Y. *I-Think-I-Can* ethic exists today, driving everything from garage rock bands to the largest software companies in the world.

Unfortunately, in many cities, the dot-com invasion has raised rents exponentially and forced many of our beloved artists out of affordable live/work spaces. Because of this, and decreases in private, corporate, and federal funding, artists have, more than ever, had to take production and distribution into their own hands. The documentary will cover these facets of the struggle as artists attempt to survive, create and form communities against a backdrop of adversity.[7]

The intended locations for shooting are: San Francisco, Oakland, New York, Los Angeles, and Denver.[8] The crew will travel to these cities and interview the artists in their own studios and neighborhoods.

7. *Little Mike helped with some of the wording of these three paragraphs.*

8. *There was a girl there that I liked. She got a boyfriend, so I didn't end up shooting in Denver. Who says all motives in my art are pure?*

BRIEF TREATMENT

Stylistically, we are taking a different approach than many other documentaries: We do not consider it a violation of the "purity" of the process to actually use good production values. We do makeup, some set design, good lighting, and high quality synch sound. We feel that the best looking footage will augment, not detract from, the impact of the subjects' words.

We are interviewing people in their own settings: their homes, studios, kitchens. And in many cases, we bring our young interns literally "to the table" to provide more dynamic and natural feedback, and avoid the "one-static-shot-on-a-talking-head" aspect that weighs down so many promising projects.

AUDIENCE AND DISTRIBUTION STRATEGY

The intended target audience is a wide swath of the population, similar to that of public television: mainly those who wish to be culturally informed and are curious about the workings of the mind of the artist. The selected subjects however, will undoubtedly also attract a hip, urbane Gen-X/Y contingent.

This film will attempt to get inside the heads of several artists, and present their life in a format that will be compelling and accessible to all. It is the filmmakers' wish to create a viable document that will appeal to the common human theme of inquiry.

> "It's all about art. All artists just wanna reach beyond the mundane and scratch into something real. Whether you're painting the ceiling of the chapel or banging out three shaky chords in the garage, you are declaring your intentions to smear your fingerprints on the veil of the infinite."
>
> —Cash Newmann (musician)[9]

This film will explore that sentiment and the modern manifestation of its thread that runs throughout all cultures and throughout the ages.

FUNDRAISING PLAN

Money is being sought primarily through queries of corporate foundations and funds (public and private) that have financed fiscally sponsored documentaries in the past.

---

9. *A fictitious character in my novel. Quoted him anyway. I know I used this again in this book, but it works, damn it. And it's* **my** *book. Write your own if you don't like it!*

Also through contributions of friends and family, and in-kind donations of goods and services of local and national companies.[10]

The *Foundation Center* has been most helpful in the research of available funds.

The intent is to attempt to make a return on the cost via licensing for broadcast, festival inclusion, and ticket sales.

We will partner with an indie label to produce a soundtrack album/CD-ROM (music and spoken word), which will aid in promotion and help us garner attention for the project via college radio, etc.

Once completed the film will be circulated via independent film and video festivals with the producers leaving open prospects for DVD, VHS, cable and Internet Distribution.

PROJECT STATUS AND COMPLETION TIMELINE:

Timeline to complete: 9-12 months after funding.

The project is currently in the early stages. The thesis has been formulated, all the interviewees have been contacted and confirmed; and resources, locations, and personnel have been reserved. Several interviews have already been conducted. More funding will allow the work to continue.

BREAKDOWN:

Filming: 3-5 months (depending on scheduling conflicts of subjects)

Synching, editing, post-production: 3-5 months

Beginning of promotion: 2 months

PROJECT BUDGET

The budget of $158,836 is enumerated below. We feel it is an adequate summary of needed monies, and is a realistic estimation for a broadcast-quality production. Many documentaries are conservative in their estimate of costs and require completion donations or bond sales in the final stages of production. We are planning ahead in an attempt to avoid this.

10. *It's important to make it clear to potential funders that the full burden will not fall upon them, and you plan to try to get money from other people too. This will make them more likely to donate.*

The documentary will be shot on high resolution Mini-DV (with a few shorter segments shot on 16 mm film). This will allow for a higher shooting ratio, while maintaining quality. Our budget of $158,836 breaks down as:

◆ $138,836 for production of the documentary (including stock; transportation; rental of lighting and sound gear; hotel; feeding interviewees—who are working for free; editing; and misc.).

◆ $20,000 for promotion (printing posters, purchasing magazine ads and radio time, dubbing tapes and mailing to festivals, festival entrance fees, and traveling to festivals).

◆ $2,500 has already been spent by the filmmakers from in-kind pre-production.

◆ $5,000 in cash has been raised.

◆ $6,000 in in-kind donations of equipment and services have been received.

We are seeking grants for any part of the remaining $153,836.

Description	Total
CREW	
MICHAEL DEAN, director/producer	26,000 *
D.P.	5,000
SOUNDMAN,	1,500
ASSISTANT CAMERA	1,500
MAKEUP	1,000
RESEARCH	1,300
PRE-PRODUCTION EXPENSES	5,000
PROPERTIES	500
SUBTOTAL	**41,800**
PRODUCTION	
CAMERA PURCHASE, Canon XL-1	3,500
COMPUTER PURCHASE, Sony Vaio	3,000
COMPUTER SPEAKERS	400
FLUID HEAD TRIPOD	500
ANALOG VIDEO CAMERA	500

Description	Total
DIGITAL EDITING	8,000
POST-PRODUCTION	2,000
MEMBERSHIPS	125
SOUND PAC RENTALS	2,000
VIDEO AND FILM STOCK, AND PROCESSING	3,400
16MM TRANSFER	1,000
SONG CLEARANCE	2,000
PROJECTION COPIES	5,000
SUPPLIES	1,200
SLATE AND OTHER COSTS	400
ADR	750
STOCK SHOTS	400
TITLES (MAIN & END)	750
INSURANCE ON CAMERA	400
CITY FILMING FEE	100
VIDEO TAPE DUPLICATION	4,000
SUBTOTAL	**39,425**
LOGISTICS	
PARKING	500
HOTEL	1,800
FEEDING TALENT AND CREW	3,000
CAR RENTAL	500
FOUR PLANE TICKETS TO NYC AND L.A.	4,000
AIRPORT PICKUPS	480
SUBTOTAL	**10,280**
ADMINISTRATIVE EXPENSES	
ISP, DOMAIN AND WEB DESIGN:	1,200
POSTAGE, FEDEX & STATIONARY	1,000
XEROX	300
LEGAL EXPENSE & FEES	5,000

Description	Total
TRADEMARK	325
TELEPHONE	1,000
SUBTOTAL	**8,825**
PROMOTION	
PUBLICITY	8,000
FESTIVAL ENTRANCE FEES	2,000
TRAVEL TO FESTIVALS	2000
RADIO ADS	2,000
PRINT ADS	5,000
PRINTING POSTERS	1,000
SUBTOTAL	**20,000**
PROJECT SUBTOTAL	120,330
FRINGES 20%	24,066
PROJECT SUBTOTAL WITH FRINGES	144,396
10% INTER. FOR ARTS ADMIN FEE	14,440
TOTAL WITH ALLOWANCES	**$158,836**

*As of this writing, I have not paid myself this yet. No money to do so.

KEY PERSONNEL

Michael W. Dean's writing and directing experience includes *Still Rockin' in the Free World*, a promotional film produced for Warner Brothers.

His first novel, *Starving in the Company of Beautiful Women*, was recently published by Kittyfeet Press (ISBN 0-9705392-0-7, Library of Congress number: 00-108701).

Dean has produced a screenplay based on the book and is in the process of concurrently producing an independent feature-length film, also with Peter Spicer.

Dean has worked for 20 years independently producing art (films, videos, music, and books), and spent two years as a singer on a major label. He has experiences from both sides of the independent fence, and understands the advantages and disadvantages of both approaches.

Dean graduated from *San Francisco City College* and has been invited back as a frequent guest lecturer on media technologies and their place in commerce and art.

He is a member of *Film Arts Foundation*.

"Michael W. Dean is a talented and dedicated artist with a steadfast work ethic. I'm sure that he will be enjoyed for years to come."—*Author (2.13.61 Press) Don Bajema*

——————————

Director of photography, Peter Spicer, studied film at *The Academy of Art College* of San Francisco, and worked for eight years as a television production director in Oregon. He has produced many short films, as well as the feature *The New Chase*.

——————————

Trailer editor Jeff Gottlieb[11] worked on many independent features, as well as corporate presentations for *Atlantic Records*, *McGraw/Hill Publishing*, *New Line Cinema*, *Panasonic*, and on commercial films, including *Freddy's Dead: The Final Nightmare*.

Actual Budget for D.I.Y. or DIE

So there's the query and the proposed budget. Here's a quickie breakdown of the actual costs. I had no idea what they would be when I made the first budget, as I'd never made a movie. I got help from film students writing the above budget, and I am told it is within the range of reality.

The actual budget is hard to really pin down, as I haven't added it all up yet. I have a garbage bag full of receipts in my room. Also compounding things is the fact that I haven't separated the production receipts from the promotion receipts.

But here's a ballpark breakdown of costs:

Fifty 60-minute DV tapes: $250

Travel and expenses to NYC and D.C.: $750 (Just me. No crew. Stayed with friends. No rental car.)

Paid out of my pocket in cash to Miles up front for editing: $750

11. *I hadn't found Miles yet, who did the actual editing on the movie proper. And I did the editing for the extras on the DVD. I also did the page layout and design of the DVD cover.*

Seven trips flying from Los Angeles to San Francisco to edit with Miles, 5 X 500= $2,500

(I paid for five of the trips…a woman I was sleeping with paid for two. I stayed with her and other friends. No rental car. All travel includes meals, taxi, bus, subway, etc. I travel very cheap.)

Trip to Utah to show rough cut at Lost Film Fest @ Sundance (I consider this a production cost rather than a promotion cost, as we took notes and made final editing changes based on suggestions. Stayed in hotel. Got rental car.)= $1,000

Misc. (FedEx, test copies, shipping, etc.)= $800

Total production budget: $6,050

I would guess that the promotion budget was about $14,000. (Just based on output for tapes, mailing, driving, phone, Internet, etc.)

So, production + promotion total= $20,050.

As of this writing, I've taken in about $15,000, which leaves my loss at about $5,000. Coupled with the fact that a lot of people have seen the film, I would say that means that this is a very successful independent film![12]

I have a new thing to say to people I like in the independent art world. When they're off to make a film or act or play a gig, I don't say "Break a leg!" (or even the music-specific one I made up: "Break a string"). I say "Break even!"

So...

Put all your money back into your art no matter how much you make. Save a little to treat yourself or your loved ones, but it's all about art. Fight for art against adversity like you'd fight for your little sister if she were picked on by bullies.

And if you live simply, you can live well and be happy on less. I never buy expensive clothes. Most people who do are posers who aren't committed to art. They're into the image, not the work. You should always work as if the money is coming. I did the authoring for my DVD without thinking that I would ever have money to

---

12. As this goes to press, six months after this was written, I have started to make a tiny profit on the movie.

have a bunch pressed. As I was working on it, I got the advance for this book. I wrote my proposal for this book and my agent pitched it. I got an offer from the publisher that included a two-month deadline. I finished my book before the publisher even saw it.

Be into free trade, but don't be a capitalist piggy. If you take the lion's share, you're depriving someone else. I ain't a communist, but some people are just too rich and others too poor. I like to even the score of the universe a little by living larger on less, and creating more. Do it yourself or your art will die. Do it yourself because no one's going to do it for you.

$30

Chapter 3

Producing

Producing is basically pulling rabbits out of hats and getting people to do your bidding. The producing section is longer than the directing section because, in my mind, getting everything done is actually more important than the role of the director. I think that in Hollywood, the role of the director is overplayed. It isn't rocket science. But making everything come together and function smoothly is.

"Producer" is a job title in film that can mean anything. It can be the secretary that the director is dating that he wants to help out. (That's usually "associate producer.") It can be the person handling day-to-day logistics on the set—procuring the special effects people, dealing with deliveries, finding mandolin strings, making sure catering shows up, and delegating duties to underlings (this is the "line producer"). It can be the silent investor who puts money into the project (executive producer). Or it can be the rich person or company that finds the story and matches it with a director and star (just plain Producer with a capital P). That guy is the most powerful, and is basically a banker making an investment. On that level, it ain't art, baby, it's business.

On a small level, a *$30 Film School* level, you may need a producer, which in your case will probably mean a line producer—the person to get the day-to-day stuff done so you, the director, can concentrate on making art. On a small film, the director (and sometimes the actors and camerapeople) ends up helping with production also.

I did almost all of it myself for *D.I.Y. or DIE*. I was the producer as well as the director on that project. And it exhausted me. But no one who would do it as well as I would wanted to help, so I did it myself.

RULE NUMBER ONE: Make something cool that people want to get involved with.

My friend, Newt, got excited when I was finishing up *D.I.Y. or DIE*. He went out and bought a one-chip Mini-DV camera for 700 bucks. I spent a few minutes showing him how to use it and how to do sound. I spent an hour teaching him to edit, and then copied a program for him and helped him set up his computer to edit. It was less than four hours on my part. A month later, he had 20 people involved in helping him make a great movie called *PropStars L.A.*, about theatrical rock bands in Los Angeles. Five months later, the finished film debuted to a receptive audience at the Silver Lake Film Festival. Newt was smart: He made a film that wasn't about him (even though his band, Insecto, was one of the bands in it).

Free Help

On *D.I.Y. or DIE*, I had film students with several more years experience than me working for free on the project, because I had a good idea. Film schools are full of people who have the technical part down, but don't really know what to point their camera at. Make friends with them.

Find interns who want to learn with you and treat them well. Call them helpers or assistants, not interns. That's less of an "I'm better than you" thing. (Doesn't "intern" sound like "internment"—the word for holding someone prisoner?) Make it a gang. A family. Thank them several times a day and mean it. Help them out. Call them up when you have tickets to a show. Buy them lunch. First rule of D.I.Y. filmmaking is: **If you can't pay people, at least feed them.** And buy them beer if they like that sort of thing. (At the end of the shoot, not the beginning!)

And get their addresses and send them a copy of the finished film, without them asking.

And don't try to sleep with your interns. You need reliable help way more than you need to get laid.

Don't be sleazy with people.

I end up *not* having interns, mainly because most people who reply to my ads are looking for an "in" to Hollywood. They want to bring coffee to the guy who brings coffee to the guy who brings coffee to the guy who brings coffee to Steven Spielberg.

I'm not the guy to get them that job. Plus, they are often not as motivated as they claim to be, and I end up spending more time trying to get them to do stuff when I could just *do it myself*. I would need an intern whose only job was to herd all the other interns. Seriously. But you may have better luck than me, especially if you don't live in Hollywood.

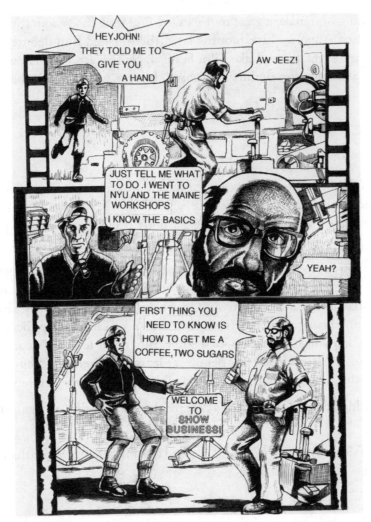

Figure 3.1 *Cartoon by Theo Pingarelli.*

Managing artists is like herding cats. I ride people hard. I think people working for free should work as hard and as quickly as people working for pay. Otherwise, I don't have time for them. This is why I end up doing almost everything myself.

(Important note…on the "extras" part of the D.I.Y. DVD, where I'm interviewed on TV and bitching about flaky interns, I am *not* bitching about the people who actually helped make the film. I am bitching about people who offered to help, didn't, and were more trouble than if they'd never contacted me.)

I end up disappointed and resentful often when I let people help, because no one is as committed to my projects as me. For instance, a guy answered my intern ad and wanted to make a cover for the VHS tapes of my film (I'd released the first thousand copies of D.I.Y. in paper sleeves with no cover). I thought this was a good idea and he came up with a cool cover design, with my text. He said he could even save me money by printing them free at work and sending the completed covers to the duplication place.

Well, it turned out that I made a dozen phone calls to him, and many e-mails and he still flaked. In the end, my tape sat at the presser, waiting for him, delaying me fulfilling orders. People had sent me their money in good faith and I kept them hanging because I trusted a flaky stranger. He ended up costing me $65, because I had to go to Kinko's to print the cover and then Priority Mail it on a Saturday. I could have gotten it done for free two months earlier if he'd simply said, "I'll never get this done and I will piss you off and cost you lots of money with my well-meaning flakiness. You should just go somewhere else right now."

Good free help is hard to find. Basically, I could have designed a good cover myself in far less time without stressing, but I was doing him a favor by trying to let him help. I wish people like this would save me time and money by saying, "I don't take myself seriously enough to keep my word."

D.I.Y. is not a badge of honor; it's survival. I've spent *way* more time waiting for and teaching some interns than they've ever saved me. From now on if someone wants to help, they're gonna have to wait outside my house for three days without food or encouragement before I'll even consider it. *Fight Club* used this motif; the writer got the idea from monasteries. This is how they used to test prospective Buddhist monks.

Keep in mind that the cool thing about filmmaking is that everyone (including you) is replaceable. In a good way, but also in a dangerous way. The reason there are so many reality TV shows now is that a few years back, the TV writers threatened to strike for better terms. The producers basically said, "We don't need you."[1] Reality shows don't require much writing, and the cameraman is the director.

In fact, a friend of mine is working as a casting assistant on a new reality show where people are going to be put to grueling tests and have to go days without

---

1. *It's kind of the realization of that sarcastic line in* The Player *about getting rid of those darned writers, directors, and actors.*

sleep. They will experience physical stress that may actually come close to killing them. Like my friend Michael Woody predicted 10 years ago about people's desperation to be before the camera: "TV is becoming closer and closer to Rollerball." I didn't believe it at the time, but he was right.

The fact that you are replaceable is also a no-stars thing. It's another reason that DV-filmmaking is the new folk music, the new punk rock, the new medium accessible to everyone to help tell their own story. It's the song, not the singer. And it's cooler than being in a garage band because it's more powerful, easier, and you aren't stuck with the same three losers forever. You get to work with different losers!

But don't treat people expendably. Love them. And if you make any money, **share it!**

A lot of wanna-be helpers are just people-pleasers who will string you along. Again, I'd rather you tell me "no," than say "sure" and then not follow through and leave me hanging when I could have done it myself or gotten someone else to get it done right. I've missed a lot of deadlines over this.

(Another reason I work alone is that I talk to myself out loud while I work, which kinda freaks some people out.)

People working for free should be reliable. There is a saying, you can get two out of three of these things: Fast/cheap/good. Fast and cheap. Fast and good. Cheap and good. Any two, but not all three. This is one reason I don't usually work with interns. I, and I alone, have the dedication to do everything fast AND cheap AND good.

There's that old cliché, "Waste is a thief." I wholeheartedly concur. I have a "two strikes" rule with people being late or flaky without calling ("Hi, this is Bill, and I'm gonna be a little flaky today...."). I'm too busy and life's too short and someone being late is really bad. It shows they seriously don't respect you.

Traffic is bad everywhere, but especially in L.A. I always try to leave early, arrive early, and wait for the person. It is best to show up for appointments between 5 and 10 minutes early and wait. Not earlier (you'll bug them) and not later (you'll be late). If it's in public rather than their office, be the first one there.

Excerpt from a letter to someone who cancelled on me:

> I just mean that indecision seems like waste to me. Waste of expectations, time, resources. You don't know me, but if you did, you'd know that I am very very punctual and very into keeping the Word. I sometimes make appointments six months in advance to meet people for lunch or whatever, and I show up on time without a reminder. I hate having plans canceled, and it makes me not want to spend as much energy on a person or their project, because I assume future plans will be canceled.
>
> My being less interested in such people is not a tactic; it's a response.

Letter to the last intern I'll probably ever have:

> Subject: The road to my starvation is paved with your good intentions.
>
> I hate to keep harping on this, but I don't want you to think "Golly jeez, Michael Dean sure is being mean about this. I MEANT well. And offered to save him money and now he's blaming me because I didn't."
>
> TO CLARIFY: Last we talked, you said you would make and send the VHS covers off to the presser.
>
> If you had simply told me several weeks (and months) ago, before many many e-mails and phone calls, if you had simply said, "I will not get this done in time," I would have gotten it done myself. I could have designed it myself (I do like your design, by the way) in an hour with no phone calls or e-mails or heartaches or hassles. I know a lot of people who would have printed them and mailed them free, but none can do it on no notice. So you did cost me actual money. (And time. And hassle. And anger.)
>
> I just spent three hours running around in hellish traffic undoing what you didn't do, but said you'd do. I should have been at home working on a deadline on a paid writing project.
>
> The copies were $36.30 total. I couldn't afford to laser print them (which I could have had done free with notice) so I photocopied them and they look like crap. But it had to get done. I spent a long time driving around, and then time waiting in line at the post office. Mailing them priority to get them there on Monday,[2] which is WAY after

2. *By the way, Monday at any post office sucks. Go any other day.*

they should have been done, cost $28.05. So this cost me SITXY-FIVE DOLLARS which is all my money in the world, more or less.

If you ever want to donate this amount to the project, it would go a long way to undo this, in my mind.

I also lost the goodwill of customers and distributors who are gonna get them way late because of this.

So the moral of the story is, you did me a huge disservice. I wish to God you'd just said "I can't do this in a timely manner." You would have done me a huge favor.

Michael W. Dean
Doin' it myself. Again.

Later I felt like telling him, "You'll never work in this town for free again." He apologized and sent me some money, but he will never work for me again.

But if You Must...

Here's a letter I posted to get interns:

INTERNS WANTED

Los Angeles (Silver Lake) filmmaker needs interns to help with Web stuff, typing, and admin help to distribute documentary on Independent artists. It's called, D.I.Y. OR DIE: HOW TO SURVIVE AS AN INDEPENDENT ARTIST.

Great learning experience, no pay. You don't need to live in L.A. We have stuff that can be done over the Web or on the phone.

We just got back from showing it at Lost Film at Sundance.

FEATURING interviews with:

Lydia Lunch, Ian MacKaye (Fugazi), J Mascis, Jim Rose (Jim Rose Sideshow), J.G. Thirlwell (Foetus), Mike Watt, Richard Kern (Filmmaker), Ron Asheton (Stooges),

Madigan Shive (Bonfire Madigan), Dave Brockie (Gwar), Jill Morley (Filmmaker) and 24 others

Shot in San Francisco, Washington D.C., New York, and Los Angeles.

contact Michael Dean 213-_____
intern@_____.com

When potential interns e-mail me, I usually search their name and also their e-mail online to see if they've left a trail. I've dodged a couple of *total* loonies this way.

Location Producing

Forget permits. You don't need them. Film any location, anywhere, any time. Some cities charge you to film on the street. But if you're small and mobile enough, you can *always* slip under the radar. If you get questioned, be polite and say, "We're film students working on a project." You are….students of *$30 Film School*. But it might help if someone on your crew really is a student at an accredited school and can produce an I.D.

That one works if you have a crew, that is, more than one person with equipment, like a camera, sound, and light person. If you have less than that, you can pretty much say, "We're tourists," and get over.

Be quick, be accurate, be nice. We filmed a scene for a movie at Grace Cathedral in San Francisco without permission. It was a scene where a Catholic schoolboy was at the altar telling a priest that he had sold his soul to the Devil. We got the shot twice, then got kicked out. But we got the shot.

Always bring security. Especially in the city. Bring two or more big, level-headed people who will guard the equipment with their life while you're busy paying attention to other crap.

And this is kind of a no-brainer, but put a card in your camera case and stickers on anything else valuable with your phone number on it. If you lose it, someone honest might actually find it. However, don't put stickers or tape on your camera, because the sticky stuff on the back can end up gumming up the mechanisms that make it work.

Direct your own traffic. Reserve your own parking spaces. Big movie productions screw up traffic all the time. Driving in Los Angeles is hell for this reason. Of course, you can't afford to pay what it costs to do this. And it probably wouldn't be legal to do so yourself. Maybe someone could set up their own roadblock if they needed to, just for a few minutes. Wearing overalls might help.

Be sensible with this. Don't cause accidents.

I have this um, friend, see, who simply, um "borrowed" some of those temp signs that cities use for keeping one side of a block open. Then parked all his crew's vehicles there for an hour for free. You know those signs that say something like "TOW-AWAY. TEMPORARY NO STOPPING 3PM-7PM". They attach easily with wires, and they get the job done (see Figure 3.2).

Of course, I would never condone or recommend that you do anything illegal.

Advance your shoots. This is important to do always. For instance, when I have a shoot planned, I always call, or have someone call, the actors and crew the night before and remind them. Same with appointments. It's part of keeping your word.

Figure 3.2 *Um, my friend, uh.....MADE these signs.*

And don't be late. And call on the way if you are going to be late. Make sure you always have everyone's cell number on you at any shoot or event or anywhere you're going to meet people. And when I'm meeting them in a public place, I always ask what they look like, so I'm not bugging everyone who walks in with, "Are you Bill?" "Are you Bill?" "Are you Bill?"

Bring duplicates. Of all resources, equipment, and personnel. Something will break, someone will flake, etc. Bring extra tape, batteries, camera, people, whatever. This goes for the production and editing phases too. When making the D.I.Y. documentary, we didn't have any live footage of the band Fugazi, and they weren't touring before we planned to complete the thing. I posted all over the Internet looking for some, and got someone who said they would send it to us. Then I realized that counting on a stranger I had never met was a risky bet, so I kept posting. By the time we finished and were ready to show, we had some footage of Fugazi, but not from the first person. Not only did they not come through, the second backup person didn't come through! Only the third person who said they'd send a tape (Dave Redman) actually did. And it kicked ass: three-camera, already edited footage of an *amazing* show.

One time I wanted to do a scene in a playground with 10 women. They all said they'd show. Only two showed. I ended up rewriting the scene and making it work, but it was a drag. I should have thought ahead and gotten 20 people; then I would have had 4. Or I could have just gotten more reliable people.

Credit everyone who helps. In any way, no mater how small. It doesn't cost you anything to add another name to the credits, and it will make everyone feel good, including you.

Feel free to credit *$30 Film School* in your film also, if we helped you. We like being in credits!

People Skills, Drive, and Adversity

Newt and I were up all night and day doing the sound editing on his documentary, *PropStars L.A.*, until 5 p.m. the night it premiered in the Silver Lake Film Festival. It was showing at 8 p.m., but we got it done, done well, and pulled it off. (The film had gotten into the festival based on a trailer.)

When we showed up, the viewing room was icy cold. Too cold for people to be in and be comfortable. I had walked out of a showing the night before for the same reason. But this was *our* showing, so I took care of it. I went through the chain of command and found the person who had control of the air conditioning and politely asked him to turn it down. He did.

Be confident, but not cocky. Develop the skills to pull off anything, under any circumstances. Be thankful, especially if you start to make a little money. Show grace and aplomb regardless of the situation. People skills and responsibility are the things that make all the difference when you are trying to change the world as an independent filmmaker. It will be a lifetime of things like this. In *$30 Film School*, you never "make it" and get to "graduate" to where you never have to lift a finger. D.I.Y., damn it. And love it!

Overcoming Adversity

Most indie films are funded on credit cards. I didn't have credit cards at the time I made my film and couldn't get them. So I had to be a little more creative. You must learn to pull rabbit after rabbit out of the many hats that an indie filmmaker has to wear.

Have you ever had a museum fly you to another city to lecture people who hang on your every word? And not had the 10 bucks it took to get to the airport? I have. Ah, the joys of indie filmmaking.

Some of the best things start out with great ideas and no funding. It is said that George Washington had to borrow money to travel to his inauguration. A lot of D.I.Y. filmmaking is all about dealing with the little you have: making it work, no matter what. Pulling a cat out of a hat, over and over and over. Turning that li'l frown upside down.

For example, I paid 150 bucks to have 1,500 D.I.Y. stickers printed. When I got them, I realized that I had misspelled "independent" as "independant" artist.

Stickerguy.com was really cool and reprinted them correctly for half price, even though it was my fault. I was really distraught about whether to throw the wrong-printed ones away. I thought about sending them to a friend in Germany, but someone pointed out that the German public school system is so good that kids there would have probably noticed it quicker than an American.

I'm sending them to a man in Greece who's gonna give them out there. When he sent me an e-mail that said, "I your film want show Greece soon send plase can you?" I knew I had my answer. Doubt anyone there will notice.

The moral is: Make the best with what you have, in an interesting way. And be as creative as you like in the process. Do *everything* as art. The best you can.

Punk Rock Drop Ship

The first time I ordered 1,000 VHS copies of my movie, I had to drive an hour to the presser to pick them up. I didn't have room for that many in my car, even though it's a big one. I already had about 200 orders, and 100 more people I wanted to send them out to for promo. So I came up with this idea: I got 300 mailers and addressed them. I drove 40 miles to the presser (in Anaheim), opened up a few boxes of VHS tapes at the warehouse, and spent a long time packaging them up to send out. Drove to a post office nearby, stood in line, and mailed the 300 single packages. I did some proofreading on printed-out pages of this book while in line to make best use of that time. Drove back to the presser and the 700 that were left fit in my car. Barely.

When I first came to L.A. I was staying on Newt's couch and didn't know where I was going to live. Then I moved in with an insane person and had to move out quickly to my current studio apartment in the Silver Lake district (the only neighborhood in L.A. that looks/feels like San Francisco). So I got a post office box at a camera store. It seems like a real office address too (1634 W. Sunset Blvd, Suite 222, Los Angeles, CA 90026). The Sunset Blvd. part sounds classy to people not in L.A. People in L.A., however, know that it ain't Hollywood. It's Echo Park, sort of in "The Hood." Much of Alison Anders' film *Mi Vida Loca* was filmed on that block.

I hammer away every day until everything's done. It's just doing business as fast as I think...DSL (or T1) speed, thought, and action. My friend says I use broadband communication with the world. Rapid-fire e-mail, speech, phone calls, etc. It allows me to get an immense amount of quality art done and out to the world. It also allows me to piss people off by remote control on a daily basis. I make people mad because no one seems willing to work like I do.

Getting Things for Free

You can get almost anything free if you ask for it. I asked a lot of friends for money when making my first film (Having non-profit status to make their donations tax-deductible made this easier.) I got two weeks use of the *amazing* laptop I'm typing on in this Vancouver café by asking an Internet pen pal in Seattle. I'd never met him, I simply had been nice to him before, when I thought there was nothing he could do for me. And it came back to help me.

Be creative. I recently got a Spam from a film stuff rental supplier in New York City. Rather than deleting it or being mean in response, I wrote the supplier, told him about our project, and asked if he had any used equipment he'd donate for a tax write-off and mention on the Web site. He replied, "What do you need?" I returned a wish list, and got a much-needed Beta deck. Win-win. Art Karma in action.

The scene in the beginning of *D.I.Y. or DIE* where I'm introducing the movie in a really nice studio was a good example. I got use of the studio (One/Eleven in San Francisco) free. I just called them, explained the project, and asked if we could record our voiceovers in their place, in exchange for credit in the film and on the Web site. I sent them to the trailer online, they called me back and said, "Fine."

Getting Paid

A good thing to know about getting people to do your bidding: You need to present things in terms of their benefit, not yours. You don't tell the distributor, "I know that that payment isn't due to me for six more weeks, but I need it now. I'm *starving*, damn it!" Instead you say, "I know that that payment isn't due to me for six more weeks, but if you can make an exception this once, it will help both of us. I'm using part of it to send out promos to writers and people with really big mouths who will love it and talk it up, so when it hits stores next month, there will be a bigger buzz."

Then when you get the money, you actually spend part of it to send out promos to writers and people with really big mouths who will love it and talk it up, so when it hits stores next month, there will be a bigger buzz.

Part of surviving as an independent artist is generating invoices. Actually print up sheets that show what you are owed and when you expect to be paid. You send them to people when a job is completed, or when you put something on consignment. The payment term for consignment is usually 90 days (but what they don't sell, they will return to you). To be paid for a job is usually between 7 and 30 days. I usually put 10 days. Don't call and ask for your money ahead of time, no matter how broke you are. But then feel free to call them the day after you don't get it and politely remind them that you are owed money. Don't be bitchy, just call them. If they say, "The check's in the mail," and you have doubts, you can ask them to fax you a confirmation.

Big companies have rooms full of people who have the dedicated job of doing both sides of this all day, every day.

INVOICE

1/12/2003

D.I.Y. or DIE documentary

Pay to:
MICHAEL DEAN 1634 W. Sunset Blvd. #222, Los Angeles, CA 90026
213-XXX-XXXX

From Joe Blow's Records
Lawrence KS.

20 VHS copies of
D.I.Y. OR DIE: HOW TO SURVIVE AS AN INDEPENDENT ARTIST
6 dollars each wholesale = $120

10 copies of
D.I.Y. OR DIE: HOW TO SURVIVE AS AN INDEPENDENT ARTIST
On DVD

7 dollars each wholesale = $70

Total due if all sold: $190

TERMS: 90 days FOB*

Thank you!
Michael Dean

The "FOB" stands for "Freight on Buyer," which means the buyer pays the shipping.

INVOICE

1/12/2003

Amount: $300

Owed by:
Kitty Farnsworth
Los Angeles, CA

Pay to:
MICHAEL DEAN 1634 W. Sunset Blvd. #222, Los Angeles, CA 90026
213-XXX-XXXX

FOR: Editing actor's reel for Kitty Farnsworth. Job is completed.

TERMS: DUE NOW

Thank you!
Michael Dean

Paying People

Richard Kern says, "Pay them, even if it's a dollar..." Most people say, "Sure, use my music for free, but pay me if you make a million dollars." I won't promise this. There are enough people who make great music that will let me use it for free that it is not something I have to pay for. I can get it elsewhere or make my own. I get it in writing that I will never have to pay for it. Then later if I do make a million dollars I might pay them, but I don't want to be contractually obligated to do so. My art is so time-intensive that if I got a million dollars tomorrow and deducted my expenses, it wouldn't work out to much more than minimum wage. Seriously.

Some would think that this is parasitic or "un-punk." Flug it. I ain't practicing to be the mayor of Mohawk Town, and my ideas make sense in my head. It's just the realities of independent no-budget filmmaking.

Basically, I am not D.I.Y. to wave a banner. I'm not trying to be anti-commercial. I am D.I.Y. out of necessity, and I like to be able to live with myself. I am not opposed to commercial ventures. I am just smart enough not to take the first crappy deal that comes along. If you are used to doing absolutely everything yourself, and don't mind it, you have more bargaining power anyway when it comes to making deals.

One of the most important tips to getting things done is to keep your word. I know this is one of the main points in that silly new-age-bestseller-du-jour *Agreements* book, but heck. My momma taught me this when I was three.

I recently went to hear Lynn Breedlove read from her amazing novel, *Godspeed*.[4] I told her that the DVDs would be out in a few days, and she asked if I could get some to her in San Francisco for her tour. I told her I'd send them. I got them the next day, and spent money I barely had to priority mail her a box of them to sell on her tour on consignment. I got them to her the day before her tour. She wrote me a thank-you note, and sounded surprised. She said, "Wow. A man of action who keeps his word."

Keeping your word is rare to the point that it actually seems odd when someone does it. I think that's kind of sad. I like to help change this trend.

Most independent films are made on "spec," meaning people get paid when money is made. I promised Miles, my editor, a certain percentage (a pretty good percentage) of any profit. When I signed my distribution deal with Music Video Distributors (MVD), I sent Miles a check. He was shocked. People involved in independent film are so used to not getting paid that it's shocking when you pay them.

Pay them. It's the most fun you'll ever have shocking someone.

I know how to sell without selling out. I do it by making something good, knowing what I want, not settling for less, and mainly treating people well. It all comes back.

Getting Groovy People in Your Film

I just ask people. I'll ask anyone to do anything. All they can do is say "No."

That's how I got all the groovy people in the flick to be in it...just asked them...I knew a lot of them already, so it was easy. I also had some fortuitous events—went to interview Watt, and he happened to be playing with Mascis and Asheton, so I got three for one that day.

Ran into Jim Rose, who I'd never met, walking down the street in San Francisco, and asked him if I could do it right there, on the street. He said, "I'm doing A&E

3. *It's about a womanizing, rock 'n' roll, drug-addicted San Francisco bike messenger searching for God. Just like my novel! But it's a very different and unique story.*

today, and the Discovery Channel tomorrow, but come to the Wednesday show early and we'll do it at 6 p.m."

Getting hold of Lydia Lunch was an ironic one. She's kinda guarded about her contact info since she, by nature, attracts so many loonies. So I spent six months going back and forth with her manager, who lives in Europe. When we finally set it up, I went to her house, which unbeknownst to me while I was trying to contact her, was a block away from me.

I'm a total poser in these photos. I don't shoot on Super-8; I shoot on DV, and this is a Super-8 camera that doesn't work. I bought it from my junkie neighbor for five bucks....she told me it worked. After the photo shoot, I gave the camera to Lydia to make art out of.

Figure 3.3 *B & W photo Lydia Lunch took of me.*

I didn't just ask Lydia to take photos so I could have the cachet of an indie-famous name on my photo credit (though that was a nice byproduct). I actually only know one other photographer in L.A., and she's very flaky from smoking too much pot. It's funny...this other chick is not a household name and acts more like one than Lydia does. I knew that if I asked this other chick, first of all she would have taken a week to return my call, then would have acted like she was doing me a big favor by taking 10 minutes of photos in exchange for 10 hours of page layout. Instead, I e-mailed Lydia on Thursday, she replied Friday, and I went over Saturday. She was very clear that I should be on time, bring film, and that she only had a half-hour. I made a little half-page contract, putting in writing that it was for no pay, but that I owed her page layout on her next book, we both signed, and that was it. Very professional, no nonsense. Lydia has that no-B.S. sensibility and a clear understanding of boundaries in all human exchanges. I love that in a human.

By the way, just because you interview someone and they're nice to you doesn't make you friends. They're not necessarily being friendly to you, they're being friendly to the audience on the other end of your camera lens. And you **will** have dreams about the people during editing; it's natural. You'll be looking at them and listening to them 12 hours a day on a screen. They will work their way into your head. This doesn't mean that you are friends (unless you are friends). Again, did they invite you to their wedding?

Lydia's just cool and I just asked her.

How I Produced My Film

I do everything myself, with help. I multitask about 14 hours a day, always on art. Train yourself to do this. That's the key to being a producer. A producer *produces* results. Learn to produce.

Skills I utilized in making and promoting my movie:

> Music editing
> Music recording
> Writing music
> Playing bass
> Playing guitar
> Singing
> Mastering music on a computer
> Shooting video
> Taking photos (silver and digital)
> Manipulating photos in Photoshop
> Doing page layout in Quark

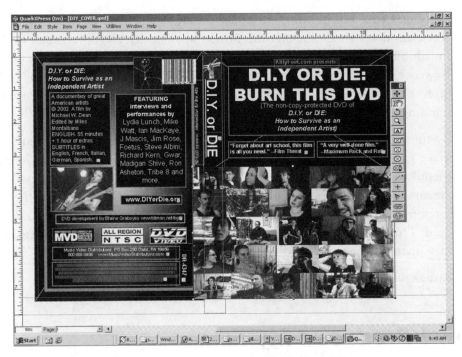

Figure 3.4 *My Quark page layout for the* D.I.Y or DIE *DVD cover.*

Creating fonts

Writing a treatment for documentary

Writing copy for voiceover

Writing ad copy

Writing press releases

Writing business correspondence

Promotion via e-mail

Research

Proofreading

Scanning and archiving documents

Network administration

Installing, maintaining, and troubleshooting new hardware and software

I.T.

Hanging up flyers on the street

Finding and overseeing interns

Organizing people in my town and via e-mail

Web design

Non-linear video editing

Linear video editing

Soldering

Day-to-day operations (getting and answering mail, going to post office, getting VHS copies made, shipping orders)

Fundraising

Record keeping

Bookkeeping

Taxes

Contacting companies for in-kind donations

Directing

Producing

I learned a lot of these as I went along. You can too.

I do everything one day at a time, with a lot of planning ahead of time. The inspiration for the next one will hit me sooner or later, probably while I'm standing in line at the post office or something equally mundane. (That's why I never leave the house without a pen!) Here's a rundown on how I "produced" *D.I.Y. or DIE:*

◆ Several smart film students ran camera for free. They knew the technical aspects, but school hadn't taught them what to point their cameras at. I had an idea, so they were more than happy to work for me for free. I treated them with respect, and credited them—two things you don't always get at school.

◆ You need to be fearless in everything. I met Peter Spicer, one of my favorite camera people, by walking up to him on the street because he had a camera in his hand. I risked being embarrassed and didn't care. We ended up working together a lot.

Not everybody was into this though: I'd placed an ad looking for help. Some film students came by my house and seemed disappointed that I worked out of my home. They would rather wait and wait for a chance to be on the waiting list to be a nameless assistant on a Hollywood film than sit down with me and actually *make* films.

◆ The documentary was originally based in San Francisco and later I moved to Los Angeles. Interviews were conducted in both cities.

◆ The project started as an eight-page query to San Francisco's *Intersection for the Arts*, requesting umbrella non-profit status. The query was approved, and we set about the task of submitting proposals to over 300 foundations. One responded, donating enough money to cover some expenses and buy one plane ticket to the East Coast to conduct more interviews. Someone else donated a fast computer.

◆ The New York and D.C. interviews were conducted three weeks after the World Trade Center and Pentagon attacks of Sept 11th, 2001. The tickets were booked a month prior, and I considered not going, but went anyway, to complete the project.

◆ Any available method was used to get to the subjects' homes and studios: planes, subways, taxis, city buses, interstate buses, borrowed cars, and even a bicycle.

◆ I crashed with friends in different cities while completing various phases of the process.

◆ The camera operators, who had their own three-chip Mini-DV cameras, worked for free in exchange for the enjoyment of being involved in a cool project. This free help was found mostly through the Internet, often on Craigslist, run by Craig Newmark, one of the interviewees.

◆ When people with three-chip cameras were unavailable, I did the interviews myself, using a borrowed one-chip camera, with no external microphone, only camera sound.

◆ Interns helped with phone calls, typing, and carrying equipment. These interns were also found on Craigslist, mostly film students wanting some production experience.

◆ We received in-kind donations of goods and services from a few local and national companies. A couple of friends also chipped in a little money. And I spent a few thousand out of pocket.

◆ Copies of the final movie were sent to magazines and microcinemas using recycled VHS tapes donated by a friend at a cable access television station.

◆ I said "Thank you" to everyone involved, and absolutely meant it.

Some have complained that *D.I.Y. or DIE* is less "how" to make art and more "why." But folks who say that are delusional. This ain't *Making Art for Dummies*. It's not laid at your feet. It's basically a crash course in being pure of heart enough to make dirty, pretty, kick-ass changes in the world. Watch my film a couple of times. If you're meant to, you'll get it all, and then some.

Conclusion

Producing is the talent of using all your other talents together to make things happen. Be creative, be fearless, and be humble. People want to help people who are living large, but not rubbing it in other people's faces. There is a certain magic to getting everything done for nothing. And you can cultivate this by helping others. It *will* come back to you.

$30

Chapter 4

Crew, Cameras, and Medium

So far we've written, funded, and planned our film. Now it's time to actually make it. First we'll meet the people involved, and put our hands on the camera and tape or film we'll tell our story with.

Film Crew

Following are the members who make up a film crew. A big Hollywood crew will have many more jobs than this, and several people for each job. Your film crew will probably have far fewer, and each person will probably fill more than one role.

You don't need nearly this many people to make a good movie. You can do a lot yourself or have your friends help cover some of the positions. Or use your interns. This is just to get you started thinking and planning, by illustrating the many hats that get worn on a big pro shoot.

Director	Is considered God. He runs everything on the set. He tells everyone what to do, and everyone (theoretically) listens.
Assistant Director(s)	Tarts out the desires of the director to everyone else. Basically enables the director to be in more than one place at the same time. Helps keep him from going crazy.
Producer	Sometimes actually tells the director what to do, but from behind the scenes. Is in charge of getting the financing for the film.
Line Producer	Keeps the logistics of the show running on the set.
Associate Producer	Can mean anything. Sometimes means nothing. Is often a credit given for a favor. Or sometimes is an investor in the film.
Screenwriter	Writes the story. Makes up the cool words that you always attribute to some actor.

Director of photography or DP	Also called Cinematographer. The person who tells the cameraman what to do. Along with the director and writer, the DP is probably the most important person in any film.
Cameraman	The eyes of the DP. On an independent shoot, the DP and the Cameraman are often the same person.
Editor	Puts everything together behind the scenes and makes it all work after all the film is shot.
Sound mixer	Helps record the location sound on a shoot.
Boom operator	Holds the big stick with the microphone on it. Works with the sound mixer. Boom operator's job is basically to hold the microphone as close to the actors' mouths as possible without ever getting the microphone in the frame (shot) of the camera.
Music supervisor	Picks the background music for the film and decides how, when, and where it is used.
Gaffer	Head electrician. Tells the other lighting people what to do. Comes from the old Hollywood term *Grandfather* meaning the "big daddy" of the lighting and electrical team.
Best boy	Gaffer's assistant.
Lighting crew	Works for the Gaffer. Sets up lights.
Grip	In charge of moving cameras, scenery, mike stands, sandbags, and so forth.
Casting	Gets the people together to audition for all the parts, and may help audition them.
Script supervisor/ continuity	Makes sure that if the lead is wearing the watch on his left hand when they shoot a scene, that it's not on his right hand the next day when they shoot coverage for that scene.
Drivers	Cart people and things around.
Catering (craft services)	Feed people.

Makeup	Make people look good or spooky or whatever is needed, using makeup.
Property master	In charge of props, the objects people hold or use to help tell the story.
Production designer	Helps with the look of the movie. Picks out clothes, buildings, scenes, locations, art, set design, and more.
Special effects	Makes weird cool things happen. Can be "practical effects," like blowing stuff up or making someone look like they're bleeding to death. Or it can be computer effects done in the post-filming stage.
Actors	Oh yeah, them. They just bring the story to life and make it breathe.

Cameras

Cameras are the first line of defense in the war that we wage in *$30 Film School* against mediocrity, boredom, and depression. New advances in technology have brought cheap, amazing video cameras within your reach. $500 can buy you a new camera today that rivals a $100,000 commercial broadcast camera that was used to make TV shows five years ago.

Look. Try to borrow a three-chip camera if you don't have one. Three-chip Mini-DV looks way better than one-chip. However, one-chip cameras actually make an image that looks more like film in some ways than three-chip. High-8 video looks even more like film. All the color footage in *Blair Witch Project* was shot with a $400 consumer high-8 video camera.

My movie looks more like film on the DVD than when played from the mini-DV. (Especially the parts shot on one-chip rather than three-chip.) I guess the compression adds something like grain. I love it.

Three-chip cameras have a separate chip for each primary color and produce a better image. One-chip cameras do it all in one chip, which doesn't work as well. Three-chip cameras and one-chip cameras are also called 3-CCD cameras and 1-CCD cameras. CCD stands for *Charged Coupled Device*—a technical name for the image-capture chips. Three-chip cameras cost several grand new. You can get a used one-chip on eBay for about $300.

One-chip cameras are often much smaller than three-chips. The larger three-chips are about the size of a cat and look more "pro" externally as well as in image quality. The smaller one-chips are about the size of a kitten, so they're easier to hide. They're also less intimidating to people who are not used to being in front of the camera.

One-chip cameras look okay for talking-head documentary stuff, but you will really notice the difference if you're filming motion. For car races or stuff like that, you'll really want a three-chip.

Regardless, make *sure* that the camera you get has an audio input for an external microphone. You will need that.

Figure 4.1 *Aaron Jacobs with the author's cute little bite-sized one-chip JVC GR-DVL307 camcorder. It was given to Michael by filmmaker and* D.I.Y. *or* DIE *cameraman, Sage Eaton. Six of* D.I.Y. *or* DIE*'s one-chip interviews were shot with this camera.* Zapruderesque photo by Lydia Lunch.

Figure 4.2 *Adra Andrews with Noah Harald's kick-ass, big, sexy, expensive prosumer (professional/consumer) Cannon XL-1. He paid a lot of money for it. Note all the buttons and knobs and dials and pressure gauges and whatever. Noah's two beautiful features,* Life Ends Merge Left *and* Stalemate *were shot with this camera.* Photo by Lydia Lunch.

Figure 4.3 *Jennifer Berkowitz with same cool camera. Note the signature on the camera of* Fight Club *author Chuck Palahniuk. Noah got it at a reading at the Beverly Hills Public Library.* Photo by Lydia Lunch (in Lydia's "Sanford & Son" chair).

You can get used cameras on eBay, or new from any consumer electronics place like Best Buy, or at any of the many many places online that sell 'em.

If you can't get a three-chip, use what you have and make it great. About half of the interviews in *D.I.Y. or DIE* were shot on a one-chip: Beth Lisick, Courtney J. Ulrich, ck0, Craig Newmark, Dave Brockie, David Wellbeloved, Eric McFadden, Ian MacKaye (second camera and all DVD "extras" footage), J.G. Thirlwell (second camera), Jim Rose, John John Jesse, Kevin Wengler, Little Mike Martzke, Lydia Lunch, Lynn Breedlove (second camera), Maggie Estep, and Phil Sudo.

Get to know your camera. Take it out, put a tape in it, and shoot some footage with it. Each camera is a little different and you should consult the manual, but here are some of the basic parts universal to most cameras:

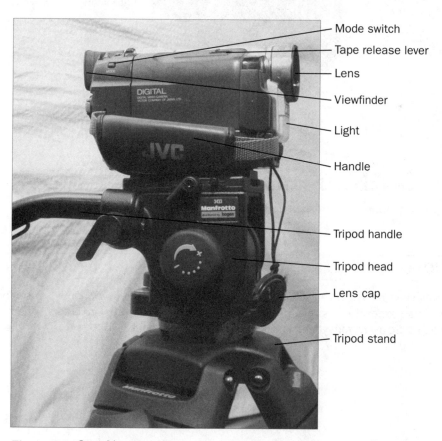

Mode switch
Tape release lever
Lens
Viewfinder
Light
Handle
Tripod handle
Tripod head
Lens cap
Tripod stand

Figure 4.4 *One chip camera on a tripod, showing the various parts.* Photo by Newtron Foto.

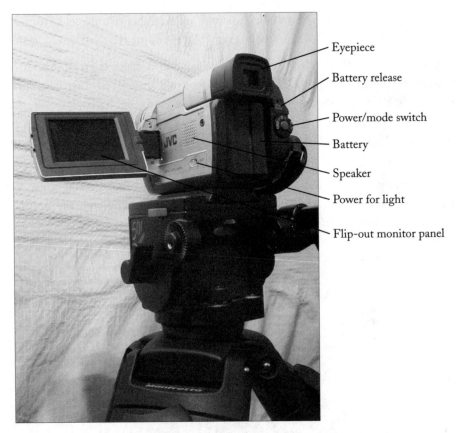

Eyepiece

Battery release

Power/mode switch

Battery

Speaker

Power for light

Flip-out monitor panel

Figure 4.5 *Same from different angle.* Photo by Newtron Foto.

NOTE

When you're shooting outside, glare can be a drag. Hoodman (www.hoodmanusa.com) makes inexpensive, cool clip-on sun shading hoods that are great for outdoor shoots to keep glare away from your mini-DV camera's monitor panel.

Figure 4.6 *Hoodman on camera.*

Figure 4.7 *Another Hoodman on a camera.*

Medium

The tape you record on is the ammo for your camera. This book mainly covers mini-DV cameras. Here we will cover the tape they use, but also touch on high-definition video as well as using actual film.

Mini-DV Versus Film

My friend is a talented filmmaker, makes cool films, and gets them in some cool festivals. She shoots on 16 mm (millimeter) and is a film snob. She says, "I can't work on video."

She stops by my house on her way home from work. She's temping at a job she hates so she can afford to shoot more. When she stops by, I'm always editing, because it costs me nothing to do so. I get to work on filmmaking out of my home 24-7, and she can only work on film about one month a year because her medium is so much more expensive.

Big Hollywood movies are mostly shot on 35 mm, a format with a much better look than video, super-8 film or 16 mm film. The bigger the frame in millimeters, the more information and thus resolution each frame holds (and the more it costs).

Video is good. It's cheap enough that you get to practice the art of filmmaking, which is more important than whether you're shooting on film or video. Storytelling, camerawork, directing, and editing will transfer over also, if you ever get the money to make the leap. This is why a lot of film school people don't make good stuff—the materials are so expensive that they don't let you touch them in the first year. In *$30 Film School*, you start shooting your first day.

Any skills you learn in DV will transfer to the next thing, when the prices come down a bit: High-definition video, or high-def (also HD). They shot the new *Star Wars* movie on it, and soon you'll be shooting on it.

Table 4.1: Dean's Power-of-Ten-Rule: Approximate price *per minute* of various movie formats, with developing.

Mini-DV video	Ten cents (stock only, no developing needed)
High-definition video	A dollar (stock only, no developing needed)
8-mm film	Ten dollars
16-mm film	One-hundred dollars
35-mm film	One-thousand dollars
70-mm film	Ten-thousand dollars

Tapes

Use name-brand tapes. But Maxell DV tapes, in my experience, are problematic. On the ones I had, the magnetic coating flaked off and damaged the camera's tape heads. Use any brand name tape, except maybe this brand.

Keep tapes dry and away from too much heat or cold (and away from magnets). Two Mini-DV tapes will fit perfectly in a cassette tape case if you break out the two things that go through the cassette hubs. Tupperware containers work well for storing all the tapes for a given project and will keep them safe. After you spill coffee or beer on a tape and ruin it forever, you'll appreciate this.

High-Definition Video

High-def is *way* better looking than Mini-DV, but the cameras currently cost over $10,000 High-def tape costs more than Mini-DV, but it's still way cheaper than film. News shows on TV are often shot on high-def.

> *High-def is going to make all of those film school snobs cry like babies…*
> *when they realize they can't get a job as a third assistant cameraman*
> *'cause they don't know dookie about video…Ha Ha Ha.*

—Film and television FX compositor Brynley Cadman

Film Look

For now, film looks better than all video. But you can still mess around with a few things in video if you have real-film envy.

Basically video looks too "real." Film has a dreamy quality to it, and it's because it has *grain*. This is actually grains of silver on the emulsion. (Keep in mind that the production process of film dumps tons of poisonous byproducts into the environment each year. Tell this to your film snob friends.)

I've actually taken a film shot on Mini-DV on a nationwide tour, and seen it projected on different equipment in a variety of environments. And it always looked pretty darn good.

Rock videos and commercials are increasingly being shot on Mini-DV. It will be a while before video replaces film (though some are trying with hi-definition video, most famously George Lucas). But Mini-DV is not only a great place to start, it's a great place to be. Digital video, and indie filmmaking in general, doesn't have to be a stepping stone.

A lot of documentaries are being shot with Mini-DV already. Watch PBS and you'll see it. Documentaries and reality TV shows are good candidates for DV, as they have a much higher shooting ratio—often 40-to-1—than scripted shows. (Shooting ratio is the amount of footage shot versus the amount actually used. A high shooting ratio means a huge budget when working with film. Not automatically so with video.) Unscripted programming needs a higher shooting ratio because people take longer to say something brilliant when you don't feed them their lines.

Using Actual Film

The main focus of this book is more or less Mini-DV, but almost all the techniques presented here will work on film too, if you want to try it.

You can get Super-8 film cameras for about 30 to 300 bucks, and 16 mm cameras for 50 to 5,000 dollars. Try eBay. Or www.EchoParkFilmCenter.org. (Tell Paulo I sent ya.)

You can actually make a good-looking flick with a low-end real film camera, but you will have problems with synch sound. These cameras have no microphone and no recording capability—they don't make sound Super-8 cameras or film any more. So you have to record sound separately. The problem is that the cheap ones are loud and they don't have a quartz drive, so the mike will pick up the motor sound even from a few feet away and also get out of synch in longer shots. But you can build a box of foam and wood around the camera to muffle the sound. You can do shots that are shorter and farther back, where you will notice "drift" in synch less than in a close up, and make it all work out. You can even edit on a computer. You can pay to have the developed film *Telecined*. Telecine is a process where they scan each frame and output the editable, high-rez electronic video file onto a beta SP tape. (Beta is a high-rez analog format used for broadcast purposes.) Or you can do "punk rock telecine," which is simply projecting it and filming the projection with a Mini-DV camera. This can look better than you would think, especially if you do some color correction in the editing program.

You can also shoot your film on film and your sound on DV. You've just gotta slate it so you can synch the sound later on the computer. This will also give you DV footage for "safety"—in case something happens to a shot on film and it doesn't turn out...this is far more likely with film than video. Also you can use the DV for the "making of" documentaries and extra material for your DVD.

You can also combine film and video. This is often done for an effect. Sometimes it is done with different film stocks. The big film *Traffic* did this quite effectively—shooting the Mexican desert scenes on high-contrast yellow filtered film and the suburban scenes on cooler stock with a blue tint. It made it easier to follow the story. You can use different film and video anywhere for any reason. The possibilities are without end.

Some indie films are shot on 35 mm for cheap using "short ends" or bits of film left over from shooting big-time Hollywood movies. You gotta know someone to get this stuff. It's free though—basically gray-market donations.

Summary

Just shoot, even if you have to use analog old-school VHS video tape. It's better to use that and start making films and making the process part of your natural rhythm than to sit around dreaming of the day you'll be able to afford good equipment. Just start making films. Today!

Chapter 5

Directing

This is the most amorphous, indefinable, and even unteachable aspect of film-making. Some even say it's something you either have or you don't have.

Directing is simply having people skills, some "big picture" vision, and the rest is indefinable "x-factor" stuff. What a director does in film is what a producer does in music. In music, the producer is the director of a recording session. They both oversee a project by other creatives, get the most money, and get to be anony-mous.[1] It's a pretty enviable position.

Basically the director's job is to interpret the script, get the best possible perfor-mances from the actors, guide the camera people, and oversee it all into a com-plete cinematographic story, using his or her own unique vision. There are a million ways to tell and show any one tale. The director uses his vision and makes it "his" story, even if someone else wrote it.

Study Films

If you want to make films, then study films. Watch them, twice. Once to enjoy them and once to dissect and learn the mechanics. Notice what happens with shots—over-the-shoulder shots, long establishing shots, medium close-ups, extreme close-ups. Listen to the background music and sound effects and see when and why they're used.

Look at the classics, but also study newer movies you like. See what works. And when people get on you for spending too much time watching movies, you can say, with a straight face, "I'm working." Watch as many movies as possible. Big crappy Hollywood ones, good Hollywood ones, great indie ones, and especially, bad indie ones. Watch TV, sitcoms, the news, cartoons (especially *The Simpsons*). It's all good. Take notes. Save receipts. Movie rentals and tickets are tax-deductible for filmmakers. Rent DVDs and listen to director's commentaries.

1. I've met a huge Hollywood director, and he is able to be totally anonymous. We were standing in a crowd of people and no one was bugging him. I've hung out with far less famous and influential people and seen them mobbed in public.

The first movies, back in the day, were basically just a stage play with a camera in the audience. Then someone (Orson Welles, among others) realized that the camera can go places the audience never could, and used this as a tool to make new realities. Nowadays, cameras, with the aid of computers, go: through walls, into the atom, inside a brain, along the path of a bullet, and even through slices of time and space.

Making an Effective Film

As a director, you want to train your eye and brain to be able to make the right decisions on the fly in order to "direct" the camera, actors, and crew while ultimately picturing how it will be edited in the end. Your job is to coordinate the "Big Picture."

One reason that many indie films aren't good is because the script and actors aren't very good. I'm all for giving everyone a chance, but there are also great writers and actors who will work with your budget, even if you don't have one. You can find them through Internet bulletin boards like Craigslist, and through putting up flyers at film schools, writing departments, and acting departments of universities and high schools. (Younger actors tend to be hard to work with though. This, as well as child labor laws, is why in Hollywood they usually have people five years older than the character playing the role. I often have trouble with suspension of disbelief on this front.)

Suspension of Disbelief is a basic premise of having a film be effective. As a director, your number-one priority is to make a final product that people can get lost in. You have to be able to get them to forget they're watching images projected on a wall, and imagine that they're looking at real people. *Suspension of Disbelief* is an important quality, always, even in the most hallucinatory fiction fantasy story.

Basically what you are looking for in good actors is believability. What you are looking for in *great* actors is the Gift—the God-given gift, that which cannot be taught. Great actors reach through the lens, through the screen, into the viewers' hearts and grab them. Hard.

Table Reading

Whether you or someone else wrote the script, do a *table reading*. This means sitting down at a table with your actors and reading the parts out loud (without acting) and seeing what works. Make changes based on this. You'd be amazed at how easy it is to see the whole picture this way. Audio or video tape it. Study it.

Many directors also write. If you wrote the script, you might want to use your non-actor friends for the table reading. It might be even better to use friends here than the actors you're going to film, as the actors may have too much input and get confused and want to do the lines the old way after you make changes. (Of course, some people actually make movies as a committee, some anarchist collectives work this way. I can't. I ain't got time for a vote on everything. That's why I quit playing in bands.) But whatever works. In that case you'd want to involve the actors. Your call. Personally, actors drive me buggy. More egotistical than rock musicians in most cases, if such a thing is possible. I can't even work with a partner. Some can, but I'm a control freak with a short temper who gets cranky around others easily. (Maybe *that's* why I do it myself.)

Controlling the Shoot

Once you have your actors rehearsed, you can shoot. In *$30 Film School*, you can shoot yourself, or have a cameraman. Be extra nice to cameramen. They tend to be cranky. They all want to direct. My friend Bink says, "They're like bass players." I take this to mean "necessary, but upset that they're not running the show." I've found it to be often the truth.

Get the Shot!

Which leads to one big rule of directing: Get the shot. If someone is acting like a prima donna, be they crew or cast, try to indulge them. You can be a Napoleonic little turd and fire them later. And you can yell, "You'll never work for free in this town again!" as you do it. But **get the shot**.

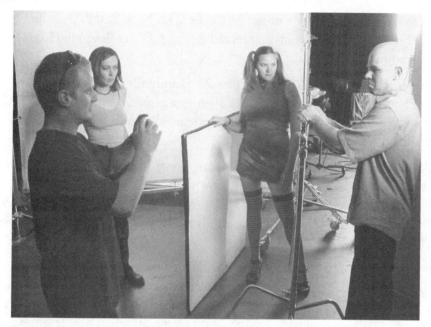

Figure 5.1 *The author (left) directing a shoot.* Photo by Newtron Foto.

Many artists tend to be cranky and hard to work with, but they don't have to be. You should align yourself with good people. However, if you misjudge someone, and find yourself in an uncomfortable situation with someone who's unhappy with their station in life and blames others, before you axe them, remember the rule: **get the shot**.

In Hollywood, they say, "fast friends to the last frame," which sort of states the same thing, but in a phonier setting.

There is a school of film called The Dogme Movement that states that everything must be shot on location, with no imported props; audio and image must be produced together, only handheld camera, only natural light, and you're not allowed to take credit for your work, and so forth. Seems to me like intentionally crippling yourself.

I hate most rules. That's one of my problems with Nick Zedd's[2] manifesto, even though he's one of my influences. It reads like rules. Film rules sound like a home-work assignment.

The other day I showed a cut of my new 22-minute film at The Echo Park Film center at an open screening that had a 10-minute limit. I made an edit of it that was 10 minutes, zero seconds, and zero frames. Was fun, but I wouldn't wanna make a life of it.

Don't be afraid to keep people from taking control of your shoot. You are the *director*. I hate it when I am doing a shoot with an actress or model and she brings her boyfriend, especially when I ask her not to. The boyfriend is baggage and he gets in the way, even if he does nothing. It's not like we're gonna make a snuff film.

It's not just boyfriends either. Any time I was in a band and a guy came to try out and brought his girlfriend along, he was automatically not hired. Because you know that you're not just hiring him, you're also getting a meddling accessory and you're gonna have to deal with her too. It pisses me off when people bring people who shouldn't be there to a shoot. Do you bring people to your work? Then don't bring people to my work.

I think this whole thing of boyfriends coming along and lurking around while I'm working bothers me because of this: I am a do-it-yourselfer because I want control over my life. I don't have a steady job, girlfriend, or roommate intentionally. I am happier alone, making art on my terms and being frequently broke and not answering to anyone, than I could ever be getting told what to do, even if it meant being rich and social and loved. So stay off my set.

One "rule" that people are told when directing is, "You never tell an actor how to say his line." I say "hogwash." I'll give an actor a few shots at trying it his way, but

---

2. *Nick Zedd is a very influential yet under-appreciated underground filmmaker. There is a line in* Pulp Fiction *that refers to a character named "Zedd"—the line is "Zedd's dead." This is referring to the fake epitaph that* Film Threat Magazine *once ran. The line is in homage to Nick Zedd (who is considered an influence on Quentin Tarantino). This is even later referenced in a* Simpsons *episode (done in Tarantino's style) that is a take-off on the torture scene from* Pulp Fiction, *where the owner of the military antique store says something like, "As soon as Zedd gets here, the party can begin."*

if it ain't working (and especially if it's a script I wrote and can totally hear in my head already), I'll feed them the line and say it out loud with the delivery I want.

Some would say this is robbing the actor of his own voice, but I will also turn around and ask an actor (or cameraman, or even intern) how he would see a certain scene delivered, shot, or even edited. This is not something most directors would do. So you see, like the producer in music, it's a difficult-to-define job description. Basically, you just use all your vision, life experiences, and skills to oversee the movie project.

The director will work with all the other key members (Director of Photography, Art Director, Music Supervisor, and so on) and give orders to carry out the whole shoot. Sometimes the director works a lot with the camera people on angles, pans, even lens and filter choices if she has a vision for that. Other times she has a camera person she just trusts with those decisions (usually someone she works with again and again on all her movies). In this case, she basically just works on directing the performances of the actors. Some directors do both. Some are incredible control freaks over every minute aspect of everything, from actors, cameras, props, art direction, sound, and editing. Sometimes, if she really has a knack for having a view of the big picture, she can be amazing with this. Others are looked at as insane. It primarily depends on the results.

Occasionally, the director is also the screenwriter. In this case, he probably has very specific ideas for how everything, especially the delivery of the lines, is to be carried out.

Some directors act more like producers, simply bringing together a good crew of people she knows work well under pressure and sort of letting the process take care of itself, intervening only when trouble arises.

On most sets, the director has the absolute final say and veto power over everyone else. (Actually, the director may be God on the set, but he is usually answering to the studio and the producers, who often know nothing about art. I want to avoid these situations. That's why I do it myself. I would need absolute control to do it otherwise.)

To be a good director, you must remain teachable, knowing you never "know it all," and you must be willing to try new things and ask questions of anyone, no matter where their job falls in the rigid conventional hierarchy of division of labor on a movie set.

Release Forms

Some would argue that this should be in the "Producing" chapter rather than the "Directing" chapter. I put it in this chapter for one reason: It has to get done. If you are the only person on the shoot, you're the director. I wanted to put this up front so you make sure and do it.

Get a release form signed by everyone. (Actors, crew, camera people, musicians, everyone.) If you do find yourself filming without a release form, point the camera at the subject and say, "What is your legal name?" If he can answer that correctly, say, "Do you consent to be filmed and have your image used for no pay?" If he says anything other than a clear "yes," turn the camera off and explain that you cannot proceed until he says yes.

If the person is over 18, this is probably enough. If she is under 18, get the parents to do this too, on the actor's behalf.

Getting releases signed can be the job of an intern or crew member, but make sure a reliable person handles this task. This is one of the most important jobs and the one you're gonna pay the most for if it gets screwed up. (Unlike other jobs, it might not become apparent that it was screwed up until years later—when someone sues you and you realize you have no papers on them.)

I usually fax or e-mail the release form to anyone who will have to sign one several days before the shoot, so everyone knows what she's going to have to sign and can discuss it ahead of time. This will prevent a nasty scene and someone storming off once you get to the location (and don't have time to find a replacement). Do send it to them, but don't require them to print it out. The actor will forget. Do that yourself.

I've noticed that the people who complain the most on any project are the ones who have the least going on in their lives. They complain about your not crediting and thanking them sufficiently, even when they're thanked as much as anyone else.

They are also the most likely to sue you. Get those release forms.

Folks who complain about release forms are also the ones most likely to sue.

The folks with the most going on in their own lives are the ones least likely to complain about how you use them in your movie, usually because they're too busy doing cool stuff to even watch the movie. People with nothing of their own will pick apart your stuff sometimes if you let them do something in it.

And make sure you keep the signed release forms so they are available years later if you need them. Putting them in a fireproof safe or a bank safe deposit box wouldn't be out of the question.

Sample Release Forms

These are also on the CD-ROM in electronic template format for you to personalize and use. (This is offered for illustrative purposes only. These are just the forms that I use. Consider consulting an attorney before using these. Laws may vary from state to state and country to country. Use at your own risk. Inclusion does not constitute legal advice. Blah blah blah, etc.)

Video Operator /Photographer Form

Get in writing permission to use images, performances, and results of work for free, forever, without limits. This is not being piggy. You can pay them later if you want, you just don't want them demanding payment while you're still losing money. Also, you don't want them to put limits on how you can use them in your work and make you change it after its done. This way, you have the maximum amount of creative control. Just be fair. It's nice to play fair.

I put some of myself into everything. Here are some release forms I wrote. (Feel free to change them and use them if you need one. And you do need one. You might wanna take the Gwar part out, unless you're shooting Gwar. And replace my name with yours unless your name is Michael W. Dean.)

This first form, *Photographer Release Form*, is pretty all-inclusive, and could be used for video operators, still camera operators, and such. The second one, *Subject Form*, could be used for interview subjects for a documentary or actors in a drama or comedy. The third, *Music Release Form*, is to get permission to use people's music, recorded or live, in your film. I would use it whether I were filming an artist's performance, or using an artist's CD as background music.

Photographer Release Form

I, _____, (herein called " Videographer") hereby release full rights to reproduce and display pictures, video, film, or photos I may have taken or art I have produced, in whole or in part, to Michael W. Dean. These rights shall include but not be limited to, altered images, electronic images, and all other reproductions of these images, for use on the Web sites, CD-ROMs, record albums, posters, plays, movies, and any other media produced and/or owned by Michael W. Dean or as advertisement for such media.

This contract is limited to footage for the movie *D.I.Y. OR DIE: How to Survive as an Independent Artist*.

I release Michael W. Dean and those acting with his authority from any responsibility, damage, or liability which may result from the taking and reproduction of said footage or still pictures; this shall include, but not be limited to, any claims for libel or invasion of privacy. Michael W. Dean may use, and exploit, or also not use, any and all of these photos or footage. I understand that I will not be paid in cash, and that the pleasure of contributing to the majestic art of Michael W. Dean is payment enough. I also understand that Michael W. Dean is under no obligation to use them. I will only be given a free ticket to a Gwar show.

I also understand that if I end up in any photos of footage, Michael W. Dean may use my image in said photos or footage, without limitation and without compensation.

By signing below I signify that I am at least 18 years of age. I also certify that I am able to contract in my own name. Michael W. Dean will take the tapes at the end of each session for safekeeping. Michael W. Dean has the right to use the images without charge, in film, Web, CD, print, and any other medium, extant or future, throughout the known (and unknown) universe. I also grant Michael W. Dean rights to assign these rights to a third party.

I REALIZE THAT AT A GWAR SHOW I MAY DIE OR BE PERMANENTLY DISFIGURED. IN THIS EVENT I WILL NOT HOLD GWAR OR MICHAEL W. DEAN OR THE VENUE RESPONSIBLE.

Signature, Videographer. _____

Subject Release Form

I hereby agree to appear in the film (also known as "documentary") currently called *D.I.Y. or DIE: How to Survive as an Independent Artist*, and I hereby irrevocably grant Michael W. Dean, and his licensees, agents, successors, and assigns, the right (but not the obligation), in perpetuity throughout the world, in all media, now or hereafter known, to use (in any manner he deems appropriate, and without limitation) in and in connection with the documentary, by whatever means exhibited, advertised, my appearance in the documentary, still photographs of me, recordings of my voice taken or made of me by it, and my actual or fictitious name. I will not be paid or otherwise reimbursed for said use.

On my own behalf, and on behalf of my heirs, next of kin, executors, administrators, successors and assigns, I hereby release Michael W. Dean, his agents, licensees, successors and assigns, from any and all claims, liabilities, and damages arising out of the rights granted hereunder, or the exercise thereof.

I authorize Michael W. Dean to use my image in perpetuity throughout the known universe in any mediums extant or later invented.

Date:_____

Signature:_____

Printed Name:_____

Name for Screen Credit (if different):_____

Street Address:_____

City:_____State:_____Zip_____

e-mail address:_____

Telephone Number:_____

_____

Additional consent to use music sung or played by me, as agreed:_____

Limitations:_____

Initial:_____

Music Release Form

I _____hereby allow use of some of my songs in the film (also known as "documentary") called *D.I.Y. or DIE: How to Survive as an Independent Artist*, and I hereby irrevocably grant Michael W. Dean, the rights to use my work and image in his film.

No payment is expected or implied. I will be credited for said use, and linked on the movie's Web site. Michael will also always brag to lots of people about how cool my music is.

On my own behalf, and on behalf of my heirs, next of kin, executors, administrators, successors and assigns, I hereby release Michael W. Dean, his agents, licensees, successors, and assigns, from any and all claims, liabilities and damages arising out of the rights granted hereunder, or the exercise thereof.

I authorize Michael W. Dean to use my music and image in this film in perpetuity throughout the known universe in any mediums extant or later invented.

Date: _____

Signature: _____

Printed Name: _____

Street Address: _____

City: _____ State: _____ Zip_____

Telephone Number: _____

Michael W. Dean loves you and thanks you. He will only use your songs for good, never for evil.

Please sign and mail to:

MICHAEL W. DEAN 1634 W. Sunset Blvd. #222, Los Angeles, CA 90026

Summary

So...where the producer basically helps the trains run on time, the director drives the train. The director is in charge of *everything*, and moves the other members of the crew as his brush to paint the bigger picture.

Now...let's actually get shooting.

Chapter 6

Filming and Recording Techniques

This is where we actually start making a film. We now need to learn the basics of using a camera, as well as getting good sound, which is imperative in the overall scheme of making a professional-level film. It doesn't take long to get these technical skills down, and then you can concentrate on having fun making great art.

Filming Techniques

Filming techniques are the brushes in your pallet. You can quickly master the basic shots and movements that are universal to all movie making, and then go on to develop your own style using these brushes.

Shooting Basics

All you really need to do is make your shots in focus, well lit, and with good sound. If you get good at quickly and consistently achieving all that, you're doing better than most indie filmmakers, and then you can really concentrate on the story. Mini-DV is much more forgiving than film with regards to amount and color of light you need to use. My friend Newt shoots most of his mini-DV shots using a single bright bulb from the 99-Cent store. (See Figures 6.1 through 6.7.)

But you can get as elaborate and creative as you want, and borrow all the tricks used by big-money shoots, even without the big money, and get amazing results.

Watch how shots are framed in movies. It's not random. The amount of space around a character, and the angle, is crucial to the look and feel. Stuff in the background is important. You can tell another story by background action that compliments, or even intentionally conflicts with, the story being told in the foreground. Sometimes the stuff going on in the background of a shot is more important than the stuff in the foreground. Especially in comedy. Look for it.

It's usually good to have people look right past the lens, not into it. If you have one of those little red "on" lights on the front of your camera, have people play to it,

Figure 6.1 *Newt's 99-cent light.* All photos in this chapter, unless otherwise noted, are by Newtron Foto.

Figure 6.2 *Newt's 99-cent light in its 99-cent fixture.*

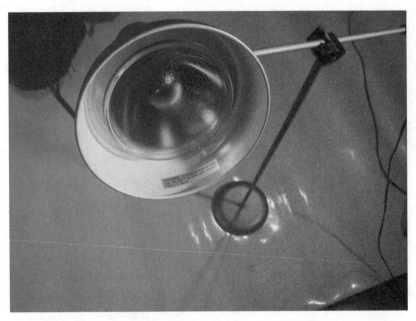

Figure 6.3 *More of Newt's 99-cent light in its 99-cent fixture.*

Figure 6.4 *Well-lit shot (model: Traci Burr).*

Figure 6.5 *Another well-lit shot.*

Figure 6.6 *Too much light—washed out.*

Figure 6.7 *Out-of-focus shot.*

not the lens. Unless they are *breaking the fourth wall*, i.e. addressing the camera directly in a way that admits and acknowledges that a camera is being addressed.

Sometimes the best camerawork is not obvious. Woody Allen's films look beautiful, and have great camerawork, though it doesn't jump out and demand to be noticed. The camerawork isn't a showoff. It's like Michael Urbano's drum playing (Smash Mouth, Cheryl Crow, Cracker). His drumming is great but doesn't jump out or call attention to itself. It serves the song. You notice the story and acting, not the camerawork. Also amazing is that Woody Allen gets huge stars to act for scale (the minimum pay the union will allow…usually reserved for unknowns) because he's Woody Allen. This is D.I.Y. on a bigger scale.

Camera Basics

Basically you want good focus and exposure. *Focus* moves the lens inside your camera until the subject you're shooting is no longer blurry. *Exposure* changes the amount of light entering the camera. It varies on how much light you have available, and what type of mood you're looking for. These are controlled by two main knobs somewhere on your camera. Placement is different for all of them. Find these controls and practice until using them is second nature. Other basic things to remember:

◆ For better image while filming, go into the menu and turn off the camera's autofocus. Autofocus is an amateur no-brainer function that should be disabled in the camera settings for most good filmmaking. I forgot and left it on for some of *D.I.Y.* and it makes the lens look like it's "breathing" as it continuously tries to refocus to the subtle movements of the subjects as they speak and gesticulate. Do the focus manually—you'll have better control over everything.

◆ Also, don't forget to white balance—point the camera at a white piece of paper each time you set up a scene, and find the place on the menu to reset the white to zero. Remember those instructions you threw in the trash? Take them out of the trash. The menus are different on every camera.

◆ Make sure the lighting is good. It's not hard to do. Mini-DV is way more forgiving with variances in exposure and even focus than film.

◆ What you see through the small black and white viewfinder is a more accurate representation of the brightness and contrast that is actually printing to the tape than the bigger flip-out color monitor. I use both—color for color and the black and white one for contrast.

◆ Using the color flip-out monitor will kill your batteries faster though. And you should always buy an extra battery or three and keep them charged and available on a shoot. If indoors, I use the AC adapter whenever I can to save batteries. There's nothing sadder than ripping along with a shoot and running out of charged batteries.

Most cameras also have some different settings on the menu for Night Vision, Black and White, Sepia Tone, Wide Screen, and so forth. These are cool, but keep in mind that anything you add in the camera (as opposed to in the editing), you will not be able to take out. You'll be stuck with it. Of all the settings available, Night Vision is probably the most useful because it's not an effect per se, just the ability to film in almost no light.

Shots

There are several main types of shots that make up most of what is used in films. Of course, you might invent a few more for us to add to this palette. I hope you do.

Master Shot

This is a shot to establish a scene, to give the viewer a reference point (see Figure 6.8). Like, if the scene is a couple talking by a bridge in Paris, the master shot will usually be a wide shot from fairly far away to show where they are, i.e. in Paris by a bridge. This provides "coverage" and also is used for cutting away to later in the scene.

Figure 6.8 *Establishing (master) two-shot (models: left, Jillian Suzanne. right, Traci Burr).*

Then we often move into a...

Medium Close-Up

This is a shot done from two to five feet away. Now we can see the faces of the people (see Figure 6.9).

Then we might move in closer for a close-up (see Figure 6.10).

Two-Shot

A close tight shot where the two people from the chest up fill the screen (see Figure 6.11).

Figure 6.9 *Medium close-up.*

Figure 6.10 *Close-up (model: Hannah Crum).*

Figure 6.11 *Two-shot.*

Then once they are talking, an...

Over-the-Shoulder Shot

Watch how common this is when people are talking. The point of view switches in the editing from behind the person talking, over their shoulder, to show the reactions of the other person (see Figures 6.12 and 6.13).

This you will skillfully combine in the editing to also show the face of the person talking in a medium close-up (shown in Figure 6.9). Taken from about a foot or two away. One person's head films the frame. Occasionally we want to cut to an...

Extreme Close-Up

Part of one person's face fills the screen, usually eyes or eyes and mouth (see Figure 6.14). Can produce anxiety in the viewer, and is often used for this effect.

These shots are all shot separately. You, as the director, have to understand how they are used, and direct the actors and the camera person in achieving them. Often, you'll want to do several takes, for more "coverage" (covering your butt to make sure you have enough good material to select from during editing).

Figure 6.12 *Over-the-shoulder shot (Traci Burr on right).*

Figure 6.13 *Another over-the-shoulder shot. (Hannah Crum on left).*

Figure 6.14 *Extreme close-up.*

You want to get enough takes, but not so many that it becomes complicated to pick and choose when editing. At first or when in doubt, it is probably better to get more. But with experience (and better actors), you should be able to nail many performances and shots in one or two takes.

Handheld Camera Shots

Handheld camera shots (see Figure 6.15) work differently from those done on tripods. They are less restricting: they give a feeling of movement and action. They can seem kind of amateur, but are often used to effect by "pros" to make slick productions look "edgy" (think MTV and many reality TV shows).

My productions by nature are pretty "edgy" already. So instead, I go for slick and end up way edgier than pros trying to come down to my world. I don't use handheld shots to try and look "street" because I already *am* street. I use handheld shots for momentum.

If I had *D.I.Y. or DIE* to do over, I would have used fewer tripod shots and more handheld shots. The little bit of handheld we used really opened up the feel. (Like

Figure 6.15 *Danny Plotnick doing handheld with an 8 mm film camera.* I'm Not Fascinating (The Movie!) photo by Anthony Bedard.

the second camera on the Ian MacKaye interview, and the entire Little Mike interview.)

A handheld camera implies action more than a tripod setup, but it makes the viewer uncomfortable if overused. Or even seasick—think *Blair Witch Project*. Handheld can also be used as an effect (see Figure 6.16). Notice in the movie *Wall Street* that most of the film is tripod shots until the protagonist's world starts falling apart. Then it's mostly handheld.

Figure 6.16 *Handheld camera shot.*

Tripod Shots

Tripod shots (see Figure 6.17) are rock-steady, but kinda boring if overused. They can be done without a tripod if need be. In *D.I.Y. or DIE*, I often just set the camera on some books.

Keep in mind that you want to be careful about shooting people, especially women, from below. It's really easy to get too much double chin (see Figure 6.18). Slightly above tends to work better if they have any kind of chin action going on.

Figure 6.17 *Tripod camera shot.*

Figure 6.18 *Chin exaggerated when shot from below.*

NOTE

There is an old saying that "The camera adds ten pounds". What this really means is that the camera exaggerates anything you've got. If you're shooting an emaciated person, he's not gonna look healthy. He's going to look ten pounds *more* emaciated.

Dutch Tilts

A Dutch tilt is when the camera is at an angle that makes the room look slanted. Cool, but disorienting, especially if overused. Think "Batman" (the TV show, not the movie). It was named for a Dutch director who liked them a lot. (Or was it a director named Dutch?)

Dutch tilts are extra cool when done from or near a *worm's eye view*, which is a shot done from a foot or lower off the ground (see Figure 6.19). Shooting from below tends to make a subject look imposing and larger than life. Shooting from above (*bird's eye view*) tends to make the subject look and feel smaller (see Figure 6.20).

Figure 6.19 *Worm's eye view shot with cameraperson on the floor. Model: Jillian Suzanne.*

Figure 6.20 *Bird's eye view shot with cameraperson on a ladder.*

Dollies and Rolling Shots

Dolly or rolling shots actually have the camera moving on a smooth track. Think a cross between handheld and tripod. You can replicate this with a baby carriage if need be. Or a wheelchair. Or a skateboard. Or a car. Or a bicycle. Use your imagination. You can duplicate anything, including *Steadicam* (good for smooth running shots). For a steadicam, you need a gyro-powered stability motor added to the camera housing. It's not hard to build similar housings if you can't afford to buy one. And *aerial* shots (see Figures 6.21 and 6.22) can be achieved if you stretch what you have. (Get up in a building, a tree, or a ladder, or use a balloon on a rope.) Anything the big boys do, you can too if you get clever.

Point of View

Point of view (POV) describes whose eyes the camera is supposed to be looking through. It is often indicated in the action direction of a script. It can be the person talking, the person being talked to, or often an omniscient observer, an imaginary non-character who sees everything. In some movies, it is a combination of all of these. Look at this when you study a film, and keep it in mind when you write. You'll get a feel for it and soon be acting on it in your direction.

Figure 6.21 *A group shot done from on a ladder.*

Figure 6.22 *The author on a ladder, getting an aerial shot.*

Lighting

Study lighting in films. Then get a couple of cheap lights from a camera store, hardware store, or garage sale. Experiment with different colors. Experiment with different angles. Try things. The whole point of *$30 Film School* is to get out there and do it, rather than reading about it. That's the only way to really learn.

Hollywood movies use very elaborate lighting equipment and setups to maintain total control over every aspect of the lighting. It's an art unto itself.

You probably won't have access to this kind of equipment, but I'll show it to you anyway, as you can get an idea of little lights you can buy, and how to approximate the techniques used when money is no object. (See Figures 6.23 through 6.25.)

Lighting can be used to simulate anything. In most Hollywood movies, it is even used to simulate natural and ambient lighting. Scenes that look like they are lit by the sun or the moon or where you see lightning or a shimmering reflection of water on the roof of a boat were almost always done with artificial lighting, baffles, gels, motors, and other artificial means. Simulating natural effects with electrical means makes a lot of sense because you have absolute control over the outcome, whereas with nature, you are at the whims of chance. (See Figures 6.26 through 6.28.)

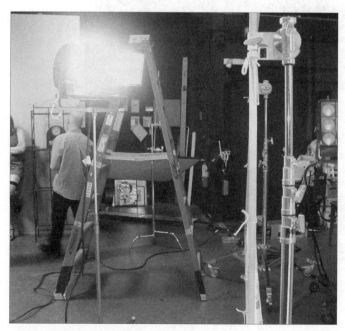

Figure 6.23 *Behind the scenes on a set.*

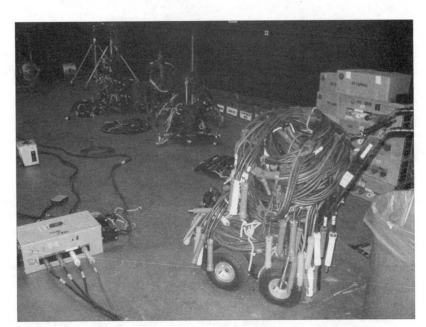

Figure 6.24 *Electrical connectors and ballast used to power big lights.*

Figure 6.25 *Fun pro light stuff.*

Figure 6.26 *Fake daylight 1.*

Figure 6.27 *Fake daylight 2.*

Figure 6.28 *Fake daylight with lights and clamps visible.*

Figures 6.29 through 6.32 demonstrate how some of these lighting effects were achieved:

Figure 6.29 *Fake daylight backstage 1.*

Figure 6.30 *Fake daylight backstage 2.*

Figure 6.31 *Fake daylight backstage 3.*

Figure 6.32 *Fake daylight backstage 4.*

Lighting is not used only to illuminate the scene; it goes beyond that. It can set the mood. For instance, notice that lighting someone from below makes them look sinister, and from above, angelic (see Figures 6.33 and 6.34).

Figure 6.33 *Lighting from below looks sinister.*   **Figure 6.34** *Lighting from above looks angelic.*

Also notice that in a lot of movies and TV shows, there's a little smoke in the air. You may not notice it as smoke, but it adds depth to the shot, makes film seem three-dimensional, when film and video is, in fact, a two-dimensional medium. You can get liquid and hardware to make this smoke at a film rental supply shop, magic shop, or rock-and-roll music store. Or you can improvise by burning dried sage, although it may bug your actors and crew.

Waving a bounce card in the air before a take will help diffuse the smoke and make it more evenly distributed, which is good, unless you are trying to make it look like there is smoke in the room; then it's probably fine as is.

Bounce Cards

A bounce card is a large (2' by 2' or bigger) piece of white Foamcore (available at an art supply shop) or a foldable device covered with silver fabric that bounces ambient natural light or electric light into a subject's face. This helps to avoid the appearance of actors being in the dark or having unwanted shadows fall across their faces. This is important and is an easy way to make any shot look more professional.

It also can be used on props. Many shots involve the use of several bounce cards: one or more for each actor, and one or more each for several key objects, props, or areas in a scene. You can set up stands to hold them at the proper angle, prop them up against objects, or have them held by your loving crew members. Keep in mind that if the subject moves or the Sun moves, the bounce card must move also. It is sometimes someone's dedicated job to hold and move these cards. (See Figures 6.35 through 6.37.)

Figure 6.35 *A large bounce card.*

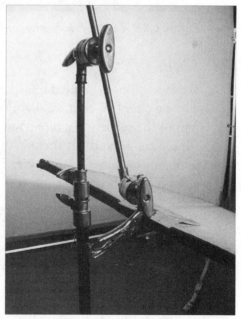

Figure 6.36 *A C-clamp holding a bounce card.*

Figure 6.37 *A hand-held bounce card.*

Gels

Gels are sheets of colored transparent cellophane used to change the color of light coming out of an electrical light (see Figure 6.38). They can also be used over the lens of the camera as a filter. You can buy sheets of them at camera supply or art supply shops, and cut them as needed. Make sure they don't touch the actual lamp; movie lamps can get very hot, and they will melt or burn if they come in contact with the bulb.

Scrims

Scrims are anything you put in front of the light to diffuse light and make it less harsh (see Figures 6.39 and 6.40). They can be metal, wood, or fabric, and can either clip on the face of the light or be mounted in front of it with a C-stand.

Notice that in Figure 6.40, the walls are fake and only go as high as a little above the camera line. This is a living room movie set permanently set up to teach film students to light Hollywood sets. Sitcoms are often done this way: making the room a three-sided façade rather than a real six-sided room is cheaper, and gives much more flexibility in how you light it, film it, and mike it.

Figure 6.38 *Hannah with a sheet of gel.*

Figure 6.39 *Fabric scrim on C-stand in front of light panel under huge overhead light.*

Figure 6.40 *Hannah with various small metal scrims that mount on the front of small lights.*

A Cucalorus (also called a Cookie) is a special wooden scrim used to simulate the look of sunlight through leaves (see Figure 6.41). Buy 'em or make 'em.

Figure 6.41 *A Cucalorus set up.*

Baffles

Baffles are pieces of fabric, white or black, set up behind lights to diffuse reflected light, to give a more "natural" feel to the light in an area. (See Figure 6.42.)

Book Lighting

Book lighting is setting up two lighting units on either side of a translucent baffle, to *bookend* the light (see Figure 6.43). The subject could be on either side of this setup and look good because there would be light in front of them, and the light coming through the back would eliminate shadows.

C-Stands

A C-stand is an all-purpose adjustable stand and clamp for holding lights, scrims, baffles, and so forth. You can buy 'em at camera supply shops, hardware stores, or make 'em. (See Figure 6.39.)

Figure 6.42 *A Cucalorus set up with a baffle behind it.*

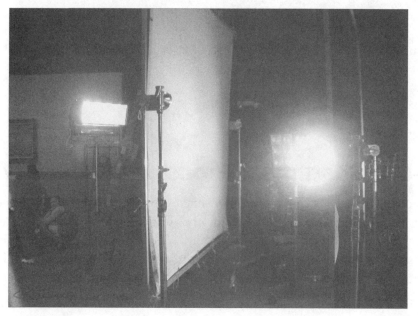

Figure 6.43 *Book lighting.*

Sandbags

Sandbags are literally that. Bags filled with sand (see Figure 6.44). They are heavy and are used to make stands stay in place and not tip over or move. Simply lay the sandbag over the bottom of the stands. The less they touch the ground, the more effective they are. The idea is to have them laying over the stand supports but not touching the ground so all their weight is put into keeping the device in place. You can buy 'em at camera supply shops and hardware stores, or you can make 'em.

Figure 6.44 *Hannah with a sandbag.*

Make-Up, Costumes, Props, and Scenery

Be as elaborate as you want to be with make-up. Sometimes makeup is used merely to bring out the cheekbones and other features of the subjects. You need less of it with video than you would with film. Make-up can also denote sexiness, the absurd, horror, death, blood, disease, scars, track marks, gangrene, old age, anything you like (see Figure 6.45).

Color is important in costumes. Make your world vivid, unless you are intention- ally trying to denote a bland place to serve the story. Make your universe breathe

Figure 6.45 *Cool make-up in Rusty Nails' film,* Grethel & Hansel. Photo by Chris Rejano.

on tape. And know that the clothes do make the man. Try dressing in rags and approaching people to ask directions and then try the same thing when you're well-groomed and wearing a suit. Notice the difference in their reactions to you. (When I say things like this, I'm not being rhetorical. These are *$30 Film School* homework assignments.) Costuming contributes a lot toward how we perceive the believability of an actor. This is why politicians, televangelists, and used car salesmen always try to look good.

Stuff people hold or use is called props. A lot of attention to detail can go into this, but it doesn't have to. You can make it like a play where they'll use a wooden mock-up of a gun and demand some imagination. Or you can be as detailed as big-budget movies where people spend months painstakingly painting and crafting everyday objects to have an exact look and feel.

Check out the movie *Amelie.* It is amazingly vivid in set design and props. Every object is very strategically chosen and intentionally placed, with color choices relating one object to another. The director worked hard on this with the cinematographer to make each scene pop. (They also did some cool color correction in post to make this even more vivid.)

(*Post* means *Post-Production*, i.e. doing something in the editing after the film is shot, rather than in *Production*, i.e. while shooting.)

A prop should serve a purpose. There's an old saying, "If you show a gun in act one, you'd better use it in act three." Don't throw anything in meaninglessly. Consider its impact and give it the consideration it deserves. Make sure the prop is well lit, well photographed, and looks like what it's supposed to look like.

Scenery can be as elaborate or as barren as you need. Sometimes, you don't need to overdo it, and you certainly don't need to if you don't have the budget. I was watching Nick Zedd's "Police State" in Seattle with my friend Kurt Shute. I said, "Wow, this is low budget as all get out...they don't even try to make that room look like a police station." Kurt said, "It's great. It doesn't have to look real. It's a play."

And then it hit me...that's a key in cheap filmmaking. *It's a play*. A lot of films with no money try to do things that look like they had money, fall short, and look cheesy. Better to just have good acting, good camera work, good dialogue, and good ideas. Zedd had this. And the acting is better than great: It might not even be acting. I'm pretty sure they actually *are* beating him up. Zedd would probably do that for his art. I think one of them is a real homeless person. Why *not* hire real bums? They can use the work. And a lot of the bums in Los Angeles are really handsome. They probably used to be movie stars.

Camera Techniques and Effects

The Rule of 180

There is a *Rule of 180* taught in film schools. I'm too dyslexic to really understand it. I am told I break it all the time, but my shots work anyway.

Okay, basically, the rule is this: You don't usually want to edit from one shot to another shot of the same scene if they are filmed from an angle of more than 180 degrees from each other. If you do, you confuse the viewer unnecessarily. For instance, if you were showing a football game, you don't want to cut to a shot from the other side of the guy running, because it will seem like he switched directions and ran the wrong way for a minute. When you break this rule, it's called "crossing the axis."

This is much more noticeable on steady shots than in handheld ones. Break this rule if needed, but first know that it exists. I broke it intentionally in one scene in *I Left My Pants in San Diego*. It's the scene near the end where the skating bunny-boy saves the girl on the sidewalk from choking. I broke the rule three times: in the "Worm's Eye View" edit, at the "Shaking Hands" edit, and a third time when Bunnyboy skates away, but is actually skating towards the spot where he just saved the girl from choking.

Framing

Shots should be well framed, unless you are intentionally framing them unconventionally for effect. Basically, you want good *nose room* (amount of space in front of the person's face) and good *head room* (amount of space above the person's head). (See Figures 6.46 through 6.50.)

Figure 6.46 *No nose room (also poorly lit).*

Figure 6.47 *Good nose room.*

Figure 6.48 *No head room—frame cut off.*

Figure 6.50 *Good headroom.*

Figure 6.49 *Too much head room.*

In *D.I.Y. or DIE*, I often intentionally framed extra space to the left or to the right of whoever was speaking. My idea was to treat their words as if the words were a character. They don't like this stuff in film school. I am told it breaks some other rule also, but I'm not sure which one.

Pan

Panning is when you move the camera from side to side to get a whole scene you can't get in one static shot. You want to work towards having a smooth motion when doing this, whether you are going hand-held or locked down on a tripod.

You can also, if need be, simulate a pan action in the post, but it is a different look and feel. This sort of panning is more suited to moving along a high-rez scan of a still image, like a poster or a record cover. You can do an extremely smooth pan in post, in the editing program rather than with a camera movement. We did this in *D.I.Y. or DIE*. Look for it when we show John John Jessie's painting and the Stooges album cover.

I mention examples from my film *D.I.Y. or DIE* a lot. I recommend you get it. In a way, this book is a companion piece to the movie and vice versa. A trailer for the film is included on the CD-ROM with this book, and the whole film is available on DVD and VHS in most Tower Records stores.

Zoom

Zooming is using the focus on the camera to manually pull closer to or away from the subject. People new to filmmaking tend to overdo this because it's neat and they feel in control. But overdoing it looks cheap and amateurish. Look how sparingly it's used in the films you like; look at where and why it's used; and experiment with it yourself until you're comfortable with the results.

Zooming, too, can be simulated in editing, but it's a different sort of animal. Doing it in post will show an apparent degradation of the image (because you are amplifying the same limited number of pixels that were captured from the big picture for your smaller picture). This does not happen as much when you zoom while shooting.

Filters

You can get filters to screw on over the lens of the camera, or you can make your own. Filters change the look of the image printing to the tape. The advantage is that you can instantly get a new look without the huge render times you would have if you added the effect in post. The disadvantage is that you're stuck with whatever you use: you cannot undo it in post.

You can buy filters made specifically to fit over your camera lens from a camera store or online. You can also get adapter rings that will make filters made to fit bigger film cameras work on your Mini-DV camera. You can also just get lighting gels and tape them over the lens. (Make sure none of the gum from the tape gets into the inside of the camera.) See *I Left My Heart in San Diego* for use of a red filter. Also watch the movie *Fight Club*—most of it is shot with a blue filter, which makes it look cool (as opposed to "warm") and kind of spooky. You can also use a filter to shoot in daylight that simulates night. Many night shots are done this way. It's far easier to do this than to get a good shot at night. The filter you use is called a *Day-as-Night* filter.

It's easy to tell when this is done in movies—just look at the shadows and the reflections on water—they are far more intense from the sun in Day-as-Night shots than they would be in a night shot.

Blue Screen

Blue screen, or ChromaKey, allows you to shoot a subject against a blue or green solid-painted wall, and then later *key out* that color in the editing program. Then you can insert another background behind them, and make them appear to fly, or be in a far-off location, or anything you can imagine.

You can do blue screen at home. Just paint a wall solid blue for people or solid green for objects. (Either color will work for either in a pinch.) Then you ChromaKey them out in the editing program.

Filming Computer Monitors

When you see someone on the news talking in her office, the computer monitor behind her usually has lines running top to bottom. This interference is caused by the fact that screens display at 60 cycles per second (also called 60 Hertz or 60 Hz). Many video cameras capture at a *dropped frame rate*, a sort of computer Voodoo leap year thang that somehow adjusts itself to what technically works out to 29.97 FPS (frames per second) rather than the actual 30 FPS. The reasons aren't important and I shan't go into them here (Okay, I don't know), but the result is a drag—those lines on the screen. If it were 30 FPS, it would be no problem; 30 goes evenly into 60 Hz. But it's a little less than that, so you see the beats.

An analogous situation is when you're tuning your guitar and the notes are almost in but not quite, and you hear beats in the tone....a sort of "wha wha wha" pattern.

Basically the number of beats is the number of cycles per second off...if one note is at 440 and one is 443 cycles per second, you'll hear three beats per second. As you get closer and closer into tune, the beats get slower and slower until you're in tune and they stop.

Another analogy here would be that drop-frame rate is to video what equal temperament tuning is to music; a compromise: humans trying to fit the parameters of nature into rigid manmade strictures.

Out here in California, some creative people consider the incredible amount of math that is required to imitate nature to actually be proof of the existence of God.[1]

Nothing in the preceding paragraph is important, but it was fun. It actually will be important when you start doing subtitles on your DVD and must make sure they line up with the speaking throughout—keeping them from drifting out of synch. What is important is how to get rid of those crappy lines if you have to shoot a scene that includes a computer monitor.

In Windows:

1. Right mouse click on the desktop.
2. Select Properties/Setting/Advanced/Monitor.

On a Mac: Click on Monitors/Control Panel.

Make sure it's set at 60 Hz. Then in your camera settings change your camera to a 1/30th shutter speed (or 1/60th if it has that). (This varies from camera to camera...check the manual.) That should work.

Film Grain

The easiest way to fake film grain is to stretch some pantyhose over the lens of your Mini-DV camera and lock them down with duct tape or a strong rubber band. This can actually look surprisingly like film. It sometimes won't work if you are shooting in direct sunlight....the sun will reflect on the pantyhose and you'll see the sun, not the grain. Also, it won't work if you have the autofocus on because the camera will try to focus on the pantyhose, not the subject.

---

1. Fibonacci numbers are the real proof. And the Golden Section is actually the same as some film screen ratio. Search "Fibonacci numbers" or "Golden Section" on google.com for an amazing plethora of baffling and intriguing Web sites on this subject.

You can also do it in the editing. This will be covered later in Chapter 8, "Editing Images."

Publicity Stills

Bring someone on each shoot with a regular still film camera to take stills for promo posters, the Web, and other places you might need a still photo. They will look much better than frame captures (see Chapter 7, "Computers").

I didn't know about needing stills when I did *D.I.Y. or DIE*, and I ended up having to do screen captures. They look crappy, especially when printed. (DV frame captures are only 72 d.p.i. (dots per inch) in resolution, whereas most scanned photos for printing are between 300 and 1200 d.p.i.) I wish I'd known to even bring along a disposable camera. My publicity shots would have looked better.

A 35 mm camera is often used, but in my experience, a good megapixel digital camera is fine. Whereas it will be a few years before digital movies look as good as a projected 35 mm movie, right now digital stills from a digital still camera can take huge-rez pictures that look incredible when printed. Technology will catch up with this on moving pictures soon. I guarantee.

Recording Techniques

One thing I knew getting into filmmaking (a thing that isn't common knowledge but should be) is that excellent sound is about 10 times more important than an excellent image in terms of how people perceive the professionalism of a movie, and how much they enjoy watching it.

Student films often seem like student films because of poor sound. And it's inexcusable, because it takes 15 minutes or less to teach someone how to do good sound. I've seen fourth-year film school shorts with horrible sound. These schools and teachers should be ashamed for taking people's money.

Recording Sound on Location

Most of the sound in *I Left My Pants in San Diego* (the training film on the CD-ROM included with this book) is camera sound, and is not great. This is because I didn't have access to any good recorders or mikes at the time. A couple of scenes are shot synch, with a dictaphone in the subject's pocket, but overall it's not a great example of sound on a film shoot (except for the fact that many of the shots are intentionally quite close so as to get serviceable camera sound).

I did take the sound into SoundForge and tweak it a little when the file was locked. (The project is *locked* after all the edits are made, and the length is not going to change. Then the sound can be exported and worked on without affecting the synch.) I applied a tiny bit of compression to the whole thing, and also adjusted the levels a little bit. We show how to do this in Chapter 9, "Editing Audio."

Excellent sound isn't that hard to get: just stick a microphone *in front of or directly above* the subject. Not too close unless they're very quiet, as it will be *too* loud, and will distort. Try different things to get the right balance. (See Figure 6.51.)

If an external mike isn't available, or the camera doesn't have an input jack for one, then you have to use camera sound (the microphone that is built into the camera). Put the camera about 15 inches (maximum) from the subject's mouth. You can go a little farther if you have a *great* mike. But not too far. I am always amazed that people film with camcorders with no external mike from, like, 8 or 15 feet away and then wonder why they can't hear their subjects talking.

Figure 6.51 *Mike placement in Danny Plotnick's film,* Swingers' Serenade. Photo by Robert Toren.

Have your people talk clearly, and make sure all noisy stuff in the room is off (cell phones, computers, refrigerators, open doors, everything). (See Figures 6.52 and 6.53.)

Figure 6.52 *Quiet on the set.*

Figure 6.53 *Quiet on the set. I mean it!*

Stuff clothing or pillows under the doors to further deaden noise. Even ask the neighbors to be quiet. Be bold but polite. You're making art for the ages. Don't be afraid to ask anyone anything, although they might, in turn, ask you to put them in your film. Be sure you have enough release forms handy at all times, and make it clear to people who beg to be in it that they will not be paid no matter how many billions of dollars the film generates.

You can also use a lavaliere (clip-on) mike, like the newscasters use. Hide it if you're doing a drama; don't if it's a documentary.

The best microphones for film sound, be they boom mikes or lavaliere mikes, are powered condenser mikes. This means they have a battery pack that you will need to remember to turn on to use, and turn off when not using. You may also need a line transformer and an adapter to plug it directly into the camera. This will be covered in the manual. If it's not, ask at the store where you bought the camera.

A boom is basically a long stick you use to get the microphone near the subject. (See Figure 6.54.)

You can buy quality booms at any photo supply store, or in a pinch, just duct tape a microphone to a broom handle! (See Figure 6.55.)

Figure 6.54 *Proper boom stance.*

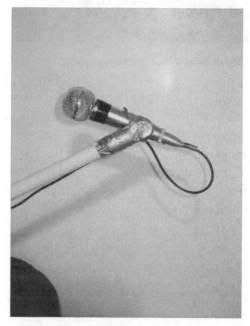

Figure 6.55 *Punk-rock boom stand.*

Try to keep your boom and mike out of the picture. Doing that is someone's dedicated job in a big Hollywood shoot. It's tricky. You will even occasionally see the microphone accidentally dip into view for a split second in some lower budget movies. (See Figure 6.56.)

Figure 6.56 *Punk-rock boom stand in use.*

If you're shooting outside, use a windscreen to cut down on noise. This might help indoors also if you have someone with a lot of *sibilance* (sssssssss sounds) or *plosives* (excessive B, D, and P sounds) in their speech. You can make one using socks, mesh, or other fabrics to cover the microphone. Again, experiment. Windscreens can cut down the high end of the audio spectrum—the place where treble lives—so only use them if you need to, and you may have to adjust the high end a bit in post

You (or your sound person) should bring some headphones and plug them into the camera to monitor the sound. Do a check to make sure it's not too quiet, or so loud that it's distorted. Adjust the microphone distance until it seems right.

There is probably a switch called *attenuation* on your camera. This turns down the sensitivity of the microphone by a set number of decibels. You can use this when recording in very loud environments (such as rock bands). But remember to turn it back for your next normal volume scene.

Slating for Synch Sound

Slating is using a clapper to put a visual cue with an audio cue to allow sound to be synched (synchronized). In film, unlike video, there is no sound recording track on the stock. It is done on a separate recorder, and synched up later. The editor does this by finding the first frame where the clapper is closed, and lining it up with the sound of the "clap" produced at the same time. Thus, the audio matches the video, and people's lips move when they should.

To summarize:

You can do audio on your Mini-DV in three ways:

◆ First is to just use camera sound.

◆ Better is to use an external microphone plugged into the input on the camera.

◆ Best is an external mike going into a separate digital recording device, like a mini-disc recorder or DAT (digital audio tape) recorder. You can run the microphone or microphones through a mixer to set ideal levels, and so forth. This will give you more control and better sound, but you will have to slate each shot and synch in the computer later.

Slate every shot, even if you are going direct into the camera. Even if you don't have a slate, you can just clap your hands clearly in front of the lens (see Figures 6.57 through 6.59). This will help if later you decide to take the sound out to Pro Tools and tweak it. For more on Pro Tools and tweaking sound, see Chapter 9, "Editing Audio."

It is important for the editor (possibly you, so it's *extra* important) to be able to quickly find which scene and take they are dealing with. That's why you say the name of the film, the scene, and take each time you slate. Like "My Kick-Ass Movie, scene 22 (or Bathroom Junkie Scene), take four." Pause, then clap the clapper (on which you've also written "My Kick-Ass Movie, scene 22 (or Bathroom Junkie Scene), take four" in dry erase marker. Update the dry erase text (or use masking tape and regular Magic Marker) and spoken take number with each take…this makes it easier to find the right take when editing.

Figure 6.57 *Slating without a clapper.*

Figure 6.58 *Slating without a clapper 2.*

Figure 6.59 *Slating without a clapper 3.*

There should then be a five-second-or-so pause before the actor or interviewer begins speaking. This allows the tape to get up to correct speed, and gives some space (*handles*) around talking, which makes editing easier.

This is also a good time for me to tell you to not cut off your interviewees when doing a documentary. My interview style was sometimes more conversation than interview, and I think I would do it differently now. It was hell sometimes in editing, trying to find in- and out-points where I wasn't talking over the last or first thing they said. If you talk other than asking questions when you interview, pause a second or two when the interviewee is done before you start speaking again.

If you don't have a clapper, use your hands. Just make sure to keep them in frame and parallel to the lens. And write the take number and name on a piece of paper and hold it in front of the lens before you do the clap. You can do all this slating yourself, or if you have a sound person or intern, she can do it. Or the lighting person sometimes takes this task. Or if you are fortunate enough to have a bevy of interns, the slate can be one person's dedicated job. Also, he (or you) should take notes about each take, what worked, what didn't, and what got screwed up. This also makes editing easier later.

Your crew needs to know that they must be deathly silent during takes—even going so far as holding their collective breath during a particularly quiet scene—and not chatter a lot between takes. It doesn't take much people-static to drive the director and actors too nuts to operate.

Finally, be sure to record a couple of minutes of *room tone*. Room tone is just the ambient sound of a room with no one talking or moving. We will use it later in editing to mix low under dialogue, especially dialogue recorded later (ADR) to make it sound more realistic or to hide edits.

Homework

Make a three-minute movie, and make it tell a complete story. It could be a documentary on a friend, a love story, a horror film, or an infomercial for an imaginary product. I would recommend, despite my "storytelling is overrated" command, to just make sure it tells a whole story with a beginning, a middle, and an end. Later you can get funky and break the tradition of the linear narrative. Then make a ten-minute film. Then twenty, and so on until you work your way up to a feature. It's always good to figure out the rules before you smash them. Salvador Dali learned to draw standard figures before he got freaky, ya know.

Of course, I threw this out the window from near the gate. I made two five-minute shorts, one on Super-8 in high school; then years later I helped conceptualize (with Li'l Mike and Charles Cohen) and edit an eight-minute promo of my San Francisco band, Bomb. Then nothing for ten years. Then when Mini-DV technology caught up with me and my filmic desires, I made a feature-length documentary of 30 people shot in four cities, on both coasts. Yikes!

So...

Now that we've mastered the basics of getting the image *into* the camera and the sound onto the tape, it's time to move on and take steps towards cooking this stuff down into a real, complete movie.

Chapter 7

Computers

L ike desktop publishing before it, desktop video is the new *killer app* that's now helping drive the sales of computers. Technology is making exponential leaps all the time. *Moore's Law* dictates that every 18 months computers double in speed and drop by half in price. That makes for a lot of computer at a pretty darned low price these days.

The technology involved in digital filmmaking can turn any bedroom or garage into a TV and movie studio that has a world broadcast area. Good ideas combined with planning, experience, and care can make stunning films for almost no money that look nearly as good as films costing millions of dollars.

The basic technological components of desktop filmmaking are

◆ A mini-DV camera

◆ A mini-DV tape

◆ A FireWire cable

◆ A FireWire card

◆ A computer

◆ An editing program

You can get all this combined for under $2,000 and make films that can be projected in a theater, made into VHS tapes and DVDs, and streamed on the Internet, with the ability to touch people everywhere.

Computers make digital filmmaking possible. They reproduce the tasks of editing, formerly done by actually cutting film, and they eliminate the need for film. A $1,000 computer running a good editing program today can do everything that a $100,000 Avid system did ten years ago.

How Much Computer Do You Need?

You need a fast computer to edit video. The slowest computer I would try to edit video on would probably be an Apple G3 or a Pentium III PC with 512 MB of RAM. And either way, you'll want at least 40 gigs of hard drive space.

The one I'm currently using is a 1.7 GHz Pentium 4 machine with a gig of RAM, a FireWire card, and two 80-gig hard drives. It's about equal to a Mac G4 and much cheaper. I used it to edit all the extra video features on the *D.I.Y. or DIE* DVD. It worked fine. I also made *I Left My Pants* on it. I would say this much power and RAM and hard drive is about right for entry level "I'm gonna make full-length movies and compete with the big boys' filmmaking."

I paid 300 bucks extra and added an internal DVD burner, and another $250 for an external FireWire drive for backing up whole editing projects in case of a hard disk failure.

My computer is generic—non-brand name, made by a local "screwdriver shop"— people who just specialize in putting them together from new parts. They sell a lot of them, have a low profit margin, and make their bucks on volume. Their boxes are fully guaranteed but come with no tech support, but I don't need it. It cost about one-third what a new brand-name 'puter would cost ($850 in August of 2002). The prices drop frequently. An equivalent box would have cost $10,000 three years ago. I never buy off-the-shelf brand name computers. They cost more and are loaded with a bunch of bundled crap that represents marketing deals rather than usefulness. Give me a bare bones, lightning-fast box made by some neighbor-hood nerd or family-run screwdriver shop and let me load what I want on it.

If you get a Mac, get a G4. The G3 will work for short projects, and if you already have one, get started learning. But a G3 is too slow to effectively edit big projects. Longer movies with many edits tend to get buggy and crash even with lots of power, and they do so faster and more frequently (on both Macs and PCs) with less processor speed and RAM. The new G4s are great machines and come standard with FireWire cards, fast processors, DVD burners, big hard drives, and even editing software: iMovie.

On PCs, I find that Windows 2000 is far more stable than 98, ME, or XP. It's also better for video editing, despite what the marketing trolls in Redmond tell you. Normally, Win2K is considered to be only for large networks, but it works great with a single machine. ME and XP are okay, but more what I call "Grandmaware"—software designed for mindless generic users who don't want to think, want to be told where they want to go today, and don't want to be able to make changes. Windows 2000 is not only more stable, but you can change things in it easier when you need to. ME and XP come with a video editing utility, sort of an iMovie knockoff. Nothing to get excited about, but it works.

PC Versus Mac

It used to be, about 10 years ago, that artists only used Apple Macs, and only soulless bureaucrats (well, and writers) used PCs. The differences between the two in interface and operation has merged so much closer that now everyone uses both. Some people get really mad if you suggest this, but they are basically clinging to what used to be.

A common argument is that Apples are more stable than PCs because Apple makes both the hardware and the software for an Apple. PCs are made by anybody, and are usually loaded with some version of Windows. It used to be that PCs crashed more, because all manufacturers didn't have all the technical info available to them. (Microsoft allegedly favored giving it to only manufacturers that partnered with them.) But technology and antitrust remedies have opened this up and leveled the playing field more.

For my money, PCs are more stable than Macs. They are way cheaper, software is more readily available, and you can tinker with them more easily. It's kind of like owning an American car. They're made to be opened up and easily customized. I love 'em.

Then there's the argument that Microsoft is an evil empire and Apple is touchy-feely thinky-diffy. Maybe at one time. But Apple is just as competitive as MS in a lot of ways, and probably just as creepy because they paint themselves as fuzzy Berkeley hippies. But heck, both companies make stuff that me and my friends really like to use, so, whatever…

The only big downside I can see to PCs is that they are much more vulnerable to attack by *virii* (plural of virus). This is partly because of their internal architecture and partly because there are so many more PCs that virus writers can hit more machines by writing for them. However, if you keep an updated virus program running, scan often, and download free service packs occasionally, you will be fine. I've been on computers for 10 years and have never been taken down by or lost data to a virus.

On the subject of service packs, Mac sort of does the same thing, but it's not free. Every few years they seem to completely revamp the OS (operating system) and sell it to you for a lot of money. It's difficult to update, and most of your programs will not work on the new one. Microsoft does this too, but their programs are far more backward compatible than Apple's. A new Apple OS usually has a higher learning curve than a Microsoft OS too.

One big advantage Macs do have though is that Final Cut Pro, an Apple product, is only available for the Mac. It will probably never be ported to the PC platform, because digital media (hardware *and* software—iMacs, G4s, iPods, iMovie, iTunes, iPhoto, Final Cut Pro, and DVD Studio Pro) is what's keeping Apple alive at the moment.

If you're starting out, I would say that if you can find compelling reasons that you have to use Final Cut, get a Mac. Otherwise, I'd get a PC. It's up to you. If you already have a Mac, you're fine. Go with it. In *$30 Film School*, we use what we can get and make it great.

On either system, you can hook a monitor to your computer so you can watch your editing bigger and better looking than you can on your little computer screen. I can't afford a dedicated monitor yet, but I have an S-Video on my computer's video card. It goes out to my VCR, which goes to my TV, so I can watch my output on the TV. If you don't have this, you can just output a tape and hook your camera through the VCR.

FireWire

FireWire is the hardware/software protocol that enables digital video to work. (See Figures 7.1, 7.2, and 7.3.) The hardware is a combination of:

1. The FireWire port on the camera or deck
2. The FireWire cable
3. The FireWire card in your computer

You need FireWire to edit Mini-DV because none of the other ports on a computer (USB 1, Parallel Port, Serial Port) are fast enough to import the huge file sizes that are produced with video without dropping frames and losing the import. Also, FireWire is set up to enable "device control," the computer and the camera "speaking" to each other, that is, sending commands back and forth to each other to enable editing to become automated. We will have more on this later in Chapter 8, "Editing Images."

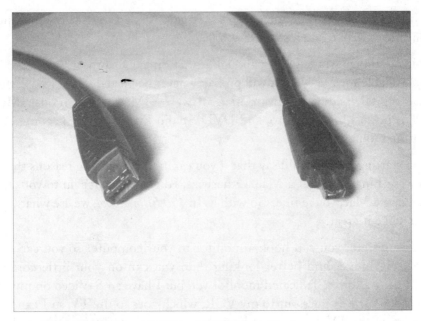

Figure 7.1 *FireWire cable.* Photo by Newtron Foto.

Figure 7.2 *FireWire cable in camera.* Photo by Newtron Foto.

Figure 7.3 *The other end of the FireWire cable plugged into the FireWire card in the back of the computer.* Photo by Newtron Foto.

If your computer comes with a FireWire card, you're set. (All new Macs and most high-end PCs do.) If it doesn't, you'll have to buy one. You can get them as cheap as 25 bucks, and, unlike analog sound cards, which are usually better if they cost more, there really isn't a lot of reason to spend a lot more than that on a FireWire card. Because they're only interfacing an already digital signal to a digital conduit, they don't have to convert anything and don't get much better with more money.

If you buy one, simply put it in one of the available slots inside your computer and insert the CD that comes with it. It should plug-and-play on Windows, but the CD will help that process, so use it.

After it is recognized in the device manager, you should be good to go and be able to start importing your footage into the computer for editing. Once this is done, you're ready to edit.

NOTE

If you're using analog video rather than digital video, you'll need an analog capture card, which starts around 120 bucks and goes up. FireWire cards start at about 25 bucks, and you don't get a much better one if you pay more. Basically, they don't have to do as much because the signal's already digital. With analog video and sound cards, you usually get a much better signal if you spend more money.

Internal and External DVD Burners

If your computer does not come with a built-in DVD burner, you'll need to buy one. They average about $250 as of this writing. All the name brand ones are pretty good: Panasonic, Pioneer, Ricoh, Toshiba, Memorex. I did have a long, drawn-out, horrible experience with the customer service division of Shecom Ikebana. And in addition, I'm *still* waiting on my rebate, almost a year later. That is one of only two negative recommendations in this entire book.

"Burners" don't actually "burn." They do alter the substrate of the DVD disk with a laser, but very little heat is produced. Don't expect smoke to pour out of your computer. It's just a word.

Internal DVD burners attach to any available slot, right above or below your existing CD drive. They are all plug-and-play and usually come with software drivers, in case the drivers are not found in your operating system. They also usually come with some DVD authoring program, such as MyDVD by Sonic Solutions (I refer to them as simply "Sonic" in much of this book). A tutorial for this program is given later in Chapter 10, "Your Own DVD."

Internal DVD burners are more convenient to use than external, but they're all good. Most of the hardware out there is very similar, and it's more about what you do with it than the marketing behind it. Just get one and start burning.

External FireWire Drives

External FireWire drives are great for increasing your storage capabilities when working on large projects, or for backing up large amounts of data. I bought a generic 120-gig drive on eBay for 200 bucks. You plug it into the wall, plug the cable into the FireWire drive in your computer, and it's instantly recognized in My Computer and assigned a drive letter (see Figure 7.4). From there, you can drag files as you would to any internal drive. You can also take it to someone else's house or studio, plug it into their system, and collaborate with them.

Software

Software consists of the tools that make your computer do anything you need. You can buy it, or in some cases you can get good stuff as Shareware or Freeware.

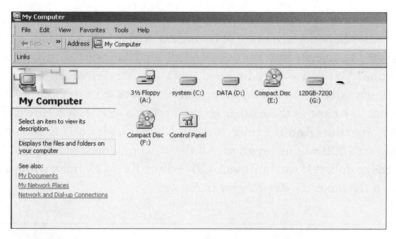

Figure 7.4 *My FireWire drive is assigned the letter G.*

◆ Shareware is software that is free to use, and you are on the honor system to send a payment if you like it.

◆ Freeware is free.

Some people also copy it from friends or download it on Kazaa Lite. Of course, this is illegal and I would never recommend you do anything illegal. Some people also download software on Kazaa Lite, try it out, and then buy the licensed version if they like it. This is quasi-legal.

By buying a registered version, you will have access to tech support, which can be very helpful. You will also be contributing to the software company's continuing to be able to make cool stuff. And you will be paying the salaries of computer programmers, who are, in many cases, true artists in their own right.

Editing

There are lots of non-linear computer editing software solutions: Avid Express, cinestream, Premiere, Final Cut Pro, Vegas Video, iMovie, and more. They are as different as they are similar, i.e. they all use very similar interfaces but have slight differences that make it a bit of a task to learn them all. I use cinestream. It's pretty basic, but very easy to use, and I don't do much that's very complicated in my editing. Another system might be better for you. Try the demos and read literature and talk to people to find out which one's right for you. Final Cut Pro and Avid are deeper programs and are more the industry standard, but they also have a higher learning curve. It's easy to jump onto cinestream, Vegas Video, or Premiere and go. Avid does have the advantage of having exportable Edit Decision lists that can be imported seamlessly into a pro Avid (dedicated hardware/software combination) system. You can even edit good work in iMovie, which comes free installed on new Mac computers now, or can be purchased for about 30 bucks online. It's not as robust as these other programs, but is very easy to use and is a great starter program. (And the price is right. I like the idea of *$30 Film School* grads editing on a $30 editing program. All the other programs mentioned above cost hundreds of dollars if you buy them.) My editor, Kevin Harreld, wrote a very good book on the subject: *iMovie 2 Fast & Easy*.

> **NOTE**
>
> For much more on editing video and a better look at editing programs, see Chapter 8, "Editing Images."

Writing

The program Final Draft (from a company also called Final Draft) is an excellent, elegant, simple-to-use, dedicated word processor for writing scripts.

Ignore the fact that they market it in a way that makes it seem like if you buy it, you'll get rich and famous…you won't. High-quality, huge-selling scripts were written without it, and far many more horrible, unsellable, unproducable scripts are made daily using it. In the hands of a talented person (like you), however, it can make great looking scripts easily from your quality words. Final Draft practically automates the process of doing all the separate formatting for standard script layout—the different indenting for character names, action, dialogue, transitions, and so forth. You just hit Return or the Tab key to go where you need to go.

The layout Final Draft gives is not only industry-standard, but for people like us, who don't care about The Industry, it makes great looking, easy-to-read scripts that will make things smoother for you and your actors (see Figure 7.5).

I like Final Draft because it's one of those rare things in life—like aspirin—that actually does what it's supposed to do, does it quite well, and doesn't try to do a lot more. This is a good model for business, art, and everything else. More people should emulate it.

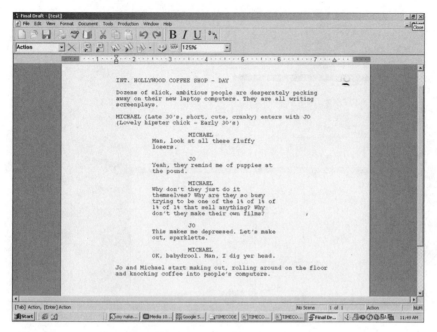

Figure 7.5 *Screen shot of Final Draft.*

Throw away the ads for screenwriting classes that come with the program. And don't ever look at that corny video on the CD. It's aimed at wannabees, and you ain't one of those. But the program itself is great. I love it. It also has utilities built in that make helpful production lists of how many times each character speaks and what the locations are for each scene. And one of my favorites, just for fun, it will make a list of all the cussing in your story. It also has a creepy robot voice utility that will read your screenplay out loud. This isn't as good as a table reading with real humans, but it's actually better than not reading it aloud at all. I tried it once through an entire script and made some changes based on hearing Mister Roboto drone through my words.

Make a Scene Report (shown in Figures 7.6 and 7.7) in Final Draft (useful for looking at the "big picture" by making index cards as described in Chapter 1, "Writing").

You can also view the script by scenes from within the program by using the Scene Navigator (see Figures 7.8 and 7.9).

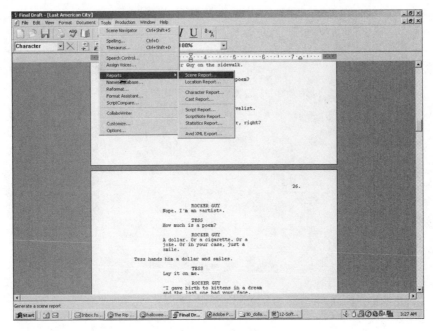

Figure 7.6 *Making a scene report in Final Draft.*

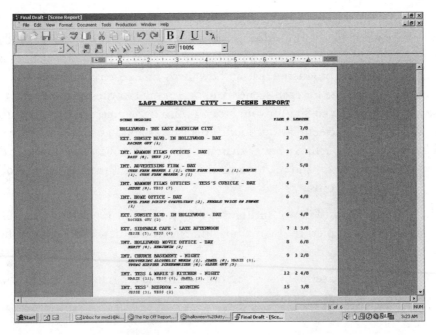

Figure 7.7 *Scene report in Final Draft.*

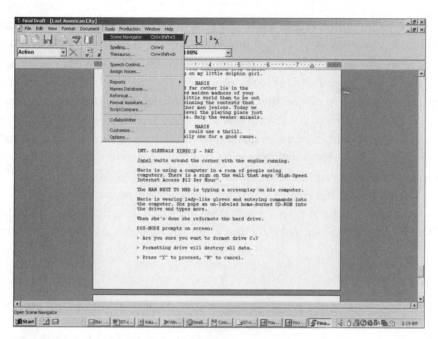

Figure 7.8 *Accessing the Scene Navigator.*

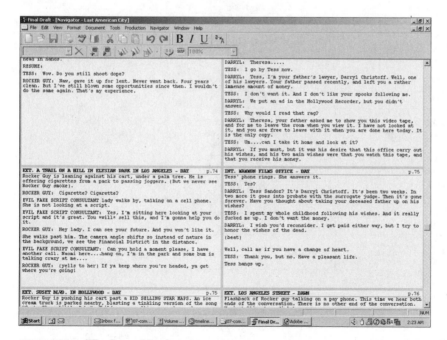

Figure 7.9 *The Scene Navigator.*

The Final Draft company also has a new program called Final Draft AV, which is aimed more at non-writers. It's a simple two-column interface, one side is what's to be on the movie or TV screen, the other is words and music that occur at the same time (see Figure 7.10). It looks promising, but presently it's too limited for most of my uses. It might be great for someone without a lot of writing experience: Kids starting out? TV executives after they fire the writers? Producers of reality TV shows? But it seems to me you could do much the same thing with two columns in your regular word processing program. To try it out, I wrote a simple script for the training film on this book's CD-ROM, *I Left My Pants in San Diego*. It worked well for this, because it was only very loosely scripted. I was more writing a treatment (outline) than an actual script. The later versions of Final Draft AV will have timecode support. At that point it may become quite useful to me.

Compositing

Compositing is basically doing effects on your computer. The term comes from the practice, in the days before non-linear editing, of editors using layered pieces of film to create special effects in a machine called an Optical Printer.

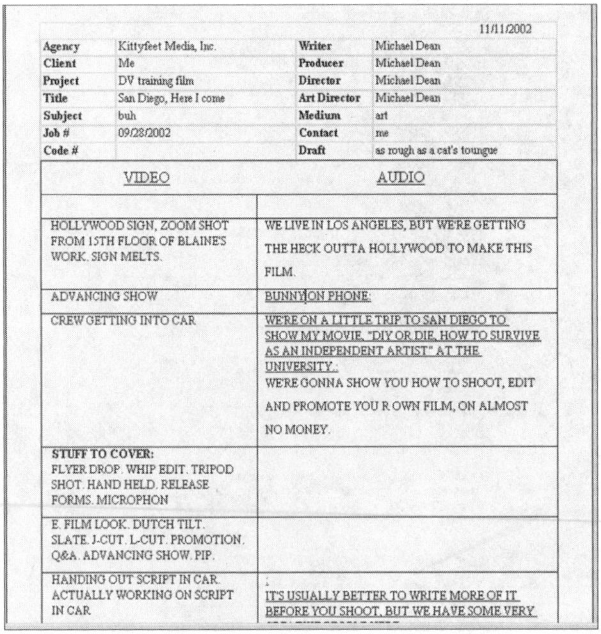

11/11/2002

Agency	Kittyfeet Media, Inc.	**Writer**	Michael Dean
Client	Me	**Producer**	Michael Dean
Project	DV training film	**Director**	Michael Dean
Title	San Diego, Here I come	**Art Director**	Michael Dean
Subject	buh	**Medium**	art
Job #	09/28/2002	**Contact**	me
Code #		**Draft**	as rough as a cat's toungue

VIDEO	AUDIO
HOLLYWOOD SIGN, ZOOM SHOT FROM 15TH FLOOR OF BLAINE'S WORK. SIGN MELTS.	WE LIVE IN LOS ANGELES, BUT WE'RE GETTING THE HECK OUTTA HOLLYWOOD TO MAKE THIS FILM.
ADVANCING SHOW	BUNNY ON PHONE:
CREW GETTING INTO CAR	WE'RE ON A LITTLE TRIP TO SAN DIEGO TO SHOW MY MOVIE, "DIY OR DIE, HOW TO SURVIVE AS AN INDEPENDENT ARTIST" AT THE UNIVERSITY.: WE'RE GONNA SHOW YOU HOW TO SHOOT, EDIT AND PROMOTE YOU R OWN FILM, ON ALMOST NO MONEY.
STUFF TO COVER: FLYER DROP. WHIP EDIT. TRIPOD SHOT. HAND HELD. RELEASE FORMS. MICROPHON	
E. FILM LOOK. DUTCH TILT. SLATE. J-CUT. L-CUT. PROMOTION. Q&A. ADVANCING SHOW. PIP.	
HANDING OUT SCRIPT IN CAR. ACTUALLY WORKING ON SCRIPT IN CAR	IT'S USUALLY BETTER TO WRITE MORE OF IT BEFORE YOU SHOOT, BUT WE HAVE SOME VERY

Figure 7.10 *Final Draft AV.*

You can do some very simple compositing in most editing programs, but it's often easier and can produce more robust results to do it in a separate program. Discreet's Combustion is a very high-end program that can do unbelievable things, but it's very expensive and has a high learning curve. Cheaper and easier to use, but still robust, is Adobe's After Effects. One thing that makes it great is that it supports a number of third-party plug-ins. *Plug-ins* are tiny programs that work within another program to extend its functionalities.

NOTE

For much more on editing video and a better look at compositing programs, see Chapter 8, "Editing Images."

Page Layout

Page Layout programs like Quark and PageMaker allow you to prepare the files for covers for your DVDs, VHS, and albums. You can do book covers, flyers, posters, all sorts of stuff. This isn't really a filmmaking issue, but it is a promotion and packaging issue.

Both are fairly easy to use, and both can produce an archive ready to send to the printer. I like Quark and used it to design the cover of the DVD and VHS for *D.I.Y. or DIE*, as well as my novel. (Someone pointed out that the movie cover looks a lot like the novel cover. I didn't notice this until after they were both in stores. It's true. I may be a novice, but I have a style!)

When doing page layout…remember, the images should be CMYK high-rez, not RGB low-rez.

CMYK mode is a four-color model used in printing rather than the three-color model used in Web graphics and video. We don't need to know the theory of this, but we do need to know the rule: If it's going to print, it should be CMYK. If it's going to be viewed on a screen, RGB.

You can, however, use Web-rez images in print if you make them print smaller, as the relative resolution will increase. Take your big 72 d.p.i. Web-rez RGB image and make it CMYK in Photoshop (image/mode), then make it smaller in Photoshop (image/image size) or Quark (drag the edges of picture box to resize, then click once on the image, then Ctrl + Shift + F to fit picture to box), and they'll look okay. I did this in Quark with all the images on the cover of *D.I.Y. or DIE*. (See Figures 7.11, 7.12, and 7.13.)

Figure 7.11 *Converting mode in Photoshop.*

Figure 7.12 *Resizing in Photoshop.*

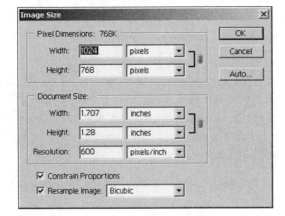

Figure 7.13 *Resizing in Photoshop 2.*

When you collect for output in Quark (File/ Collect For Output), everything will be included except the fonts. This is because the company doesn't want to violate copyrights by including the fonts made by others. Check with your printer to see if she has all the fonts you used, and include them in the archive if she doesn't. In Quark, check Usage under Utilities to see which fonts and images are used (see Figure 7.14). Make sure all the images and fonts are included on the CD or Zip disk you bring to the printer.

Figure 7.14 *Collect for Output in Quark.*

Quark has a lot of third-party Xtensions (the Quark-specific term for plug-ins) available to do a number of cool tasks. Check Quark.com for links to these companies.

Handheld Hardware and Software

Handheld computers, commonly miscalled "Palm Pilots," are great for on-the-go filmmakers. You can keep all your production, contact, and logistical information at a fingertip-ready state, as well as write as easily as you do on paper, but in a form that is later editable on a computer—all at a fraction of the cost and weight of a laptop computer.

I use Handspring Visor Deluxe with a little fold-up keyboard; I like it. It runs on the same operating system as a Palm Pilot but has a larger pen area and reading area without being much bigger (see Figures 7.15 and 7.16).

I like the Handspring with the Tarugus. Together they cost under $150, weigh less than a pound, and are a little bigger than a pack of smokes. It's cooler than a laptop. Laptops weigh between four and ten pounds. Sure, you can do more on them, but if all you're doing is typing text (which is most of what I do on a computer), the Handspring/Tarugus combo is da bomb. A laptop is so heavy that you have to think, "Am I gonna need this?" when you leave the house or hotel. The Handspring/Targus combo is light enough that you can just take it with you in your shoulder bag, purse, or backpack and be spontaneous.

Figure 7.15 *Photo of Handspring and collapsible Targus keyboard.*

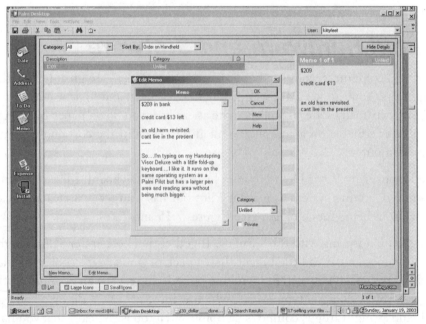

Figure 7.16 *Palm desktop.*

I use the Internet for mapping. I find it pretty amazing that computers can do this…it seems so *human*. Dealing with numbers seems very computer-intuitive, but when they start giving me explicit and (usually) accurate driving directions, I get a little nervous. But I do it, and I load my route into my Handspring Palm unit before I jump on the plane. I put my plane info, rental car numbers, etc. in there too.

I select the text only on these map pages, car info, and so forth and paste it into a Word document. I remove the junk formatting, then save this as text, and drag that text file onto a little freeware utility on my desktop called MakeDoc (see Figure 7.17).

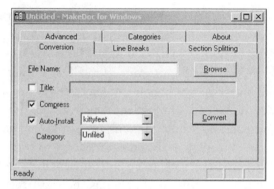

Figure 7.17 *MakeDoc (available free on shareware.com).*

MakeDoc turns it into Palm format and drops it directly into my Handspring folder for instant installation next time I synchronize my PDA. I also do this with my contact numbers and anything else I'll need on the road. I don't bother painstakingly entering each field into their database. I just have a searchable raw text document. That's fine for my needs. Then I have all the data I'll need for the whole trip.

Screen Shots

All the places in this book where there's a shot of what the screen looks like to illustrate a particular point are *screen shots*. You might have occasion to take them at some point for some reason: to edit into a movie, to put in a book, to e-mail to a friend when asking her how to troubleshoot something or to help her learn something.

To take a screen shot in Windows, press the "PrtScrn" button in the upper-right corner of your keyboard. Press it firmly and hard. Then open up Photoshop or another image editing utility. Press Ctrl+N. You will get a new blank document the same size as the image on the clipboard. Then press CTRL[1] + V to paste. Then edit and save.

To take a screenshot on a Mac, hold down the Apple key, the Shift key, and the 3 key. It is automatically saved to the hard disk as "Picture 1," "Picture 2," and "Picture 3."

Web Export

To make stuff Web-ready from your NLE program, export to *Cleaner*—a third-party program from Discreet that comes bundled (as a light version) with most editing suites. There you have the option to save it as Real Media, CD-quality Quicktime, DVD MPEG-2, Windows Media, or even Palm PDA format. You can select large, medium, or small file sizes. The bigger you select, the better it will look, but the longer it will take to download. Only select the streaming option if your server is set up for that and you know how to configure stuff. I just select non-streaming and let people save it to play over and over. I used to offer it in more than one format because I wanted everyone to be able to view it. Windows Media is the smallest file size, but Quicktime probably has the most installed users. And Real Media *looks* really good, so go figure.

Then I got the non-light (full) version of Cleaner, which also will export to MPEG video format. This is the best to use, as it will open on *any* computer, usually in QuickTime on a Mac and Windows Media Player on a PC. That's also the format that I used for the *Left My Pants* video on the CD, although that is a much higher bit rate and file size than I would have used on a Web-download version.

PDF Export

Adobe Acrobat is the freeware program to make .pdf (portable document format) files. This is a great way to share text and graphic documents while retaining more perfect layout control than a Web page, with lower file size than a scanned image. Most people have the Acrobat Reader on their computer.

---

1. Command key (⌘) on a Mac equals CTRL on a PC.

A relatively inexpensive Adobe program, Acrobat Distiller, is used to create these .pdf files (see Figure 7.18). It can be used as a freestanding utility, or configured to add drop-down menus in Photoshop or Microsoft Word to export directly from those programs to .pdf without having to open Distiller (see Figures 7.19 and 7.20). Both Acrobat and Acrobat Distiller (the network version that is more robust than Acrobat even when used on a single machine) are available at www.adobe.com.

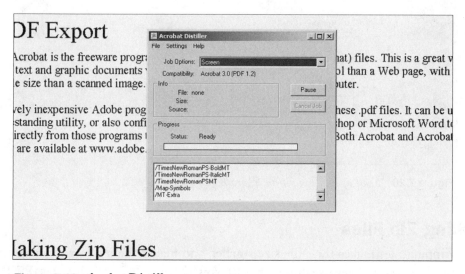

Figure 7.18 *Acrobat Distiller.*

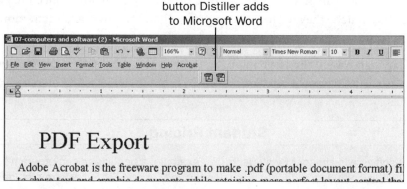

Figure 7.19 *"Convert to .pdf" button that Distiller adds to Microsoft Word.*

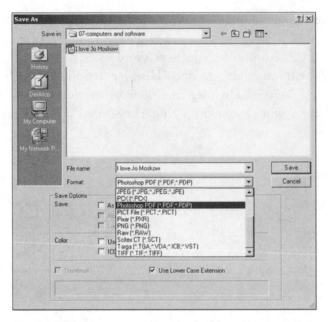

Figure 7.20 *"Save as .pdf" menu in Photoshop.*

Making Zip Files

Zipping files makes their file size smaller, and makes them easier to share across the Internet and across computer platforms (Mac to PC and vice versa) without getting corrupted and ending up unable to be read. A zipped word-processing document can be as little as 1/10 its original size. Zipping won't reduce image files or music files much (they're already compressed), but it will make them more stable to transmit.

A popular shareware utility for zipping and unzipping files is WinZip (see Figure 7.21), available at www.winzip.com.

Student Pricing

A lot of software is cheaper for students. For example, a popular editing program lists for $999, but is $299 for students. They don't usually check. Tell 'em you're a student at *$30 Film School*. (Print and show the I.D. on the CD if they ask.)

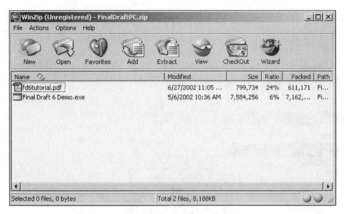

Figure 7.21 *WinZip.*

Troubleshooting

Sometimes random problems will occur on your computer after an upgrade or after installing some program. You will have problems and errors, and you will feel you are going nuts dealing with computer crap when you just want to get down to making art.

Big corporations have people whose full-time job is taking care of this junk. But you aren't a big corporation. You'll have to do it yourself or get a friend to do it.

Troubleshooting can involve reading the manual—most have a "common problems" or "troubleshooting" section, and many programs include searchable versions in Adobe Acrobat format in addition to the "treeware" or paper versions. Sometimes you have to just work backwards by intuition. I usually try to remember when things were working and what I changed since then. Sometimes I take notes while installing. Sometimes I use a utility like Norton GoBack that can take me back to a previous configuration when things were good. Or you can use Ghost to make a complete backup of your hard drive on a removable drive or device.

Sometimes even if you make a bunch of changes, the problem (or benefit) will not show up until you reboot. When troubleshooting, I usually reboot the program, device, and computer, in that order, until everything works. Very occasionally, software will become corrupted and stop working, or begin to be very buggy. In this case, I often uninstall the program (through Windows' Uninstaller utility) and reinstall it from the disk from scratch. Sometimes your preferences will be saved and sometimes you'll have to reset them all manually.

Most programs have a Help Menu. It usually appears in the top right of the program menus. From here you can access tutorials or search terms (see Figure 7.22).

From there, you can usually type the word you are looking for, hit Return on the keyboard, and get the info you need (see Figure 7.23).

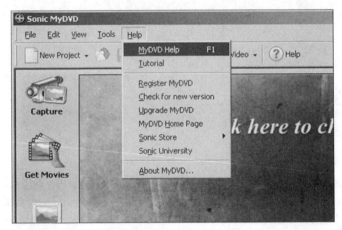

Figure 7.22 *The Help Menu of Sonic Solutions' MyDVD.*

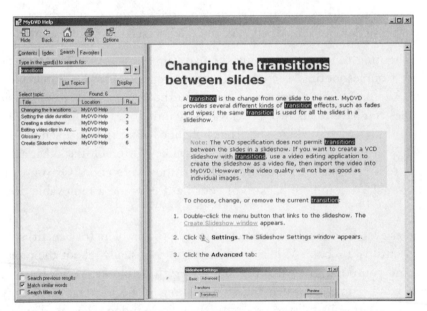

Figure 7.23 *Searching the word "transitions" in the Help Menu of Sonic Solutions' MyDVD.*

Protecting Your Computer

Some people don't want to learn to create, so they just destroy. They become virus writers or unethical hackers (crackers). Some people can't come up with a good business idea, so they just e-mail a dumb one to everyone in the world. That's where Spam comes from.

Even Spam without malicious code attached is a hassle. It's junk e-mail. Reading it and manually deleting it takes time, and that wasted time adds up. Learn to protect yourself against both Spam and virii. Getting rid of them will give you more time to concentrate on art.

SpamAssassin

SpamAssassin is a program (free from www.Spamassassin.org) that actually works to block spam. You have to ask the system administrator for your Internet service provider to put it on his end, then set up a filter on your end to send anything with the word "spam" in the subject line into the trash. (Or ask the Sys Admin to do that on his end, after you've run the program for a week to check for false positives and false negatives.) It kicks ass. I've gone from about 100 pieces of Spam a day to about five!

Many I.S.P.s, especially smaller ones without much bureaucracy, will be glad to do this. It makes their customers happy and actually cuts down on the amount of bandwidth they use, which saves them money.

SpamAssassin assigns different "points" to different criteria, and if it reaches a certain amount, it adds the word "SPAM" at the top. Here's an example:

"SPAM: Content analysis details: (7.5 hits, 5 required)

SPAM: Hit! (2.7 points) Subject contains lots of white space

SPAM: Hit! (1.0 point) From: ends in numbers

SPAM: Hit! (0.6 points) From: does not include a real name

SPAM: Hit! (0.5 points) Subject has an exclamation mark

SPAM: Hit! (0.6 points) BODY: Uses words and phrases which indicate porn (12)

SPAM: Hit! (0.1 points) BODY: Uses words and phrases which indicate porn (10)

SPAM: Hit! (2.0 points) Subject contains a unique ID number"

Another way to minimize Spam is not to put your e-mail address anywhere on the Internet. Spammers and people who sell address lists to them have programs (*bots*) that just follow link after link on the Web to harvest e-mail addresses.

When you post on sites, have a separate Web mail account to use. When using Craigslist, choose the Anonymous option. Instead of putting your address as text or a clickable link on your Web site, just make an image file of it. It won't be clickable but any smart person will know to type it into their mail program to write you. There's also a Java Script that creates the address on the fly. It's supposed to be invulnerable to the harvesting bots, but I don't know. I think they might be programmed to read it now. Maybe not. I tried it on one of my sites, and I haven't gotten any spam at that address yet.

Virus Protection

If you're going to *live* on your computer like I do, you need to protect it against virii and other garbage. I use Norton Antivirus. It's cheap, and it works. Scan for virii frequently, keep your virus software updated, and make sure you download the latest virus definitions (see Figure 7.24). I do all three, and run a complete scan at least once a week. Configure Norton Antivirus to check your e-mail and all downloaded items. And even then, still right-click and run a virus scan on anything you download, especially from KazaaLite or any file-sharing utility.

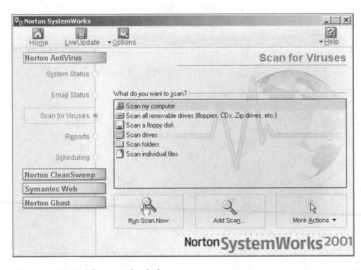

Figure 7.24 *Norton Antivirus.*

Keep in mind that some e-mail problems aren't virii at all. Most e-mails that ask you to e-mail them to everyone you know, offer something amazing, or try to scare you and make you act *now* are hoaxes.

Bill Gates does not want to pay you to forward e-mails, and you don't need to delete some file on your hard drive you've never heard of. And it's often not a virus, but an operating system component. These e-mails are wastes of time and resources. And you've got things to do. Ignore them.

Before acting on one of these, I search a few key words from it on a search engine along with the word "hoax" and see what comes up. Also, a lot of the more common ones are listed at www.snopes.com under Computers and Inboxer Rebellion.

Service Packs

If you're on a PC, every six months or so, go to Microsoft.com, download service packs for your operating system, and install them. It's just a few clicks, and very easy. This will help to ensure that you are protected against newly discovered vulnerabilities in security.

Firewall

I use ZoneAlarm (www.ZoneAlarm.com) (see Figure 7.25). The free version kicks ass. Just configure it to allow or block each program.

There are a couple of programs that you should allow even though the names sound a little suspect. They are just part of normal Windows operation. One is "Use dll as an app," and "Distributed com systems" is another. Just don't allow server rights to anything except a server or a Kazaa-type program.

Spyware

So, in case you don't know, there is a new thing called "spyware," which puts programs on your computer without your knowledge. These programs do stuff like make ads pop up at you, or (more scary) keep track of when and where you surf to send that info back to some company. Those companies then make your marketing profiles more robust so they can sell your e-mail address to marketers to specifically target you based on your preferences. It's sort of like basing their business plan on a legal virus.

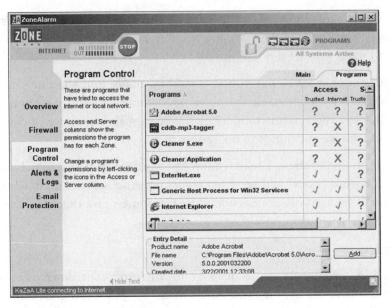

Figure 7.25 *ZoneAlarm.*

Sometimes spyware is installed during the installation of an unrelated program. Kazaa adds 11 programs! Kazaa charges these 11 companies money to put that garbage in there. (That's why you should use the hacked version, KazaaLite from kazaalite.com. The spyware has been removed in KazaaLite.)

Spyware, apparently, is the new Internet business model…the old one (giving everything away and getting rich) didn't work, it seems.

You can download AdAware (www.lavasoftusa.com) free to remove spyware on a regular basis (see Figure 7.26). If you have Kazaa, uninstall it, run AdAware, delete the spyware, then download and install KazaaLite.

Maintenance

Gently vacuum the dust out of your computer once in a while. Dust will kill a computer over time. Run regular maintenance to keep it humming and happy, such as defragging the disks: Start/programs/accessories/system tools/disc defragmenter in Windows 2000.

Vacuuming regularly and running the defrag utility are pretty much all I do to my computers, and they all run nearly flawlessly. Much of this is because I'm running Windows 2000. It is the most trouble-free operating system I've used.

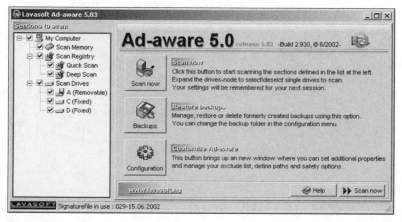

Figure 7.26 *AdAware.*

Conclusion

If you have an inquisitive mind, learning new programs will probably come pretty easily to you. I took classes in college on using Word and Excel, and after that, almost never looked at a software manual. I usually get a new program and am creating in it within minutes. A lot of the interface is the same: File, Edit, View, Insert, and so forth. Also, the same basic keyboard commands work in a lot of programs (Ctrl+S for save, and so forth). It isn't usually until I get fairly deep into a program that I consult the online Help menu or go on the Interweb to look for answers.

Demos for several of the programs mentioned above are included on the CD-ROM that comes with this book. I invite you to try them all. Get the software you need, by any means necessary.

Be willing to try new stuff, but don't spend all your time in front of a computer. Get out there and film, and also make sure you take time to live life and experience new things so you can actually make movies *about* something.

Chapter 8

Editing Images

Editing is the organization of shots after the shooting is done. It's the process of making sense out of chaos, and it's what makes a real movie out of a pile of tapes. Editing is an art unto itself, and can make or break a production. It has the power to make the mundane interesting, and the interesting magical.

When people first started editing on video (in television studios originally), the systems were linear. This was a hassle. It meant that if you put together clips A, B, C, D, E, F, G, and H in order and then later decided to switch the order of A and B, you had to start over. They were basically editing from one big VCR to the next.

Computer editing systems are, again, like film, non-linear. They're also far easier to use than film. You just move stuff around on the screen in a timeline with your mouse.

Basic Editing

There are a number of non-linear editing (NLE) programs that are useful for editing. One very high-end program, fast becoming the industry standard, is Apple's Final Cut Pro (FCP). It lists for $1,000. Adobe's Premiere is not as robust as FCP, but is a perfectly serviceable program and costs half as much. Because it's cheaper, I put a demo on the CD-ROM, and I'll demonstrate some basic editing techniques with it. I'll also show you some of the same techniques in Sonic Foundry's Vegas (also on the CD-ROM) and also in Discreet's CineStream. I won't show you every command in every program, but will show enough for you to see how these editing programs are similar and how they are different.

> **NOTE**
>
> I learned editing on CineStream, the PC version. It has since been discontinued, and is only available for the Mac. The screenshots here are the PC version, but the interface is almost identical to the Mac version, so they are included to help our Mac-usin' friends.

Sonic Foundry's Vegas Video (also called "Vegas") is an NLE video editing system that also supports multitracking audio capabilities. We will explore this audio part more in the next chapter.

The Vegas Video 4 Suite also comes bundled with Vegas + DVD, a good DVD-authoring program.

Many of the interfaces and techniques are identical or similar in these programs, so many skills will transfer from one program to another.

> **NOTE**
>
> I skipped learning this for my first movie, and simply hired a professional editor using FCP and worked with him. This allowed me to make a great-looking film the first time out, and I pay him a good double-digit percentage of all royalties I receive from sales. I did learn editing myself to do the "extras" part on the DVD. It didn't take long—about a week—to get the basics.

We will talk in Chapter 10, "Your Own DVD," about a program called ShowBiz that you can get free with your DVD burner.

If you are using a Mac, iMovie comes already loaded on the new Apples. PCs with Windows XP now come with a very basic video editor.

Working in an Editing Program

When you open your program, you get the new project window (see Figures 8.1 through 8.3). The default in both Premiere and CineStream is to have it automatically set on Mini-DV preferences. This is what you want. Just click on OK and save your new project from the file menu (see Figures 8.4 through 8.9).

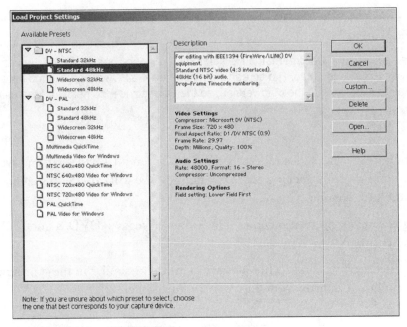

Figure 8.1 *New project window in Premiere.*

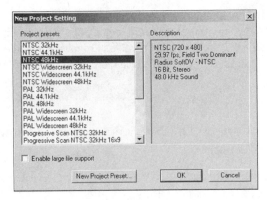

Figure 8.2 *New project screen in CineStream.*

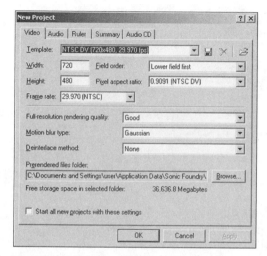

Figure 8.3 *New project screen in Vegas.*

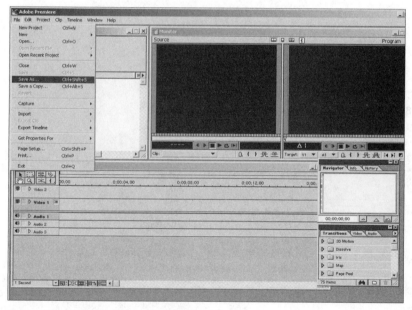

Figure 8.4 *Saving a new project in Premiere.*

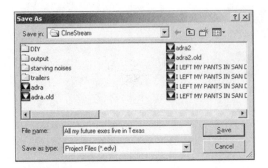

Figure 8.5 *Saving a new project in CineStream.*

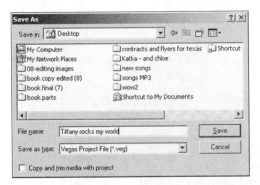

Figure 8.6 *Saving a new project in Vegas.*

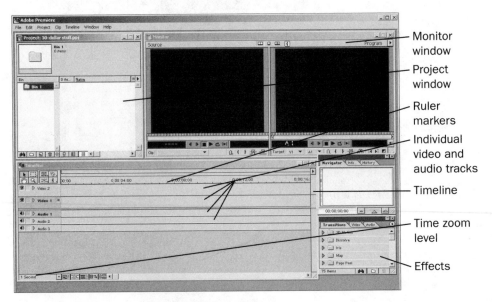

Figure 8.7 *The parts of the Premiere interface.*

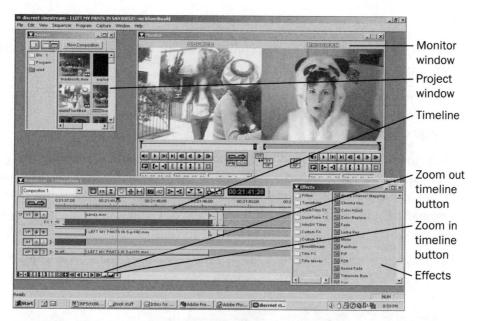

Figure 8.8 *The parts of the CineStream interface.*

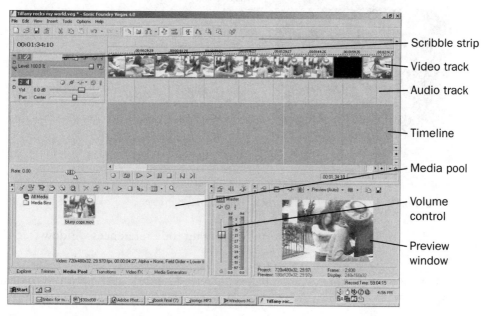

Figure 8.9 *The parts of the Vegas interface.*

Capture

You must first get the footage from your camera into your computer. This is called "capturing" or "importing" your footage.

You should only import clips that you want to use because the files are huge (DV is 13 gigabytes—about 13,000 megs—per hour) and your hard drive will fill up very quickly.

Once you get your camera working, import your footage. CineStream configures automatically, but in Premiere, you'll need to set your preferences for the particular brand and model of camera you are using. You can try and see if it is detected automatically, but if it isn't, you'll have to set it. It's in a different place in each program.

In Premiere, go to File/Capture/Movie capture/ to open the Movie Capture settings window (see Figure 8.10).

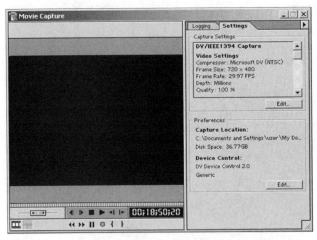

Figure 8.10 *Movie Capture settings window in Premiere.*

Click on the bottom "edit" button to bring up the Preferences window (see Figure 8.11).

Click on the "Options" button below "Device Control" at the bottom to bring up the DV Device Control Options window (see Figure 8.12).

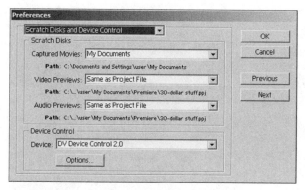

Figure 8.11 *Preferences window in Premiere.*

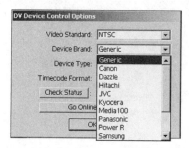

Figure 8.12 *DV Device Control Options window in Premiere.*

Pick your camera's make from the drop-down menu under "Device Brand." If your camera is not listed on the drop-down menu, simply select "generic." Hit "OK" on both windows.

Then you're ready to capture. You can capture in two ways: one is by selecting the scenes you want to capture with in and out points and then letting the program automatically rewind and seek and import only those parts. This happens through what is called "Device Control," the protocol by which FireWire seamlessly integrates and talks back and forth from the camera or deck to the computer via the actual FireWire cable. It's pretty cool when it works, almost as ghost-machine-like as a player piano. The camera, or deck, controlled by your in and out points, fast-forwards to the next segment you've picked, plays it at normal speed and inputs it, and then fast-forwards to the next part, slows down to normal and inputs that, and so on. The only problem is that it can screw up from a million different variables (any type of timecode break causes most of them) and get "lost." Then you have to manually import the parts anyway. (See Figures 8.13 through 8.16.)

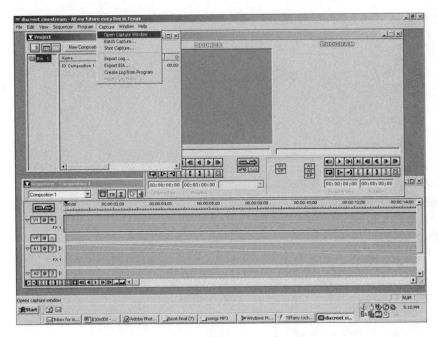

Figure 8.13 *Accessing Capture Window in CineStream.*

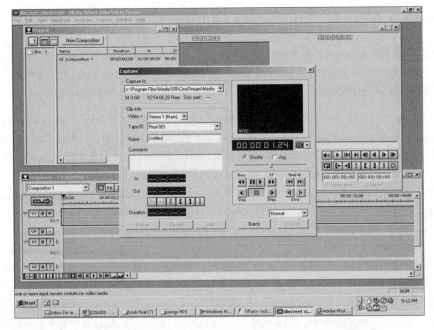

Figure 8.14 *Capture Window in CineStream.*

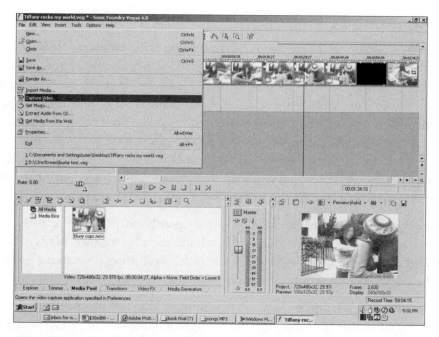

Figure 8.15 *Accessing Capture Window in Vegas.*

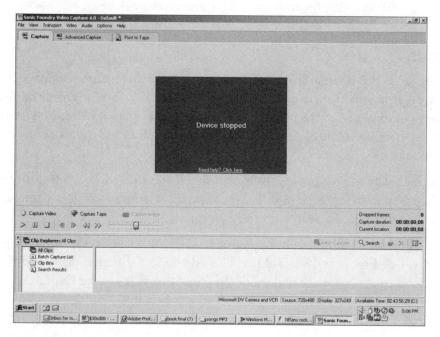

Figure 8.16 *Capture Window in Vegas.*

Troubleshooting

A few common errors I have encountered involve using an older DV camera as a deck to import video, and getting a Please Use Cleaning Cassette error message in the camera monitor a lot. Sometimes I need to actually clean. (Running a cleaning cassette—a special cleaning device the size and shape of a DV tape that you buy at a camera store—should be a last step. It is not good to do it too often because it can scratch the heads.) More often, I need to simply rewind or fast-forward a bit, then reboot the camera. Remember, DV cameras are just little computers, and when computers don't do what you want them to, try rebooting (shutting the computer down properly and then starting it back up).

I've also gotten this error message to stop by gently hitting the side of an older camera, Fonzie style. This is what DH is talking about to me in *I Left My Pants in San Diego* where he says, "I've heard of 'hittin' it', but hitting the *camera?*"—I'd just hit the camera before shooting that bit.

A timecode break (sometimes caused simply by the end of one scene and the beginning of another on your tape, for example, where you stopped recording and then started again) can also show up as a false Please Use Cleaning Cassette error. These troubleshooting tips will work for a timecode break too.

Timecode

Timecode is the internal machine language that allows synchronization to occur between programs, devices, and media (see Figure 8.17). You can enable or disable viewing of timecode in the program or camera. It is displayed as four sets of numbers, separated by semicolons or colons, representing hours, minutes, seconds, and frames of video.

I just manually import to begin with and forget most device controls. Six of one, half a dozen of the other. You still have to watch the stuff, make your choices, and do some rewinding regardless.

Bringing video into your editing program is remarkably easy. Open the Capture window (see Figures 8.18 and 8.19). This will be in a different place in different programs. In Premiere, it's under File. In CineStream, it's under Capture.

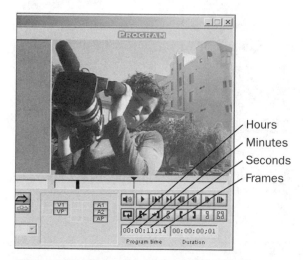

Figure 8.17 *Screenshot of timecode in CineStream.*

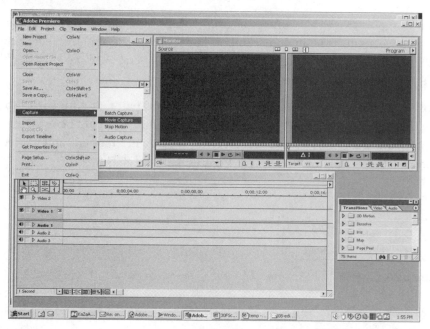

Figure 8.18 *Opening the Capture Dialog box in Premiere.*

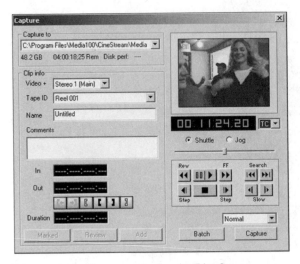

Figure 8.19 *Capture window in CineStream.*

You can import from your camera or from a deck. A deck costs some money but will save wear and tear on your camera. For a cheaper alternative, some people graduate from a 1-chip camera and buy a 3-chip camera, but keep their 1-chip to use as a deck.

Hook the camera to the FireWire card on your computer, and turn your camera on with a tape in it and the camera on Play. Your camera should be recognized by the program. If it is not, you will get an error message in Premiere, and whited-out Capture controls in CineStream (see Figures 8.20 and 8.21).

Figure 8.20 *Camera Not Recognized error message in Premiere.*

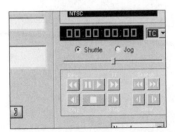

Figure 8.21 *Whited-out Capture dialog controls in CineStream.*

If you see such an error, reboot (restart) the program. If that doesn't work, you may have to set the name of the camera in the Camera Preference Setting dialog box (see Figure 8.22). If your camera is not listed, use the generic setting.

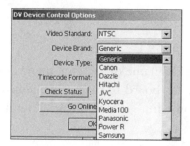

Figure 8.22 *Camera preference setting dialog box in Premiere.*

Use the little arrows below the Capture window to control the camera (see Figure 8.23). It's just like a tape recorder. The arrow pointing to the left means play, the arrow pointing to the right means rewind, the square means stop, and the round red button means record (capture).

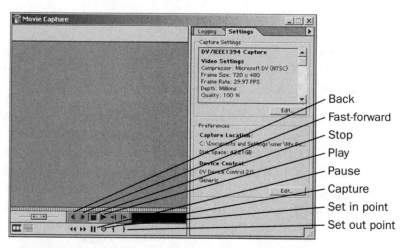

Figure 8.23 *The Movie Capture dialog box in Premiere.*

Use the rewind, fast-forward, and play parts to get the section you want to import. Hit the red "record" (capture) button to capture the part you want, and "stop" to stop importing. Try to record *handles* (extra footage before and after) of about five seconds to make it easier to edit. This makes transitions (fades and such) possible. You can't butt two clips together and dissolve them without handles; there is nothing to dissolve from. If you dissolve from nothing, you'll end up with a weird color bar thing in the middle of your fade. This looks cool and might be used as an effect once in a movie, but if you're going for a smooth dissolve, it ain't what you want.

Working with Video Clips

After you import your clip, name it by typing the name of the clip, then click on OK (see Figure 8.24) or press Enter on the keyboard to save. Give your clips descriptive names to help you later when you edit. "Jillian waving," "Jennifer's redemption take 3," stuff like that.

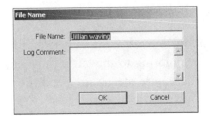

Figure 8.24 *Name the clip.*

The clip name becomes the file name. So you can search that way if need be. Sometimes when looking for a clip I've previously captured, I'll right-click in the capture folder and search by name, date, size, or file type.

You can arrange clips in separate folders by scene, part, day, actor, or whatever will help you edit and make sense of the jumble that will become your art. Most editing programs have a folder analogy interface of some kind, usually called *bins* after the physical bins they used in days of yore to store actual film (see Figure 8.25). (Okay, studios still use bins and real film. But not for long—video will probably almost completely replace film within 10 years at the rate of current technological advances.) *Attack of the Clones* was all done on high-def digital. No film was used at all.

Note that if you import and save other clips without naming them, the program will automatically just add sequential numbers to the new clips, "Jillian waving 1," "Jillian waving 2," "Jillian waving 3," etc.

You can also get footage into your program by using the Import feature (see Figures 8.26 through 8.29). This is useful if you have previously captured clips

Figure 8.25 *Bins in Premiere.*

Figure 8.26 *Import command in Premiere.*

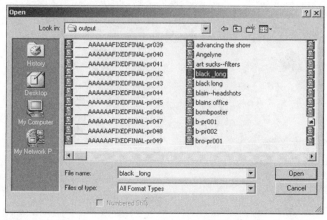

Figure 8.27 *Importing in Premiere.*

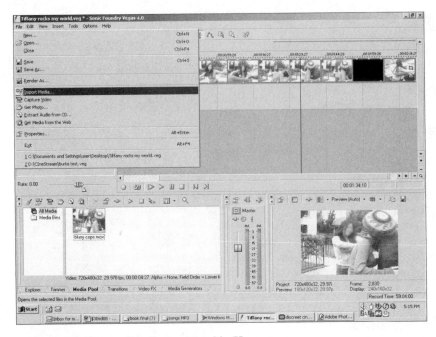

Figure 8.28 *Import Media command in Vegas.*

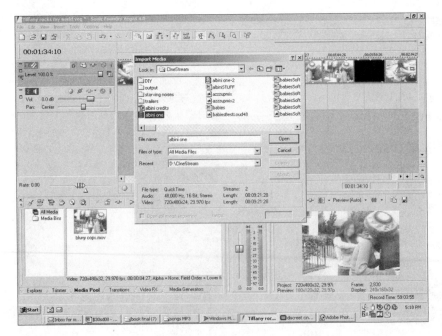

Figure 8.29 *Importing in Vegas.*

from another project, or even another program. Or if someone gives you clips on a CD or removable drive that need to go into your project.

You can drag scanned still images in almost any file format into the timeline. (We did this with Kevin Wengler's black and white photos on *I Left My Pants*.) They sometimes add an interesting mood or change of mood. You can also use PAN filters to imitate camera moves on still images. (More on this later.)

High-resolution images will look better than Web-rez pictures, but use what you have; see what works and how you like it. You can also import audio clips in a number of formats: .aiff, .wav, and even MP3.

Once you've got your clips into the program, by capturing and/or importing, then you can start the fun part—the actual editing!

Click on the Thumbnail View button at the bottom of the project window in Premiere (see Figure 8.30) or the Picture View Button in CineStream (see Figure 8.31) to see a tiny thumbnail of the first frame in each clip. This combined with the names (You *did* give them descriptive names, right?) should help you get a mental picture of what could and should go where.

This is not required in Vegas because the files show in the Media Pool in Thumbnail view by default.

The actual editing takes place in the Timeline, the rectangular bottom-half of the program interface, and the Monitor Window (see Figure 8.32). They are both pretty easy to work with, once you realize that on the timeline, going from left to

Figure 8.30 *Click on the Thumbnail View button in Premiere.*

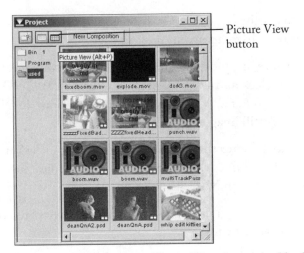

Picture View button

Figure 8.31 *Click on the Picture View button in CineStream.*

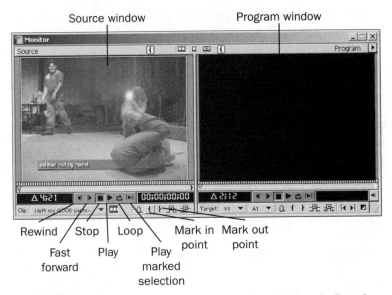

Source window   Program window

Rewind Stop Loop   Mark in Mark out
                        point   point

Fast   Play Play
forward   marked
              selection

Figure 8.32 *The control buttons in the Monitor Window in Premiere.*

right represents time, and from top to bottom are different clips; and the Monitor window basically works like two TV sets, the left being the incoming clips, and the right being the edited result.

Zooming the View in the Timeline

You can zoom in or zoom out on the amount of time displayed in the timeline. This is useful at different points in the editing process, for looking at the big picture (zoomed out), or working on minutia of individual frames or transitions (zoomed in).

This is done slightly differently in different programs. In CineStream, you just click on the Zoom In button or the Zoom Out button on the right of the toolbar at the bottom left of the sequencer (see Figure 8.33).

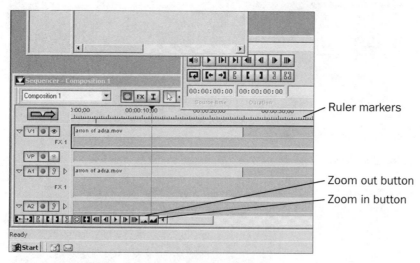

Figure 8.33 *The Zoom In button and Zoom Out buttons in CineStream.*

Note that in CineStream, one single ruler marker on the timeline always represents a single frame. Therefore, the timeline will look different zoomed in vs. zoomed out (see Figures 8.34 and 8.35). You will see fewer or more markers in a given window.

To zoom in or out in Premiere, you click on the Time Zoom Level button in the bottom-left corner of the tile line (see Figure 8.36).

This will expose the Time Zoom Level Chooser, a list of time choices (see Figure 8.37). Picking any choice will change the amount of time each ruler marker represents. The choices vary from one frame (approx. 1/30th of a second) up through eight minutes.

In Vegas, you simply click on the plus or minus markers on the Zoom Tool on the bottom-right side of the Timeline Window (see Figure 8.38).

Figure 8.34 *CineStream zoomed in. Note fewer visible ruler markers.*

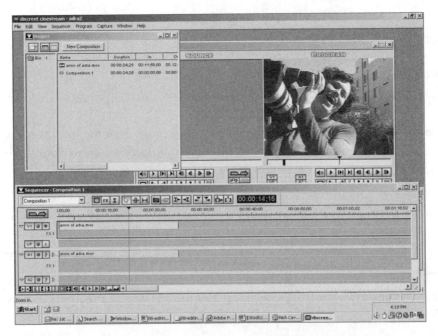

Figure 8.35 *CineStream zoomed out. Note more visible ruler markers.*

Figure 8.36 *Time Zoom Level button in Premiere.*

Figure 8.37 *Time Zoom Level Chooser exposed in Premiere.*

Figure 8.38 *Zoom Tool in Vegas.*

Getting Clips into the Timeline

In most NLE programs, there are two ways to get your clips into the timeline. The first is simply holding the mouse button down, dragging a clip into the timeline, and releasing it. From there you can hold down and drag the beginning and end points or cut them to make it longer or shorter. Keep in mind that you are only cutting a reference to the clip, not the actual clip, so don't worry about hurting your clips. In computer editing programs, you can make as many changes as you like without altering your media.

The other way to get your movie clip into the timeline is to double-click the clip in the Project window. It will then appear in the left (Source) side of the Monitor window. Then you can mark in- and out-points (using the Mark in and Mark out commands) to decide which parts you want to use. Then put your cursor on the picture in the window itself and drag the edited part you want to use into the timeline. Put it at the beginning or end of the clip you want to have it come before or after, and *Voila!* You're editing.

NOTE

In Premiere, still images behave differently in the Project window. When double-clicked, rather than appearing in the monitor, they open up in their own window. However, they can still be dragged into the timeline and incorporated into the project like moving images.

The loop button (available on both the Source Window and the Program Window) is useful for playing a selection over and over while choosing in- and out-points (see Figure 8.39).

Loop buttons

Figure 8.39 *Loop buttons.*

You can also mark in- and out-points in the Monitor window by pressing I or O on the keyboard.

Once the clips are in the timeline, you can also hold down the mouse cursor on the clips themselves and move them around, back and forth, and overlap them (see Figures 8.40 through 8.42). You can put audio under them, and add text and effects.

Note that the timeline is called the Sequencer in CineStream.

You can trim the clips in the timeline by using the Razor tool, or move them using the Selection tool (see Figure 8.43).

In Vegas, you can simply slide the clips back and forth in the timeline to change the length. You can also right-click on a video or audio track in the timeline and click "open in trimmer" to cut them.

Once you get a few clips into the timeline, click your mouse cursor at the beginning of the timeline and start playing it by pressing the Spacebar. (This command will start and stop playing in almost any video or audio program.) Your rough edit will play in the right (Program) side of the Monitor window. You can look at it, and make more changes until you like what you see.

Figure 8.40 *Clips in a timeline in Premiere.*

Figure 8.41 *Clips in the Sequencer in CineStream.*

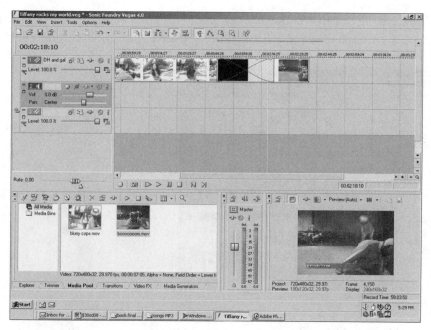

Figure 8.42 *Clips in a timeline in Vegas.*

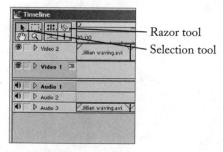

Figure 8.43 *Razor and Selection tools in the timeline window in Premiere.*

Adding Transitions and Effects

Most programs have a list of ready-made transitions that you can drag into the timeline. Click on the names list in the Effects Window to expose more choices. Both of the videos need to reside on the same track before you add a transition. Drag an effect into the timeline by holding down the mouse cursor. Double-click on the transition in the timeline to open up the Effects Properties dialog box.

In Premiere, click on Window/Show Transitions to bring up the Transitions Palette (list of transition and effects choices). (See Figures 8.44 through 8.46.)

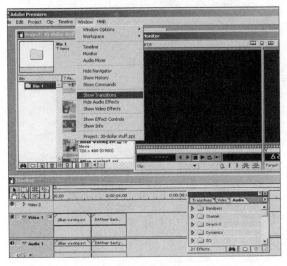

Figure 8.44 *Revealing the Transitions Palette in Premiere.*

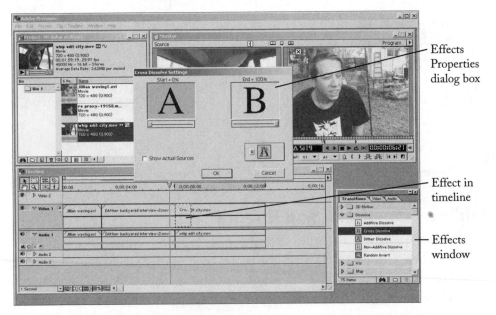

Effects Properties dialog box

Effect in timeline

Effects window

Figure 8.45 *Using Effects in Premiere.*

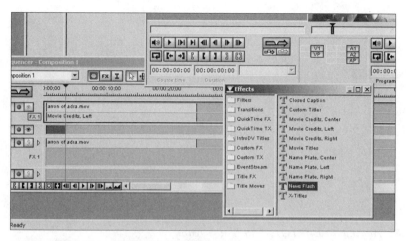

Figure 8.46 *Using Effects in CineStream.*

Note that in Premiere, you drag the effects onto the clip in the timeline. In CineStream, you drag it under the clip into a separate Effects track—called the *FX track* (see Figure 8.47). If the Effects track is not showing, you can add a new FX track (see Figure 8.48).

Figure 8.47 *Enabling the viewing of Effects in CineStream.*

Figure 8.48 *Adding an Effects track in CineStream.*

To add transitions or video effects in Vegas, click on the Transitions Tab or the Video FX tab by the Media Pool (see Figure 8.49).

Pick the transition or FX you want, and drag it onto the part in the timeline that you wish to affect. A window will pop up where you can set the properties for the event (see Figure 8.50).

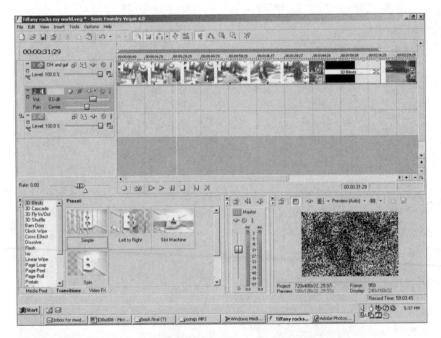

Figure 8.49 *Transitions tab clicked in Vegas.*

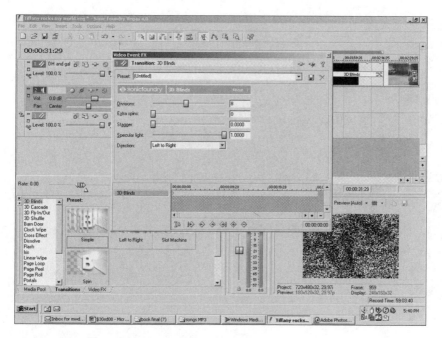

Figure 8.50 *Transitions Properties Window in Vegas.*

Set it how you want, then render.

Adding Text

To add text in Premiere, you create a title. Select File/New/Title (see Figure 8.51).

Then you get a window with editable text that can be laid over the images. Start typing your text. You can change the font, color, and alignment from the toolbar on the right of this window. You can click on Styles at the bottom to get default styles that look good.

When your title looks the way you'd like it to, press Ctrl + S to save (or Apple + S on a Mac). Give it a name (I used "punker title") and save. Or you can just close the window, and you will be prompted to name and save your title. It will then appear as a still image in the Project Window.

To bring text into the timeline, first you have to add another video track. Go to timeline/add video track. A new track will appear in the timeline, above the existing video track (see Figure 8.52).

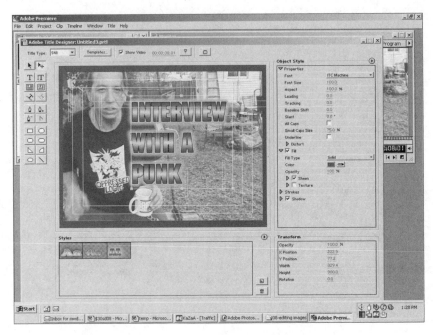

Figure 8.51 *Title Window in Premiere.*

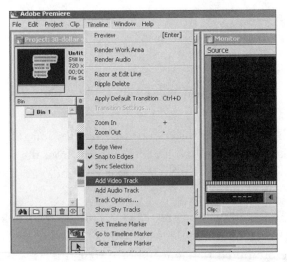

Figure 8.52 *Adding a video track in Premiere.*

Then you drag the title into the video track, add in- and out-points, render (see the "Rendering and Mixing" section later in this chapter), and your titles will appear over your movie. (See Figures 8.53 and 8.54.)

In CineStream, the titles are in the Effects window (see Figure 8.55).

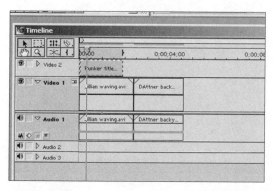

Figure 8.53 *Added video track (Video 2) with Title inserted.*

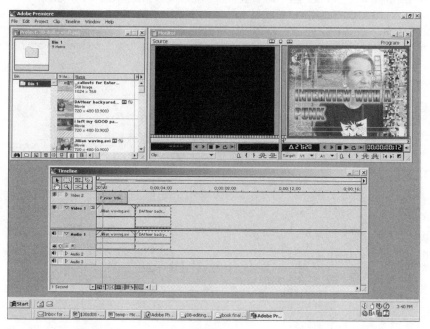

Figure 8.54 *Appearance of title in Program Window of Monitor after rendering.*

Figure 8.55 *Title window in CineStream.*

You edit text by double-clicking on it and typing your replacement text (see Figure 8.56). Then click on OK.

NOTE

Screenshot in this chapter are from Premiere 6.5, the current version. The demo on the CD-ROM is 6.0, the latest version of demo available at this writing. The interface is different. I would recommend checking www.Adobe.com to see if a later demo is available when you are ready to try these steps, if you don't have a fully functioning version yet.

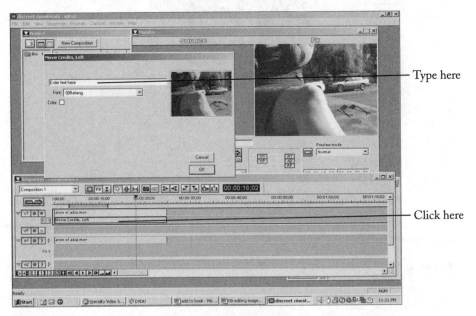

Figure 8.56 *Entering and editing titles in CineStream.*

To add text in Vegas, click on View/Media generators (see Figure 8.57).

Select "Text" on the far bottom left (see Figure 8.58).

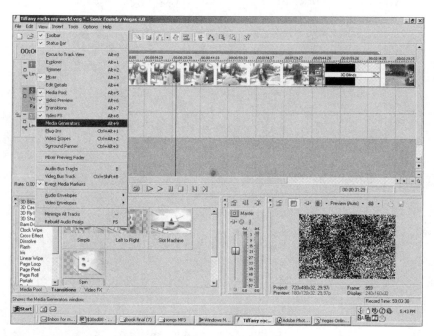

Figure 8.57 *Click on View/Media generators.*

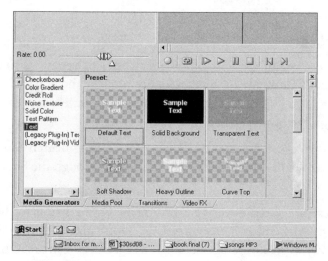

Figure 8.58 *Text presets in Vegas.*

Pick a style you like, and drag it onto the timeline. A window will open containing the word "sample." Highlight the word "sample" and type the text you want to replace it with. Then render to see the changes (see Figure 8.59).

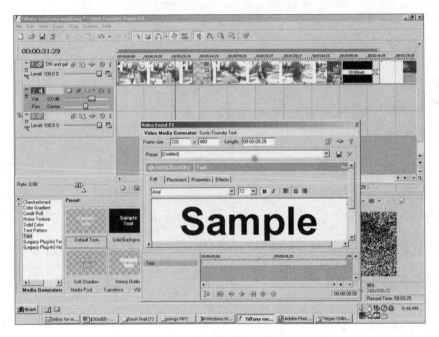

Figure 8.59 *Text Generator Window in Vegas.*

Titles and Credits

Titles usually come at the beginning of the film and tell the viewers what they're about to see. Titles should normally be short. Credits come at the end, tell who did what, and can be a little longer. Opening titles often also have a few credits, usually only the director, the producer, and principal actors.

Credits and titles can be as simple as static images or as complicated as little movies unto themselves, like the computer composited "trip through the brain" at the beginning of *Fight Club*.

Make sure you have credits. Credit everyone who helped. You owe it to them, especially if you didn't pay them. It is their payment. Don't make the mistake I made on *Burn This DVD* of making them scroll so fast that you can't read them easily without freeze frame. (This will be fixed at some point if I get money to do a new version.)

Most programs have a place to do credits. In CineStream you drag a title in from under the effects. You can use them for simple scrolling one-liners such as all the identification titles in *Left My Pants* (CineLook and Background action), or you can have long scrolling text like that at the end of *Left My Pants*. The credits in *D.I.Y. or DIE* were done in Combustion, a high-end compositing program that is better suited to more complicated actions than it is to simple credits.

You will have to render any moving or scrolling credits, and this can take a while, so do a test on a short section first. You also have to render short "one-liners" of text laid over video, like in *Left My Pants* where I have phrases like "CineLook" and "Worm's Eye View" show up. Those only take a few seconds to render.

NOTE

You can also do much simpler credits by simply producing single frames in Photoshop or Illustrator. I did this for the "We don't like Pepsi" at the end of *D.I.Y. or DIE*. Make the frame 720 × 480 and use NTSC-safe colors from the color picker.

Titles and credits don't have to be done on a computer. You can paint or draw real objects and film them. I always liked Nick Zedd's *Police State*, in which he actually spray paints the credits on a police car for the camera. And it's a real honest-to-God NYC police car. This goes down in my book as the cheapest, most effective, and ballsiest opening credits ever.

Rendering and Mixdown

You will have to "Render" most transitions, effects, and text to see them. (Timeline/Render work area in Premiere. Program/Overwrite All Program Tracks in CineStream. File/Render in most other programs.) Rendering tells the computer to *cook* the changes and make a new file (see Figures 8.60 and 8.61). This can take a while—up to several days for a long project with much fancy stuff (depending on the speed of the computer, and the complexity and length of the project). But for what we're doing, a short project with just a few things, it will only take a few minutes. Examples of Rendering in Vegas are shown in Figures 8.62 and 8.63.

(The rendering command in CineStream is called "overwrite" not "render.")

Figure 8.60 *Rendering in Premiere.*

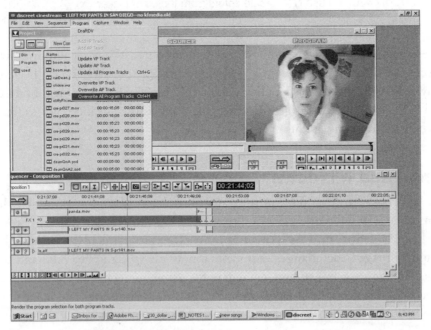

Figure 8.61 *Rendering in CineStream.*

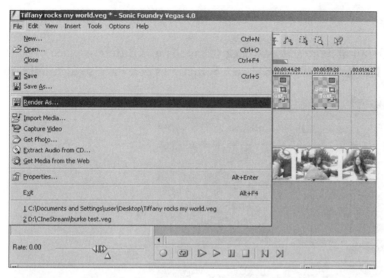

Figure 8.62 *Rendering in Vegas.*

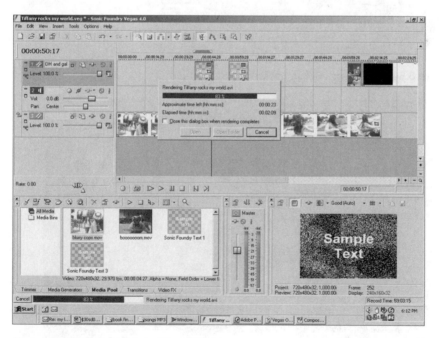

Figure 8.63 *Rendering in Vegas 2.*

Mixdown

Exporting the final rendered mix back to tape is in a different place in each program (see Figures 8.64 through 8.66). Sometimes you have to also hold down a

Figure 8.64 *Exporting back to the camera in Premiere.*

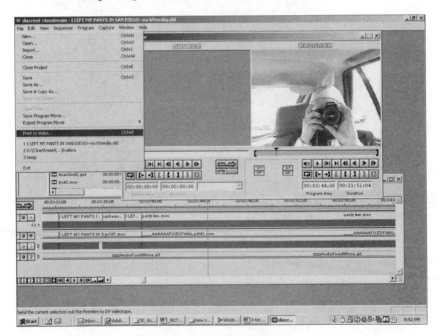

Figure 8.65 *Exporting back to the camera in CineStream.*

key (different in different programs—the Shift key in CineStream) to get it to work. The Record button is grayed out until you do. This is so you don't accidentally print to tape when you don't mean to.

You may have to reboot the program if the camera is on and hooked up but not recognized (see Figure 8.67).

In Vegas, you must select the DV device from the list at Options/Preferences/Video Device (see Figures 8.68 and 8.69). Then set your device and follow the prompts.

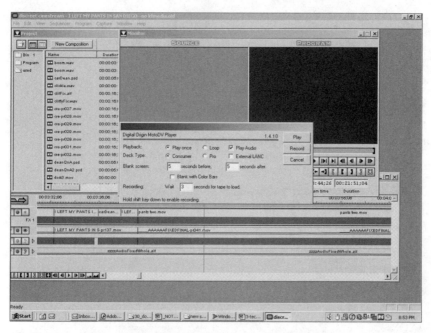

Figure 8.66 *More on exporting back to the camera in CineStream.*

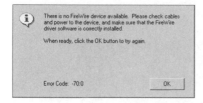

Figure 8.67 *Camera Not Recognized error message during output in CineStream.*

Figure 8.68 *Accessing Options/Preferences/Video Device in Vegas.*

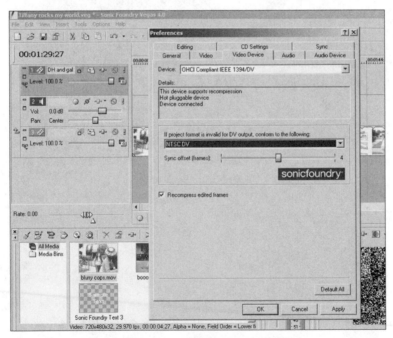

Figure 8.69 *Accessing Options/Preferences/Video Device in Vegas 2.*

Then choose Tools/Print Video to DV Tape and follow the prompts (see Figure 8.70).

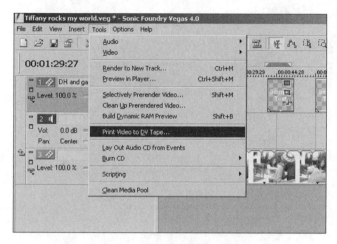

Figure 8.70 *Tools/Print Video to DV Tape.*

In the Print to Tape dialog box of CineStream, you can specify how many seconds the camera or deck should wait before it starts to print (four or five seconds is usually enough to get up to speed). You can also specify what's seen next, color test bars or black screen, and the amount of time this happens (again, four or five seconds is usually good), and the number of seconds after (see Figure 8.71). I usually mark in- and out-points (I and O on the keyboard while clicked in the timeline in most programs) for the section I want to render. Then I render to affect my transitions and effects and print to tape (see Figure 8.72).

Bam! A real film.

Use your camera's RCA jack outputs to hook it to your TV. Sit back and watch. Make notes. Make editing changes based on the notes. Repeat again and again and again until satisfied.

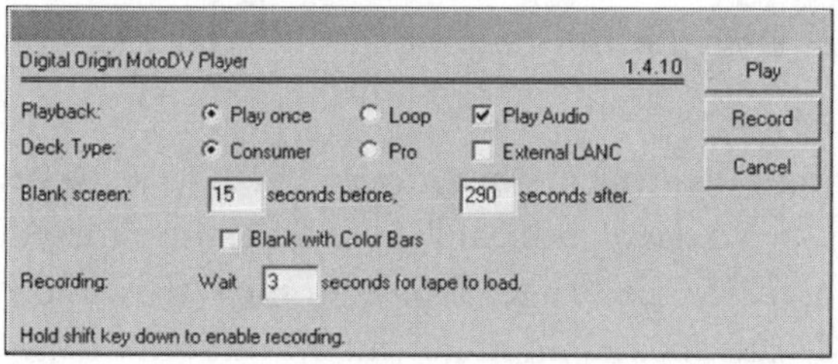

Figure 8.71 *Print to Tape dialog box in CineStream.*

Figure 8.72 *Setting in- and out-points in CineStream.*

A more detailed explanation of this formula is: Look at all the footage, write out on paper the cuts you want to use, make an outline, and start capturing. Then drag all the clips into the timeline and start moving them around to get a feel for how the thing is going to look. Don't worry too much yet about transitions, effects, volume between tracks, and so forth. Get it to a good point and print to tape. Step away from the computer. Watch it on a TV screen. Take notes. Then go back and make the changes, and output a better version. Watch that. Doing this will kind of direct you on how to direct your editing (or editor).

The TV is going to cut off about 10 percent on all edges of what you see on your computer screen. So you have to make all titles *title-safe*, which means don't take it all the way to the edge. So if you (or the program) don't wrap the text, the subtitles may look fine on your computer, but will cut off on a TV. Make sure you look at your stuff on a TV also.

Keep this title-safe issue in mind. It is true of anything you plan to show on a TV rather than just project onto a screen. Look back at Figure 8.51, the Title Window in Premiere has a white square inside the image. This is to show the cut off point for title-safe. Anything outside this square might get cut off on some TVs.

We will more thoroughly cover the concept of making your work title-safe in Chapter 10, "Your Own DVD."

Advanced Editing

So far this chapter has covered the basic stuff you'll need to make a good-looking film. The details and minutia of these editing programs are amazingly deep—some of them have 500-page manuals, and we couldn't possibly cover one, let alone all of them, in depth. We are going to just give you short introductions for the rest of the chapter, to let you know what exists and pique your interest for further study. So if you want to skip on to the next chapter, feel free. You can come back to this later when you want to learn more.

More on Transitions

If you look at really professionally done movies, ones that have great flow and rhythm, 95 percent of the transitions are only three things: cuts, dissolves, and split edits.

◆ *Cuts* are just that: straight cuts from one scene to another. This is the most common transition. Cuts work well almost anywhere. Straight cut transitions are often used in scenes where two people are talking back and forth. They're also used in scenes with two people on the phone or on walkie-talkies in separate locations. Cutting back and forth between the people talking helps make sense of the fact that different people are talking to each other in different locations.

◆ *Dissolves* are when one scene morphs into another, where you can see one fading out while the other is fading in (see Figure 8.73). This can be used sparingly to bring continuity between scenes that are not as obviously related as above. In some programs, you can set the length of the dissolves; in others, it's preset.

◆ *Split Edits* are cuts where video from the previous scene carries over into the audio of the next scene (J-cut), or, conversely, where audio from the previous scene carries over into the video of the next scene (L-cut). This transition is the glue that provides much of the sense of flow in films and TV (see Figures 8.74 and 8.75). Short ones (a second or less) make edits less abrupt. Longer ones provide interesting juxtapositions, augmentations, or contrasts. Look for them and see how often they're used, and why.

Figure 8.73 *Applying a dissolve in CineStream.*

Figure 8.74 *Screenshot of L-cut in CineStream.*

Figure 8.75 *Screenshot of J-cut in CineStream.*

Go for a good sense of pacing, and only use crazy effects if there's a reason. Like Lisa said on *The Simpsons*, "There's more wipes than just star wipes." A lot of people, when they first get on a computer editing system, go nuts with the special effects, because they can. That stuff isn't really in there because real filmmakers want it, it's in there because it's easy to program. It's just more bells and whistles, more dancing baloney to keep programmers employed and drive the price up.

Using more than cuts, dissolves, and split edits (unless sparingly and for a reason) tends to cheapen your vision and turns something cool into something that looks like Grandpa's vacation footage.

Use anything you want, but *think* about why you're using it. People tend to do better breaking rules once they know the rules. The best abstract painters mastered realism first. Kevin Smith did a fairly straight movie with *Clerks,* and afterwards did the complex and convoluted plotlines in *Dogma* that also worked well.

Sync Sound

If you recorded sound directly to the camera, you won't have to do anything to sync (synchronize) it with the video. It will already be synced. If you recorded it separately on a DAT machine or mini-disc recorder to give you more versatility, you'll have to sync it. Do this by bringing the video and the sound in, then scrubbing (move the timeline back and forth). Keep doing this until you line up the clap sound with the first frame with no light coming between the clapper and the slate. Then you lock them and you have sync sound (select Both, Right click/Lock). It can help if you add a *marker* on the timeline where the audio clap sound is. In most programs, this is done by pressing Ctrl+M on the keyboard. The marker does not affect the program; it's just for you to see. (You may have to expand the timeline to be able to see individual frames to do this.)

You can also add markers in sound editing programs such as Sonic Foundry's SoundForge. Most anything with a timeline interface works similarly.

Sound

You can even out the level between different clips in the sound program by pulling a sound filter from the Filter menu and dragging it to the FX track under the clip. Raise or lower the level, and render. You can also add fade-ins and fade-outs like this. In some programs (for example, Vegas) you can add cross-fades (where one track fades in while another fades out—like an audio dissolve) by pulling the sound fade filters across each other. In other programs (for instance, CineStream) you do it by pulling a "cross-fade audio" transition from the Transitions menu (see Figures 8.76 and 8.77).

To reveal the Audio Dissolve Palette in Premiere, click Window/Show Audio Effects (see Figure 8.78).

You will have drop-down options on this palette that will be reveled by clicking on the triangles. After picking the option you want, drag it onto the audio you want to affect in the timeline (see Figure 8.79). An Effects Control Palette will open up. From here, you can set the variables for the effect.

After doing this, render the section of the file, and listen to your changes.

In Vegas, you simply drag the end of one audio clip over another audio clip and slide it back and forth until it is the length you want your audio cross-fade to be (see Figure 8.80). You will see curved bands that show where this occurs. Then render, and the cross-fade will be audible.

Sound will be covered in more depth in Chapter 9, "Editing Audio."

Figure 8.76 *Picking an audio dissolve in CineStream.*

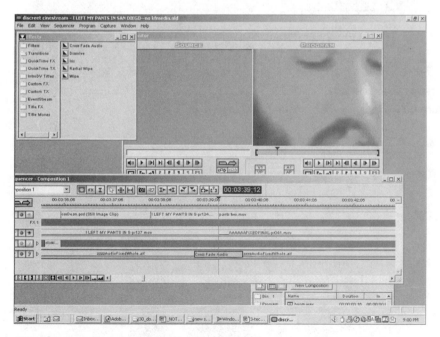

Figure 8.77 *Applying audio dissolve in CineStream.*

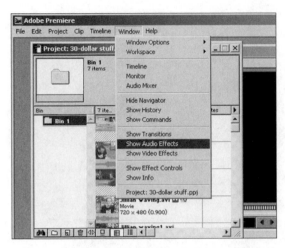

Figure 8.78 *Revealing the Audio Dissolve Palette in Premiere.*

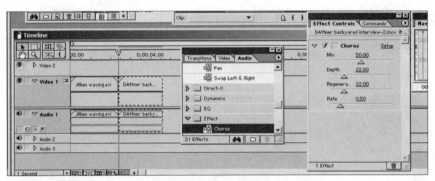

Figure 8.79 *Applying chorus to audio in Premiere.*

Figure 8.80 *Audio cross fade in Vegas.*

Slow and Fast Motion

You can change the settings on your camera to make something shoot in slow or fast motion, or you can do it in editing. Doing it in the camera changes the rate at which the scene is captured (fewer frames per second for fast motion, more for slower). Sometimes scenes are shot at a higher frame rate to capture more detail and then adjusted in editing to make them appear normal. This is usually done with film, not video. An example is the plane crash scene in *Fight Club*. Or the action sequences in John Woo movies.

I find it better to do slow and fast motion exclusively in the editing, not the camera, because this gives me more control. Basically, you just set in- and out-points, change the time in the properties, and then render (see Figures 8.81 and 8.82).

To change the speed in Premiere, simply choose Clip/Speed (see Figure 8.83).

And change to a new speed by percentage or by duration (see Figure 8.84). Then render the clip.

Figure 8.81 *Speed picker in CineStream.*

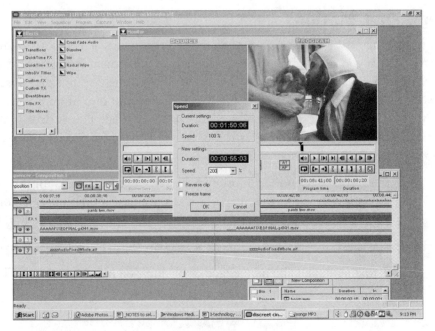

Figure 8.82 *Speed change in CineStream.*

Figure 8.83 *Accessing Speed Change window in Premiere.*

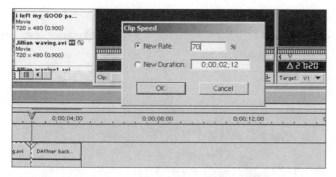

Figure 8.84 *Setting speed change in Premiere.*

Slish Editing

Taking blocks of single frames out of a timeline is called Slish Editing. It can produce cool bizarre results, especially when combined with accelerating, decelerating, and repeating small sections. It's more or less cutting combined with slow and fast motion in small sections. There are examples in *I Left My Pants in San Diego.*

The possibilities for variations in look and feel in this type of editing are endless. Mess around with it and you'll dig the results.

Whip Edits

A whip edit is when you quickly pull the camera away and create a blur at the end of a shot, and start the next shot by starting with a moving camera and ending on the stationary subject, who then begins his line. Then in the editing program, you find a blurry spot in the middle and match them. The result can be a cool illusion that one scene jumped and morphed into the next. This works best if the frames at the split are similar in color and brightness.

This was (over)used combined with a Dutch Tilt a lot on the now-defunct TV cop show, *Nash Bridges.* (They added a cool *Whoosh!* sound effect with it also.)

Again, I did this for you in *I Left My Pants in San Diego.*

Picture in Picture

You know what this looks like. One small box inside the bigger box of the full screen. Really cool, makes action seem more active. But don't overdo it.

Usually you drag both video files into the timeline (you may have to add a second track for it) and then drag a filter called *PIP* (picture in picture) under one, set the preferences, and render it (see Figure 8.85).

Figure 8.85 *Screenshot of PIP in CineStream.*

Pan

A filter you drag into the timeline to make a still image look like a camera move. Especially useful in documentaries that utilize a lot of historical still images. Set angle, speed, and direction, and then render.

Mood

You can affect the mood a lot with editing…fast cuts, long shots, etc. Most of all, a scene is affected in its perception by what follows and precedes it. Watch for this in movies, and experiment.

Another thing to work on is where you make an edit. If there is music, you will often do well to cut on the beat. If there isn't music, look for a place where it feels natural (or unnatural, if that's what you're going for). Take cues from the movement of the actors and work with their motion.

Blue Screen

Making blue screen shots work is a function of editing. You can later add any background you want. Just drag the source video filmed against any solid color into the timeline, drag the new background below it, drag a ChromaKey filter in, and then match and set the color you want to key out with the new background.

> **NOTE**
>
> You can use colors other than blue or green for your blue screen shots, but blue and green are used because they do not exist in skin tones. If you use white, red, yellow, brown, or black, some people's skin will be keyed out in parts. If the clothes match the background, it can be an issue. I first noticed this when watching the weather report as a child and noticed that the weather map was showing through spots in the weatherman's tie.

Subliminals

I kind of hate the idea of teaching a large group of people how to do subliminals, because they are powerful and can influence people in odd ways. But I feel that if you are reading this book, you aren't about all that BS. I'll tell you about it, but you must promise to use your new powers for good, never for evil.

One frame of anything can get by most people unnoticed. Drop it into your timeline. If you want to make people not consciously notice it and have it truly get by, make sure the color does not change very much and the sound does not change at all (use the sound from the source material and not from the single frame).

Subliminals were used very effectively in *The Shining*. Single-frame subliminals are a plot device in the movie *Fight Club*. You do notice the single frames of Tyler that are inserted. And you notice the pornography in the movie theater scene even though you don't directly see it because the sound and color changes. If you make the backgrounds closer, people won't be tipped off.

Remember…for good, never for evil.

Film Look

You can fake film look on video using a post-production plug-in for your editing program to simulate film grain and scratches. I use DigiEffects's CineLook, a third-party plug-in for Adobe After Effects (see Figures 8.86 and 8.87).

Figure 8.86 *After Effects.*

Figure 8.87 *CineLook in After Effects.*

After Effects is a compositing effects program. I edit in CineStream but use After Effects for this purpose only. You can approximate a number of different actual film stocks from the drop-down menu or create your own. You can also create beautiful and/or horrifying psychedelic looks.

There are usually two main parts to film look treatments: grain and damage. Film damage simulates scratches in poorly stored film. This look is very overused in the media, and in my opinion, is cheesy and cliché. We used it in the beginning and end of *D.I.Y. or DIE* with the flyergrrrl and Xeroxgrrrl sequences, but as a joke, sort of poking fun at this overuse. In serious film-look simulations, I just go with the grain and minimize or forget the damage.

Again, I think this is one of those things where people use effects because they can. Film look is the page-curl edit of the millennium.

The only problem with a post-production film look is the horrendous render times. There's an unbelievable amount of math your computer has to do to simulate reality. To render one minute of uncompressed video with film look on my Pentium 4 machine with a 1.7 Ghz processor with a gig of RAM takes about 20 minutes. This means a feature film would take over a day. If you do actually render a whole movie, make sure you do a test on a small segment, then do it in maybe four smaller sections. It's less likely to crash that way, and if it does, you won't have to do the whole thing over.

Note that you can't touch so much as one key on your computer, or the mouse, while rendering, or it may crash. The same is true with outputting a movie to tape.

TIP

Keep your cat, ferret, and baby out of the room while you do these operations. Kitty walking across the keyboard is cute while you're typing a letter, and screamingly frustrating 27 hours into a 40-hour render.

Do CineLook last, after the picture is locked (when the exact length is not going to change anymore, when all the transitions have been rendered, and all that is left to do is the final sound tweak). This will give you more freedom, and you will only have to render the media you actually use in the project. (Be sure in your program to make frequent backup copies.) Since non-linear digital editing suites only replicate the "sheet music" pointing to the huge media files and not the media files themselves, you can do this easily without using much hard drive space. Simply name the project with successive numbers, such as DIY1.edv, DIY2.edv, DIY3.edv, DIY4.edv, and so on. (You don't increase the whole hard drive space size until you render.)

My friend Newt takes it further and saves it with a file name that reflects the project name, the date, and the *time*. Like: PropStars9_19_630am.edv.

This is incredibly useful, especially in final edits, and when dealing with a deadline. We were doing edits on his film *PropStars L.A.* up to two hours before it debuted! We worked 24 hours straight, at one point taking turns napping for a few minutes on my bed while the other worked. Newt would get stuck, wake me up, I'd say "Let me drive" (sit in the computer chair). I'd fix the problem for him and go back to bed.

We ended up with a perfect version that would not output to tape for some reason. (Explained in the Software section. It was a codec issue, but we didn't know at the time, and were on a deadline.) We used his time-named file system to remember when it was working, and output from there.

This file saving idea isn't a bad idea when working in any computer program. For me, a lot of art evolves over many nights with hundreds of thousands of mouse clicks. (That's what the MouseCount program on the CD is for…counting those clicks!) I know I have the tendency to over-tweak something to the point where it's done and perfect and then keep messing with it until it's worse. Keeping time-marked versions helps with this.

If you forget to name files with date and time file names, you can always arrange the icons in the folder according to age (see Figure 8.88). (Right click/Arrange icons/By date.)

This methodology of troubleshooting, mentally reverse-engineering everything until you find the problem, is part of the process of filmmaking. I developed this type of thought while playing music as a teenager. If you get no sound out of the amp, it's either the amp, the cables, the effects peddles, a battery, or the guitar. I would substitute an amp, cable, effects peddle, battery, or guitar that I *knew* was working into the chain until I found the problem.

Actually, it is rare to have this type of analytical thought coupled with artistic ability. One is left-brained; the other is right-brained. This is a problem with many

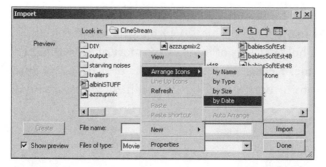

Figure 8.88 *Searching by date of creation when importing files.*

artists: they are flaky and also have poor business sense—a reason they often hire managers and agents.

If you really want to be in total control, and do everything yourself, you have to exercise your full brain.

Backup

I back up everything all the time in all programs by hitting the Ctrl+S key combination frequently; on a Mac, it's Apple+S. I don't like Autosave—it takes a second to work, and you can't input at that exact instant, so it interrupts my flow. In most programs, if the default is to have Autosave on, I turn it off. I disable Autosave under Options and instead just save on the keyboard instinctively every few minutes, or whenever I do a bunch of work I am particularly pleased with and wouldn't want to lose. I also write longer e-mails in a word processing program and then cut and paste them into my e-mail program. You will never get an e-mail from me that begins: "I wrote you a really long e-mail, but my computer crashed, so I had to start over."

You can also back up entire Mini-DV tapes by running a FireWire cable from one camera to the other. Remember, when you record with this or print-to-tape on the computer, you put the *Slave* (camera being recorded to) as well as the *Master* (camera or computer with media to be recorded) on Play, not Record. The Slave will recognize that a FireWire device has been plugged in and give you a "DV IN" on the display. If you don't see that, reboot the camera. (Turn it off and then turn it on again.)

I also back up a lot of important stuff from my computer onto a FireWire drive and even data DVDs. I use a rerecordable DVD for this and put it at a friend's house. A data DVD will hold 4.7 gigs of info. That's most of everything I need to back up at any given time. Keep backups in your car or a friend's house. Your house can get broken into or burn down, but it's unlikely your car and another house will also.

Plug-Ins

One fun little feature of *I Left My Pants* is that I couldn't figure out how to do a mask in CineStream to edit someone's face out (the guy in red wouldn't sign a release form). So I exported the section from CineStream as a Quicktime file, and imported it into Quicktime Pro. I used Quicktime to export an image sequence of PNG files, opened 275 individual frames up in Photoshop, blurred each one out by hand, re-imported the sequence into Quicktime and rendered it back into a Quicktime movie. Then I imported this back into CineStream and replaced the original section in the timeline. This took about 40 minutes.

The next day my friend JP Kelly gave me a plug-in for After Effects, called Cop Blur. It's the look they use to hide bystanders' faces on the TV show *Cops*. Even though I had that and used it later in the faux-street fight scene in *I Left My Pants*, I'm glad I had the experience of doing it frame-by-frame myself once.

One plug-in I like a lot is DigiEffects' CineLook. It is pretty good at faking film grain. There's a demo of it, Cop Blur, and a bunch of other cool plug-ins on the CD.

To use Cop Blur or any other animation (tracking) effect in After Effects (and many other animation and editing programs), you have to set Key Frames to show that program where to track the image (see Figure 8.89). You set as many key frames as you need, and during the render, the program fills in the "tween" or in-between material (see Figures 8.90 and 8.91). Pretty magical.

Setting key frames is different in every program.

JP made the explosion in After Effects, e-mailed it to me as an uncompressed QuickTime movie, and I added it into the flick with After Effects.

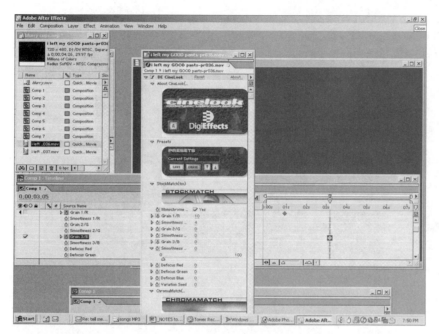

Figure 8.89 *Setting key frames in CineLook within Adobe After Effects.*

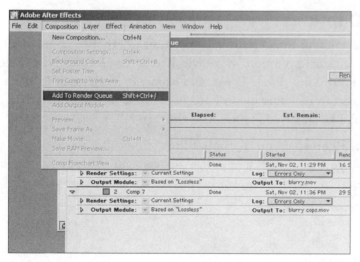

Figure 8.90 *Rendering in CineLook within Adobe After Effects.*

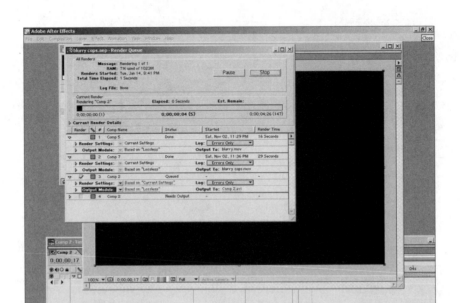

Figure 8.91 *More rendering in CineLook within Adobe After Effects.*

Taking Frame Captures

A movie is a collection of single frames. If you want to export a single frame, say, to use on your Web site to promote the movie, here's how: In your NLE timeline, select an in- and out-point of one frame, and export to file in the file menu. You may have to convert from a bitmap in Photoshop. Make sure to de-interlace them so they don't look like crap (see Figures 8.92 through 8.97).

Open the file in Photoshop, go to Tools/Filter/Video/De-interlace, and press Enter. Those squiggly lines will disappear. Also, the auto-contrast feature under Image/Adjust/Autocontrast is a nice help most of the time, especially with dark images.

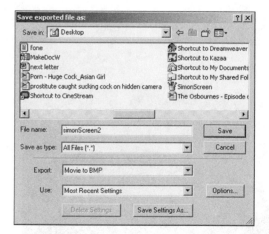

Figure 8.92 *Frame export in CineStream.*

Figure 8.93 *Raw screen capture from Mini-DV video. Note squiggle lines.*

Figure 8.94 *De-interlaced version of this image.*

Figure 8.95 *A different raw screen capture from Mini-DV video. Note squiggle lines.*

Figure 8.96 *De-interlaced version of second image.*

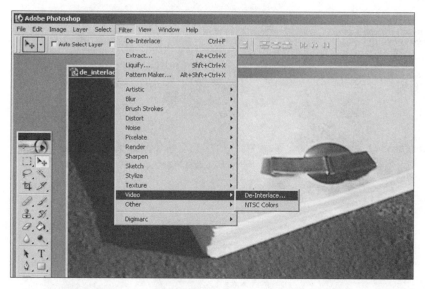

Figure 8.97 *Screenshot of Photoshop de-interlacing.*

Trailers

Trailers are the little one-minute or so teasers they show before other movies. They are ads for an upcoming film. It's good to make one; you can put them on the Internet or on DVDs or show them in with other films to promote your film.

Go for a quick sense of pacing, and try to capture the attention and make people want to see the film. That's more important than trying to tell the story. You don't need to. The movie will tell the story. You just want to get people to the movie.

By the way, when you're cutting a trailer, it's okay to use a few outtakes that did not end up in the movie.

Encoding for DVDs

To make DVDs, you first have to encode your movie into a format the program will accept. Many of the lower-end wizard-driven consumer programs will accept .avi files, which are easy to output from your editing program. Select your in- and out-points, highlight the timeline files, and export (see Figures 8.98 through 8.102).

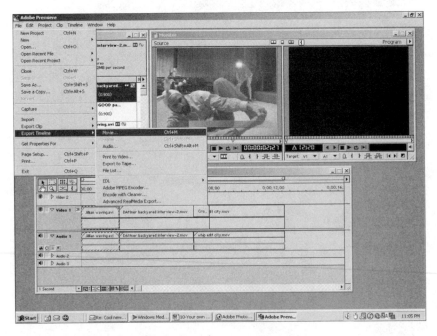

Figure 8.98 *Export to File in Premiere.*

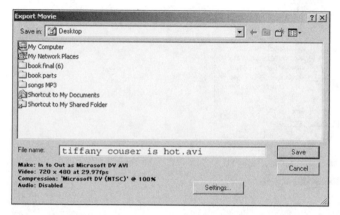

Figure 8.99 *Saving the .avi file in Premiere.*

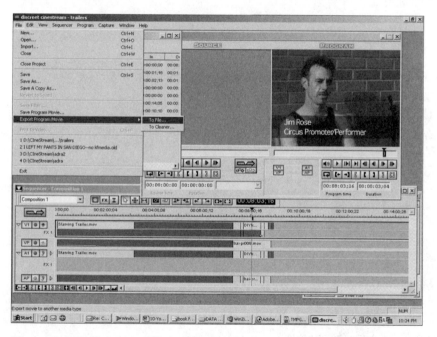

Figure 8.100 *Export to File in CineStream.*

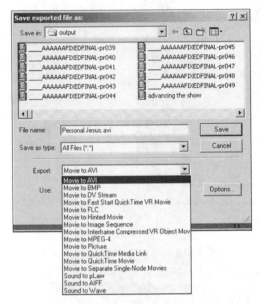

Figure 8.101 *Picking .avi as the file format to export to in CineStream.*

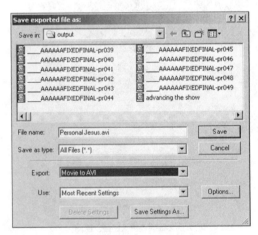

Figure 8.102 *Save the .avi file.*

The higher-end programs (like Sonic Creator and Producer and Fusion Sonic Scenarist, Ulead MediaStudio Pro, Apple DVDSP—the ones you'll need to do really cool stuff, like adding subtitles) require MPEG files.

You can turn movies into MPEG DVD format, using a software encoder like Cleaner. ($529 from www.discreet.com—also available in a light version bundled free with many video editing suites. (See Figure 8.103 through 8.105.) For about $200 more, you can get Cleaner Streaming Studio, which includes CineStream. (Cleaner EZ5 comes with this demo of Premiere.)

Because this is *$30 Film School*, not *$500 Film School*, I'm gonna spend more time on a shareware utility that will also encode, called *TMPGEnc* (www.tmpgenc.net). It's free to use for the first 30 days. It's not as easy to use, and the encodes aren't quite as good-looking, fast, or as small in file size as those from Cleaner. But the price is right. I put a time-limited, *working* copy of this program on the CD that comes with this book.

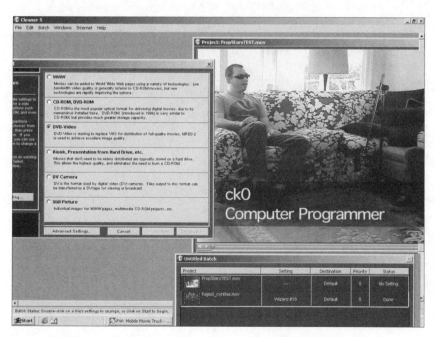

Figure 8.103 *Screenshot of Cleaner.*

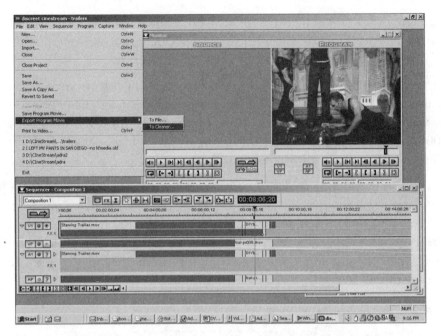

Figure 8.104 *Exporting to Cleaner.*

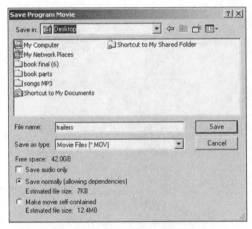

Figure 8.105 *Exporting to Cleaner 2.*

TMPGEnc will not export directly out of your editing program like Cleaner. You will have to do one extra step first before you encode: convert your movie to .avi format from your editing program (see Figures 8.106 through 8.109).

Then, to encode a movie in TMPGEnc, open the program.

The wizard will guide you through. Pick "DVD NTSC"

Hit "Next"

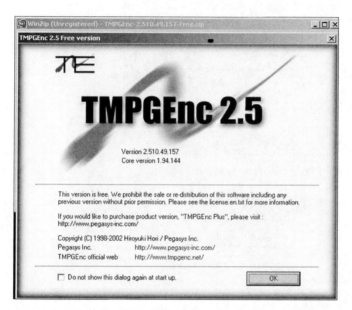

Figure 8.106 *TMPGEnc.*

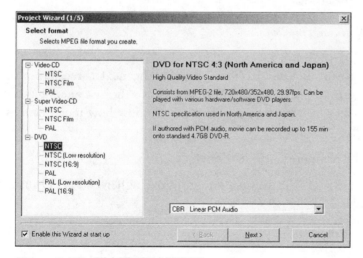

Figure 8.107 *Pick "DVD NTSC."*

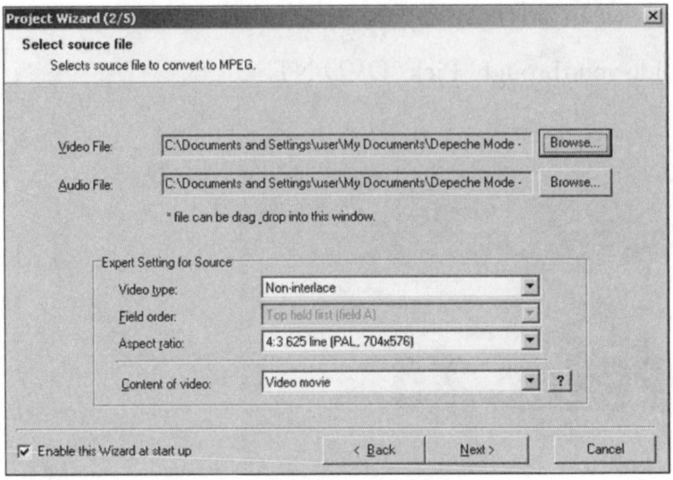

Figure 8.108 *Click the Video File/Browse button.*

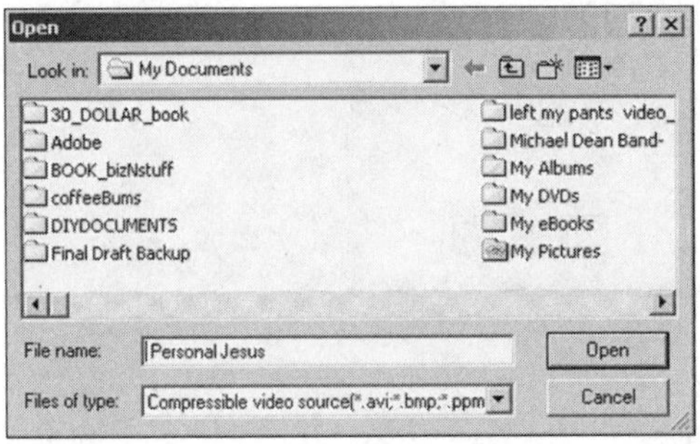

Figure 8.109 *Pick your .avi movie file.*

Click on Open. Keep clicking on Next through the next three panes of the Wizard without setting any changes. When you get to the last one, press OK to begin encoding. You can watch the progress bar to know how much time is left (see Figure 8.110).

Step away from the computer until it's done.

This will output an MPEG file you can import into a higher-end DVD authoring environment.

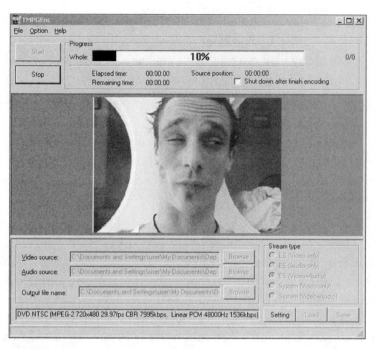

Figure 8.110 *TMPGEnc working.*

Editing Theory

My process for making art, any art, is this: Put down way too much, and then edit. Like those painters who slather on layers of paint and then scrape it off, I work by process of elimination. I'm like the sculptor who looks at a block of marble and says, "There's an angel in there, I just have to let her out." I work in increments, and make each draft as complete as possible.

When I was making *D.I.Y. or DIE*, I shot about 45 hours of interviews, then I imported it all, picked about 6 hours of what I thought was golden, output that to tape, and brought it to the editor, Miles Montalbano, and we worked from there. That's the only way I can work, the only way I can visualize and concentrate.

Part of the reason I work this way is that it somehow is the only way to make sense of my left/right brain connection. The rest of it is a fear of death. I write a whole novel from start to finish, then edit and improve as I add more and take away more. I just print it out, go through with a red pen and circle changes. I enter the changes into the computer and make the master file. Then I print it out again and go through it again. All the while though, I am adding more to the master file. I do this about five times, and a book is done. I think the idea is that if I die, I want there to be *something* of my new project...for someone else (that I trust) to finish editing or to be enough of a work in progress to stand on its own.

Newspaper articles are written like this, the headline is the most important part, the first paragraph tells the story, and subsequent paragraphs fill in details, until you get to the last sentence and it's probably just superfluous opinion. (This is called "The inverted triangle format"....although I had an English teacher who called it the "crotch format" because it was shaped, in importance, like the bottom half of a bikini.)

Historically, this was because stories were sent in by telegraph, and lines often got knocked down. They wanted to be able to have *some* story if the line died mid-tap. Later when more trustworthy methods of transmission were developed (culminating in the Internet, which can survive far more than a cut wire), journalists kept this format because people were used to it. Also, it is useful for busy people to get the gist of the day's news without having to read entire articles. Also, this makes it easier for editors to edit for length; they simply cut whatever they need from the bottom to fit the day's ads into the paper, and the article still makes sense.

The "put down way too much, and then edit" method is just my way. I tell you about it only to inspire, not to dictate. Find your own way.

Editing Advice and History

You can practice editing by "fixing" movies you almost love. Don't dig that obligatory romantic interest in your favorite war movie? Cut it out. Do you hate Jar Jar Binks? The story works better without him, etc.

When people first started editing video, it was linear with two decks, going from one to the other. (This is called *stacking*.) Or you can use two VCRs. Just stop and start the tape.

If you don't have a computer or a friend with one, and can't do non-linear editing (NLE) or find someone else to do it, you can edit by stacking with two VCRs or a VCR and your camera. This is harder than non-linear editing, because if you want to make a change at the beginning you have to start over, but it will actually make you visualize the whole story better.

When people first edited, it was on film. Film is a non-linear medium. In other words, if you put together clips A, B, C, D, E, F, G, and H in order and then later decide to switch the order of A and B, you don't have to start over. You just cut them, switch them and splice them together.

When big budget movies are shot today on 35 mm, editors still edit by cutting and splicing the actual film. (Actually, the editor doesn't do that. It's the dedicated job of a person called a *Negative Cutter.*) But those cuts are executed following exacting decisions made by an *Editor* working on a computerized non-linear editing system. It's usually the Avid—a very expensive, dedicated hardware/software combination—but increasingly this is done with Final Cut Pro (Apple) and even CineStream (Discreet) or Avid Express. The film is Telecined (*Telecine* is the process of scanning each frame to make a digital copy) and edited it on an NLE in the computer system. This makes it easier to try infinite numbers of things that would be difficult with actual film.

When the director and editor agree on all the decisions (and often in Hollywood, the fat, non-artistic banker financing the film has a say in this), the editing program exports a text list of all the changes called an EDL (edit decision list). This lists timecode and frame numbers of which clips go where and how they transition. Then the conventional film cutter dude makes the old-fashioned cuts based on this list. Then he makes a copy of this and makes all the projection prints from that master print.

If you are working strictly in video (which is the focus of this book, although we will touch on working with film), you will bypass this. What you shoot, and what you edit will not be simply representational; it will be the actual product. And it looks pretty good. Not as great as film, but infinitely more affordable. You can always pay a lot of money and have a film print made for projection of the final project. You used to have to do this for film festivals, but most festivals can now project from a DV or Beta tape. That just saved you about $10,000.

No-Budget Focus Groups

Kind of related to the table reading, but later, during editing. Don't torture your friends with your first draft of an edit, but after three or four improved takes on the above process, you might enlist a few good friends or helpers who like and understand movies to watch it with you. After doing this a few times, you'll quickly see who has constructive criticism and who's a goofball not to be invited to future showings.

We showed a polished rough cut of *D.I.Y. or DIE* at the Lost Film Fest at Sundance in Park City, Utah. It showed twice, to about 40 people total. I talked to *every* one of them and got feedback. The things that came up again and again and made sense, we implemented. Basically, it was "You need background music" (it had none at that point) and "We want to see more of the people doing their art" (which we added).

Don't make concessions based on BS Hollywood expectations though—don't add a gratuitous happy ending on a movie that doesn't need it, for instance. Go see the movie *The Player* for a good take on this.

Editing is often considered the most important phase, and it's good to have someone you trust to watch and help with advice. It's easy to think everything we do is golden, and it's good to have a BS detector.

A character in my novel states, "Everything that can be done has been done. Being a great artist consists simply of being a good editor."

I look at editing as a natural extrapolation of what I do every day with everything I do: It is simply putting things in their proper places in a creative way. I feel the same way—process oriented—when I'm answering e-mail or out doing errands or petting the cat. It's all editing. It's all about taking in all the information the world pushes your way and filtering out the static and keeping what's good, and putting it in a sensible order.

One thing that I find quite useful is watching movies with the sound off. That way you can separate yourself from suspending your disbelief and really see how the thing was made. Look at the lighting, the editing, the camerawork, and so forth. (I learned this technique because I end up flying a lot but sometimes can't afford five bucks to rent the stupid headphones.)

Making Mistakes Work

The thing at the end of *I left My Pants in San Diego*—when Joshua Leonard is speaking and the right side of the frame looks bizarre—is actually my camera heads needing cleaning. I thought it looked cool so I left it. The same thing is in

D.I.Y. or DIE: Burn This DVD when I'm filming myself being interviewed in Vancouver on that CBC morning drive-time show.

The volume of the background music that plays behind some of the menus on *D.I.Y. or DIE: Burn This DVD* was WAY louder than the program material within each menu on the first pressing. This was an accident, but I immediately noticed it on the test disk, and left it intentionally. I *wanted* people to have to ride the volume on the project to keep them from getting too complacent when they listened to it. It made it a non-passive experience.

(I should point out that many powerful artists are never satisfied with their work. John Lennon is said to have hated listening to Beatles albums because all he heard was the mistakes.)

I got bored with this and fixed it on the second pressing. You can tell the second pressing because the menu music is not oppressively loud, and because the *First Play* (the menu you first see when the DVD starts up) and *Setup* menus have different music, not the same music.

And just so you know, that groovy repetitive bass figure on the first play menu is a snip of the Bach flute from the *Web Links* menu slowed waaaaaay down in SoundForge. It was played by my friend Suraya Keating and is leftover audio from the production of the *Starving* trailer. (I played on all the music on the menus except this flute.)

When we shot the *D.I.Y. or DIE* footage, the first interview shot was Mike Watt. I lucked out when I went to interview him; he was playing with Ron Asheton and J Mascis, so I got to interview them also.

There were a bunch of cups from the venue on the table that said "Pepsi" on them. They were actually full of water, but regardless, they ended up in frame for all three of these interviews. The student cameraman who was lending us his skills on that shoot left them in frame. I don't know that he did it intentionally, but maybe he did. They probably teach you to do that in film school.

I was so excited to be working on my film after *weeks* of planning that I didn't bother to even look through the viewfinder, so I didn't notice or say anything. So basically, not one, but *three* of the interviews, 10 percent of the film, of this anticommercialism art film, ended up with inadvertent, unpaid product placement for what is, in my opinion, one of the most aesthetically questionable products in the world.

We meant to pixilate it out, but that takes time, and I was spending my virtual dollars getting my editor to actually finish the thing. So taking those Pepsi cups out got moved to the back burner and never got done. So I added a thing at the end, done on my computer, with my limited knowledge and ability that did not look as good as the rest of the film. It was after the first false ending, after the credits, when the audience usually starts clapping and leaving. After Ian MacKaye comes back up and says the thing about playing piano and never failing. After the static frame comes up and says "NOW GO MAKE YOUR OWN MOVIE." And people laugh and clap again. After this, I added my crappy little thing over a reprised snip of the theme song that says, "WE DO NOT LIKE PEPSI." Then another one comes up that says, "WE DO NOT DRINK PEPSI." And finally, "THE CUPS WERE FULL OF WATER."

People *love* this. I may take it out and pay Miles or someone to pixel blur the cups at some point, but I may not. I kind of like this anti-product placement.

And our lawyer, Marc Alain Steier, Esq. (who works pro bono on the project), says that the wording here is perfectly legal. If we'd said anything like "Pepsi sucks," that might get us in trouble. But saying we don't drink it is a fact, not an opinion, and non-slanderous under fair use.

Again, make the best with what you have, in an interesting way.

Collaborating

Editing really is the glue that holds a picture together. It can make a big difference in the mood of a film. The editor is the director's friend, but sometimes they have differences. I worked with Miles on *D.I.Y. or DIE*, and love what he did. We got along great, but he did it differently than I would have. I made many of the decisions, but let him dictate the overall feel because he had more experience than I. He did a wonderful job, but knowing now what I know, if I had it to do over, I would have made it a little more psychedelic and fast-paced. Probably less stately. Picture my editing on the *D.I.Y.* DVD extras and *Left My Pants*, but done with Miles' skill, the way he did the movie itself.

Working with an editor can be a collaborative effort like it was for us, or it can be frustrating and almost argumentative like it was for some friends of mine. Basically, the bottom line is if you learn to do it yourself, you won't have to work through someone else's hands, and you'll be freer to work alone or choose to work with someone else when you want to, not because you have to. I'm still learning, and will probably still work with an editor for my next film. But since I have more experience now myself, I will be more proactive in my interactions with him or her, and will certainly do a little of the editing myself.

Conclusion

They say that movies are directed for a second time in the editing, and that documentaries are directed for the first time in the editing. There is some truth to this, but editing is not a replacement for a lack of planning. Outline. Script. Think things out. Don't count on "fixing it in the mix." Write, plan, research. Make drawings (storyboards) of what you plan to film. Shoot great images and then use the editing phase to make it even better, rather than using editing as turd polishing.

Chapter 9

Editing Audio

We've already learned that sound is actually more important than image in affecting how people perceive the professionalism of a movie. We've learned how to get good source sound on a shoot. We've learned about using sound in the video program. So now let's learn how to make the audio in your films as great as we possibly can. Here we'll cover the use of software to make soundtracks and improve overall sound, and also how to dub dialogue to improve our films.

Basic Sound Program Use

Sound editing programs, like image editing programs, have made quick work of processes that used to take hours of work, years of training, and hundreds of thousands of dollars worth of equipment.

Three programs on my hard drive replace the following physical devices and also do things that these devices could never do: 24-track tape recorder, mixing board, variable speed tape recorder, sampler, synthesizer, tone generator, splicing deck, noise reduction unit, noise gate, oscilloscope, tuner, slate, pitch shifter, wah wah, echo box, reverb plate, distortion, graphic EQ, parametric EQ, limiter, phase shifter, Dolby encoder, compressor, pre-amp, chorus, vibrato…heck, and even two turntables and a microphone.

Jump in with us now as we explore the world of high-quality low-budget digital sound manipulation for desktop filmmaking.

Using Acid

Sonic Foundry's Acid is a very simple-to-use software utility that can easily allow even non-musicians to make great-sounding background music. All it takes is patience and a sense of flow, which you will need to develop anyway to shoot and edit.

I use Acid a lot. My good friend Cliff Truesdell (who actually *is* a good musician: check out www.clifftruesdell.com) used Acid to make the spooky cool instrumental piece called "Thelemic Eye" that we used as some of the background music in *D.I.Y. or DIE.*

Acid does one thing only, but it does that one thing very well: It takes different audio loops and stretches them to match each other in a coherent manner. Acid will do in seconds what people used to spend all day trying to do with two turntables and a tape machine. Then you import the ensuing rhythm track directly into your video editing program to use as background. Or first, you can take it into Sound Forge or ProTools to edit, then bring it into Vegas and add other sounds, live instruments, or even vocals. There are several different levels of Acid, for any budget. Acid Pro is the high-end version with the most depth. Acid Music is the mid-level version. Acid Style is the beginner (and least expensive) version.

Here's a lesson on using Acid to make some background music for your movie. (A demo version is included on the CD—although it times out at two minutes and has to be restarted. Try to get a full version somehow.)

Open Acid. Save the project with a descriptive name (see Figure 9.1).

Figure 9.1 *Save the project.*

Select File, Open. Open all the files in the Noises/Acid files folder on the CD-ROM that comes with this book (see Figures 9.2 and 9.3). I made these sample audio loops in Sonic Foundry's Sound Forge using parts of previously existing songs of mine, but you can use any audio sample in Acid. Acid recognizes both .wav and .aiff format files. You can even buy ready-made CDs of great rhythm tracks from Sonic Foundry. These are specially prepared and have special internal meta information which make them loop better, and give better results when matching tempos.

NOTE

.wav (pronounced "wave") files are a standard Windows media format. .aiff is a standard Apple format. Most computers and almost all audio and video programs can read both formats nowadays. For all practical purposes, one format does not have any large advantage over the other. They both sound almost identical and have almost the same file size.

The Acid interface will automatically create tracks for each sound file (see Figure 9.4).

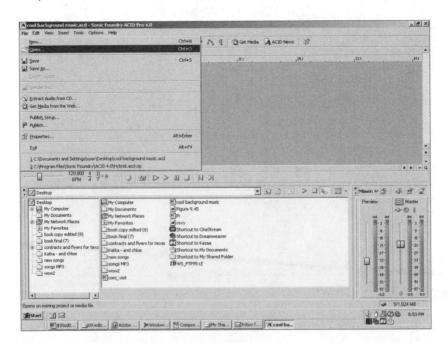

Figure 9.2 *Open all the files in the folder.*

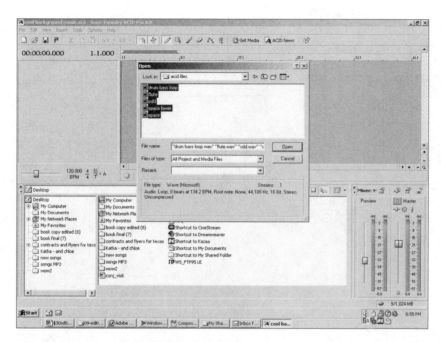

Figure 9.3 *Open all the files in the folder 2.*

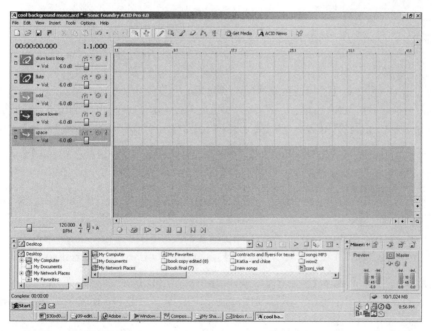

Figure 9.4 *Tracks in Acid.*

We are basically going to be using two tools in this demonstration, the Draw Tool and the Erase Tool (see Figure 9.5).

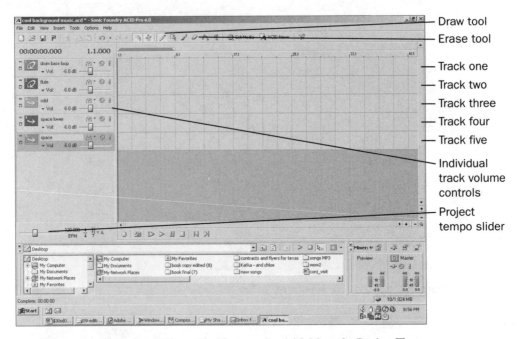

Figure 9.5 *Draw Tool and Erase Tool buttons in Acid. Note the Project Tempo Slider and the Individual Track Volume Controls. We will use those too.*

Click on the Draw Tool button. Using the Draw Tool (it looks like a pencil), hold the left mouse button down and draw a line across the drum bass loop track. Then release the mouse. You will get a track of solid drum bass loop (see Figure 9.6).

Hit the Spacebar to begin playback. You will notice that Acid has looped the short audio track to create a longer rhythm track.

If it seems slower or faster than you like, you can adjust the Project Tempo Slider to the desired speed. Note that a variance of only a few BPM (beats per minute) can make a big difference in the mood of a piece. I brought this project from the default of 120 BPM up to 159 BPM. This gave it a hard industrial sound.

Now, using the Draw Tool, draw some more audio in the rest of the tracks (see Figure 9.7). But this time, lift and release it here and there to allow the sound to start and stop.

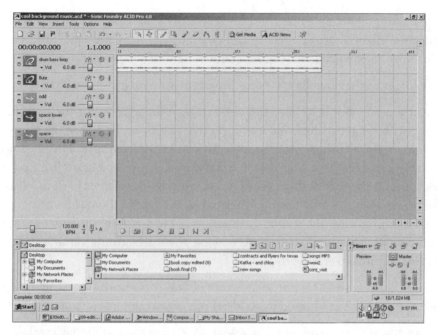

Figure 9.6 *A single track with audio in Acid.*

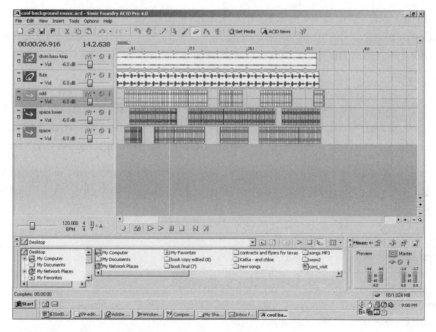

Figure 9.7 *Several tracks with audio in Acid.*

After making changes, press the Home key on your keyboard to return to the beginning of the piece. Listen to the changes again by pressing the Spacebar again. Keep making changes until it sounds the way you want it.

Don't forget to periodically save your project as you go. Just press Ctrl+s.

A good way to work is to have the basic track you are using for the beat, usually the one with the most rhythmic sound (in this case drum bass loop) go all the way through, or almost all the way through. (It can be interesting to have it drop out for a few measures, as it does here near the end—note in Figure 9.7 that other tracks take up the beat at that point until drum bass loop comes back in.) I usually build on the basic beat by having other tracks come in and out. It is often a good rule of thumb to have the rest of the tracks build in a way that there's not much at first but more as the song goes on. Of course there are infinite variations, but this is a good formula to start with.

So now that you've got some tracks down, you can remove parts by using the Erase tool. That's how I build in Acid—I put down a lot, then take away.

You can adjust the individual track volumes by using the Individual Track Volume Controls. This will help give you a balance you like.

When we get a sound we're satisfied with, it's time to render it, close Acid, and use our new background music (see Figures 9.8 through 9.10). Select File, Render As and then from the drop-down menu, select Mixed Wave file.

Close the Dialog Window.

The file I got out of this exercise is on the CD in the Noises folder; it's called Cool Background Music. I had to convert it to an MP3, because the disk was almost full and it wouldn't fit as a Wave file, but you can listen to it and see what I made.

You will now have a complete piece you can use as background music in your film, and it only took a few minutes and no musical training. Now close Acid and open the Sound Forge demo.

TIP

Muska & Lipman has two great books that explore Acid and Sound Forge in much more detail than we have room for here: *ACID Power!* By David Franks, and *Sound Forge 6 Power!* by Scott Garrigus.

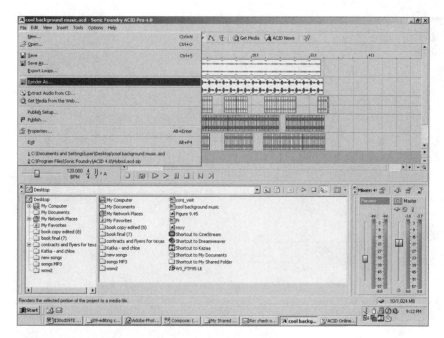

Figure 9.8 *Pick "Render As" from the File menu.*

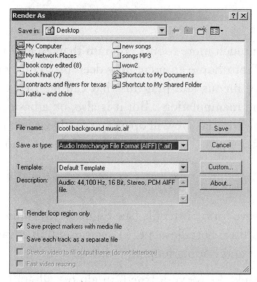

Figure 9.9 *Type a file name to save your new Acid soundtrack.*

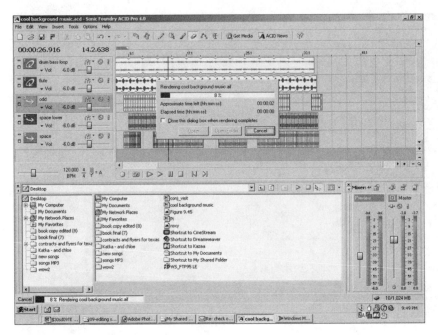

Figure 9.10 *Acid soundtrack rendering.*

Using Sound Forge

Sonic Foundry's Sound Forge is a much more robust program than Acid. I think of it as the audio equivalent of Photoshop—an incredibly deep program (with a 500-page manual) with dozens of menus and plug-ins that can be used for an almost unlimited number of sound manipulations. But it is also, on a basic level, easy to use. For the first part of this tutorial, we will open up the file we just made in Acid (see Figures 9.11 and 9.12), apply a little EQ, reverb, and flange, and then save the file

First, use File/Open to bring in the file we just made.

Note that you can see the actual wave form of the file (see Figure 9.13). This takes the place of having a dedicated hardware oscilloscope. (This is useful in advanced editing for finding altering regions and finding looping points.)

Hit the Spacebar to begin playback. As we've learned, in almost all audio and media programs, this will stop and start playback. As in Acid, hitting the "home key" on the keyboard when the program is stopped will bring you back to the beginning of the file. Now let's do a little EQ. EQ stands for "equalization," which

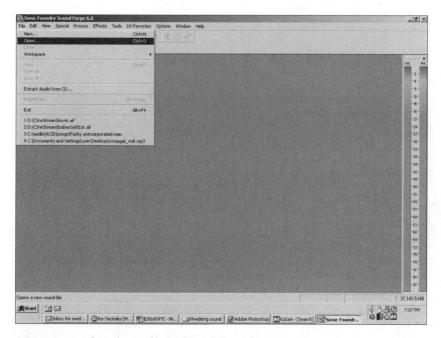

Figure 9.11 *Opening a file in Sound Forge.*

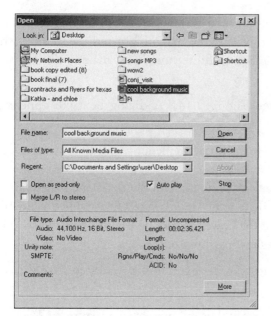

Figure 9.12 *Opening a file in Sound Forge 2.*

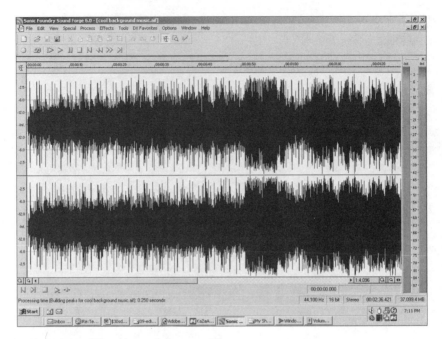

Figure 9.13 *Wave form of the open file.*

is the mix of different frequencies present in the overall sound of a file. If there's too much low end, it will sound muffled. Too much high, and the sound is shrill. Changing the EQ of a sound file is a useful technique for making any file sound better.

Select Process/EQ/Graphic (see Figure 9.14). A dialog box will appear (see Figure 9.15).

Hit the Reset button. This will return all the frequency bands to zero, which is no boost and no cut. At this setting, no EQ is applied. Try boosting the bass by sliding the far left two sliders all the way to the top and the third one half-way to the top (see Figure 9.16). Click on OK to apply. It will take a little while for the file to render. The speed will depend on the power of your computer. You will see a little task bar in the lower-left corner showing the progress.

When the file is done redrawing, play it again, and notice that it sounds a lot deeper because it now has more bass.

There is a drop-down menu with several useful presets (see Figure 9.17).

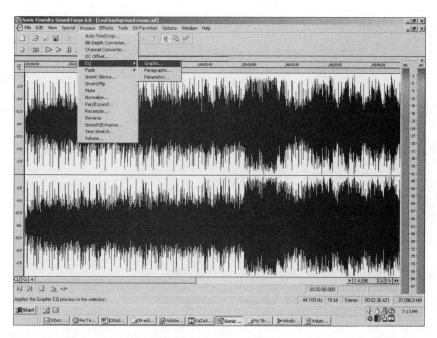

Figure 9.14 *Accessing the EQ dialog box.*

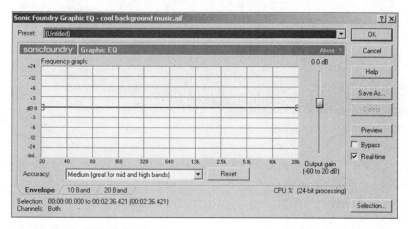

Figure 9.15 *EQ dialog box.*

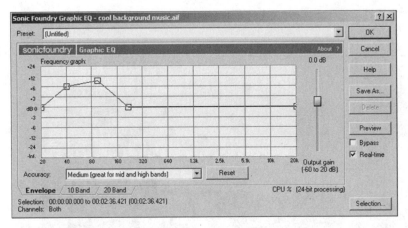

Figure 9.16 *Boosting bass EQ.*

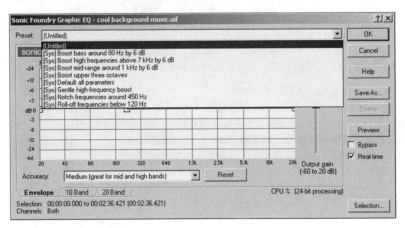

Figure 9.17 *EQ drop-down menu.*

Experiment with these later and listen to how the sound is altered. Make copies of each file before altering it in Sound Forge, because it will overwrite the file and you will not be able to go back to your original once you've saved the changes.

Click on OK, then click Save As from the file menu and save the altered file with a new file name

Now we will apply some reverb. *Reverb* (short for *Reverberation*) adds depth and warmth to a sound by imitating the sound of short echoes. If you clap your hands in a large empty auditorium, you will hear some reverb. If you do the same in a small closet full of clothes, you will hear none.

Select Effects/Reverb to access the Reverb Dialog Box (see Figures 9.18 and 9.19).

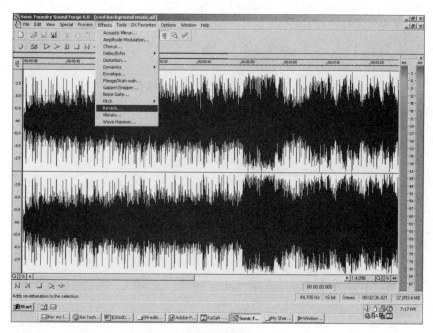

Figure 9.18 *Accessing the Reverb Dialog Box.*

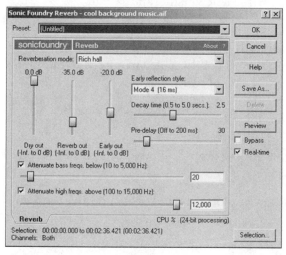

Figure 9.19 *The Reverb Dialog Box.*

Go to the drop-down menu and select Long Hall. Click on the "Preview" button for a real-time preview of what it will sound like. If you like it, click on OK, wait for the changes to render, then play the file (see Figure 9.20). Notice how different it now sounds.

The Real-Time Preview Button is available for all the effects in Sound Forge.

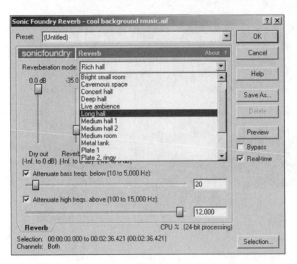

Figure 9.20 *The Reverb Dialog Box drop-down menu.*

Now click on "Save As", give the file a new name, and save it.

Finally, we'll add a little Flange. *Flange* is an effect that makes a file sort of sound like it's inside a jet engine, in a really cool way. It's used on a lot of rock records to make them sound trippy. As soon as you hear it, I'm sure you'll go, "Oh, *that's* what that is."

Select Effects/Flange-Wah-Wah to open the Flange Dialog Box (see Figures 9.21 and 9.22).

Get the preset Slow Flange 2 from the drop-down menu, and click OK. Listen to the file. Save.

You can repeat these steps for even more flange. You can do this with any of the controls in Sound Forge. Doing any of these processes twice will add twice as much of the effect.

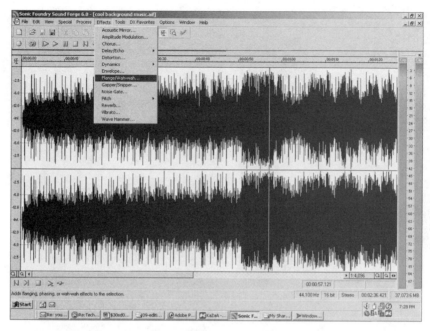

Figure 9.21 *Opening the Flange Dialog Box.*

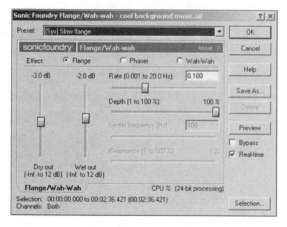

Figure 9.22 *The Flange Dialog Box.*

You can also highlight just a part of a file and process only that part (see Figure 9.23). (If you highlight none, the entire file is affected.) You highlight by holding down the mouse button and sweeping the cursor over just part of the file.

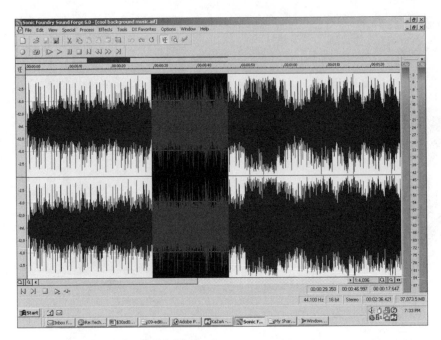

Figure 9.23 *Part of a file highlighted.*

Now close Sound Forge and import your groovy new file into your video editing program; lay it under some video clips and try it out (see Figures 9.24 through 9.29). Pretty neat, eh?

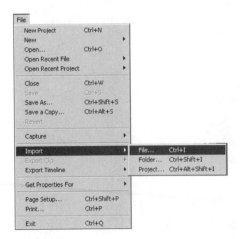

Figure 9.24 *Importing audio in Premiere.*

NOTE

You may have some extraneous new small .skf and .sfl files in the same folder as your final product. They will have file names like cool background music.sfk and cool background music.aif.sfl. They are just meta disc image files created by Sound Forge (and Acid and Vegas) to help them work. They are sort of digital poop left behind and can be safely deleted.

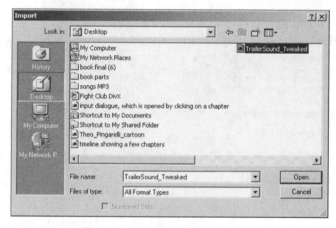

Figure 9.25 *Importing audio in Premiere 2.*

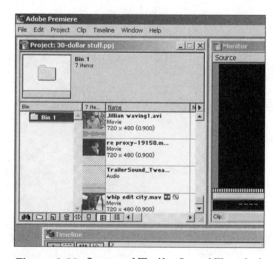

Figure 9.26 *Imported Trailer Sound Tweaked audio file in project window in Premiere.*

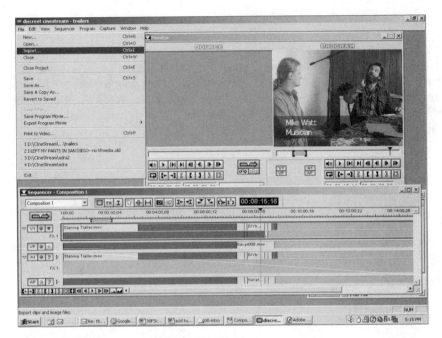

Figure 9.27 *Importing audio in CineStream.*

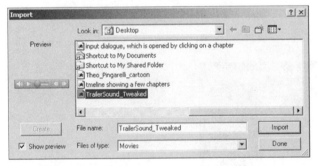

Figure 9.28 *Importing audio in CineStream 2.*

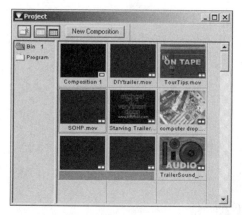

Figure 9.29 *Imported Trailer Sound Tweaked audio in project window in CineStream.*

You may have to adjust the volume of your background music in either the video editing program or Sound Forge (Process/Volume) so it doesn't overpower the talking (see Figures 9.30 and 9.31). Experiment until you get a mix you like.

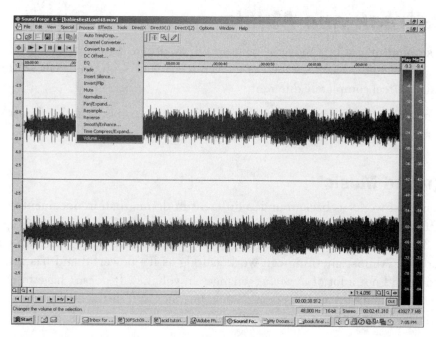

Figure 9.30 *Accessing volume dialog box in Sound Forge.*

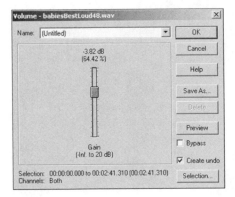

Figure 9.31 *Altering volume in Sound Forge.*

Move the slider to get the desired effect. If the number is above 100 percent, you are raising the volume. Below 100 percent, you are lowering it. When you get what you want, click OK and Save the file.

Soundtrack and Music

Background music in a movie is far from unimportant. It really helps drive how the audience perceives the mood of a given scene. The same scene with different music can feel completely different.

Sound effects can be intentionally loud and jarring, or more subtle, almost subliminal. Either way, they have a big effect on how we are moved by cinema.

Background Music

Music that works as background is different in drama than in documentary. For documentaries, you want music that is unobtrusive to put under the people speaking. Hip hop without the rapping is great—it's *made* for talking over. Trip hop is good too. Almost anything can work as long as it's powerful and has a steady rhythm and not a lot of *dynamics* (changes in volume). It doesn't have to exactly correspond in mood to the person talking, but shouldn't distract. It's *background*. I call it "beds," though I don't know if that's a real term.

CAUTION

Unless you're using your own compositions (like the stuff you did in Acid), get permission. Don't use music by people you don't know if you ever think your film will be shown anywhere. There are a million starving musicians who make great tunes who would be honored to have their stuff in a film. Get your terms in writing. Don't screw them over, but also steer clear of folks with a prima donna attitude. I had one lady in a project who wanted all kinds of rights and provisions when I had famous people who sold a thousand times as many records saying, "Sure, use our stuff." I politely offered to take her and her song out of the film, not out of spite, but out of logistics. She quickly changed her tune.

Film music (mood music in drama or comedy) can have much more variance in dynamics and intensity. It can actually move the scene. It is also best if it is instrumental when someone's talking over it, but this is not as imperative as with documentary. And when it's not under someone talking, music with singing works fine.

Foley

Foley is the term for the sounds in the movie that are not music or speaking. Footsteps, rustling of leaves, the sound of a syringe popping through a junkie's skin—these sounds are all added later, often faked, and made separately.

TIP

There is an excellent tutorial on the Extras section of the DVD of the film *Suicide Kings* that explains this quite well. It's called "Tunnel Scene Tutorial." It demonstrates Foley, as well as sound effects and music quite well. Check it out—you can turn off various aspects of the tunnel scene, have just the music, just the dialogue, just the sound effects, which in this case is Foley, as well as creepy little barely audible echo-like noises that really add to the overall feel of a movie. Listen for them after you check this out. You'll see how much they are used in movies and get ideas for original ways to use them yourself.

You can record your own Foley sounds, or alter existing sounds in a program like Sound Forge. Go nuts. This is one of the most fun parts of making movies.

You can also find sounds online and download them and alter them in sound programs: add echo, change pitch, resample the sampling rate, play them backwards, add distortion, or all of the above and more. I search online with the name of the sound I'm looking for followed by .wav or .aiff. Try meow.wav or foghorn.aiff on Google.com and see what you get. Also keep in mind that some of these sounds are copyrighted. Ask permission, get it in writing, and credit use of them.

Advanced Sound Program Use

I'm not going to get extremely deep into any of these programs. Each one would be a book unto itself. But I'll cover a few more techniques and programs you may find useful.

Acid, Sound Forge, and Vegas Video are all separate programs made by Sonic Foundry, but they all work well together in concert with each other. It is sort of reminiscent of how a graphic designer would use Photoshop and Illustrator.

For instance, you can right-click on a track in Vegas and have the option to open that track in SoundForge and edit it, without even leaving Vegas. Keep in mind that this will be destructive editing; it will overwrite the original track, so you should save backup copies until you become very adept at using it and know exactly what the results of each action will be.

There are other programs like ProTools that are even deeper. I'm not going to go into them other than to mention them. ProTools does most of what Acid, Sound Forge, and Vegas do combined, but it is harder to use. There is a free version of ProTools available at Digidesign.com.

Tweaking Audio in Post

Get the best sound you can when shooting and working in your NLE video editing program. Then you can take the whole sound timeline out as a single file and tweak it in post. In Hollywood, they have very well-paid people who do this all day long. You'll probably have to do it yourself, or get a friend to do it.

I spend a good bit of time on this in a given project. I go through and listen and adjust sound levels, fix bad EQ, remove noise in sections, apply fade-ins and -outs as needed, even add some subtle effects. It takes me about three hours to adjust the sound on a one-hour movie, and I'm very fast. It took a lot longer the first time I did it.

I do this after the film is locked. (*Locked* means that the timeline will not change. It also has to be locked before you can export the audio as a single stereo file and tweak in and re-import it. If it isn't, it won't sync up with changes you make after exporting audio.) I try to get the sound levels as close as possible for everything in the program using sound level filters and rendering, then export the whole thing and tweak it part by part in Sound Forge, then re-import it and it should sync up and sound better. You have to make sure not to do any editing that adds time to the timeline, which will put your project out of sync. Some echoes do, for instance, so does some pitch manipulation. You might do well to save various versions as you go (this is easy because audio files are not nearly as big as video files) and check the exact length before reimporting. (See Figures 9.32 through 9.35.)

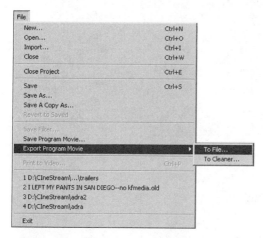

Figure 9.32 *Exporting audio in CineStream.*

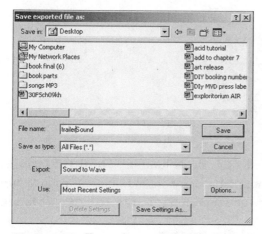

Figure 9.33 *Exporting audio in CineStream 2.*

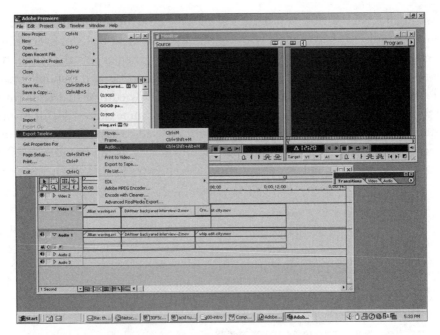

Figure 9.34 *Exporting audio in Premiere.*

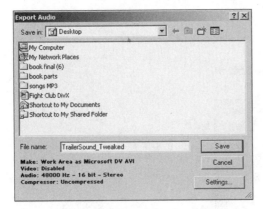

Figure 9.35 *Exporting audio in Premiere 2.*

I add a tiny bit of compression and a tiny bit of limiting. The default settings for both compression and limiting are pretty darned good, but you can experiment with both if you find it affecting the sound too much or too little. (See Figures 9.36 through 9.39.)

Note that the drop-down menu here is the Hyperprism DX menu, which is not available in Sound Forge out of the box. Hyperprism DX is a set of third-party plug-ins. More on plug-ins in a moment.

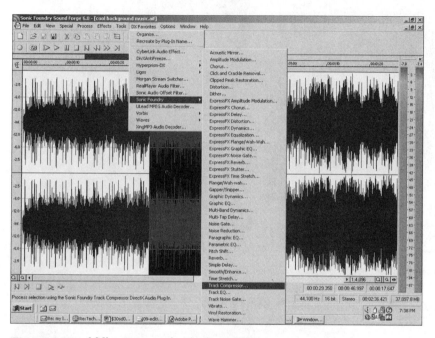

Figure 9.36 *Adding compression in Sound Forge.*

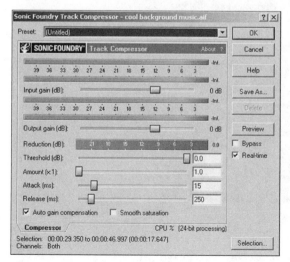

Figure 9.37 *Compression Dialog Window in Sound Forge.*

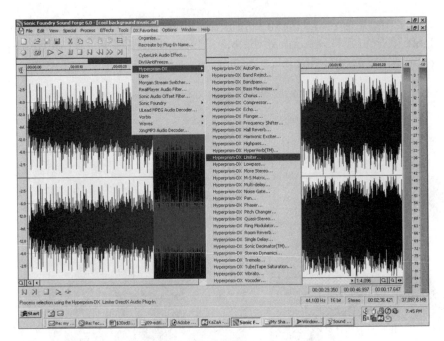

Figure 9.38 *Adding limiting in Sound Forge.*

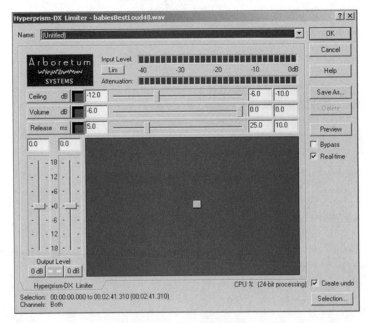

Figure 9.39 *Limiting Dialog Window in Sound Forge.*

There is some limiting available as a drop-down option from the Compression Dialog Window, but it is not as robust as the Hyperprism DX plug-in.

Experiment to find the best settings. You might have to do it in sections: Music has different needs than voice, and music with voice has still other needs. There are also presets you might try. For some operations, noise reduction in Sound Forge for instance, you may need a plug-in. (A *plug-in* is a little add-on program that extends the functionality of another program. Some are made by the same company that makes the main program; some are third-party add-ons.)

TIP

For *D.I.Y. or DIE*, after we finished the entire edit and got the sound the best we could (even between individual cuts, a few mono cuts synthesized into stereo, and so forth), we added a two-pop (two clicks audio and video added together in Final Cut) before the project, and exported the entire audio to a CD and mailed it to a ProTools expert to tweak. He burned another CD of the fixed sound, and mailed it back to us. It sounded much more even and just generally better overall. We synced it to the two-pop and replaced the project sound with the final tweaked audio in the timeline.

When I had the entire audio back from the audio tweaker, I also put it all up on my Web site as a download. I took the .wav file and converted this to an MP3 in Sound Forge with the MP3 plug-in. The Real Audio file was created using Real Producer, the basic form of which is free from Real.com.

A lot of my collaboration is done via snail mail, e-mail, FTP, and FedEx. It's a global economy, and you can even find global volunteers on a good project. The cool credits on *D.I.Y.* were done by my friend Bink Cadman in Vancouver, and he uploaded the final 200-meg file to my Web site via FTP. I downloaded it and dropped it seamlessly into the timeline.

Noise Reduction

The Sound Forge Noise Reduction plug-in can work wonders, but it takes some experience and skill. Otherwise it makes your program material sound over processed. My friend Adam Hauck recently sent me some music taken off of one of my records, and I e-mailed him back and said, "You're using too much Sound Forge Noise Reduction plug-in." He wrote back, "How the heck did you know? I'm downright baffled."

Basically, I said, "Because I have it, I've used it, and I've decided not to use it much. Most of the time I use it, it sounds like there are robots whispering under the music." (I used a little too much on the Maggie Estep interview on the *D.I.Y.* DVD, for example.)

Actually, in the hands of a skilled pro, it can work wonders. I had a friend in San Fran who was making a good bit of scratch restoring bootleg tapes of sixties hippie music live shows for some bootleg record producer. You really have to work with it though. It tends to work really well on constant sounds like motor or electrical hum, and really poorly on non-constant sounds, like wind.

Basically, after installing the plug-in (there is a demo on the CD), it will appear in one of the Direct X drop-down menus in Sound Forge (alphabetically as Sonic Foundry Noise Reduction). (See Figures 9.40 and 9.41.)

You open it while you already have a file open, check the Capture noiseprint checkbox (near the bottom left of the Noise Reduction plug-in dialog box), and you find a place in the file with no music or talking. Then you hold the mouse down to highlight and sample a short bit of silence by hitting the "Preview" button (see Figure 9.42).

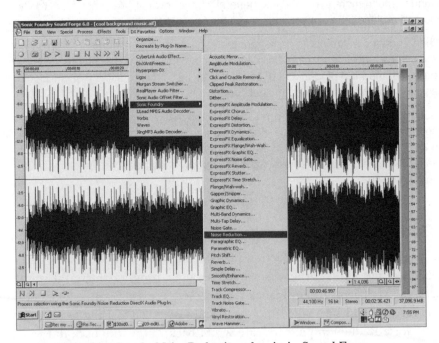

Figure 9.40 *Opening the Noise Reduction plug-in in Sound Forge.*

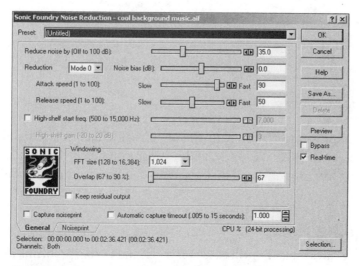

Figure 9.41 *Noise Reduction plug-in dialog box.*

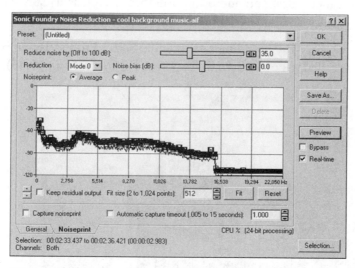

Figure 9.42 *Capture Noise print pane of Noise Reduction plug-in dialog box.*

A quarter-second to two seconds is good. It takes a *noise print* of the background noise in that selection. Then you "Save as" and name it (you might want to use the same preset again) (see Figure 9.43).

Then close the plug-in, deselect the silent part, and click anywhere in the file. Reopen the plug-in, and click OK to apply it to the whole file.

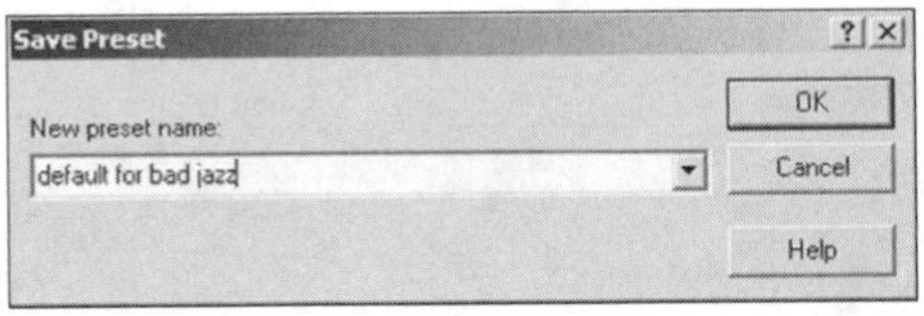

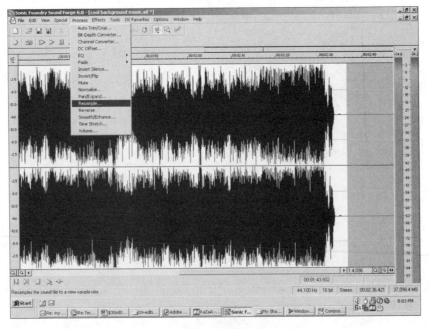

Figure 9.43 *Saving Noiseprint settings.*

You can control the amount of noise reduction with the Reduce noise by slider at the top of the noiseprint pane. Too little, and it doesn't do much. Too much, and you get the "whispering robot" digital artifacts. Experiment until you find the right amount.

Changing Sampling Rate

Different sampling rates on audio will cause playback and export problems in your NLE. Editing programs usually change everything to DV standard (48,000 Hz, 16-bit stereo, also called 48k), and audio imported from CDs is usually 44,100 Hz. This can be glitchy, but you can fix it and then re-import it.

Sound Forge can resample the sampling rate of a file. Select Process/Resample to open the Resampling dialog box in Sound Forge (see Figures 9.44 and 9.45).

Figure 9.44 *Changing the sampling rate in Sound Forge.*

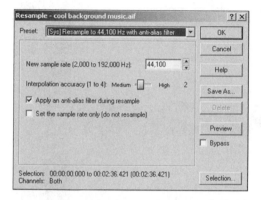

Figure 9.45 *Resampling dialog box in Sound Forge.*

You can set the new sampling rate by typing it in manually or picking one of the standard jobs from the drop-down menu (see Figure 9.46).

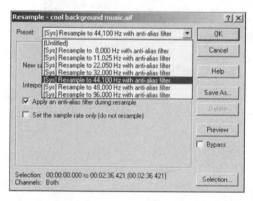

Figure 9.46 *Drop-down menu choices in resampling dialog box.*

If this changes the pitch, you can fix that (Effects/Pitch/Shift). (See Figures 9.47 and 9.48.) Note that the set the sample rate only box must be checked.

Usually bringing it up or down 2 semitones (adjust the slider, or type 2 for up and -2 for down) will correct this when going from 44.1k to 48k or vice versa.

Otherwise, experiment with the right number of semitones to raise or lower until it sounds like it did before resampling. Be sure to save a copy of the original file to revert to, especially if resampling and shifting changes the file length, which will get the video and audio out of sync when you reimport.

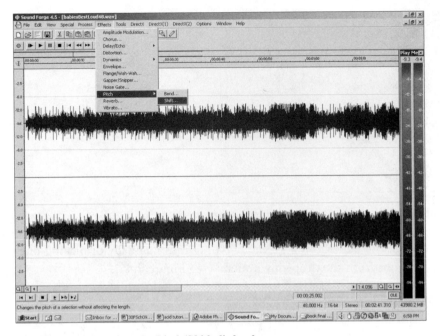

Figure 9.47 *Opening the Pitch/Shift dialog box.*

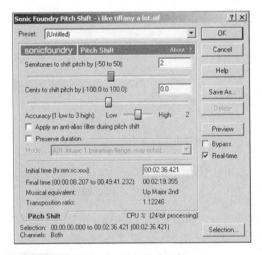

Figure 9.48 *Pitch shift dialog box.*

You can see the exact length of a file, as well as the sampling rate, file size, and other properties in Sound Forge by looking in the bottom-right corner of the main display (see Figure 9.49).

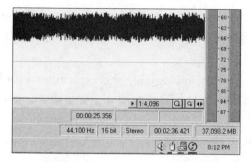

Figure 9.49 *The Properties display in the bottom-right corner of Sound Forge.*

On the Extras section of the *D.I.Y. or DIE* DVD, the audio on the Tour Tips short by Danny Plotnick ended up out of sync and pitch-shifted up a couple of semitones because the audio on the tape I was given was 44,100 Hz sampling rate. It should have been Mini-DV standard—48,000 Hz. The editing software compensated, and it ended up out of sync. I didn't notice. I probably would have noticed on any other trailer, but this one is all voiceover, and is a kind of parody of the "serious voiceover guy" style of delivery, so it seemed like it should sound odd.

Most people who saw it didn't think anything was wrong with it, and it still brought a smile to their faces, but I know how Danny felt. When my novel came out, the first printing had about 10 percent of the copies with some pages out of order near the middle. Also, a pressing of a *Bomb* CD had a skip. And there was an issue with the first pressing of the *D.I.Y.* DVD.

My assumption (because I've had this issue before) is that Danny brought sound into the project off of a CD. CD sound is 44,100 Hz. It probably set the sample rate of the After Effects project to 44,100 rather than 48,000.

I was really bummed and sorry that it happened. If I were a lot more experienced, I might have noticed this. But I was just overwhelmed with trying to make something cool and also promote all the folks who I admire. There was nothing I could do. It was already pressed when Danny got a copy and told me. Would have cost about $10,000 to fix, and would have meant destroying 5,000 copies.

I apologized to Danny for my part, then chalked it up to experience. Danny's primarily a film guy, and me, I'm new to all this. We're both still learning about digital video. There's a lot to learn. If I had noticed this issue with Danny's movie before the creation of the DVD glass master, I would have exported the audio from the clip to an .aiff file, imported it into Sound Forge, resampled it, and brought it back into the project.

I posted this notice on the Web site about it, apologizing and explaining. I told my friend Mike Kelley about it, and he responded, "Art making is all about problem solving."

Or as Sandy Doell (the really smart editor on this book) said, "Art is a process, not a result."

Making Audio Loops in Sound Forge

As we've seen, loops are good for importing into other programs like Acid. You can then construct rhythms and soundtracks out of them by combining other sounds.

In Sound Forge, select part of the waveform by holding down your mouse cursor and moving it along the file (see Figures 9.50 and 9.51).

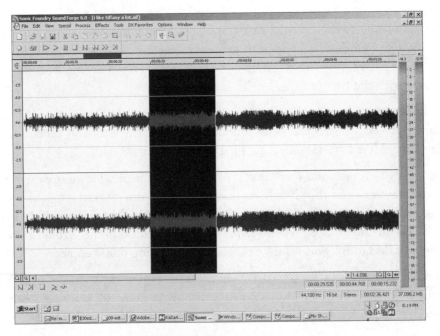

Figure 9.50 *Select part of the waveform.*

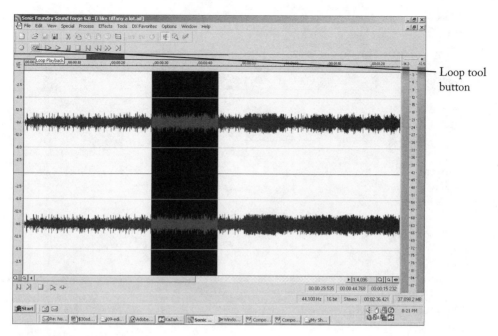

Loop tool
button

Figure 9.51 *Sound Forge's Loop Tool button.*

Click the loop button, and move the mouse cursor back and forth while holding down the left mouse button. Play around until you find a section that loops well. Then copy that section to a new file and Save.

This is how I did the looping menu audio backgrounds for the *D.I.Y.* DVD menus and the "Acid files" on the CD used in the tutorial at the beginning of this chapter. You can also make drum loops from drum parts on records.

Video in Sound Forge

You can open a video file in Sound Forge; it's just like opening an audio file (see Figure 9.52). You can't do much to edit the video, but you can edit the audio and then resave it. The video will display key frames at the top of the window so you can follow where the video is in relation to the audio.

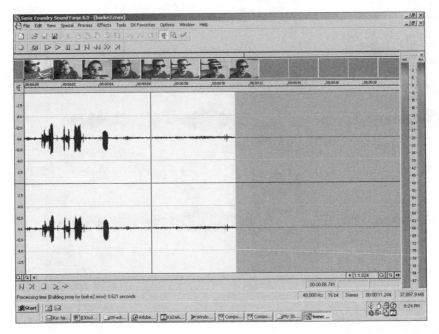

Figure 9.52 *A Quicktime file of director Burke Roberts opened up in Sound Forge.*

Quicktime Pro

Quicktime Pro is a really cool utility. It's made for viewing video files, but it's also sort of a Swiss Army Knife for editing. I use it a lot to change one file type into another. Quicktime can turn almost any image type into almost any other, and almost any audio type into almost any other. Sound Forge can do the audio part just as well, but it takes longer to open up. I often use smaller programs when juggling around between mediums, because they open almost instantly and don't use up much memory. This is good when you have several programs open.

Usually an NLE will deal with audio file types the same. But sometimes, for no reason, it won't want to open or display one type, and you'll want to change it to another that it can open. Sometimes it will open the file, but will play back stuttery. There is no rhyme or reason to it, no one type is better than the other, but sometimes voodoo computer makes programs cranky.

To turn a .wav file into an .aiff file, first open Quicktime Pro, then bring the file in through the File/Import menu (see Figures 9.53 through 9.55).

Figure 9.53 *Accessing Import Dialog Box in QuickTime Pro.*

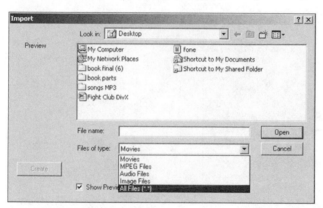

Figure 9.54 *Setting selection for all file types in Import Dialog Box.*

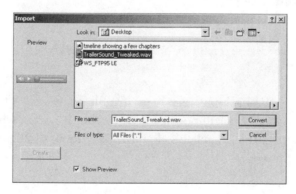

Figure 9.55 *Importing a .wav file.*

Then choose the type of file you want to export to from the Export Dialog Box and hit save (see Figures 9.56 and 9.57).

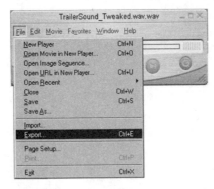

Figure 9.56 *Opening the Export Dialog box.*

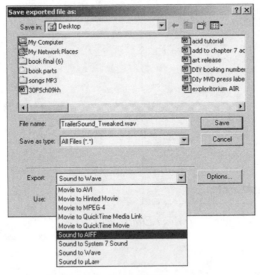

Figure 9.57 *Selecting .aiff file type to export to in the drop-down menu of the Export dialog box.*

Quicktime Pro also turns an MP3 back into a .wav or .aiff file really well. This is a really useful thing. It's not what QuickTime was made for, but it's often what I use it for. You can use .wav and .aiff more reliably than MP3s without problems in your audio and video editing programs.

QuickTime also turns a Midi file into an editable .wav or .aiff file. Just go to File/Import to bring the Midi file in, then File/Export to make a new file. This is a good way to collaborate over the Web with people making music for you. Midi music, by nature, sounds very filmic, and the file sizes are tiny, because they are basically just the sheet music, not the sound themselves. We used some Midi medley versions of my old band, Bomb, as background in *D.I.Y. or DIE*. Michael Woody did them, and they are on the CD-ROM for you to use as well.

The free version of QuickTime only plays and doesn't have any of these editing or exporting features. But the upgrade to Pro is only $30. Both are available at www.apple.com/quicktime

Many NLE programs actually use Quicktime Pro within their internal operations. If you look in the project folders for CineStream, Final Cut Pro, or Premiere after working on a project, you will see many large uncompressed .mov format (Quicktime) files.

The editing program is just an elaborate way of controlling an iteration of Quicktime within the computer. All three of these programs even install Quicktime Pro during the installation of the program to enable this. If you have either of these three programs, you already have Quicktime Pro.

Multitracking and ADR in Vegas

Vegas Video is a NLE video editing system that also supports multitracking audio capabilities (see Figure 9.58). You can record a whole band, one instrument at a time. Or bring in existing files and add vocals.

As we mentioned previously, Vegas Video can be used for editing video, audio, or both at the same time. The audio portion is easy to use, with a very intuitive interface. Basically, the audio portion has all the tools that you would have on an analog multitrack recorder combined with a mixing board. Vegas Video just adds an extra line to the timeline, and two editing windows, just like any other NLE system.

Dialog Replacement—sometimes called ADR (Automated Dialog Replacement) or Looping—is basically recording over the dialog in a particular scene. Sometimes good sound isn't available when a scene is shot. Or later it is discovered

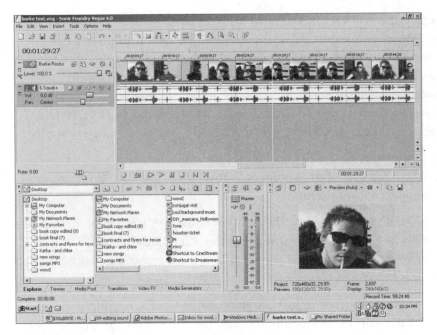

Figure 9.58 *Vegas interface.*

in the editing that it isn't as good as the rest of the sound in the film. For instance, an outdoor shot will have wind distorting the talking.

What you do is get the actors to come in and watch the scene a few times to get used to it. You set up a microphone and give them headphones and have them rerecord it into the editing program while watching the footage. Some people are way better at it than others, and some scenes are easier to do than others. If it's shot from far away, it's easy to do because you can't see their lips moving as well. A close-up is harder to do. (Think badly dubbed Kung Fu movies.)

Don't forget the Room Tone we had you record a few chapters back when you were on the set. You can put it under the ADR or any dialogue to "open it up" and make it sound more natural. ADR is usually recorded in an acoustically "dead" room (dampened with absorbent material on the walls like egg cartons, foam rubber, or fabric) to give you the most options later. You can always add reverb; it's impossible to subtract it. Added room tone will help the ADR match the original takes.

To do ADR in Vegas Video, open the program and import your existing video project with the audio intact (see Figures 9.59 and 9.60).

Figure 9.59 *Importing video in Vegas Video.*

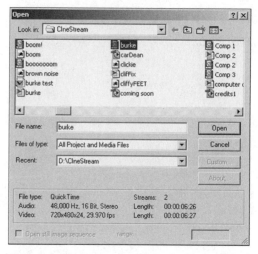

Figure 9.60 *Importing video in Vegas Video 2.*

Add a new audio track and name it by double-clicking on the scribble strip and typing a descriptive name (like "ADR Burke"). (See Figure 9.61.)

Click the red Arm for record button (see Figure 9.62).

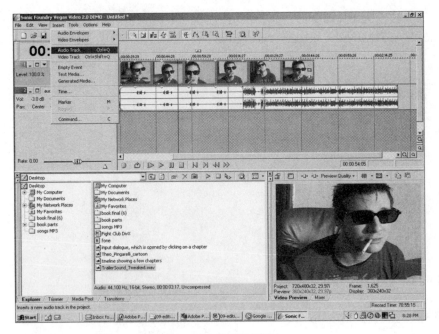

Figure 9.61 *Adding an audio track in Vegas Video.*

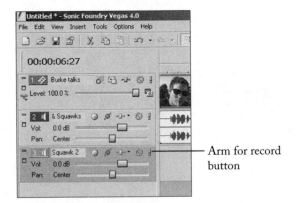

— Arm for record
button

Figure 9.62 *Click the red Arm for record button.*

Vegas will ask you where to save the file. Pick a location from the Browse button and name the file (see Figures 9.63 and 9.64).

When you are ready to record, you still need to set the audio levels. Have your subject speak into the microphone while you watch the meters where it says "master." You want to have the average rate come as close to going into the red without

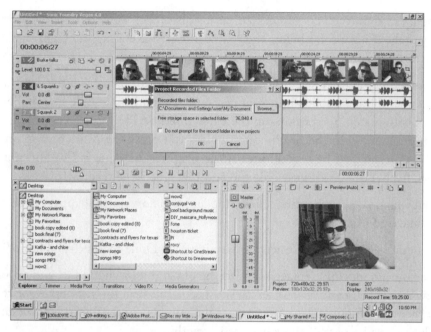

Figure 9.63 *Pick a location and name the file.*

Figure 9.64 *Pick a location and name the file 2.*

going up into the red very often. Red means distortion. You don't want distortion. Conversely, if it's too far below the red, you don't have a high enough signal-to-noise ratio, which will result in poor sound.

When you get a good level, hit the red Record button and have the actor speak into a microphone hooked into your computer's sound card while he watches and attempts to match his speaking in the video monitor. He will also be able to hear his original audio in the headphones, unless you press the Mute button on that track (which might be a good idea if the original dialogue is Off and not just quiet). In that case, he'll hear only the new dialogue as he records it.

When you are done recording, click Stop and a dialog box will appear to save the new take (see Figure 9.65).

If you don't like it, you don't need to save it. Click Done to save (see Figure 9.66).

Then you can mix and replace between the old and new vocal take, and export to a new track. You can try as often as you need, and save the new takes, or record over them (see Figure 9.67). You can use the numbers in the Timecode window to mark a particular part to come back to it exactly.

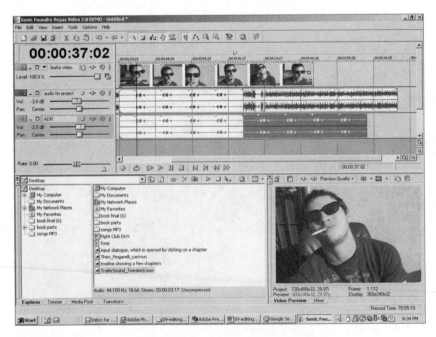

Figure 9.65 *New track of ADR.*

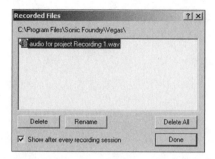

Figure 9.66 *Save Take dialog box.*

Figure 9.67 *Saving the new video file.*

Conclusion

While *getting* good sound on location is the most important part of a shoot, *maintaining* and even *improving* good sound is one of the most vital parts of post-production. The availability of simple-to-use programs combined with the basic techniques we've just learned will keep your project professional all the way through the next phase—making copies for public distribution.

$30

Chapter 10

Your Own DVD

You've finished your film, and you've poured your heart into it. Now let's share it with the world (including the parts of the world that do not speak your native language). Making DVDs is easy, and DVDs have many advantages over VHS tapes, including support for subtitles in multiple languages. We will explore the basics of DVD production, as well as some advanced techniques if you really want to get into it.

Basic DVD Authoring

Creating a DVD design interface is called *DVD authoring*. The process resembles Web design in many ways. You are making clickable interfaces that take the user to a different file, which brings up different media. These files look and sound great and are huge compared to Web files. Because they are viewed on a local system instead of the Internet, they load instantly.

You can author basic DVDs at home, using software like Apple DVD Studio; or Sonic Solutions DVDit or MyDVD; or Sonic Foundry's DVD Architect (bundled with the Vegas +DVD suite). Making the DVD is pretty much point-and-click in some programs. The less-expensive consumer-oriented authoring environments like Sonic MyDVD have *wizards* that walk you through. They are not as robust as more professional-oriented programs like Sonic DVD creator (see Figure 10.1), but are good to start with, especially if you're on a budget.

Adaptec has a cool hardware/software suite called Videoh! DVD video converter kit. It includes an external video card for converting analog video (like older footage you may only have on VHS or high-8 video) or DV via RCA or S-Video input, and uses hardware conversion (as opposed to simple software encoding— this yields better rates and speed). It converts files to MPEG and inputs into the computer via USB 2.0 (or the slower 1.2 if that's all you have). It's a good, consumer grade, no-brainer video editing and DVD production setup. It comes bundled with free software—Sonic MyDVD as well as a very simple editing program called ShowBiz.

The DVD authoring program I'm going to do most of my demonstrations in is Sonic's MyDVD (see Figure 10.2). It is not on the CD, because it's too large to fit with all the other stuff I have on there. But a full *working* (not demo) version of it

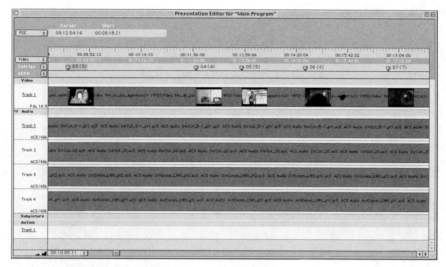

Figure 10.1 *Sonic DVD creator.*

Figure 10.2 *The MyDVD splash screen.*

is included free on its own CD bundled with almost every DVD burner sold in America. So if you're ready to make DVDs and have a burner, you probably have MyDVD already.

Just like NLE video editors, many DVD authoring programs have similar interfaces, so learning this program will transfer over to other, more professional products, especially ones by the same company. Sonic makes many programs that cost more and can do more and are more complicated to use than MyDVD. But MyDVD is good, and comes free with many burners and it will get you started. (See Figure 10.3.)

Figure 10.3 *The MyDVD interface.*

Back in Chapter 8, "Editing Images," we learned how to output and encode our movie projects into files we can import for DVD. You still have those files, right?

After installing MyDVD, open it up.

Highlight DVD video on the left (see Figure 10.4) and click on Create or modify a DVD video project.

Name your project and save (see Figures 10.5 and 10.6).

Click on the Edit Style button (see Figure 10.7).

The Edit Styles window will open up (see Figure 10.8).

Click on one of the default styles (see Figure 10.9). Note that here you can edit many aspects of the look and layout, including substituting one of your own background images instead of using their generic defaults (see Figure 10.10). I recommend this. (You can also create styles and upload them for other users to use and download theirs free at http://styles.mydvd.com.)

Figure 10.4 *Click Create or modify a DVD video project.*

Figure 10.5 *Name your project and save.*

Figure 10.6 *Name your project and save 2.*

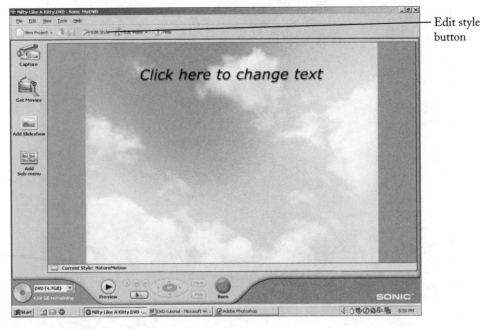

Figure 10.7 *Click on the Edit Style button.*

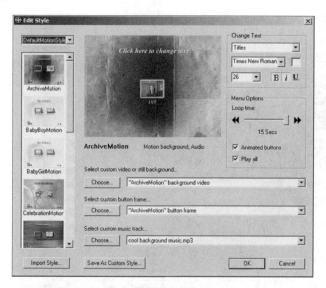

Figure 10.8 *The Edit Style window.*

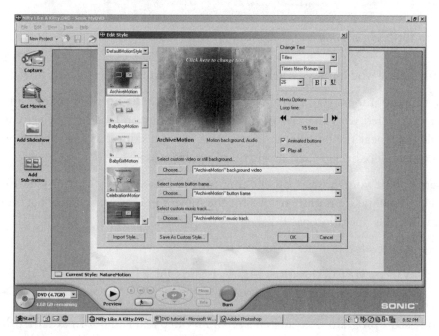

Figure 10.9 *Click on one of the default styles.*

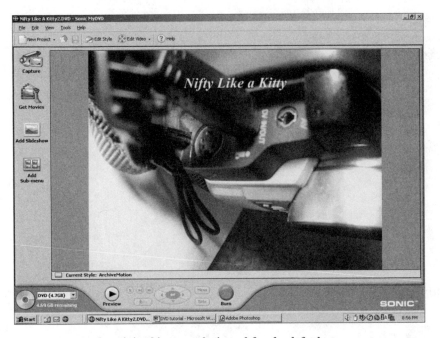

Figure 10.10 *An original image substituted for the defaults.*

Double-click where it says Click here to change text to add your own title.

You can also import your own music here to replace the horribly pedestrian ones that are offered with the program. Click on the button that says Select custom music track near the bottom on Figure 10.8. Try selecting the music track on the CD called Cool background music that I made in Acid.

Then import your movies by clicking on the Get Movies button (see Figure 10.11). It will take a minute or two for the movies to import. A status bar will tell you when this operation has finished.

The supported file formats include:

Video: MPEG-1, MPEG-2, AVI, and QuickTime.

Audio: WAV, MPA, and MP3

If you used a program that created a separate video and audio format rather than a video format with audio built in, it can deal with that too. Simply put both the video and audio files in the same folder, import the video, and MyDVD will automatically import the audio and sync it up. How cool is that?

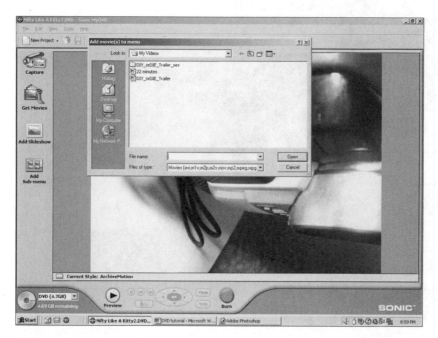

Figure 10.11 *Import your movies by clicking on the Get Movies button.*

Buttons are automatically generated for each movie, using the file names. You can double-click on the text (where it has the name of the file) to type different titles. A frame from early on in the video will automatically appear as the clickable link button on the menu interface (see Figure 10.12).

TIP

Note the little indicator at the bottom left of the interface window that tells how much media your project is using. It will show what amount of the available 4.7 gigs are used. This is so you will know when to quit adding media.

If you wish, you can click on the Add Sub-Menu button on the left to add more movie buttons.

You can double-click on the text (where it says Untitled) to type your own titles, or just let it automatically name it the same thing as the movie you drag in (see Figure 10.13).

Figure 10.12 *Automatically generated link buttons.*

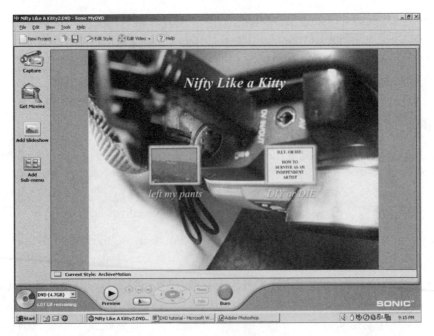

Figure 10.13 *Add your own text.*

Click once to highlight the New Movie button, then import the next movie. Don't forget to keep clicking on the Save project button at the top periodically. It looks like a little floppy disk.

Click the Preview button (see Figure 10.14). You will activate the grayed-out interface at the bottom that looks like the controls on a DVD player. This will allow you to play and navigate the project as it now stands. This is great, as it will keep you from having to burn and waste disks. You can make the changes playing as a virtual disk off your hard drive, and only actually burn when you are satisfied.

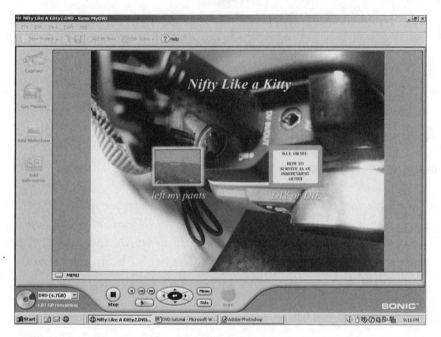

Figure 10.14 *Preview mode.*

Double-clicking on any of the movie menu buttons will bring up a dialog box that actually enables you to trim the movie and do simple edits from within the project without going back into your editing program! (See Figure 10.15.)

You can also right-click on the movie and click "edit movie" to open it up in ShowBiz and edit it. (More on ShowBiz right after we're done making this DVD.)

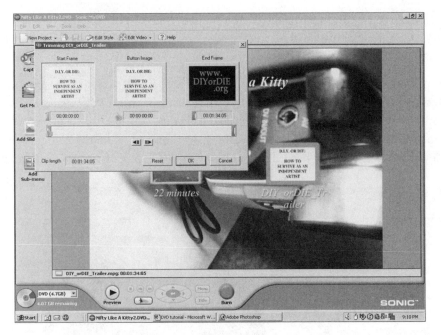

Figure 10.15 *Trim Edit dialog box.*

You can enable the TV Safe Zone dotted guide lines to see what will get cut off when you play it on a TV rather than a computer. (View/Show TV Safe Zone.) ("TV Safe Zone" is MyDVD's name for making words and images title-safe. Remember, we covered making title-safe in Chapter 8, "Editing Images.")

TIP

Keep all your images and text inside these lines. (See Figures 10.16 and 10.17.)

Clicking the Build Motion Menu button (the one with an icon of a little guy running) at the bottom will render the motion menu. This will make a moving menu out of the movie button using the first few seconds of the film. This is *very* cool. Try it.

Hit Stop at any time to go back and edit the project more.

There are many options we didn't explore, but they are all covered in the Help menu and the tutorial available at startup. I just wanted to get you started on this amazingly fun trip of DVD authoring.

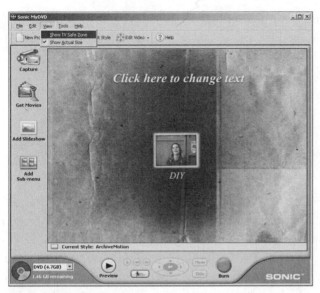

Figure 10.16 *Enabling TV Safe Zone.*

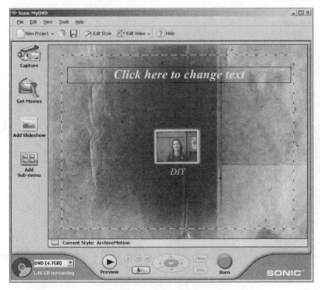

Figure 10.17 *TV Safe Zone guidelines enabled.*

When you're happy with your project, put a blank DVD in your burner. Hit the red Burn button. The Make Disc Setup dialog box will appear (see Figure 10.18).

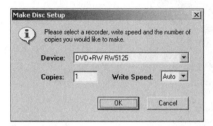

Figure 10.18 *Make Disc Setup dialog box.*

Click OK.

Preparing and burning the disc will take a while. The program has to further encode all the media. Don't do anything else on your computer while this is happening or it may crash. A status bar in the bottom-left corner will tell you how this is progressing (see Figure 10.19).

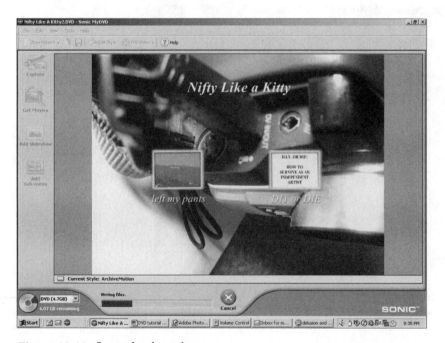

Figure 10.19 *Status bar in action.*

When this is finished, you will have a real DVD of your project that you can play on any DVD player, or even use as a master to get copies replicated at a replication house!

Congratulations.

Other Cool Things MyDVD Does

MyDVD has several additional capacities that make it a very cool all-around beginner-to-intermediate DVD creation suite. These include making Video CDs, doing simple video editing, and even converting from video directly to DVD without requiring any intermediary steps.

Video CDs

If you don't have a DVD burner but have MyDVD, you can also author Video CD (VCD). Video CDs are burnable on any CD burner and use the same file formats as DVDs. They don't look as good, don't hold as much media—700 megs versus the 4,700 megs or 4.7 gigs a DVD holds—but are playable on virtually any computer, and even many new DVD players.

To do this, when you open MyDVD, highlight the Video CD option on the left and then click Create or Modify a Video CD Project and follow the prompts (see Figure 10.20).

The interface and process is virtually identical to the steps we just took to author a DVD, except the file size is lower, and the output is to a CD. You can actually get a pretty good looking encode of a movie on a CD, especially if it's shorter than an hour. (See Figure 10.21.)

Note again the little indicator at the bottom left of the interface window that tells how much media your project is using. It will show what amount is still available of the 650 megs (or 700 megs depending on the capacity of your CD). The program will detect this. This is so you will know when to quit adding media.

Video Editing

MyDVD also includes a free, very basic, video editing program called ArcSoft ShowBiz. So if you can't afford to buy an editing program, you can actually edit and make DVDs with the software on the CD that comes with your burner.

Figure 10.20 *Click Create or Modify a Video CD Project.*

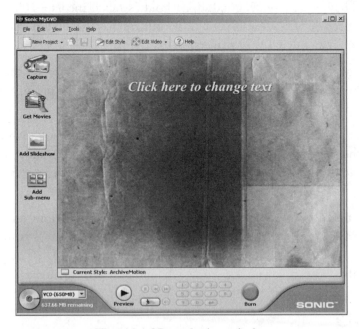

Figure 10.21 *The video CD authoring window.*

To do this, when you open MyDVD, highlight the Edit Video option on the left and then click Launch The Video Editor. (See Figure 10.22.)

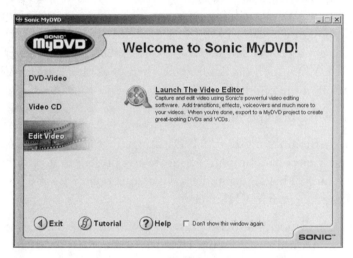

Figure 10.22 *Click Launch The Video Editor.*

This will open ArcSoft ShowBiz (see Figure 10.23). You can click on Learn The Basics for a very easy tutorial.

From this screen, you can also access a tutorial on using the DVD function or Video CD creation function.

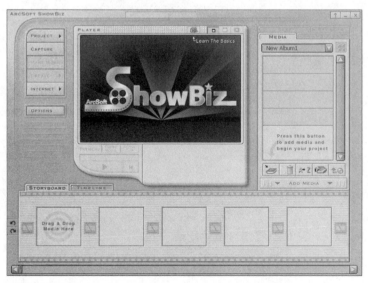

Figure 10.23 *ArcSoft ShowBiz.*

Video-to-DVD

MyDVD can also import from a camera directly into the program via FireWire and bypass the need to use a video editing program. This limits your opportunity for much control (although you can clip the length of videos, that's about it), but is a very basic way to get a project started. To do this, when you open MyDVD, highlight the Video DVD option on the left and then click the Transfer Video Direct-to-DVD option in the middle (see Figures 10.24 and 10.25).

From there, just follow the prompts of the wizard.

Unfortunately, this is the only mode in MyDVD where you can add *Chapter Points*, places where a viewer can jump into a movie at a preset point rather than starting at the beginning. This ability to be navigated is one of the things that make DVDs infinitely cooler than VHS tapes.

To do this, click on the Transfer Video Direct-to-DVD menu, and the wizard menus will appear automatically (see Figure 10.26).

In the wizard, you can edit your menu style from the Edit Style button.

Name the project and pick the place to save your data: DVD if you want to go straight to DVD, or Record to Hard Disk if you want to first make a disc image and preview it. Click Next. The Video Direct-to-DVD capture window will

Figure 10.24 *Click Transfer Video Direct-to-DVD.*

Figure 10.25 *The Transfer Video Direct–to–DVD menu.*

Figure 10.26 *The Transfer Video Direct–to–DVD wizard.*

appear (see Figure 10.27). If you have your camera on and plugged into your FireWire port, MyDVD should automatically detect it and begin displaying the first image.

Figure 10.27 *The Video Direct-to-DVD Capture window.*

Here you can set Chapter Points where it says Create Chapter Points. You can either preset them at intervals you choose, or do it manually as you capture, by hitting the Spacebar on the keyboard.

Click Finish when you are done and remove your completed DVD from your burner.

Edit DVD

MyDVD is totally unique in its ability to edit a DVD that has already been burned. You can take a project you've done, put the DVD back in, and change it. To do so, click File/Edit DVD-VCD (see Figure 10.28).

This will open the Browse for Folder dialog box to pick the drive that the DVD is in (see Figure 10.29).

After highlighting the correct drive letter, click OK to open the project in Edit mode (see Figure 10.30). From there, it's just like authoring a project before you burned it, like in our tutorial above.

Figure 10.28 *Click File/Edit DVD-VCD.*

Figure 10.29 *The Browse for Folder dialog box.*

Figure10.30 *Project in DVD editing mode.*

You can skip past advanced DVD authoring to output if you want, and come back later to learn about other programs, and about subtitles.

Encoding

We made *D.I.Y. or DIE: BURN THIS DVD* a DVD-5, the lowest capacity DVD, but also the only one that home burners can adequately reproduce so people could burn copies of it. It's amazing the amount of data you can fit on a 4.7 gig disc. Especially if you get the encoding done as hardware encoding. Hardware encoding uses dedicated proprietary hardware and software combinations to do an amazing job. SD-2000 and SD-1000 are some of the better ones, both made by Sonic Solutions. They compress (encode) a movie in real time, and the file size is smaller and looks better.

The downside is that the stuff costs about $35,000.

With hardware or software encoding, you can set a different encode rate for different things. Usually, you use a slightly higher rate for the main movie than for the extras. We did. The higher rate uses more file size on the disc, but it looks better.

To change the bit rate in TMPGEnc, instead of skipping over this screen like we did in the tutorial in Chapter 8, raise or lower the slider to the right of the Average video bit rate (see Figure 10.31). Note that the estimated file size will change, as reflected in the status bar at the bottom.

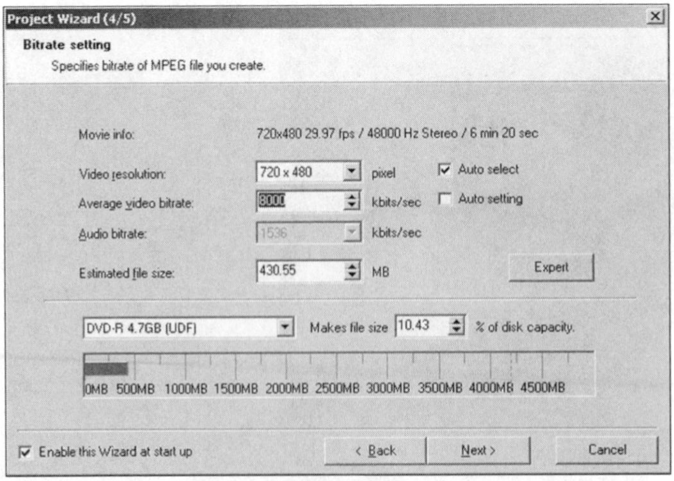

Figure 10.31 *Setting to change the bitrate in TMPGEnc.*

I first tried encoding *D.I.Y. or DIE* using Cleaner. It cooked my 55-minute movie to a 3-gig file. Actually, a DVD movie is often encoded into two separate files: audio and video. (This is to make it easier to integrate different language tracks and commentary.) The video is in a special MPEG-2 format, and the audio is in .wav format. So it was a 2.3-gig video file and a 700-meg audio file.

On my 1.7 Ghz Pentium IV system with a gig of RAM, this encoding took 24 hours. It looked pretty good.

Then I had Blaine Graboyes try an encode using Sonic Solutions Sonic SD-2000 encoder hardware stuff. It took 55 minutes, was less than 2 gigs total for audio and video, and looked great.

A lot of this also has to do with Blaine. He set in- and out-points, based on his extensive experience, to change the encoding rate for different parts. The stuff I did in Cleaner was one click. I just let it run.

Blaine is my genius DVD authoring guy who worked for free because he was so into the project. No, he won't do your project free. Don't bug him. He's by far the coolest person I've met in Los Angeles—very unlike what most people think of when they think of the cutthroat L.A. entertainment biz. He's very well employed doing great work for big movie studios and record companies, but saw my post on Craigslist and took time to author my DVD for free because he liked the project and the anti-copy-protection aspect of it. He even slaved away on it with me on the weekends when he could have been out having fun in the sun.

I had a few other people answer my "Free DVD authoring Wanted" Internet posting with mean e-mails like, "Why don't you get some money and then call me." These posts were written by people who had little or no professional experience and worked out of their homes, and didn't have access to the amazing equipment that Blaine has. Blaine is many levels above these people on professionalism, experience, reputation, and access to equipment. He was one of the first people to work authoring DVDs, back in 1996 when DVDs launched. This was years ago when most people had not even heard of DVDs. He helped make them a household word. He now gets some of the highest profile jobs around. Blaine did the authoring on the official DVD of the 2002 Super Bowl.

This is something I have encountered time and time again: Often, very employed, professional, expensive, and often famous (in their niche) people are willing to help a good project for free, whereas the wannabees and me-toos who are filled with ego and frustrated that they ain't got it going on, not only won't help, but treat me poorly for even asking.

You can also have people do jobs on spec (speculation). This means they work for free, and get paid when and only if you make a profit. Be sure to put your terms in writing.

Advanced DVD Authoring

Once you've mastered the basics of a point-and-click DVD authoring environment like MyDVD, you might want to consider moving up to the hard stuff. It's a little more challenging to use, but you can really expand the capability of DVDs by learning to create in the more professional programs.

Subtitles

One of the things that makes a Digital Versatile Disk, or DVD, so versatile (and you thought it was Digital Video Disk, didn't you?) is its ability to support multiple language streams, camera angles, and subtitles. I'm going to concentrate on subtitles, since they promote universal understanding of your message, and I've actually created them.

I'm gonna cover this pretty well, as I feel it's very important. I think that making your thoughts available to people all over the world is the whole point of making art.

Sure, English is spoken and understood a little bit almost everywhere. But people are much more willing to watch something subtitled well in their native tongue than they are to watch it in a foreign one. People in other countries are not as resistant to subtitles as we Americans are. In most of the world, they are considered quite normal.

Before you go to the trouble of creating subtitles, you should check to see if your program supports them. (Check the Help menu or Web site for the program, as this may change in later versions.)

These programs do not support importing subtitles: Apple iDVD, Sonic ReelDVD, and MyDVD.

These programs do: Sonic Creator and Producer and Fusion Sonic Scenarist, Ulead Media Studio Pro, and Apple DVD Studio Pro.

For *D.I.Y. or DIE*, Blaine used Sonic's DVD Creator (for Mac),Version 2.1. and used a Subtitle Text file to bring into the program.

To create this file, you must first transcribe the whole thing in English. What I did was export the whole audio to one file in my editing program (Export movie/To file/.aiff in CineStream) and then chop it into six chunks. I converted each of these to MP3 files with AudioGrabber (see Figure 10.32) and uploaded them to a folder on my Web site and sent the URL to my assistants (see Figure 10.33).

(AudioGrabber is free shareware from www.dezines.com/audio.) (Mac users can get iTunes free from Apple: www.apple.com/itunes.)

Four of my assistants around the country helped me transcribe the files in English. This took a day. I took the final MS Word files that they e-mailed back to me, printed them out, and checked them. I made corrections, and assembled them into one master file. I e-mailed this to a friend on the East Coast and had her check it against her VHS copy of the movie[1]. She caught a couple more mistakes. Then I created Excel spreadsheets to have people do translations in (see Figure 10.34).

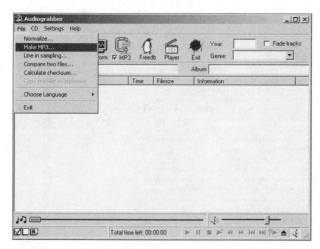

Figure 10.32 *Screenshot of AudioGrabber.*

1. *I love being self-employed, sleeping late and living on the West Coast. Because of the three-hour time difference, there's almost always East Coast business for me in my e-mail inbox by the time I wake up.*

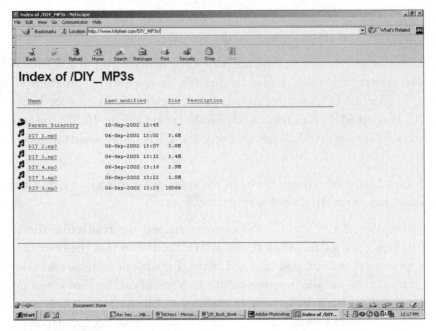

Figure 10.33 *Screenshot of uploaded, non-linked files on my Web site.*

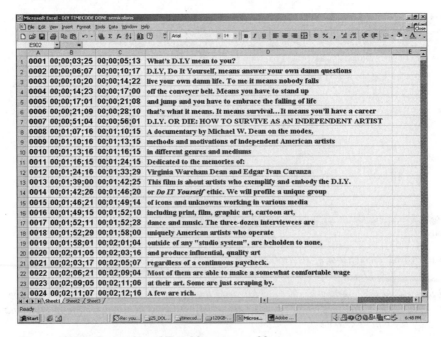

Figure 10.34 *Screenshot of Excel language table.*

To do this, you start each column with an apostrophe ('). This lets Excel know that you are just dealing with the sheet as a chart, not using any formulas. That way it won't try to reformat the numbers.

Type '0001 in the first cell, and '0002 in the second (see Figures 10.35 and 10.36).

Then select both cells, hold the mouse key down, and drag down the page (see Figures 10.37 and 10.38).

Then in the fourth column, I had to manually cut and paste and make lines of subtitles that were between 40 and 70 characters long (with spaces). This seems like a good readable amount. Keep in mind that some authoring programs will wrap the line after 43 characters. Some won't. I had to go in and insert carriage return breaks manually for very long lines. And make sure the subtitles are Title-safe.

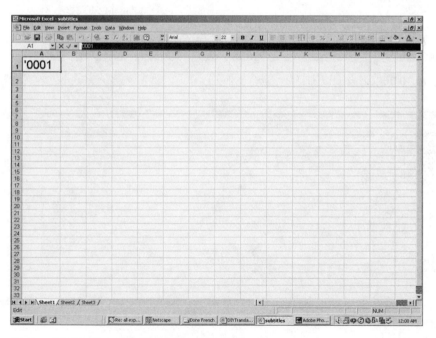

Figure 10.35 *Creating Excel language table.*

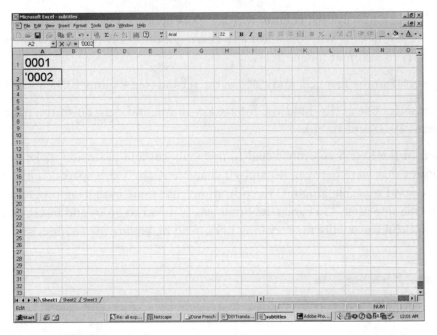

Figure 10.36 *Creating Excel language table 2.*

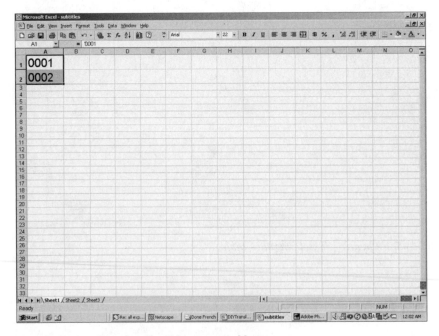

Figure 10.37 *Creating Excel language table 3.*

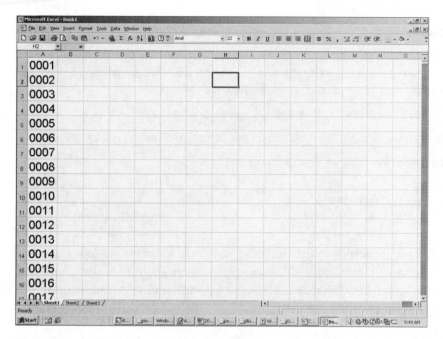

Figure 10.38 *Creating Excel language table 4.*

So, then I posted on Craigslist to get translators. Here's my post:

NEED TRANSLATION HELP

NEED TRANSLATION HELP for cool movie. German, Spanish, Italian, French. Project has non-profit status.

So, we have a very cool finished documentary project, *D.I.Y. OR DIE: How to Survive as an Independent Artist.*

It's toured the country, played in Europe, shown on TV in five states, and is in the Silver Lake Film Fest. It's a well-done film that shows a powerful group of artists who work regardless of a continuous paycheck.

Craig from Craigslist is in this film.

We are working on the DVD right now, and we need people to translate an English transcription into French, Spanish, German, and Italian for subtitles.

We are releasing the DVD with no copy protection and no regional restrictions and encouraging people to copy it. The name of the DVD is *D.I.Y. or DIE: Burn this DVD.* It's a labor of love to spread kick-ass art throughout the whole world.

WHAT WE NEED IS smart cool folks to translate for subtitles. And also check translations of others. We need it done this week.

No pay, but much thanks, and a free copy of the final DVD (with your name in the
credits.) Also, letter of recommendation for job reference.

We have 501c3 non-profit status, letter available if needed.

We're in Los Angeles, but you can do this in your own home via Internet.

Must have MS Excel on your computer.

Love and art,
Michael W. Dean

I got a bigger response for this than anything I've ever posted. I got responses
from all over the world. I think people who are multilingual are into spreading
understanding because they understand how frustrating it is to be misunderstood.

So, within hours I had an army of people translating sections into French,
German, Italian, and Spanish.

I sent people Excel sheets, and also the same text uninterrupted in a Word document, so they could see the flow of the paragraph easier. I made another Excel
spreadsheet to keep track of work flow. Once one was done, I had someone else who
spoke each language check it. Once those were done, I had someone check it again.

Then I checked that on the AltaVista BabbleFish translation page:
http://world.altavista.com.

Computer translation programs are not yet good enough to do the whole translation job, but they can help check to see if the person knows what they are doing. I
mean, it's still gonna translate looking like "All your base are belong to us," but I
caught a couple of things, like someone forgetting the little mark over the N in
Spanish that makes the difference between the word for "years" and the word for
"anuses."

While this was being done, one other guy and I (mostly I) logged timecode for the
1,002 lines of subtitles in the whole film. This took almost a week of 4-hour days.
I had to find where each line began and ended in the film, and then copy and paste
the exact timecode into a table in Excel. This would be used later to create a tab-
delimited list to feed the computer with the DVD authoring program. One had to
be created for each language, but it was pretty easy once the English was done,
because they more or less all lined up the same (see Figures 10.39 and 10.40).

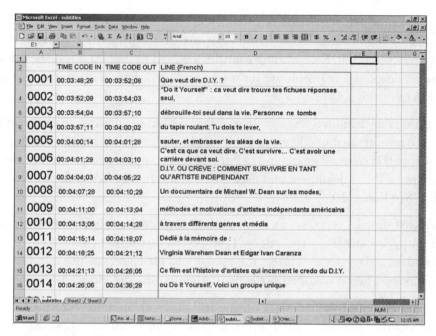

Figure 10.39 *French Excel language table.*

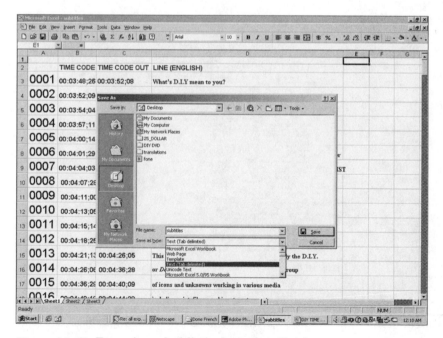

Figure 10.40 *Exporting tab-delimited text from Excel.*

Keep in mind that the translations will not line up exactly line for line. This is because of the differences in sentence structure in different languages. Don't worry much about it. People using subtitles are used to this. And it matters less in documentaries, where people are mostly just talking, than in dramas, where talking has to match action.

Exporting tab-delimited text from Excel worked, but required some workarounds. The program tended to add extra quote marks and such. It was still dealing with my text as if it were a formula instead of just text. I copied and pasted the spreadsheet into a Word document and used that to import. The Word file worked perfectly. (See Figure 10.41.)

Once we burned a test disc, we noticed that some of the subtitles were not title-safe and got cut off on the edges. I simply went through the Word file and inserted a carriage return (insert the cursor and hit Enter) in the middle of the longer ones. Then it wrapped perfectly on the next disc to two readable lines.

It's best to have a second or two of title still onscreen after the subjects are done talking so the viewer can catch up reading, but this often wasn't possible in our film, because it's mostly continuous talking. I often just added one frame in the

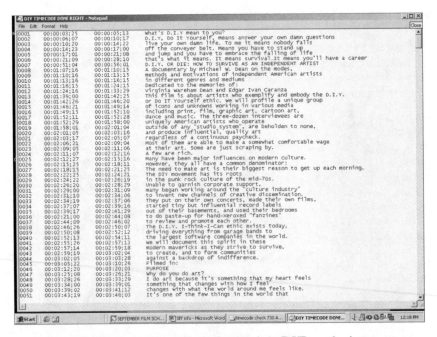

Figure 10.41 *Final text file ready for import into DVD authoring program.*

timecode manually and made the timecode for the beginning of one line start a frame after the end of the last line, within the same person's segment.

It goes without saying, but don't have one person's subtitles roll over into the next person's image. Also note that subtitles are converted to image files in the program, so they do take up some file space in the project. Not much, but some. Having over five languages will degrade the amount of available space on the disc, and on a DVD-5 will require encoding at a slightly lower bit rate, which may make the movie look a little less vibrant.

When you're done, import into your authoring program. This is done differently in each program—check the Help menus. In Sonic DVD Creator, it's:

Presentation/Import Subtitles/Text subtitles script. (See Figures 10.42 and 10.43.)

Then burn a test disc. If you don't have a burner, make a DVD disc image on your hard drive (usually one of the options under the Output menu). Watch the English portion, and make sure everything lines up correctly. We had a problem with our first disc, but it was an issue of one machine reading Drop-Frame Mode and one in Non-Drop Frame. It started out okay, but by the end of the 55-minute movie, it was four seconds off. We fixed this, and a couple of places where lines

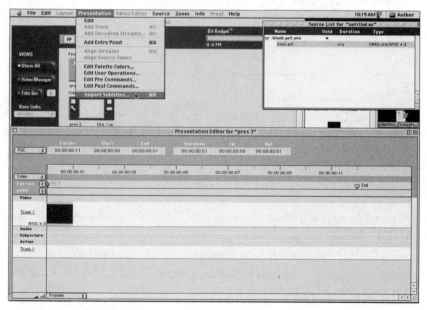

Figure 10.42 *Importing subtitle file in Sonic DVD Creator.*

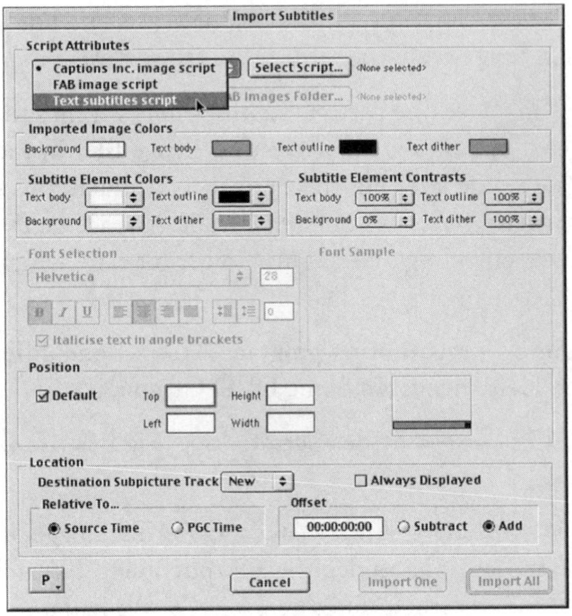

Figure 10.43 *Importing subtitle file in Sonic DVD Creator 2.*

overlapped or were missing. (Because I accidentally cut and pasted the in-point the same as the out-point. Hey—three mistakes in 1,003 lines—that's pretty good.) Then Blaine outputted it to a DLT tape (digital linear tape—more on this later) and I sent it off to the presser (duplication house).

NOTE

A cool side note: Once I learned all this crap about logging timecode, I actually got some paying jobs doing this myself for other people. And for the translations, I paid the best of the folks who worked for me for free. So it all works out in the end. Art Karma and Green Karma in action....

It's important to know if your project is in Drop-Frame Mode or Non-Drop-Frame (NDF) Mode, because if the clips are in one and the project is in the other, your sync will drift by about four seconds per hour. This will make people's lips move wrong, and make your film look like a badly dubbed Kung Fu movie.

Drop-Frame Mode is DV standard. You can tell by looking at your camera settings if it's in DF mode. You set the mode in the project presets when you open a new project. If you do nothing, it will usually default to Drop Frame. You can tell the mode in the editing program by looking at the time code display. In Non-Drop-Frame Mode, the numbers are separated by all colons (see Figure 10.44).

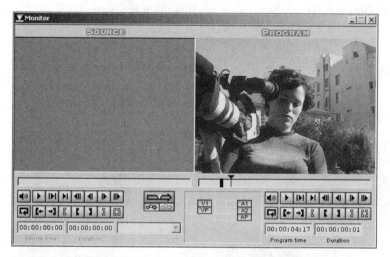

Figure 10.44 *Non-Drop-Frame timecode in CineStream.*

In Drop-Frame Mode, the numbers are separated by either all semicolons or a semicolon in the third field (see Figure 10.45). Either way, if you see semicolons, it's DF mode.

Figure 10.45 *Screenshot of Drop-Frame timecode in CineStream.*

Menus

The menu for the subtitle setup has flags for each language (see Figure 10.46). Note that I broke convention and used a British flag, not an American flag, for English and a Spanish flag rather than a Mexican flag for Spanish. This is because I wanted to honor the counties of origin.

Figure 10.46 *Flags on Subtitle menu of* D.I.Y. *or* DIE *DVD. (Photo is of my daughter, Amelia, and me.)*

Square Pixels

There is an issue with DVD background menus on TV screens of square pixels versus non-square pixels. You have to make your titles at 720 × 540 pixels and then squash them to 720 × 480 (standard DV resolution). This will compensate for the difference. If you made them at 720 × 480 and need to resize them, crop part off to get them to 640 × 480 and scale them up to 720 × 540 to keep the shapes of things good, so a circle doesn't look like an egg.

You can resize things in Photoshop by using Image/Image size and unchecking the tick mark that says Constrain Proportions. (See Figure 10.47.) This is normally on, and changing one axis will change the other. With it unchecked, it will change the shape of the rectangle, that is, changing the height will not change the width, and vice versa.

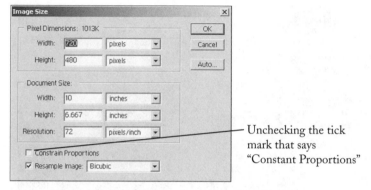

Unchecking the tick mark that says "Constant Proportions"

Figure 10.47 *Constraining image proportions in Photoshop.*

PAL Versus NTSC, Link Licensing, Region Restrictions, and Copy Protection

Most DVD authoring programs have a preset that enables you to make a new project that is either NTSC or PAL (see Figure 10.48). I make them NTSC because that will play in a PAL player, while a PAL DVD will not play in a NTSC player.

Figure 10.48 *The NTSC/PAL menu is the second thing to come up when you open DVDit.*

In advanced programs, you can also put region restrictions so a project will play only on machines made in certain parts of the world. This is one more example of "the Man" using technology in a futile attempt to control the flow of information that wants to be free. Forget it. (The default is no region restrictions, so if you do nothing, you'll have a disc that plays everywhere and anywhere.)

Figure 10.49 *Weblinks menu of* D.I.Y. or DIE *DVD.*

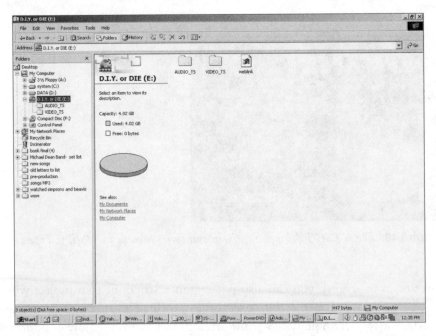

Figure 10.50 *Weblinks HTML file on* D.I.Y. or DIE *DVD in Explorer.*

Putting a clickable Web link in most programs actually involves having to pay a royalty and go through their central server. This is an unbelievable (in my mind) idea: that someone actually patented having a clickable link. Evil. So, the way we got around that was to make an actual HTML page with the links and just put it in the main volume and put instructions on the Weblinks page telling the user to simply open that up on their computer (see Figures 10.49 and 10.50). Ha.

How to add copy protection, (and why you shouldn't) will be covered in Chapter 14, "Copy Protection and Rights."

DVD (and VHS) Replication

You can get DVD copies mass produced for about a buck-fifty each (about the same as VHS), with a cover, in lots of 500. They will cost more if you order less, and less if you order more. You should shop around, online or in the *Yellow Pages*, to find good work at a good price. Or ask someone in your area where they went. After 1,000 units, there is a price break where DVDs start to get cheaper than video tapes.

I've gotten DVDs done in Canada (www.duplication.ca), and VHS done in Anaheim (www.newstylemedia.com). The both do great work, but there is a tradeoff for both. With Canada, I don't have to pay tax, but I have to pay shipping. Anaheim is a short drive, but I pay California sales tax.

We're in a global economy. You can now get things done anywhere. Shop around online. But keep in mind that shipping and taxes are a tradeoff for getting it done locally. Also, getting it done locally helps support your neighbors, so it's probably a nice, community minded thing to do.

You are supposed to report and pay taxes on the Net, but some people seem to forget to for some reason. Of course, I would never recommend you do anything illegal.

Sales of DVDs generally outnumber sales of VHS 3 to 1. And DVDs are just better. They look and sound better than VHS. They are smaller and weigh less (cheaper to warehouse and ship), and are less fragile than VHS. You can put much more material on one, access scenes more quickly, choose commentary and subtitles, and more. They last longer, don't jam, don't degenerate on repeated playings, and they're just plain sexier than those clunky old VHS tapes.

Not everyone has a DVD player yet, but that will change in a year or two. Many computers now ship with DVD players installed, and some with DVD burners. External DVD players for your TV are as low as fifty bucks, and the price is dropping. But at first, you might want to still make some VHS tapes. More people have players (though that will be wrong info in a year). It's easier to make up ten or a hundred or so VHS tapes or DVDs yourself to send out for promo than it is to commit to manufacture DVDs or tapes. (The minimum run on DVDs is usually a thousand. It's usually a couple hundred on VHS tapes.) This is changing also with the proliferation of DVD burners and software. Burners are currently about $300, and the price is dropping.

For VHS, you will provide the presser with a master tape (use the File/Print To Tape command in your editing program that you learned in Chapter 8 to make the master), usually on Mini-DV or Beta SP, and a cover art and label file on CD or Zip disk. They will want a high-rez Photoshop, Quark, or Pagemaker file, not MS Word, for the cover art. (It varies from place to place. Ask them. And ask them for templates.)

If they don't have a template, there is a Quark DVD cover and label template on the CD that comes with this book.

DVD is an amazing format, but a little more complex to get ready than making VHS copies.

I worked hard on the *D.I.Y.* DVD. I made cool menu backgrounds using art by people in the movie and other friends. I made looping audio to play behind them, mostly using my music. I made 10 cool little shorts for the Extras section (and two for Easter eggs). That's one of the most fun parts of making a DVD, and the part all filmmakers dig. Because all filmmakers dig making short films. There's a lot more fun, and a lot less stress. But the tradeoff is it's hard to make money just making shorts. So you make your feature, which makes money, and augment it on the DVD with some fun little shorts. Win-win.

There are several variations on the DVD format. Physically, they are all the same size and look the same, but they are different in capacity. ("Layer" means how many programs of material are on each side. Two-layer DVDs have information at two different depths in the plastic, accessed by the laser pointing at different angles.)

DVD-5	Holds 4.7 gigs	1 side, 1 layer
DVD-9	Holds 8.5 gigs	1 side, 2 layer
DVD-10	Holds 9.4 gigs	2 sided, 1 layer
DVD-18	Holds 17 gigs	2 sided, 2 layer

I explain this so you will know your project size options and limitations for masters.

As of this writing most replication houses cannot yet do the DVD-18 format, but this will change. And they'll come up with something that holds more after that, I'm sure.

I can't wait!

DVD burners are cool. Make sure you get the ones that can burn DVD-R (discs that can only be burned once), not just DVD+RW (re-recordable discs that can be burned, then later erased and re-burned, sort of like how you can re-record on a cassette tape). I made the mistake of getting one that only does re-recordable discs, which are like 15 bucks each. Regular Maxell write-once DVDs are a buck each if you get 50. Some blank DVDs are as cheap as 50 cents each in lots of several hundred. (The Apple ones are three bucks each for some reason.)

Always burn test discs and try them on different DVD players to make sure everything works. Watch the test discs with scrutiny. There's no reason to press 1,000 or 5,000 mistakes.

At this writing, most home burners will only make a DVD the capacity and configuration of a DVD-5 (4.7 gigs, 1 side, 1 layer). For production masters, you can only use a home-burned 4.7 gig DVD-R if you're making DVD-5s or DVD-10s. You'll need two of them for a DVD-10. You cannot use them for masters for DVD-9 or DVD-18. Those require a DLT.

When replicating DVD-5s, sometimes home-burned DVDs fail as masters, and then you still have to pay for the ruined glass master. (Replicators have to make a glass master to press from. This costs a few hundred bucks. You're better off paying 50 bucks, finding and renting a DLT deck, and outputting to that. That is relatively foolproof.)

Keep in mind that no one really uses DVD-10 any more because DVD-9 has basically the same capacity, but with DVD-10 you have to physically turn them over, which can involve interrupting the movie. Some people don't even know you're supposed to do this, and feel baffled when the movie abruptly ends in the middle. One technology-savvy friend said she went rooting through the box looking for a second disc. A double-sided DVD is just not a very intuitive way to do things, so I recommend against it.

Some DVD replication places will accept home-burned DVD as a master for a project. Others require that the project be output onto a DLT tape, a proprietary format that is hard to find decks for, even for rental, even in Los Angeles—the media capital of the world. (By the way, none of the Grandmaware[1] programs will export to DLT.) Using DLT is the safest bet and will make for flawless duplication. Other pressers will take a DVD-R, which you can record on any computer with a DVD recorder. (See Figure 10.51.)

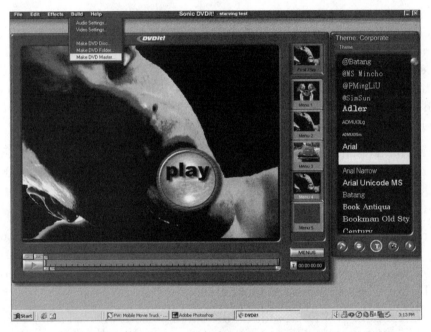

Figure 10.51 *DLT tape output in Sonic Solutions' DVDit. (Image: Screen capture from the author's trailer* Starving in the Company of Beautiful Women. *Photo by Peter Spicer.)*

---

1. Grandmaware is my term for point-and-click wizard-driven programs aimed at very basic consumers, as opposed to prosumer or pro programs. Grandmaware is easy to use, but so limited as to frustrate adept computer users who are willing to learn more to have more power and options.

Conclusion

When you complete this venture and get the duplicated art back, it's okay to take a copy and flirt with it. Take the DVD, or a pile of them, and hold them. Look at them. Pet them. Sleep with them. I do.

But don't rest too long on your accomplishments. That's not the $30 way. We want to go on to the next phase of the fun and twisted trip we're on: Promotion—actually getting our DVDs out into the hands of the many people who will eventually dig our films. Then maybe they will flirt with them, pet them, and sleep with them.

Chapter 11

Telling the World

You made something cool. Now share it with the world, Part II.

You've made your movie and made copies on VHS and DVD, and now you want to get people to want to look at it. Here's how to make your movie stand out, how to get people to want to help spread the word, and how to get some "juice" behind your art.

Using the Internet[1] for Promotion

No reference to indie filmmaking would be complete without at least a cursory mention of *The Blair Witch Project*'s Internet campaign. This film broke all the rules and came out of nowhere. It made more money than any indie film ever. And it was a lot more surprising than Robert Rodriguez's oft-cited *El Mariachi*. *El Mariachi* partially sold well because it was the precursor to *Desperado*, the big Hollywood movie with Antonio Banderas. *El Mariachi* is a fine little film, but it was basically the calling card. It had a lot of money pumped into it, but only as a marketing prequel to Desperado.

Blair Witch was the Nirvana of film, in the sense that Nirvana was a garage band that sold huge, and *Blair Witch* was a true indie film that made a heck of a lot of money (once it was given non-indie promotion). In this sense, Robert Rodriguez, while talented, smart, and funny, wasn't that important; he only proved that a guy who can make a good indie film can be a big Hollywood director. That happens all the time—it just never happens that fast or without a crew. *Blair Witch* was important because this indie flick was the *actual product*, not the calling card. (Even though *Blair Witch* heavily borrows themes from another, far lesser known movie called *The Last Broadcast*.)

1. We also call it the "Interweb1" or the "Internurd" for kicks.

Produced for $30,000[2], *Blair Witch* literally made hundreds of millions of dollars, and it's the only huge theatrical release shot on video. (To be fair, some of it was shot by Joshua Leonard on 16mm film. That's one reason he got cast. He was not only good-looking and cocky, and could improvise well on-the-fly; he was also a filmmaker in his own right, and he could actually use a camera.) See Chapter 16, "Interviews and Advice from Cool Film Folk," for an interview with Joshua.

Part of what drove the campaign for this motion-sickness inspiring romp through the woods was the Web site. It was spooky and cool and it never broke character or allowed you to un-suspend your disbelief. In short, it made you feel *involved*.

This is called *Viral Marketing*—not in the sense of a computer virus, but in the sense of an *information* virus. Information that one person desperately wishes to pass on to another. Much cooler than Adidas making people pay to wear the logo on their clothes. No, this is grassroots, one-to-one beauty at its best. And one-thousand users now means a million users later on. They're your First Adopters. Once it hits big, everyone will claim they were into it from the start. I remember seeing club shows of Nirvana where there were me and 20 other people in the audience. After they got famous, I had at least 40 people tell me that they were at that show!

Making Viral Marketing work is half science and half Voodoo. Big corporations shell out tons of bucks trying to make it happen. And they are throwing their money away, because you can't predict it. You can't buy luck, and you can't buy heart.

I did a little bit of Viral Marketing with the Web site for my film *D.I.Y. or DIE*. I made a cool community that made it easy for people to feel connected with the movie. Unlike *Blair Witch*, I invited people to do paid showings of it and split the money with me. I put everything they needed on one page, sent them a VHS, they showed it in their town, and sent me half the money. It was fun, made people feel *very* involved (because they *were*), and I *lived* off that money that summer. I can't count the times that I was starving and I'd get a check for 60 or a 100 bucks from someone in Ypsilanti, Michigan or Jacksonville, Florida. Kept me in bagels and coffee. Mmmmm…mailbox money.

And they *all* kept their word. Not one of the people who agreed to show it without me present didn't send the money. They all sent it.

---

2. *Really. Unlike* El Mariachi, *which was made for $7,000 but about $250,000 was spent practically reassembling and grooming and fluffing Rodriguez's print to be cinema-ready.*

I also periodically added downloads to the Web site to keep people coming back:

- ◆ B-roll snippets that didn't make it to the movie.

- ◆ Interviews done after the movie, with such people as Phil Sudo, interviewed not long before he died, and Steve Albini, who was not available when we filmed the movie.

- ◆ Cute stuff like footage of me getting interviewed by a high-school radio station in Indianapolis, and bitching to my friend Jo off-camera (I thought) before an interview on cable access in East Los Angeles. (This later ended up, longer, on the Extras section of the DVD. The DVD came out six months after the VHS.)

Also, I gave away an MP3 and Real Audio version of the *entire* audio portion of the movie. I've never seen this done, and it seems like a good idea. It works on its own, although you can't see who's talking, which might be even *more* effective, given the "downplaying celebrity" aspect of the film's mission statement.

I also added text updates and tour reports, and still photos from the road. You know, it's kinda like how when a kid from the ghetto makes it to the Majors, or the Olympics. It ain't just you going…it's your whole scene. You are an inspiration for people who need to be told that it's okay to be free. And you are also there, believe it or not, to be lived through vicariously by folks who may never make it off that couch. So let 'em know what's going on, but don't brag…

…Much.

Basically, offer something cool on the site, and people will come. And then they'll come back. That's the secret to the Web that few big corporations are aware of. Most big corporations spend hundreds of thousands on fancy Web sites that are hard to navigate and offer nothing without paying, or at least typing in all your demographic contact info (which they later sell). These sites are lousy.

If you give people something interesting, and put people before profits, you will do well. And maybe even make a profit.

Also, don't use crap like pop-up exit consoles and those jive-ass Java scripts that make it impossible to use the Back button on the browser. You don't make a Web site "sticky" by using selfish code that hijacks users and makes it physically difficult to leave. Those are about as welcome as an aggressive panhandler. They make you want to run in the opposite direction, and cross the Information Highway when you see it coming to avoid it in the future. And those creepy corporate tricks are totally antithetical to the mission statement of *$30 Film School*.

A majestic Web site is a great thing, but it doesn't have to cost money. Web design is one of the most overpriced services in the world. You can do it yourself, or find a friend to do it, but make it good. A lot of times if someone is starting out, and good, but has no paying clients yet, she might be willing to do your site for free so she can put it on her resume. She needn't say on the resume that she did it for free…only that it was work she did. This is not dishonest.

Have a good URL too. One people can remember.

Make an Electronic Press Kit (EPK). This is basically a zipped file with .pdf scans of all your press. Mine is three megs. Don't e-mail it to people without asking first. If they're on a dial-up connection, it will piss them off. But link it on the Web site, put a prominent link at the top, and e-mail the URL to everyone you contact. They will appreciate it. (I put all the files in my EPK on the CD, unzipped, for you to see. It's in the folder called *EPK*.)

Make your Web site about *information*. Sure, a good mood and look is great, but I am incredibly frustrated with a lot of sites. I can't count the number of hours I've wasted looking at gorgeous Flash animations and clicking through intriguing Byzantine labyrinth interfaces when I'm just looking for a damn *phone number*.

Always give low-bandwidth users the option of skipping the graphics-heavy intros and such. If they have to wait, they'll go somewhere else. The Web is the ultimate realm of us no-attention span TV babies.

A good example of the importance of a good Web site is this: When I was looking for an agent for this book, it kind of came down to two very qualified companies. I went with the one who had the Internet presence that was easier to navigate.

They say the Internet's a level playing field where any fool in his or her room has the same power to reach the world that *Time Magazine* does. Well, then how come *Time Magazine*'s site gets 10 million people a day and yours gets 10? Mine gets about 500 people a day, which is pretty good for what it is: your basic vanity personal site. More impressive is my throughput, about 6 gigabytes a month are downloaded from me, mostly video and audio, which means people are investing time in my site and getting some serious media off of it. Six gigs of throughput is about what a mid-sized corporation gets. It's huge for a personal site.

Time Magazine gets a lot of hits because they have their URL on all their magazines, billboards, late night TV infomercials, and more. Sure, anyone in the world *can* look at your site, but do they? You have to advertise. Put your name everywhere. And consider that 100 million other people are doing the same.

One thing you can do is try to get magazines like *Time* to write about you. Might be hard if you're a nobody like me. But you might get the New York *Times* or *Spin Magazine* to mention you. I have.

E-mail a one-page press release of your film (just as plain text in the body of the e-mail rather than as an attachment) and links to your Web site and Electronic Press Kit to all the independent movie magazines: *FilmThreat* and *Filmmaker Magazine*, and any special interest magazines that would cover something on your subject.

Newspapers are easier to get into than magazines, and magazines are easier than network TV. But a well-written press release is good….basically, just know the job of the person receiving it and make his job easier. Is a rock band news? No. Is a rock band with a one-handed Lithuanian lesbian drummer on the run from ethnic cleansing in Bulgaria news? Yes. Don't lie, but find your angle, find what makes you news, and send it to the appropriate editor. Their names and job descriptions should be listed on the Web site for the publication. Do your research, or get your interns to help.

(By the way, Google is the best search engine and produces the best results in general searches. It also corrects my louzy speling.)

TIP

Don't forget to register your movie on www.imdb.com and http://worldfilm.about.com. I did. It's free, and I've actually sold copies of the movie because people saw it on one of those sites.

E-Mail Promotion

I do a lot of contacting people via e-mail. That's how I get interviews and let people know what I'm doing. But I don't Spam. Spam in any form is a drag. It's wrong and counterproductive. There are ads now on the back of fortune cookie fortunes, and on the wall when you're trapped captive in the toilet stall. I find all of this visual telemarketing insulting. Don't be like this. Make great stuff, get the word out, and things will come to you.

For example, I got Chris Gore's book on indie film festivals and looked up contact info for all the Sundance winners he interviewed. I e-mailed them all with a synopsis of my film and asked if they wanted a free copy. Several did. One later helped a lot on another project. I didn't Spam him, just offered my movie free to him.

Filmmaker Melissa Brown said I spend so much time on the Internet that my computer isn't a machine, it's my roommate.

Sometimes I read an article by someone and think that they need to see my movie. I tell them about it and ask if they'd like a copy. They usually do, but it's very important to ask. (And if they say "No" or don't write back, don't bug them again. This is important.)

Just sending someone an unsolicited movie, script, or album is considered unprofessional, and seems kind of stalkerish.[3] Many professionals in the media industries have a policy of returning all movies, scripts, demo tapes, and any unsolicited items unopened. This is to keep from getting sued. This policy seems kind of pricky until you realize that people sue famous people *all the time*, imagining that the famous person has stolen their ideas. Sometimes it's even assumed to have been done with psychic powers, but is a lot easier to "prove" if the someone has actually sent something to the person's office before.

So...I send out a lot of e-mails and get a much smaller number of responses, but enough to keep stuff rolling and get my art out to The Universe without pissing off too many people. I have a pretty good feel for who will like what. I also have to make sure that I don't get pissed if someone doesn't respond, or responds curtly. The thing to do is to be so busy that you forget what you send out and then you are pleasantly surprised when they do respond. (I guess this is one area where it would help to have a support staff.) This method does piss some people off if I send them the same thing a few times, especially if they have already responded. I did this when asking some film festivals to waive their entrance fee—many will if they want your film and you ask *very* nicely. And they will tell you to tell no one. Pay if you can, but ask not to if you can't.

I have an e-mail list of over 1,200 people. Everyone on it asked to be on it, or let me put them on when I asked. It's grown from one person in 1996 when I first

3. *Although there is a story that Quentin Tarantino got into the Biz by jumping Harvey Keitel's fence and leaving the script for Reservoir Dogs and his phone number. Who knows?*

started keeping one. About five people a week ask to be added, and about two people a week ask to be removed. (Every few letters I put "To be removed, just ask" at the top. And I remove people as soon as they ask, and send them a letter that says, "done" as a reply to their request.) I try to include lots of URLs, anecdotes, and fun stuff to keep the morale up for the troops. And I send less than one posting a week. I used to send out three a week, and my attrition rate was much higher. Actually it's about three times a month.

I get people to be added to my list by having the following as the signature line on all outgoing e-mails:

> May I add you to the weekly art and cats e-list? (if you're already on it, never mind).
>
> It's the list of what I'm up to, with the movie and other stuff. Cool audio and video download links.
>
> All addresses are BCC (not showing), never shared with anyone, removed any time you ask.
>
> reply and say "add me" if you want.

Sometimes I ask my list to help me with things. When I met in San Francisco with people from PBS who were interested in the documentary, they basically said we'd have to make a bunch of changes, and that they wouldn't pay for it. I'm tapped out in virtual editing costs, so I can't do it. But they also implied that if there were a demand, they might show it anyway.

So I sent this out to my list:

> If you want to, e-mail your local PBS affiliate, and tell them you want to see the movie. *D.I.Y. or Die: How To Survive As An Independent Artist* on PBS; it just might happen. Call or e-mail them. Contact info for each town here:
>
> http://www.pbs.org/stationfinder/index.html

Another thing I use e-mail for is day-to-day detail stuff. For instance, we were about to go to press with *D.I.Y.* and make copies of the film, and I didn't know the name of the song that Foetus (J.G. Thirlwell) plays live in the segment we shot. I output the audio of that bit from CineStream, converted it to an MP3 using AudioGrabber, and e-mailed that tiny file to Jim. Within hours, he wrote back that it was "Friend or Foe," and it got listed correctly in the credits.

A lot of times I'll be e-mailing someone back and forth on a particular subject and they'll say, "Let's do this on I.M. (instant messenger) instead." I don't like using I.M.—it works *too* well. The lag in time with e-mail (especially since I type about 95 WPM—far faster than most folks, and think even faster) gives me time to multitask and get other stuff done. With I.M., I'm just using I.M. And I'm already on the computer *way* too much each day to get sucked into chatting when I need to be working.

I do use I.M. for file sharing though. If I have to get a big file to or from a collaborator, I'll log onto MS I.M., transfer the file, and sign out.

The Web and e-mail are very effective art and business tools, because they are asynchronous communication. Face-to-face office meetings and phone calls are synchronous—both parties have to be present. (Phone tag is asynchronous, but ineffective.) Someone is more likely to make a flyer for your show if they can do it on their own time in their underwear than if they have to wait for you to come over and drop off the artwork. And I love that when some intern flakes and I have to reproduce his work on a Saturday, the Quark cover templates are on my VHS presser's Web site.

TIP

E-mails shouldn't, in my opinion, try to do too much media-wise as far as displaying content and having HTML formatting. Simple text is better. Best to just have links and let people choose. Otherwise your viewers get hijacked, with browser windows opening and sometimes crashing while they're just waking up and trying to check their inbox This makes people resent your organization.

Also, it seems obvious, but if you want to be taken seriously, DON'T TYPE E-MAILS IN ALL CAPITAL LETTERS AND USE LOTS OF EXCLAMATION POINTS. THIS IS PERCEIVED AS "SHOUTING" AND TURNS OFF MOST PEOPLE IMMEDIATELY!!!!!!!!!

Rough Cuts

Sending rough cuts to festivals is a mixed bag. You might get into one where you would otherwise miss the deadline, but you might not get in at all. I recommend against it, and this is based on experience. Rough cuts rarely amaze people. And if you must send rough cuts, make sure you label them clearly with "ROUGH CUT. NOT FOR PUBLIC SHOWING." We had several instances of festivals accepting us based on a rough cut, not telling us, and then showing the rough cut. Embarrassing.

NOTE

Be creative with everything. This includes not just making the film, but all aspects, including promotion. We didn't get accepted to many film festivals for some reason (probably because I was sending out rough cuts). So, undaunted, I ended up booking paid showings (showings where they paid *me*) in bars, theaters, clubs, record stores, and basements. Nationwide! Before the thing was even finished, I had a national tour set up that would pay for me to travel and present it in person. I contacted clubs and microcinemas and sold them on the idea of showing my film, charging a cover, and giving me something between half and all of the door. Bars make money on drinks. So if no one showed up (which never happened), I didn't lose money, but when people did show up, I made money off the door, and the bar made money off drinks. Or if it wasn't in a bar, the venue and I split the door and both made money.

So rather than *paying* to enter festivals where it would only have a *chance* to be one of many films shown, I was getting *paid* to show it where it would be the featured attraction!

For more on booking a tour, see Chapter 13, "Touring."

Four-Point Plan for Effective Promotion

1. You have to have something that people totally want to see.
2. You have to bring it to everyone who can help, without hustling them.
3. You need to be utterly unrelenting.
4. And finally, thank everyone.

1. **Make something great.** We've established this, but it bears repeating. Everything you do should kick ass, whether it's making a movie or tying your

shoes. Also, never make any half-assed product, thinking, "This is just a demo" or whatever. If it is mediocre, you'll never get heard later with good stuff. And if you do, the weak demo will get bootlegged by your fans and haunt you forever. Make everything as if it's the only thing you'll ever be known for.

Find a great story, or write one, or present one, and do the best you can. This ain't just empty pep-talk, A-for-effort, wimpy new age affirmations. This is the law of the Universe and, therefore, the Law of the Jungle.

The Universe loves art. Make some, and she'll take care of you. And maybe you'll get laid and get paid along the way. Maybe not. But the art itself is the payment. You need to really believe this and live it internally and externally.

Attitude will only get you so far. A lot of young people survive on a modicum of talent, and make up for it with a lot of attitude. If you're gonna survive in the world, you must develop your talent. Be great so when you bitch as much as I do, you don't come across as "a loser complaining."

Documentaries are generally more boring than church. Ours isn't. It isn't the most amazing one I've ever seen (*Straight Outta Hunters Point*, by my friend Kevin Epps is). Ours is good for what it is, and I'm proud of it as a first effort done on almost no money. Some documentaries blow me away...some of them are the best movies I've ever seen. It's an amazing genre...a cross between news and school, presented in a cool way. And ours only took a year. Actually 11 months. Started tax day 2001, finished April Fools Day, 2002.

2. **Bring your art to everyone who can help**. Don't be afraid to ask for help, ever, any time in life, but especially here. Remaining teachable, not "knowing it all," is what will keep you from getting old. When people think they know it all, they start aging inside and out.

Sometimes people are just too cocky to ask for help, or sometimes they're afraid. Just know that what you have is good, and if it is good, then it's worth bringing to people. It's no longer you you're working for; it's the art. This makes it easier to get out and work for it. It's not you being rejected, it's the art. And somehow, even though the art is you, it's easier if you make this distinction. This somehow reminds me of how strippers use a fake name to keep that part of their personality separate.

Just get out there and have hustle for the art, not for you. You'll get to go along for the ride too....

3. **Be absolutely vigilant**. You know, if you haven't figured it out yet, this isn't just a how-to book. It's a blueprint for war. War on sloth and indecisiveness.

Get out there and have hustle for your art. Book a tour. Get helpers. You can find the phone numbers and e-mails of the people you'll need to help you online. All of them. I'm not going to give them to you for several reasons. One, if I did, it would dilute them; everyone who buys this book will e-mail all of them and piss them off. They would all have to change their e-mail addresses. If I don't put it here, you'll have to do a little work, prove that you have good motives, and have the gumption, pluck, and luck to do it yourself. Then these people will respect you more and be willing to help you anyway.

I constantly do stuff like contacting local radio and magazines and newspapers in every town I'm visiting. I don't rely on the venue to do this. The venue, however, will often provide the contact info if you ask them. I e-mail a flyer and handbill to a friend in each city. I have a friend in every city, thanks to the Internet and the fact that I rarely leave my room. When I'm on tour, I actually get to meet them! Offer to put them and a friend on the guest list in exchange for making some flyers and hanging them up. If I can, I get more than one person in each city to do this. It's that old D.I.Y. rule of "Someone will flake, be covered, don't put all your crack in one basket....." Maybe tell 5 people you trust that if they print 200 and hang them up, they get in free. Or 10 people. That means 2 or 3 might actually do it.

This is a lot of work, but do you really wanna just work a dull job and consume what your TV tells you to consume until you die? Would you rather get fat waiting for a fairy godmother to wave her funded-debt wand and make you famous? Or would you rather work your butt off to make something brilliant and show it to a few wonderful people in every city in the world?

In the book *Fight Club*, Tyler holds the gun to the head of the convenience store clerk and tells him he'll kill the clerk unless he goes back to college. The scene is also in the movie, but the book has a bit that never seems clear in the movie. He basically loves him. He says he's doing it to save him from a life of nothingness, a life of "watching TV and eating cheese."

I'm sick of hanging up flyers. I've been doing it for 25 years. But I still do it. Why? Because it's better than watching TV and eating fried cheese. By the way, don't staple flyers on trees. It kills them. We need them to breathe. Don't be selfish. Your art isn't worth more than my daughter and me being able to breathe.

Your dad's been saying it your whole life: Make something of your life. He's right. Just know that your idea of success might be different from your dad's. If he's anything like my dad, he'll be proud of you regardless. Seriously. Make something of your life.

It's easy for me to do this. I am spared. I should have been dead from drugs. Each day I wake up not addicted is a day I am willing to work my ass off for very little return because it beats the alternative. I have a tattoo of the word *Spared* on my inside left wrist to remind me of this. I got it last year, right after I got in a (sober) car accident in L.A. that came very close to killing me and my friend Tracy.

Computers, art, and computer art are great things to keep ex-addicts busy. Because the amount you can learn is *endless*. You never get bored. Addicts have a great thirst for everything, including knowledge.

Kevin Epps is saved too. He used to pound the pavement in the ghetto and get shot at. He may have been involved in things we can't mention here. So of course he'll have no problem walking up to anyone and giving them a handbill to promote his film. It beats getting shot at. He has the marketing sensibility of a street hustler.

Figure 11.1 *Cool flyer art that Patrick Roullier painted for one of Rusty Nails' films.*

Figure 11.2 *My newest tattoo.*

I think he'll do well in Hollywood. He has a sense of respect for his fellow man, which will make him rise above the crap. This is a rare and potent combination: ex-street hustler with a heart of gold. Will someone please make a movie about this man?

Part of being absolutely vigilant is doing things quickly and efficiently. Part of this means keeping on top of daily and mundane tasks like answering e-mail, having ink for your printer, and mailing out movie orders. That way when something comes up, you're not too busy putting out the day's fires to get on it *now*. When someone sends me an interview, I do it usually within hours, and I do it well. I even print it out and proof it before sending it. When an underground festival in Long Island e-mails me and wants to buy a copy of *D.I.Y.* to show, needs it in two days, and says they'll send money, I mail it priority that day and worry about the money later. I manage my time so that I can fulfill any reasonable request on behalf of the art almost as soon as I get it.

This works on the other end too. When I was designing the DVD for *D.I.Y.*, I decided that I was going to put some trailers of friends' films in there. When I toured with the film, I'd brought these trailers and some shorts to show before my movie, so it made sense. I'd show about 20 minutes of other people's stuff before my film. It was a little one-man film festival. I brought my DV camera to use as a deck and plugged it through their projector.

I didn't just bring the trailers to fill time. I wanted to spread the love and help others. That's what the *D.I.Y.* project is all about. I'd noticed that commercial DVDs from big studios have trailers, but always trailers of stuff they're selling. I wanted stuff I had no economic stake in, just cool art. So I told a bunch of friends to cut 30- to 60-second trailers and get them to me. Trailers this short will even fit uncompressed on a CD at this length. Burke Roberts cut one and brought it to me the next day. Over the next two weeks, I got the rest in the mail, or people brought them by. One guy didn't remember to, and I didn't have time to chase him. His trailer did not end up on the DVD.

The moral is: stay on top of your game so you can go into battle any time.

3. **Be creative.** Think of new ways to get your word out. I had a friend who made a rubber stamp and stamped his URL on all the money that passed through his hand. I stenciled my URL on my car.

Also, be sure to keep a few copies of your movie and press kit in your car. You never know when you might need them. If you have DVDs (which are lighter and

Figure 11.3 *The back of my 1966 Plymouth Barracuda.*

easier to carry than VHS tapes), you might even keep them in your backpack, shoulder bag, or purse.

Make T-shirts. You can do this almost free if you use spray paint and a stencil, and get shirts cheap from the Salvation Army or Goodwill. That will make each one unique!

Start a scene. One fun thing you can do until you're ready to go on tour is have a monthly thing with your band or a friend's band or different bands and show different movies by indie filmmakers each time. Most bars will love this, and you can build a scene this way, and meet other filmmakers and artists.

The bands usually know the club owners, which makes booking easier. It's good to show the films between the bands to keep the night lively and keep everyone there. Though, depending on the feel of the bands and the films, putting films before or after might be better. Sometimes bands even like to show stuff *while* they are playing. It's best to use either "found footage" (old high-school educational 16 mm prints, surgery films, and erotic stuff are sometimes good choices), or make something specifically for this purpose. Anything but hurting the ego of one of the contributing filmmakers by showing their film during a band without their permission.

You will need a digital projector and a screen. Projectors start at about $1,200 new and $500 used, but are great to have. Screens are $30 to $300. If you have these, you can go on tour a lot easier because you can play any bar or club or house. Currently, not many places have their own projector, but that will change. In a couple of years, projectors in bars will be as common as PA systems for bands are now.

Get on TV. There is a cool little-known secret that the FCC requires all cable providers at the local level to make time available free for people from the community. It's one of those bizarre cases of a huge cranky bureaucracy actually doing something cool. *All you have to do to get on TV is ask.* Just call your local cable provider and ask them how to do a public access show. Generally, you'll have to take a free four-hour class to learn how to use their equipment (even if you already know how) so you don't break it. This can usually be waived if you make your show at home and bring it in on tape.

TIP

When I went to do an interview on Adelphia Cable Access in East L.A. (some of this footage is on the tour featurette on the DVD of *DIY*), I brought my friend Jo Moskow. She rocks, and we were having a lot of fun that day. There wasn't much to this TV studio, just a big room, a blue seamless wall (seamless means curved where it joins the floor so there's no corners to cast shadows), and a few old cameras. And one rack of outdated equipment. But in fifteen minutes, one (not very well) paid guy and two volunteer interns produced a well-done three-minute bit of television (and I did two takes!). Amazing. And this was very low budget. (I must say this for big Hollywood and N.Y. money, and even local news…with a huge support staff, they can produce a one-hour show more complicated than my movie in an afternoon. And my movie took a year.)

So Jo, who I had in-frame of the TV station's cameras videotaping me to use later on the DVD, said when we left, "That's all there is to it? Wow. I thought there was a lot more to making TV." And she's right. There ain't much to it. Performing, acting, delivering the news, it's all just being a human saying stuff into a camera and a microphone and making other people care and believe. There's nothing to it. And somehow there is this illusion that it's a lot more difficult than it is. These people acting and directing and shooting and editing are not rocket scientists.

Not many people watch community access, but a lot of people have the potential to. All you have to do is make something great, put up flyers, get the word out, and you will have an audience. You will also learn a lot. Believe it or not, this experience actually works well on a resume or proposal. Especially if you're trying to work with PBS or other non-profits.

There are a million hours of TV that need filling, a zillion film festivals, unlimited Internet bandwidth, and other untapped venues. People wanna look at stuff, and most of what they look at is, again, stunningly photographed crap. Help them. Help the world. Help yourself. And maybe you'll even do what I did: Make something just for the sake of making it, to tell a story, not for money, and semi-accidentally end up making money.

I once got myself interviewed for the front page of the San Francisco *Examiner*. At one time this would have been a big deal, but *The Examiner* was sold a few years ago, and it now has one-fifth the readership it used to have. However, most people in the sticks, hell, even in N.Y.C. and L.A., missed that memo. Most people outside of San Francisco are still impressed at the mention of that paper's name, recalling its former grandeur. So I put it on the front page of my press kit. Totally honest, but a little tricky.

Figure 11.4 *Danny Plotnick risking a spill to get a cool shot.* Death Sled II: Steel Belted Romeos *photo by Dana Mendelsohn.*

Part of being creative is being willing to take risks and get dirty. In every aspect of the process. From start to finish.

TIP

I have a friend who says he often copies one of his own short movies over the black space at the end of VHS tapes he rents.

I suppose one would have to put a piece of duct tape over the tape-copy prevention slug that's knocked out on the front of commercial tapes to do this, and then remove the duct tape before you return the tape. I'm only guessing though, because this whole process would be illegal and I don't really know how my friend could do such a thing.

---

4. **Thank people**. Always. And mean it. They'll remember you. Most people trying to book things (bands in bars come to mind), act like they are owed a gig. In actuality, the booker is doing *you* a favor. If you send him an e-mail telling him how you appreciate his help, he'll remember you more than the majority who don't say thanks. Or better yet, send a postcard, which you can have fun writing on the road during your downtime. Buy stacks of postcards at truck stops. Christmas cards are good too, if you don't intently dislike Christmas, like some folks I know.

Conclusion

Basically, promoting an independent movie is a combination of making something people want to see, inventing creative ways to get it noticed, and relentless work. It's a lot of effort with no guarantees, but wouldn't you rather take a chance at making a difference than sit by and just passively consume the mediocre mass-marketed media manufactured for the lowest common denominator.

Chapter 12

Selling Your Film

You made something cool. Now share it with the world. Part III.

I didn't make my film to sell. I made it just to make it, but also to communicate with. I was planning on giving it away. Once it was done though, people wanted to see it, and I realized that it would cost money to get it out in the way that I wanted, so I had to sell some copies.

If you make something the world needs to see, the world will actually pay for the privilege of seeing it. Here's how I made a living on my first film. I'll explain the different types of distribution deals. I'll also show you how to find a good distributor, how to negotiate, and of course, how to protect yourself from the sharks.

There are basically three ways that I know of to make money on a film. (Technically, there's also product placement, but I don't do that.)

◆ Selling copies on VHS and DVD

◆ Showing it in theaters

◆ Showing it on TV

You can do all these things yourself, or you can *license* (sell) the rights to someone else to do it. If you do it yourself, you keep all the money and all the control, but you probably won't sell as many copies.

If you have someone else do it, you will have to give up some of the money and most likely some control, but you may sell more copies. People who are in the business of administering these sales are pretty good at it. They aren't usually artists; they don't divide their time between working on art and conducting business. They only do business. Their bottom line is The Dollar, and they don't usually invest energy in things that are only cool for art's sake. They want to make money.

Of course, there are also other people who act like they can do something for you and really have no experience. At best, they are amateurs, inexperienced "me-toos" jumping on the bandwagon. At worst, they are scam artists. These people exist in all enterprises, but especially in art and entertainment, because those fields are filled with beaten-down hopefuls—people who are so used to being rejected that they are sometimes drunk on the idea that someone is finally paying attention to them. The world is full of both types (and I think most of them are in Los Angeles) and both are to be avoided.

If you keep your day job, you'll never have to compromise your art. If you avoid thinking of your art as something in search of "The Big Break," you'll be a lot better off. If you think in terms of a lifetime of small breaks, and of fighting for the art and not yourself, you'll be less likely to get drunk on the soothing words of one of these slippery snake-oil salesmen.

And if one of them ever asks for money from *you*, **run**. That is not how entertainment works. If you have something genuinely worth selling, people will want to represent you for a percentage of money later. They'll even *invest* money in you, up front. If someone wants you to pay money to put out your product and slap their name on it and get some stake in your future output, tell 'em to take a long walk on a short pier. You can pay to put your own stuff out and put your own name on it and owe no one anything. I've done that a lot in my life. I've also had a lot of people invest money in my art.

It's all part of the journey of the flow of life and art and commerce.

Having Someone Else Sell It

Types of licensing:

- When someone pays you for the rights to sell copies of your film on VHS and DVD, this is called *Licensing the home video distribution rights*.
- When someone pays you for the rights to show your film in theaters, this is called *Licensing the theatrical rights*.
- When someone pays you for the rights to show your film on TV or cable, this is called *Licensing the broadcast rights*.

Some companies deal with all three. I like the idea of dealing with separate companies better. You don't have all your eggs in one blender that way, and you're more likely to come out with something intact. And you shouldn't license exclusive rights for any of them if you don't get some money up front.

Broadcast rights are often negotiated on a case-by-case basis. Big channels like Bravo and Sundance Channel will often pay a low six-figure amount for exclusive rights to show a film for six months. PBS might pay half that to show it a few times. Low-end non-profit cable networks like *Freespeech.org* will pay around $700 for non-exclusive use for six months. Local cable affiliates will show it free.

I faxed a cover letter and description of my film to every distributor listed on *Documentary.org* (a very informative and cool resource), and got nothing. The people I finally went with, MVD, contacted *me*, and did so because they'd heard of it because I'd gotten out there and four-walled it. (*Four-walling* is taking a film on tour yourself to non-traditional theaters—bars, microcinemas, homes, anywhere you can get an audience and show it.) Someone forwarded them a URL of a review of the movie in some local paper on one of my tour stops. These things do happen. If something has wings, it'll fly. But you have to get it out there a bit first to give it a chance.

One thing that you should know (and then forget) is that when people license films for broadcast, they usually pay by the minute. So longer films make more money. I knew this and still made a short feature. We made it exactly as long as we felt it needed to be: 55 minutes. We could have made it longer and maybe one day licensed it for broadcast for a few more bucks, but that would have compromised the integrity of the project. If you're out to make a lot of money, go into banking. Or munitions. Or porn. Making art is not a good bet. But if you like art, like me, just make the best art you can.

I have yet to license any broadcasts of my film. It has shown for free on a lot of cable access shows. But most of them bought a copy to do that when asked to.

Pitching Your Project

At one point, I did get a sit-down pitch session with people at PBS who had the capacity to make a decision to actually air it. It didn't get on (they more or less told me it didn't follow standard format enough), but they were very nice.

I wrote a pitch to read to them, and it could have worked, so I'll include it here. Pitch I read to PBS when they asked me to fly up to San Francisco and talk to them:

March 9, 2002. 1 p.m., Film Arts Foundation. San Francisco

Meeting with

C_____ _____ PBS

and

S_____ _____, Corporation for Public Broadcasting

D.I.Y. OR DIE: How to Survive as an Independent Artist is a persuasive presentation of a simple yet powerful idea: It's an accessible and colorful exploration of the methods and motivations of American underground artists.

The project has 501(c)3 status through *Intersection for the Arts* and was begun 11 months ago. Four weeks from today we are premiering it at ATA in San Francisco.

This documentary features interviews conducted in San Francisco, Los Angeles, New York, and D.C. with artists working in a variety of media including music, dance, print, film, and multimedia computer art. They represent diverse backgrounds, races, sexual orientations, and creeds.

The film contains six sub-sections: *Purpose, Integrity, Commerce, Self-Definition, Overcoming Adversity*, and *Giving Back*. The interviewees address each of these themes, qualities that we feel make up what it means to be a successful independent artist.

Some of the artists are well known in the underground scene: for example, performance artist, Lydia Lunch; circus entertainer, Jim Rose; and Fugazi's singer Ian MacKaye. Others are lesser known, but still produce high quality art regardless of a continuous paycheck.

The people included are given face time based on what they say rather than who they are; that is, the unknowns are given equal weight with the famous interviewees. This is to stress that the importance is attitude and commitment, rather than the synthetic fame of the star system.

The style is straightforward, yet visually compelling. We traveled to these cities and interviewed the artists in their own neighborhoods and studios, while they worked, surrounded by their own output. We also used some of their own original music as background in the film.

Since the project searches the common human thread in these artists, it will appeal to a wide demographic, whether or not they are fans of any of the individual subjects. It would also bring PBS affiliates more viewers—fans of each of these thirty-four artists.[1]

1. We shot 40 people. Finally reduced to 30 in the final edit. We were still editing at the time this pitch was made. They had only seen a rough cut.

This movie is not yet finished, but it has already struck a chord. It has been previewed in the *SF Gate* and *Film Threat Magazine*, and we were invited to the Lost Film Fest at Sundance where we showed a working edit of the film.

We already have showings booked at universities, galleries, and theaters in Los Angeles, San Francisco, Berkeley, Seattle, New York, D.C., New Orleans, Detroit, Chicago, Vancouver, Bellingham, and Muskogee.

We've created a robust Web site for the movie which has many links to do-it-yourself resources, as well as a community forum.

D.I.Y. or DIE is Part One of a trilogy I've planned to celebrate the underdog and empower the individual. I also have a treatment for a television series based on the same interview style and thesis: It would be a weekly summit showcasing independent artists for their merit and wisdom.

I guess you could say that when I grow up, I want to be the punk-rock Charlie Rose.

Our documentary ends with the suggestion, "Now go make your own film!" Encouraging this is one of the reasons the movie was made. We view digital filmmaking as the new folk music: the new medium accessible to everyone to help tell their own story. I picture a near one-to-one ratio of content producers to consumers.

***FOOTNOTE

Our interactive platform plan addresses this: We are going to make a DVD that will not only include more highlights from the 45 hours of footage we shot, but also "The 99-Cent Film School"[2] a complete mini-course on how to get started in desktop filmmaking, including free access to resources.

D.I.Y. or DIE shows how artists work, why they work, and demonstrates that everyone can make art. We want to encourage this through DVDs, the Internet, print, and lectures. Digital filmmaking can unite communities and help make individual views accessible to the many.

***FOOTNOTE

I am honored that you invited us to pitch, and it would make my year if this film were picked by PBS.[3]

2. That's where the idea for this book came from. No one was buying at 99 cents. There's a lesson here—don't charge too much for things, but don't charge too little either. Like John John Jessie says, people won't buy if something's too cheap.

3. It wasn't.

Negotiation

My name, Michael Dean, has a number of anagrams. My favorite is "Deal Machine."

I had heard somewhere that a perfect anagram for "Ronald Wilson Reagan" is "Insane Anglo Warlord." I checked this out, and it worked.

An anagram of your name is supposed to say something about your personality, so this made sense. Like "Jim Morrison" equals "Mr. Mojo Risin.'"

I *am* a deal machine; I constantly make deals. I just make sure to make deals that are good for me and don't screw others. That's basically my only rule of business. Since I cannot afford a lawyer for most things I do, I damn well had to quickly become my own jailhouse lawyer. And this took some research and thought.

If you must use a lawyer, *never* use the lawyer your distributor or movie studio or record label recommends when you negotiate with them, and never use the lawyer your manager or agent recommends when you negotiate with him. They will endorse a guy secretly sympathetic to their cause, not to yours.

You should feel free to contact people that the corporation or person has done business with and ask if they'd use them again. Agents, managers, labels, and distributors shouldn't mind you doing this if they're honest. Just don't get the list from them. They'll only give you names of people who will back them up. Do your research and snoop around. This is totally ethical. Don't try to hide it, and know that it *will* get back to them.

A business deal should always be win/win. If it's not, it's not worth doing. I don't look at a good distro (distribution) deal or a record company deal as an employer-employee relationship. I look at it as the artist simply outsourcing an important aspect of the process.

When you get to the point of needing distribution, don't jump at the first offer. They will try to get you to give it all up for nothing. Negotiate a little so you get something for something at least. It's good to talk about the different points in a contract before you get the contract, so they can save the time and money of a revision. It makes them know you're stronger, too.

Of course, if they're shrewd, they *don't* wanna save money on this revision. They want you hungry and feeling like asking for changes is putting them out. They probably have lawyers on staff to do their bidding, so it doesn't cost them extra to do your little bit. They want you to feel like you have to sign the contract the second you get it.

In some cases, agents *are* the bad guys. So are some of the larger piggy publishers, managers, publicists, record labels, distributors, and a lot of other nameless salesmen who extract a pound of flesh. Anyone who separates the artist from the means of production and from direct contact with the audience has a large potential for evil.

When bad agents and lawyers and labels and such want to sign you, they will take as long as possible to deliver the contracts. They know you're starving, want to starve you more, and don't want you to fight anything in the contract. They will intentionally starve you so they can own you easier.

And the company will sometimes not e-mail you the contract to look at and discuss before sending you a copy. They will wait and wait and wait and then overnight you two copies, usually with their own signature on them. Their "buyer's market" moves all are designed to make you desperately sign the second you get the contract.

When courting you, they are ostensibly your friend. A lot of companies talk like, "It's great to have you aboard!" and like it's a done deal, even though they haven't given you a contract, money figure, creative control, or anything else that is specified in a contract. A lot of companies, in my experience, believe that when they decide to hand an artist a contract, it will automatically get signed. Most people probably don't say "no," no mater what.

It reminds me of how, in Hollywood, when they outsource a job on a movie to a particular company, they say they "award" the job. It's just more crap of making people seem like they're being done a favor. THEY will hand you contracts trying to get it *all*. THEY will tell you that they *have to* because the first film/record/book won't make money and they need to invest in you to make a return.

Record labels, managers, agents, and publishers have been telling this lie for decades. Many of them are fat ugly middlemen, who could never make their own art. But somehow they control the central means of production.

I don't like this. I'm not a communist, and I'm not really a capitalist (in the ugly sense of someone who lives to accrue capital by any means necessary). I am a free-enterprise small businessman. I'm not as much anti-big business as I am pro-small business.

The Problem(s) with Contracts

Usually by the time people are offered a contract for anything, they are so sick of starving that they sign it. (And then it *still* takes them two months to get you the money they owe you.) Or artists hire a lawyer and try to fight the company so hard that they end up giving the lawyer all the money.

It's hard to get "them" (agents, managers, whoever) to give it up the way you want, but you can almost always do better than the standard boilerplate contract if you ask. These things are long, written in convoluted legalese, and pretty much boil down to: "We get everything; you get nothing, forever."

I write my own agreements, and do my own lawyering on simple contracts that are for under five figures. I can read, and years of temping in law firms has made me able to read through the horse piles and get to the real deal. When offered a contract, I always suggest revisions, and get some of them accepted before I sign. Most contracts offered are very one-sided in favor of the person handing it to you. I mean, they paid someone to write this duplicity, why would they spend their money to favor you?

I often write one-page agreements and hand them to people, and even companies. Usually I make them slanted a little bit in my favor, figuring they're gonna bargain me down on some points and I want to be able to give them other points in return for keeping what I really want. It's always a dance of give and take. But surprisingly often, they just sign.

CAUTION

Try as hard as you can to eliminate any clause in a contract that is worded anything like this:

"The Artist agrees to defend, indemnify and hold Company harmless from any claims, actions, damages or expenses, including attorneys' fees."

Almost all contracts contain some variation on this. I have always felt that this is an absurd and unfair clause in any contract. Especially the "including attorneys' fees" part. It basically says they can breech and you have to pay *both* sides' expenses to fight the breech.

Note that it is *attorneys'* fees—plural, not *attorney's fees*—singular. It means they can hire a bunch of them and you have to pay for it. They will just keep hiring lawyers until you not only back down, but have to file for bankruptcy.

Some publishers, lawyers, companies, distributors, and agents often try to slip something in the contract that makes it really easy for them to break the agreement, while making it really hard for you to break the agreement.

When people speak of a "three-picture deal" or a "seven-record contract," they often brag about it, as if it means the artist is set up and provided for through the next three movies or seven records. No way! It means if the company wants, they own you for that many projects. They can also drop you after one, and often still own your name and can shelf you, making you unable to work for other companies without providing you work with their company.

They'll also often try to slip something in the contract asking you to relinquish "artist's rights," "Moral Rights," or *Droit Moral.* These all basically mean "creative control." There are different degrees and interpretations of this, but by giving up *Droit Moral*, you are not only giving them the copyright, but essentially also giving them permission to take your name off the work, put someone else's name on it, release it before you think it's ready, repackage it as a larger work and not pay you, make a movie based on it and not pay you, and use it on a CD-ROM and not pay you. They can add product placement, ads, and corporate sponsors that you are totally opposed to, and not pay you for that either. They can put a Bud ad on the back cover of your book or in the credits of your movie. You are also giving up the right of trademark, i.e. the rights to use your title in a series written by someone else if the thing is successful. And not pay you.

When I was in Bomb, I was used as product placement once. I was never told it was going to happen, it came as a surprise (I found out when a friend saw the movie and told me), and I was never paid for it, because forgoing Artist's Rights in the contract permitted it. It's in *Demolition Man* (a Warner Brothers movie). There is a poster of our band on Sandra Bullock's character's office wall. At the time, I thought it was cool, but looking back, I was just a product. I ain't very into it right now. When you're on a major label, you are a product, no matter what they tell you when they're trying to sign you.

Losing and then regaining *Droit Moral* is the idea behind "director's cuts." A studio signs a hungry young director and takes *Droit Moral*. The studio edits the movie as they see fit, even if the director hates it. When and only when the director becomes famous enough to call some of the shots (usually several movies later), he demands retroactive *Droit Moral* in his new contract and gets to re-release the movie the way it should have been in the first place.

In the big Hollywood world, the writer's union has fought for the right to make sure the writer's name is on the movie, under the credit, "Written by[4]." *Written By* is even the name of their magazine. Conversely, the Director's Guild has gotten the right for directors to take their name *off* a project if they don't like the outcome. Their name is usually replaced by the fictitious moniker Alan Smithee. Search "Alan Smithee" on IMDB.com and you'll see what I mean.

I like the contract I signed with MVD for the *D.I.Y.* DVD. It was three pages of relatively plain English, and I rewrote much of it from the first draft handed me. And they approved the changes. The business relationship it defined was very similar in magnitude and complexity to a major label record deal. My contract with my literary agent was five pages, and I rewrote much of it. My deal for this book was six pages, and I demanded and got a rewrite. I didn't use a lawyer for any of this. All of this would have been impossible without a lawyer with a 75-page major movie studio or major label contract.

On the other hand, small guys can be the bad guy too, more often from ineptitude than design. Major labels, although they do everything they can to take what they want, do tend to pay in a more timely manner than small labels run by "good guy" artistic types. This is another example of why I tend to avoid doing business with well-meaning people who don't have their act together. I'd absolutely rather deal with honest "It's all business" business people who run tight ships.

Money Versus Art, and Keeping Your Day Job

One of my heroes is Steve Albini. He engineered the Nirvana record "In Utero." He was basically the producer, but turned down the "producer" credit (and an extra five million or so) and went with what he always uses, the very proletariat "Recorded by" credit. He got a few hundred thousand dollars for that record, and put it all back into his studio. He still records bands he likes for $300 a day.

He feels that the "producer" credit is an overrated, synthetic contrivance that furthers the inequity between the artist and the machine selling the art. He is on the side of the artist, not the big label. And willing to back it up by taking an immense pay cut.

4. Or, in the case of the pilot (first episode, which includes the characters and situations), the credit is "Created by." It's more lucrative to create the pilot than to write the subsequent episodes.

People like Steve putting their money where their heart is, in my opinion, is the first step towards building a more equitable art/commerce system. We need to vote with our wallets.

Steve talks about another good point on the *Extras*[5] section of the *D.I.Y or DIE* DVD: Steve says if you maintain your amateur status, you'll never make decisions you later resent based on your economic needs. You can keep your art *pure*, man.

See his amazing article, *The Problem with Music*, on my Web site.

What's the antidote to all these problems with lawyers, contracts, and selfish businessmen?

1. Like Albini says, not betting your whole life on making a living at your art.

2. Selling it yourself. Relying on someone else to get your stuff out to the world puts you at their mercy. And this tends to make the artist unhappy, and the company very happy. Without fail.

Selling It Yourself

I licensed the home rights to my first film. This is not a likely scenario. You might be better off four-walling your first movie and selling copies yourself. It is not likely that you will find someone to license it unless it's good and has something about it that touches a wide chord.

If you put it out yourself, you keep *all* the money. Just don't go through a vanity press/label/film company. They do a crappy job, and they charge a lot. For instance, for my novel, I did the page layout myself and went to a printer, not a phony "publisher" who would merely charge extra, and then take it to a printer. Same goes double for "on demand" printing. That really is generally where only crappy writers go. You're better off just posting it on the Internet.

When you have a film, book, or record deal, you get to tell your friends, "I have a deal," but you are likely to get only about 2 to 5 percent of retail on each unit sold. And they will want to alter it, chop it up, and own your next book or album. A lot

---

5. *I wanted him in the main part of the movie, but hadn't gotten a hold of him by the time we started editing. He's rather busy, and was difficult to contact.*

of film contracts work the same way. So don't quit your day job. If you have a little money in the bank, you'll have more recourse when it comes deal time.

In Person

When *D.I.Y. or DIE* first came out, I paid out of pocket to have VHS copies made up, and I sold them online and out of the trunk of my car. I sold about 1,100 like that, and made a slight profit, but I sold them on a sliding scale and often only made a couple of dollars on each one. The idea was to get them out, and that's what I did.

Just because most self-published stuff is crap doesn't mean there need be shame in self-publishing. Mark Twain was great and he self-published the first pressing of *Huckleberry Finn*. He also trademarked *Mark Twain*. Smart guy. Henry Rollins self-published all his books. Some of my favorite records were put out by the bands themselves. Same with a lot of films I love.

Online

I also sold copies online, using a PayPal account. These are easy to set up at PayPal.com. Make a Web page with a few photos, a description of the film, and a downloadable trailer. This will help people know what they're buying. Put the PayPal link on the page. Keep the file sizes of the images on the page low, so it will load quickly, even if the viewer is on a dial-up account.

Consignment

A lot of stores, particularly smaller independent movie, book, and music stores, hell, even coffee shops and clothing stores, will take VHS or DVD copies of your movie on consignment. It's kind of a drag to deal with logistically, and involves a lot of footwork and getting turned down, but it can help get the word out there. I've done it a lot, with records and CDs I've recorded, my first novel, and my movie before I got a distribution deal.

You just go into the store and say to the person behind the counter, "I made a movie. Who do I talk to about putting it in the store on consignment?" Find out who to talk to, and when they'll be there. Be polite. The are doing *you* a favor. Come back and bring between one and three copies with you. Ask the consignment person politely if they'd take a few copies. It will help if you have a professional-looking full-color package, and also if you have some kind of poster to hang in the store.

Ask them what their terms are. Usually it's 60/40 or 50/50. (You get 60 or 50 percent of the retail price, and they get 40 or 50 percent.) I usually suggest a retail price that's a few dollars lower than movies from big studios.

Get a receipt, with the terms on it (percentage, retail price, and when you should check back—usually one to three months). *Make sure* that the store's name and the person's name is on it. I have lost money by having receipts with everything on them except the name of the store, and six months later when I find it, I can't remember what store it's from.

It helps if you make posters and put them around town, and put the names of the stores that carry your product.

Go back at the stated date and ask if they've sold them, get your money, and ask if they want to take more. If they haven't sold many, don't get mad. It's not their fault.

An Elegant Concession

The best thing to do is to create something cool that people want, then find a distributor who wants it and will mass-manufacture it. It's a little different from signing it away. You keep all the rights, have the distro of a label or studio, and keep total artistic control. You don't owe them your soul or even your next project. This is the deal I have with MVD and with my literary agent and the publisher of this book. With a deal like this, you can often get between 10 and 25 percent of the retail sales price. I did.

I think that the best of both worlds (doing it yourself and having help) is to sign less-than-totally exclusive project-by-project deals with different people for each facet of distro. For *D.I.Y. or DIE*, I have a different distributor for theatrical and for home video, and I will handle the broadcast rights myself. I also have different unrelated agents for my fiction, non-fiction, and screenplays, again, all on a project-by-project basis.

I got an advance from my distro for the *D.I.Y.* DVD and negotiated (without a lawyer) to get better terms than they offered me. A shorter term, better royalty, kept Canadian rights, VHS rights, broadcast and theatrical rights, and could still sell the DVD through Dischord Records. This took a week of respectful back and forth, and was totally worth the time and effort.

This was inspired as a reaction against my problem with Bomb. We had a manager who we were contractually locked into. He was a dry drunk. While we were on tour promoting our record on Warner Brothers, he got dumped by a girl and started drinking again. He quit managing us, but didn't tell us; we were powerless anyway. He later told me he remembers sitting in his living room in his nice house in the Hollywood Hills (paid for by royalties from when he worked with Jane's Addiction; they fired him too....), drinking booze out of the bottle, and ignoring my voice on his answering machine saying, "Please pick up the phone! We're screwed. The gig cancelled and we're in the middle of Kansas and the van is broken down and it's cold and we can't afford to get towed and we're hungry." (And we were on a major label!)

Negotiation, Continued

How a nobody negotiated without a lawyer to get a good literary agent, on his own terms (a parable for any negotiation):

When I was finishing up my first movie, some kid heard about it. He wrote me an e-mail and said, "I wanna make movies too. How do you do it?" I spent about an hour writing everything I could think of and sent it to him. I kept a copy of it.

A few weeks later, someone else wrote me and asked me how to promote a movie. I spent about two hours writing everything I could think of and sent it to her. I kept a copy of it. I expanded it into a Web site called 99CentFilmSchool.com. People read it, but no one went to PayPal to pay the 99-cent tip I asked for.

I decided to expand it into a book with a CD-ROM. I expanded the Web site into the first two chapters of the book, and took the Web site down. I called the book-in-progress *$30 Film School*.

I studied online how non-fiction is sold. I realized that it is often sold with only a proposal and a sample chapter or two written. I wrote a 28-page proposal following this format exactly. It included my "credentials," which basically were nothing more than an interview on the front page of the *San Francisco Examiner*, and the fact that I had made one film, had booked a shoestring tour, and I had a lot of moxie.

I wrote a two-page query and e-mailed it to 40 agents that I found from online research. Most never wrote back. Ten wrote back and said, "Not for us." Six wrote back and said, "Please send us your proposal." I wrote back and said, "e-mail or snail mail?" Four said, "e-mail;" two said "snail mail." I sent them all out that day.

Two days later, one e-mailed back and said, "We love it and want to represent you." They attached a contract. I checked them out online. They didn't have much of a track record, and I considered them a last resort in case the other five said "no."

I e-mailed the other five agents looking at my query and said, "So-and-so sent me a contract, but I wanted to talk to you before I signed it. Have you had a chance to look at my proposal yet?" The ones who had opted for e-mail all said, "No, but I'll look at it tonight." Knowing that someone else was interested lit a fire under them.

I looked at the last-resort agent's contract and noticed that they wanted me to sign over my entire literary career, forever: non-fiction, fiction, screenplays, articles, etc. I e-mailed them back, "I have a lawyer who is acting as my agent for screenplays, so those rights are not available to sign over. As for everything else, I would be much more likely to consider this if you did this on a project-by-project basis, rather than everything I write. My old agent did this for my novel." (This is true. But he never sold my novel and we went our separate ways. I self-published my novel, D.I.Y. style. I didn't tell them that he didn't sell my book, but I wasn't lying.)

Three of the five other agents wrote back and *all* said, "We are interested in representing you." All three sent contracts. (The two who didn't reply were the two that had insisted that I send it by snail mail rather than e-mail. They had just gotten my stuff and were not operating at Internet speed...a common problem with people in the publishing industry...still stuck in an all-paper mindset. They lost out because of it. One later sent me a contract, two weeks *after* I'd already signed with my agent.)

All three of the contracts wanted me to sign over my entire literary career, forever: non-fiction, fiction, screenplays, articles, etc. But two of the agencies were heavy players with huge batting records. One was my absolute number-one choice of all—Waterside. They are one of the most powerful agents for non-fiction how-to tech books in the world. They even agented *HTML for Dummies*, which I bought in 1996 and learned Web design from.

I wrote back to all three and again said, "I have a lawyer who is acting as my agent for screenplays, so those rights are not available to sign over. As for everything else, I would be much more likely to consider this if you did this on a project-by-project basis, rather than everything I write. My old agent did this for my novel. And right now you and three other agencies (I named them all) have all sent me contracts, and one has agreed to do it only for this project. If you did that also, it would likely sway me in your direction."

My number-one choice wrote back and said "O.K." and sent an amended contract. (I wanted them so badly I would have signed their original contract, but played my cards right.) I read the contract for a day, thought about it, signed it, and faxed it to them on a Saturday, e-mailed them confirmation, and snail mailed them the signed contract.

So, this is how I got a great agent, on my terms, in a week. In all of this, I was humble and calm, not cocky, and I didn't lie. Everything I told everyone was true, and I got what I wanted. This is a good working model for negotiations. But the only way you can do this is if you have some kick-ass art to back it up.

Keep in mind that negotiations aren't always events. They are sometimes conversations. And these conversations can happen in one sitting, but usually happen over a period of time. And people are more into negotiating with people who respect them than with people who are trying to "play them." Always go for win/win, my friend, win/win.

Let the Company Do Its Job

Don't be high maintenance. Once you get a deal of any kind, with anybody, don't bug them more than you have to. People will love you and want to deal with you on your next project if you are low maintenance. If your project sells copies, and you never bother the company, and they just send you your checks, they'll love it. If you bug them every two weeks, ask them how it's selling, ask for more advances when you're broke, nit pick and just interfere in general with them doing their job, they'll hate it and not want to work with you next time.

Conversely, don't be afraid to offer suggestions if you have something that can really help. I often send MVD names of magazines that need a promo copy or something to do to help promote my movie, and they often take the suggestion. You'll have to figure out on a company-by-company basis who wants how much proactive input on your end. Hopefully, they do want some input. But keep in mind, people who market for a living know their job, and hopefully, your market. You shouldn't even work with them if they don't.

Conclusion

If you make something the world needs and have good motives, the universe will work in your favor. It's up to you to figure out what story needs to be told, and how to tell the story in a way that has some basic human thread running through it, regardless of the obscurity of the specifics. If you do that, have hustle, don't compromise, and don't screw people over, you might make your money back.

You might even make a living.

$30

Chapter 13

Touring

You made something cool. Now share it with the world. In *person*. Don't play an instrument, but always wanted to go on tour? You don't need a band! I booked a 40-city tour for me and my film that paid for itself. You can too. One of the greatest pleasures of my life has been going on tour to show my art. It's more fun alone with a film than with a rock band. I've done both.

Rock Bad, Flick Good

The difference between touring with a rock band and touring on your own with a movie. I remember the first time I took my film on tour. (This is also *called four-walling* a film.) It was five shows on the East Coast. I flew out, rented a car, and drove around from Portland, Maine to Washington, D.C., with stops in Boston, New York City, and Providence.

When I went on tour with the film, it was just me. I loved it. I was amazed as I compared it in my mind to touring 10 and 15 years earlier with a rock band. I helped pioneer touring self-booked with an alternative rock band before the term "alternative" even existed, before "The Circuit" existed. Now I'm helping pioneer taking a digital indie film on a similar tour. And I'm even playing some of the same rooms.

When you tour with a rock band, you huff and puff lifting heavy equipment. You do a sound check. You scream your lungs out, leap around, and look silly. Then you go eat at a gas station and come back and actually play the set. You scream your lungs out, leap around, and look silly again. For people, if you're lucky. At the end of the night someone hands you between $75 and $300. You get into an old van that gets nine miles to the gallon and constantly breaks down. You fill the gas tank. You split the rest of the money with three or four guys who hate you. You go to a party where three or four guys who hate you compete for some ugly girl's attention.

You go sleep in the van alone.

When you tour with a film, the club already has the VHS screener that you sent them (a *screener* is the copy of the film they preview to see if they want to book you… most people booked *D.I.Y.* without even seeing it or after seeing just the online trailer), so even if you don't show up, it gets shown, and they still pay you. You lift nothing. You show up in a new rental car that gets 40 miles to the gallon and never breaks down. Ahhhhh. That new carcinogen smell.[1] You pull a little DV tape out of your pocket and stick it in the deck. The projector lights up. Your movie shows; you sit back and relax. Then you wow people with your intelligence, wit, insight, humor, and humility in the Q&A period. This can actually be much more intimate than playing rock. At the end of the night someone hands you between $75 and $300. **You stick it in your pocket.** Afterwards, you go to a party where everyone wants to meet you and no one hates you. People want to be a part of what you have. And because filmmaking, by nature, deals with different crew members and actors instead of the same three jokers you have in a band, you can actually include folks you meet on tour in your next project.

Getting Gigs

This is the tricky part. You have to do your research, because there isn't really a "circuit" yet. I remember when I had been playing in bands a while, a magazine called *Maximum Rock N' Roll* came out. (It's still around—see my film's review on the CD-ROM.) It had constantly updated punk rock booking numbers and "scene reports" (local updates of each town) monthly. That magazine is probably the reason punk rock exists now. And it was (and is) D.I.Y. as all get out. I loved it.

There is not yet a thing like that for film, but there will be.

How I Got Gigs for My Film

I basically just did research, approached rock clubs, and asked everyone who ordered a copy of the film where it could show in their town.

◆ I e-mailed rock clubs, schools, churches, and friends. I looked on www.lostfilmfest.com and contacted the same places they were showing. I just hustled up a tour out of nowhere. Also, www.microcinema.com has a searchable nationwide database for places to show

---

1. They now say that that new car smell can give you cancer: It's all the bonding materials, plastics, and glues they use to make the car, giving off fumes as they dry.

◆ One little trick: When you can't find where to show your movie in a particular town, call the college radio station and ask around. Those cats know *everyone*.

◆ Don't send your listing and film to people who would never book it. Don't make a totally commercial rock band thing and send it to punk rock anarchists. Know your audience, and know your journalists.

◆ National Press. A lot of local press covers predominately local news. But you can make your film local news on a national level if you take it on tour and go to each town. The letter I send out for booking was more or less cut and pasted from my original funding application proposal written before I started the film, with a few updates. This also served as the basis for my press release. Your press release should state quickly and easily what's unique and why they should care. Keep it short. Booking people read a lot of these things and they have to be made to care by just reading the subject line.

◆ I wrote a stock Booking Letter and sent it to anywhere I could think of. I got a surprising number of favorable responses, usually having a show confirmed within days, sometimes within hours.

I wrote this query and kept the file on my desktop for easy access. I constantly cut and pasted it into e-mails, with slight variations, throughout the booking and promo process.

I put the "featuring interviews with" as the subject line, in a small font so it would cut and paste into an e-mail as a subject line without any line break and therefore not get cut off:

Would you book a Documentary with Lydia Lunch, Ian MacKaye, Mike Watt, **J Mascis**, Jim Rose, **Jim Thirlwell**, Richard Kern, **Ron Asheton** and more?

D.I.Y. OR DIE: HOW TO SURVIVE AS AN INDEPENDENT ARTIST

An arts documentary by MICHAEL W. DEAN

FEATURING interviews with:

Ian MacKaye (*Fugazi*), Lydia Lunch, Mike Watt (*Minutemen*), J Mascis (*Dinosaur jr.*), Jim Rose (*Jim Rose Sideshow*), Jim Thirlwell (*Foetus*), Richard Kern (Filmmaker), Ron Asheton (*Stooges*), Dave Brockie (*Gwar*) and more.

Project has 501(c)3 status through San Francisco's *Intersection for the Arts.*

> OVERVIEW:
>
> A 55-minute film on the methods and motivations of independent American artists in different genres and mediums.
>
> A celebration of the Underdog. This film profiles a fascinating group of icons and unknowns working in various media including print, film, graphic art, performance art, and music. The three dozen interviewees are mavericks who operate outside of any "studio system," are beholden to no one, and produce influential, quality art regardless of a continuous paycheck.

I sent everyone I could a description of the movie, with the subject line being names of people in the film, to get their attention. Someone asked me if this was antithetical to the anti-star stance of the movie. I say not at all. It gets people's interest, while also telling them some of what the movie's about. Then they can get in and see the real depth of it later. You gotta grab people.

Star power is power. Use whatever power you can to get seen. It's not hustling if you do it with love and joy and humor. Find a power. Sex power is power. A friend of mine made a movie about her fellow strippers and got it shown everywhere, based on the fact that it had strippers in it. It got repeat showings based on the fact that it was good.

Following Up on Bookings

Once things are booked, I do follow-ups. I send the people an e-mail with a link on my page that has all the links for promoters in one place. Downloadable press release, bio, flyer, contract, press links, trailer, and downloadable photos in both low- and high-rez for Web and print. This saves them a lot of work. Making someone's job easier makes them happy. They will like you and help you more.

Once the showing is confirmed (via e-mail before they send the contract back; the contract is just a formality), I immediately add the showing to my Web site and send them that link in an e-mail, in which I also ask for e-mail links to local press, both small punk zine stuff and big stuff. I make a press release with that city's showing on it and e-mail and fax it to all those people. I do this again two weeks before the actual show, or right before I leave for tour, whichever is later.

I try to set up, or have them set up, a radio interview in town for the day I'm there.

I save all these booking and promo contacts in my own database for the next tour also.

One suggestion on radio interviews: Jim Rose told me to never say a show is sold out (especially on the radio), even if it is. They can always get more people in there, and if not, it's not a bad idea to have a bunch of people out front who can't get in. Sounds rude to let them come down, but they will meet each other and, at least, buy copies of your art, network with each other, and make it look really good to the promoter and press and the public. And often the promoter will even add a second show the same night.

Film Festivals, Museums, and Universities

Other places to four-wall films are film festivals, museums, and colleges. Film festivals cost money to enter, and I've covered this before. Ask them to waive the fee. If it's in your town or you're planning on going regardless, you can also volunteer to help out if that will help get them to waive the fee.

My film gets shown a lot at colleges and sometimes at museums. Colleges and museums will sometimes ask me to come speak to the class also. I've been flown up and paid to speak at the Yerba Buena museum in San Francisco, paid to speak at CalArts Valencia college, and paid to speak at the Los Angeles MOCA (Museum of Contemporary Art). They showed my film also at all of these.

They usually contact you, but if you have a film that would be very applicable to showing at a museum or art school (an arts documentary is a good bet), you can send them a polite e-mail, but don't be surprised if they don't book you. Museums are usually by invitation only. Typically, someone in their inner circle sees your flick and recommends it to them.

Museums and schools sometimes pay an "honorarium" if you speak, usually $150. Sometimes they only pay it if you ask. Sometimes if you're really polite, they will pay it to you in advance. If you are asked to present and speak at a school or museum, know that it is an honor. A huge honor, and make sure you let them know that you know this. Especially before you ask for the money, and especially before you ask for it in advance.

They will need your social security number to cut the check, and they always pay by check, never cash.

Museum stores might carry your film. As far as I know, only one carries mine, the store at the Whitney in New York. Again, it's a huge honor.

When people call or e-mail or ask in person on tour for free movies for their university library or to broadcast non-profit, I ask them to buy a copy. I do this respectfully. If they can't, I often will give them one. But you'd be surprised who is able to do this. I've had several universities give me between $35 and $100 for a single copy to keep in their library or to show to classes. You may have to fill out some paperwork, give your social security number, and wait six weeks after sending the video to get paid, but so what?

If they have the money for this, you are not being creepy by asking. And $100 allows me to mail away a lot of other tapes for promo and to people who cannot afford it. It can't hurt to ask.

Touring at Film Festivals

SUNDANCE/LOST FILM FEST SCENE REPORT

January 16-20, 2002

By Michael W. Dean

Sent out to my e-mail list.

Reprinted by Mike Watt on his e-mail list.

Hey kitties. I'm sitting in our hotel room in Park City, Utah typing like a war correspondent using my Handspring Palm PDA and its collapsible portable keyboard (full-sized keys, but it folds over twice to the size of a Palm). Little Mike, Peter Spicer, and I are here to show a rough cut of our new D.I.Y. documentary (*D.I.Y. OR DIE: HOW TO SURVIVE AS AN INDEPENDENT ARTIST*) at the Lost Film Festival, one of the smallest and definitely the most independent non-Sundance festivals at Sundance. (There are ten or so other festivals that go on here the same week: Slamdance, Tromadance, No Dance, Slamdunk, Lap Dance, etc.)

Most of these festivals repute to be "non-Sundance" or anti-Sundance or such...but basically, we're all just here, it seems, to try and grab a tiny sliver of speck of a spotlight reflected off the glory of the big fest. I mean, if we didn't care about them, why come to Godforsaken Utah and almost die in a blizzard in winter...why not go to Kansas City in July? The weather would be better, and hotel rooms would be easier to find. (In fact, Little Mike and I are thinking of starting one called "Fogdance" in San Francisco. I just bought the domain name, Fogdance.com.)

Sundance, if you don't know, is a huge "independent" movie festival started about 15 years ago by Robert Redford (The Sundance Kid...get it?). It was really an independent fest when it started, and does show great films, but has been co-opted as a sort of Farm Team market for big-money Hollywood movie companies to come find the next big thing. A lot of films got "discovered" here, from *Slingblade* to *Blair Witch*...the money is snowballing down the streets of this little white bread sleepy mountain town annually, and that ain't a bad thing. It is pretty shmoozie and funny though. I mean, why fly 700 miles to freeze and hustle people who live two miles from you? (I recognize a lot of people here, and I'm not talking about the celeb sightings we've had, like John Cusak, Jason Priestly, and Buck Henry, but the people that I see on the street every day in Los Angeles. Oh...there's that guy I always see at the Fish Taco stand....)

So we get here (wearing the cute matching faux leopard-fur ski jackets that Little Mike had made and embroidered with DIYOD.ORG over the vest. Peter Spicer had a matching hat) and find out that Pete (a cameraman on our documentary) has had his luggage lost by Greyhound. (Little Mike...one of our interviewees and a big conceptual help on the doc, and I flew here and are flying back to Cali. Peter is flying back to PDX, but took a bus here...24 hours...from San Fran, to save a few bucks.) Two days later, after a million calls, Greyhound has found his luggage. We drive in a blizzard, literally, to Salt Lake City (40 miles) to pick it up, and his $2,000 camera has been stolen. We file a claim, they say it will take up to 30 days to even begin to process, and that he may only get $250 back. This is very bad and wouldn't happen on a plane.

The main D.I.Y. lesson I am learning this week is that if you try to save too much money, you lose both money and effectiveness. A friend printed 1,500 handbills for us for free at her work last month, and mailed them to us third class at my request...they never arrived in time. We had to spend $80 at a Kinko's here to duplicate that effort. I should have mailed her six bucks and had her send them first class. We thought about staying with friends to save money on a hotel room, but I'll tell you this: in sub-degree weather, I am gonna do a much better job handing out flyers to strangers on the street (which is illegal in Park City...so it takes some judgment calls) on six hours of sleeping on a hotel bed, even if my buddy is sharing it with me, than I will after two hours of sleeping on a floor at a stranger's house in a room full of people trying to party. And the hotel has a hot tub. I just spent an hour in it. I'm all pink, mellow, and feel like I'm on Valium. It's delightful.

So...there's all these Hollywood phonies here and wannabe Hollywood phonies here...but the truth is, we talked to a lot of them on the street and many are very cool, funny, and smart. We hand them a flyer, they hand us their flyer, and some actually seem to care about our film.

We are filming everything here with Little Mike's camera...we're working on footage for the DVD that we plan on making for our film...sort of a "making of the making of" thingie...we did film a lot of little skits with other filmmakers...where we'd hand them our flyer and they'd crumple it up, etc. We filmed Pete trying to get his camera back, us in the hot tub, Little Mike rolling in the snow in his swimsuit, interviews with the "man on the street" etc. It's really fun.

Let's see...we stood in front of documentaries from the "real" fest and Shpammed them (surreptitiously handed them flyers for our thing, went inside, and laid them amongst their flyers, etc.)....gave a copy of our film to Spike of the *Spike and Mike's Twisted Animation Festival.* (He was interested because his friend Jim Rose is in it.)

Met a guy from San Fran who is gonna let us use his drum & bass stuff as background music in the film. Met a really nice guy who wants to show our film at his college in Washington, met a guy from 7th Art Distribution who wants a copy, have a pocket full of business cards, will sort them out tomorrow. The two stars from *American Movie* were at our party too, but they spent about three hours locked in the owner's office, doing God knows what.

We went to an amazing Lost Film Fest presentation at the University of Utah over in Salt Lake. (Most of their showings, including ours tomorrow, are in Park City, at an Internet cafe that holds about 50 people tops.) This was in a huge beautiful hall that looked like the place you would receive the Nobel Peace Prize. And you could see the Olympic stadium out the window. By the way, they are making all the students double up and finish the semester two months early to clear the dorms for better security at the Olympics.

The Lost Film Folk are cool. It's the only fest, I believe, that doesn't aspire to replace Sundance. I think it is more out to crush the entire Hollywood system. They travel around the country doing this at many film fests and are even going to Cannes in France. (Our film is going with them.) They are the only people that I know doing something like this on these terms at this level, and it's pretty darned groovie. They are a collective and run everything by group conscience. Kinda bizarre...picture punk rock mixed with Robert's Rules of Order...sort of what I call a Chaocracy, but they get the job done.

We did an interview on a student AM station (the aptly named KUTE) in Salt Lake City yesterday...it was funny...the transmitter was so weak (one watt) that we could barely pick it up on the rent-a-car radio when we were pulling into the parking lot. I swear we could get it until we drove by a tree and it blocked the signal. But they also broadcast on the Internet. The host, Natalie, had questions from listeners for us from as far away as Germany. And she was great. Usually at interviews you talk for 15 minutes and they throw you out. We talked for 45 minutes, and we finally had to go because we were missing a good movie downstairs in the Lost Film Fest. Natalie was very cool and did her research more than most interviewers I'd ever met. She asked me questions from stuff many levels down on the Web site.

So, here we are freezing in the land of God and multiple partners, to show our humble little film. After coming back from Salt Lake that night, we got tickets (from the Lost Film Fest folks) to a party for one of the other fests in Park City. At the top of a snowy mountain (pretty dicey drive) Slamdance Film Fest had rented out an old silver mine, and had an open bar free for all with about 1,500 people in attendance. It was like the hipster high school prom in Hell. We got there at 1 a.m., and it was nuts, fun, and out of control. I went outside to use the cell phone though, and they wouldn't let me back in. I waited for 45 minutes in zero-degree weather, walking to stave off cold. (The air here feels like icy knives in your lungs. And a Palm Pilot's character recognition gets pretty abstract.) I spent a while waiting for Pete and Mike to come out with the car keys. It kinda sucked. I killed time calling people, and was so spun from the contact drunk of being around that, that I left a friend a message that I was at Tromadance. I was actually at a Slamdance Fest party. I forgot. I watched about eight drunk alterna-jocks get thrown out for fighting while I was freezing.

Saw some great films in Park City...esp. *Gigi* (from 9 to 5) (at Lost Film Fest), *Straight outta Hunter's Point* by Kevin Epps (San Fran Doc by ex-gangster...amazing, insider footage that no one else would ever have been able to get...telling a moving real life story of life in San Francisco's most notorious housing project ... see it Feb 6 & 7 at Red Vic in SF)... *Dotcom: Hot Tubs, Pork Chops and Valium* www.sneakykings.com (mockumentary comedy...funny as hell...about a failed dot com's rise, fall, rise, fall, fall, fall, etc.)....And the urban drama called *Bloody Crisis* was great: www.bloodycrisis.com.

On Saturday, the last night of Sundance, our film showed to about 40 people in folding chairs, while across town, future film millionaires received awards. It might seem nuts to fly all that way and pay about a grand for a plane, hotel, and rental car to do that, but it was worth it in every way. We had a blast. We met cool folks and saw great films. Spammed people with flyers to get the name out. Gave out lots of VHS copies of the film and some CD-ROMs of the trailer to cool folks. And I talked to a bunch of people who saw it and got comments for the final edit. Sort of a punk rock focus group. And I got back rubs from a cute girl.

We went to some other non-Sundance showings and saw films in HUGE rooms that must have cost a fortune to rent, and we were the only people there. We didn't pay a cent to show ours and feel we made out okay, despite the obstacles.

After the Lost Film Fest closed down, Kevin Epps hung out with us and slept on our hotel floor the last night. We got up really early and drove to the airport. Extra security soldiers with M-1s....more cops......I'm waiting for buttprobes for all.

LATER> I am sitting at an empty information kiosk that says "Joint Task Force Military Reception Station for 2002 Winter Olympics." So far, no one has asked me for information. I probably won't BS if they do, as airport security is frighteningly high. They are rubbing bags and your hands with a swab and then putting the swab in a portable gas chromatograph to sniff electronically for bomb stuff.

Can you imagine if my band, Bomb were still together and on tour? Could you imagine trying to take a big Anvil road case with "BOMB" stenciled on it through security? Hell...we could tour with Anthrax and have extra fun.....

Met a cool guy on the plane home who actually had a film in Sundance. His film is a short called *Casablanca*. (Really!) We talked, I gave him the last VHS of our film and we played with our Palm Pilots, beaming stuff.

Back home:

I got back to L.A. at 5 p.m. Sunday on two hours sleep. My skin is dry and itchy[2] from the cold mountain air, but I'm happy. I just slept four hours. It's 9 p.m. and I am getting up and starting my day.

2. It turned out to be scabies.

Why I Do Booking Contracts

The only reason I do contracts (and I never hassle people for money if the place closes down or whatever) is to put it in writing. I can't count the times my old band drove 500 miles to do a gig and the guy at the door says, "Who are you?" and I say, "We're called Bomb. Your boss, Bugsy, booked the show." And they guy at the door sez, "Bugsy ain't here and there's no show tonight."

I even do contracts for free showings, to make sure I know what I'm getting into. For instance, so that it actually happens, and so they can't charge money at the last minute, or add a corporate sponsor, etc. (I always put a "No corporate sponsor surprise" clause in any contract for a public showing.)

Why I Would Rather Do Shows at Commercial Theaters and Bars than at Squats Run by Well-Meaning Anarchists

When bars flake, I can sue them. I never have, but I could. Anarchists don't sign contracts (and if they did, I think it would be inherently non-legally binding somehow) and it ain't cool to sue the "scene." The reality of making this kind of tour work, however, booking plane tickets and rental cars, and betting your rent you're gonna break even, is that even one cancellation can mess it all up. That's why I book in bars. Sad that I have to depend on the financial regularity of a place that dispenses legal liquid drugs to keep things flowing.

Well-meaning anarchists who keep their dogs on strings hate money and don't pay well. And they get upset if you ask them to. They often have an unrealistic view of money and hate it because they don't earn it. Their parents usually support them.

PUBLIC SHOWING AGREEMENT

I hereby agree to screen Michael Dean's documentary, *D.I.Y. OR DIE: HOW TO SUR-VIVE AS AN INDEPENDENT ARTIST* in my town _____ at _____ (venue) on the date(s) of _____.

I will provide a projector that can project from VHS (or from RCA inputs from a DV camera that Michael Dean will provide if he makes the showing in person).

I will provide some advertising (amount consistent with what is usually done for this venue) and tell all my friends.

I will charge a low price at the door (4 dollars or less if the movie is the only feature of the evening…6 dollars or less if other films/bands/whatever are featured). I will set aside a fair portion, _____ % (must be between 50 and 90%) of the proceeds to send to the film's director, Michael Dean.

Michael Dean will try to make the showing personally to present, but this is not guaranteed.

If Michael is at the showing, he will be paid immediately after the Q&A. If he is not, I will mail the *D.I.Y. OR DIE* film portion of the night's proceeds in check form to:

MICHAEL DEAN, 1634 W. Sunset Blvd. #222, Los Angeles, CA 90026

The check will be made out to MICHAEL DEAN.

It is possible to show it additional nights without an additional contract if Michael Dean is contacted by e-mail and approves.

A copy of any promo materials for the night will be sent to:
MICHAEL DEAN, 1634 W. Sunset Blvd. #222, Los Angeles, CA 90026.

All posters, ads, and promo material must contain the line, "D.I.Y. is a fiscally sponsored project of Intersection for the Arts." and also should have the D.I.Y. Web site, listed.

Michael Dean will try to make it in person, but if he is scheduled and cannot make it, the film will still be shown and Michael will still be paid.

If Michael Dean comes in person, he will bring some short films and trailers totaling 30 minutes that he will be permitted to show before his film.

NO CORPORATE SPONSORS WILL BE ATTACHED TO THE EVENT WITHOUT WRITTEN PERMISSION OF MICHAEL W. DEAN.

THE DAY AFTER THE SHOW, I WILL E-MAIL MICHAEL DEAN AND TELL HIM HOW MUCH HIS SHARE IS AND HOW THE SHOW WENT. I WILL MAIL HIM HIS SHARE WITHIN TWO DAYS OF THE SHOWING.

Payment may alternately be made via PayPal.com at 99 Cent Film School

Signed _____

Date _____

Please sign this contract and mail to:
MICHAEL DEAN, 1634 W. Sunset Blvd. #222, Los Angeles, CA 90026

(Thank you for spreading art and goodness. MWD)

Let's Go...

I book my shows and then buy my plane tickets. I book rental cars or a reliable ride around the region I'll be visiting. I map it all out on Mapquest or Yahoo and print out the directions and all gigs and contact info and rental car details or load it into my PDA.

When you pack for tour, travel light. Use the old Boy Scout packing rule: Take the absolute minimum you can get away with taking and lay it on your bed. Then only take half of what's on your bed.

I "advance the show": Two weeks before the event, I e-mail the promoter (often it's a kid but usually a bar or college) a confirmation that I'm still coming. Then I call everyone and reconfirm the shows a week ahead of time, two days ahead of time, and often the day of the show.

This is very important. Sometimes things get cancelled if you don't. And sometimes they cancel anyway, and you wanna know about it, so you can scramble for a replacement, or just not drive out of your way and show up expecting a show. And don't rail into people if something cancels that's beyond their control. Crap happens, and a lot of the people who book these things are not professionals. They are just people into art trying to help you, nothing more.

I make these calls from my cell phone. It's important to have a cell phone plan that has real nationwide long distance. Also keep in mind when on the road that it is illegal in some states to talk on a cell phone while driving. The car rental place or AAA will know the laws. And if you are driving your own car, make sure it's in good shape, and that you have AAA. You might need it.

My friend Sandy Swears by AAA and says it's a great idea if you do much traveling. They give you free maps, and map out a TripTik, which is better than just mapping it on Yahoo. You get discounts on hotels and restaurants, they'll tow you for free, and even cover your insurance on rental cars.

Etiquette

Keep appointments, and arrive there early. Some people don't do this, especially with people they consider unimportant. Treat everyone equally well, treat everyone as though they're important, because they are. A college radio DJ on a tiny station is as important as someone interviewing you for NPR, not just in a karmatic and respectful sense, but in a careerist sense. You never know what that little guy will be doing in five years, what his station in life will be. (He may be *running* NPR.)

Allow extra time when driving; show up early by a couple of hours the day of the show, park your rental car, and go in and be nice. Don't take out on them the fact that you've been stuck in interstate traffic for hours. Remember that it's an honor to get paid to show art. Be friendly, come in, hang out, chat. Sometimes they'll feed you, but don't expect it unless you talked about it ahead of time. If the showing is in a restaurant, I usually ask for dinner and put it in the contract. And I make sure I have the signed contracts with me. Often, the person who signed it and agreed to the terms is the booker, and only there in the day. Having the contract to show to the night manager can be useful.

Test the equipment. Set it up and put your movie in. Test the public address system for sound, and also the microphone you'll be speaking on. I do this if I'm showing in a basement to 10 kids on a television set, or to 500 people in a university theater. **It's all equally important**. There were times when my band played for 10 people and we kicked ass as if it were 1,000—and good things always came of it: write-ups in cool magazines, good word of mouth, more gigs, even record deals. Even if none of these things happened, we just did a great show for 10 people who remembered it. And often, years later, there were 100 people claiming they were at that show.

Again, thank everyone. Just do. In person. On the phone. Via e-mail. Before, during, and after. These people owe you nothing. They are doing you a favor. Tell them that you appreciate it. Mean it when you say it. Thank people after showing your film. Thank people for reviewing you. Thank the people who buy a copy of your movie. Thank people who interview you. Thank people who put you up.

Crossing Borders

Most countries require you to file for work permits if you're gonna be making money there. Indie filmmakers don't need no stinking permits. We, I mean they, just go, and look straight and normal, and act like tourists. We, I mean they, FedEx product ahead to the gig in another country. You can't cross the border with product…they will, at best, charge a tariff, and at worst, not let you in for trying to work without a permit. And we, I mean they, have the name of a person we, um they, say they're visiting on the other side, in case Dudley Doright gets on the blower to check the story.

TIP

Note: It's very hard to cross borders if you have warrants. You may end up blowing your whole tour. Take care of this stuff well before you leave.

Question and Answer Period

You should do a Q&A after the film. This allows people to know you and your work better, and also makes the evening feel more like an *event*.

Often, at first no one will have a question. Just start talking a little and then ask if there are any questions. Once you've answered one, others will follow. (No one likes to go first. You might even have a plant in the audience for the first question the first few times you do this!)

Do a very short introduction before the film. They don't know you or your art yet and ain't gonna have much patience. Keep it under 40 seconds. And, very important, don't do too long of a Q&A after. Ten minutes if you are a great public speaker, five if not. Leave them wanting more. Even if they want more than that, stop at 10 minutes. (Less is always more. See the movie *Tao of Steve*.) Some people will want to leave, and you don't want them to feel trapped by the one guy who wants to know everything. He can talk to you later, as you're selling copies, or take you to his house and bug you later as you're trying to sleep.

Have copies of the movie to sell after the showing, and announce that they will be for sale after the Q&A. Announce this before the film and again at the start of the Q&A. I usually sell them "$5 to $100, sliding scale" and average about 10 bucks. That way people smile, and laugh, and the guy with only 5 bucks can still get one. And occasionally, someone gives you twenty or even two twenties for a tape. This is a good example of Art Karma in action. You make the stuff available to everyone, and end up with the same bottom line as if all you cared about was the bottom line.

(I like helping people, by the way. One of my main reasons for being on this earth is to hook people up. Doing art is only a way to meet more people to facilitate that. I'm a professional catalyst. A matchmaker for people and resources. Art is simply the delivery mechanism.)

Whenever I show my film in Los Angeles or at any event where there are industry folks around, I always preface the Q&A with "So, I do have copies of the film for sale on VHS. They're sliding scale, $5 to $20. Now I know people are gonna say to me, 'Hey man, I'm in the industry, I can help you out. You should give me a free copy.' And I really can't *give* any copies away today. But I have a special rate for industry people: (pause). $200."

It also helps to have someone else sell copies so you can talk and not have to transact at the same time.

At the Q&A, people will try to give you their art. You will end up schlepping too much stuff. Politely ask them to mail it to you. And use a P.O. box for your public persona. You don't want fans showing up on your doorstep. It sounds like it would be romantic, but trust me, it isn't.

Accommodations

The Q&A period is also a good time to mention that you are looking for a place to stay, if you haven't made previous plans. I usually say, "It's time for my punk rock hotel reservation" or "I need a floor plan" then ask for a place to stay. They giggle and then put you up. Sometimes several people will offer and you can have them bid, seeing who has the best accommodations. Don't get cocky though.

My sister says, "You can stay anywhere you want in the world rent free if you can converse intelligently in the native tongue and do dishes without being asked."

And obviously…put the people you stay with on the guest list. Don't be stingy in general with the guest list. The five bucks you miss here and there will come back to you in karma and green karma (actual money) a thousand fold.

Occasionally I'll spring for a hotel or motel. It's worth it to be well-rested and fresh to drive.

Touring the $30 way ain't like staying at the Ritz. Often, *everything* ends up being D.I.Y.—Like, I'll stay at a stranger's house, and wake up to find them gone to work, with a note that says, "Make yourself at home." I have to forage my way around the kitchen, find coffee, and use toilet paper as a coffee filter. (In some punk rock anarchist houses, I've had to use coffee filters for toilet paper.)

I recommend staying with women, not men. Women are sweeter, and they have cleaner houses and better stuff. Girls have great skin- and hair-care products. And I recommend you don't try to do them. If you must have interactions like that, let them chase you (ibid...*Tao of Steve*, but ignore the last 10 minutes of that cool indie flick. That's the dumb Hollywood ending someone tacked on to this otherwise masterpiece.)

When you're on tour, the way to keep from losing things, other than packing light, is to always make sure everything is in one pile. When you're done with your toothbrush, put it in that pile. Change your socks? Put them in that pile. And even so, take an idiot check (last look around) before leaving anywhere.

Tour Diary Entry

July 6, 2002

Vancouver. Doing two nights at the Blinding Light Cinema. Really cool, well-run microcinema.

Last night at the showing of the film, I introduced it and when the projectionist started it (showing off my crappy DV camera) the camera heads were dirty and the image played really crappy with horrible digital distortion. I yelled, "Stop it," and she stopped it. I announced to the packed house (80 people) "I'll fix it." They laughed. I ran up to the booth, cleaned the heads, rewound it, ran back, and she started it over. The cool thing about this film is that the title and the thesis of it have a built-in excuse for anything that goes wrong. In a way, when things go wrong, as long as the showing goes right, it kind of adds to the experience.

I had a blast today walking around Vancouver with Kimberley, the cool single mother I met at last night's showing. We made handbills and handed them out as she walked me and her young son around the city. It was a gorgeous day.

When I did the Q&A tonight, I said, "I wanna do a little punk rock market research. How many of you are here tonight because I handed you a flyer on the street?"

Not a single hand went up.

I said, "Well, that was three hours well spent." They all laughed.

But in reality, it really was three hours well spent. Kimberley and I had a blast and I saw a lot of the town on this idyllic warm day. And the flyers all had the film name and the URL on them, and got the name out.

What would I rather do? Sit in the hotel room? What would you rather do? "Eat cheese and watch TV"?

Doing flyers is imperative....even/especially on tour. It gets the name out in the public eye. If you get into town a day early, or hours early, you can do them yourself. But I will say that, from experience, flyers don't get people to a show nearly as much as a good mention in the local paper. That's what brings them in. But you should flyer also, as that reinforces the name in the people's eye.

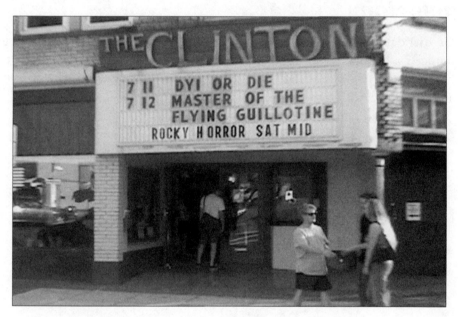

Figure 13.1 *Clinton Theater marquee and their interesting spelling.*

Never Rest

Promotion doesn't end once you get out of town. On tour I am constantly working on everything. I have no support staff and, as I've said, most of the people who say they want to intern are totally flaky. I end up spending at least an hour a day online and on the phone once I'm actually on tour. (As opposed to my 12 hours a day at home.)

At the end of the tour, you've probably at least broken even. If nothing else, it's an amazing free vacation. And even that vacation can progress into more, as film always builds on itself. If you're fair and nice and treat people well, and make something cool, each project can get a little bigger and better with more people wanting to do things for you. **Film is built on relationships**. At all levels, from the smallest indie short to the Hollywood blockbuster, it's all about people. Don't mess up. Treat people well. There's an old Vaudeville saying "Be fair to everyone: You meet the same people on the way up that you meet on the way down." Ain't that the truth....

Conclusion

Getting out and rocking the world with your art is no longer just the privilege of musicians. Make a great film and you can live like a rock star, with all the perks but none of the heavy lifting. Going on tour is a true American rite of passage, and now you can do it too.

Chapter 14

Copy Protection and Rights

Big companies spend millions of dollars to try to keep people from copying their movies, music, and software. Here's why it's a losing battle, why you shouldn't bother, and how some people get around it (and how to copy protect your own stuff if you absolutely insist).

With recent advances in technology, it is easier than ever to make near-perfect copies of media files (music, movies, photos, and even books) and trade them with friends and strangers instantaneously over the Internet without paying the artist or record company/studio/publisher.

I can understand why content producers hate this. A part of me doesn't like it. As someone who has worked sporadically as a professional musician for years, I can see the "They're stealing from us!" mentality. But a much bigger part of my psyche is a music *fan*. And fans *love* getting music and movies for free.

I think that artists should embrace these technologies. Even rich artists. I think the only people who have something to lose are the middlemen—record companies, music publishers, book publishers, film studios, and distributors. Their role is increasingly being eliminated or replaced by technology. And of course they're the ones screaming the loudest.

Tinseltown Trademarked

At the end of a movie I was watching on DVD, in the credits it said, "Hollywood Sign trademarked by Hollywood Chamber of Commerce." I thought this was funny…I never realized that this sign was anything more than a sign. I guess it's almost a character in a lot of films to the point that it needs to be paid and credited, and it even has an agent. It's more important than any actor. Hell. More important than *all* the actors. This sign is the vanity license plate of the Beast.

I thought this out loud to myself, alone in my room late at night as I realized it. Then I wanted to take a screenshot of it to e-mail to a friend in Canada who was at that moment working for free on really cool updated credits for my film. I took a screenshot of it and tried to paste it into Photoshop and couldn't edit it because it was copy protected!

Someone has even bothered to invent copy protection data for a paper medium. A friend said he scanned a page in a book to put an image in a non-commercial PowerPoint presentation. When he scanned it, the scan said "Copy" in big letters across it. Wow.

Keep in mind that copy protection involves not only the medium, but the player—Photoshop and this scanner had encoding to prevent copying. This is put in by manufacturers responding to pressure, law, or their own vested interests. Pretty soon it may be impossible to simply buy a computer without it including a lot of protection that will prevent me from doing things even with media I own the copyright on!

My point here is that I understand the protection of intellectual property. I also understand Fair Use, and I feel that locking editing capacity is locking out Fair Use. My beliefs about computers are that they are freeing and enabling and I resent any attempt to prevent me from having free and total control.

Using the Hollywood Sign in my little movie on the CD-ROM is not trademark infringement. It's satirical commentary, which is covered as Fair Use by landmark precedent cases representing recent interpretations of the free speech facets Constitution of the United States.

Why It's Okay to Copy My Movie

I feel artists should be fairly compensated, but I also feel that most media costs too much, because most of it is not going to the artist. Albums cost almost $20. Hollywood blockbusters cost nine bucks to see in a theater. This is because you aren't just paying the artist, you are paying for the first-class travel, hotels, and escort services for a bunch of chubby bald middlemen too.

The chubby bald middlemen used to say, "Yeah, but whadaya gonna do? You're just losers complaining. We own the means of production." But the Internet, personal computers, and especially Napster and all its ugly stepkids (like Kazaa) is giving Mister Have-A-Cigar a run for his flabby billions.

I have this friend, who says, "When software costs 50 bucks instead of 500 bucks and albums cost 5 bucks instead of 20 bucks, I will stop bootlegging them." Both are pressed onto round pieces of plastic that cost 20 cents to manufacture in the quantities that major labels/studios/companies use. Choke on that for a while.

This is why I released the DVD for *D.I.Y.* with no copy protection and titled it *D.I.Y. OR DIE: Burn This DVD*—to encourage people to copy it for personal use. I was protesting this crap.

I was partially inspired by a friend, Eric Bickernicks, who made a good movie that he couldn't sell and he offered the *entire thing* as a free download. I *could* sell my movie. (I'd sold 1,200 copies on VHS when I started working on the DVD, which doesn't sound like a lot, but it *is* a lot to sell in four months of an indie film. Trust me. This is good external success, and good internal success.)

The Universe doesn't care how many records you sell. The Universe cares how sweetly you sing. Art helps people. So, pass it on.

I used Napster a lot when it came out. And yes, I did go buy some of the records I "previewed." I thought it was very tacky when Metallica made such a stink (especially after bragging in the liner notes of *Garage Band Incorporated*[1] about their leaner days of making copies of their fave tunes on cassette).

Architecture is the only art form more expensive than Hollywood filmmaking. Film footage is only called "footage" because they price it by the foot. That's why they make Hollywood films appeal to the Lowest Common Denominator. They **must** guarantee an ROI (*Return On Investment*, i.e. profit). Hollywood. Heck. I'll never work in this town again. But who cares? Actually, I've *never* worked in this town.

So… copy-protection is a technical attempt to enforce a legal procedure. It used to be that movies were copyrighted, the studios made them, and we paid to see them. But technology has changed that. Starting with home video cassettes and on up through DVD burners and Internet peer-to-peer file-sharing schemes, all are threatening to undo the legal world (from the viewpoint of the Industry), or restructure the status quo, depending on how you look at it.

My intention of selling thousands of DVDs with no copy protection and an invite to bootleg for personal use was strategic. I wanted to get the movie out, and I also

---

1. *One of the most truthfully named rock records ever. Metallica used underground indie cred (credibility) to ride the major label wave. Metallica hasn't had indie cred in over a decade, but I guess no one in the organization passed that memo on. They did hire consultants who gave them an image revamping for the album* Load. *I think the consultants basically said, "Dress and do your hair like the Red Hot Chili Peppers." And they did. That's pretty much when I stopped liking them. I always liked that they looked like white trash mullet rednecks from the East Bay. That was part of their charm. Ah, committee thinking.*

was willing to sacrifice a few bucks in royalties to help foster more dialogue on piggy corporate tactics.

Screw copy protection. It is an affront to the Universe. Invented by selfish plump prigs who sell art, but don't create it or enjoy it. Whoever has their art on the most people's hard drives when he dies, wins. Anything less is grossly materialistic. Art is free. My DVD is a chain letter to the heavens.

Sure, I want to make money on this. But more than that, I wanted to get it out in the world. I feel that this movie has a purpose. Call me naïve, but I feel art has the power to change.

Why the World Needed Napster and Kazaa

Hollywood makes movies. Most of them suck. Some of them are great. If they all sucked, I wouldn't mention them. But I love movies and I hate to see squandered potential. Europe makes great films because they care about art in Europe. Stunningly photographed crap; 92 percent of all films in Hollywood are Stunningly Photographed Crap. Good films are the exception. There are tons of horrible movies with huge budgets. Most of them, actually.

Whenever there is a system in place, an industry, the thing has to keep producing product to keep everyone employed. This is why Microsoft keeps adding features I don't need to Windows, and charging me more money. And it's why Hollywood keeps making crappy movies where the cocaine budget for one day, hell, one *shot*, is 10 times the full production and promotion budget of indie movies that have made the world a better place.

There is a theory called *Gaia's Garden* that says that Mother Earth protects herself: If there's too many people, the Earth provides a flood. Or an earthquake. Or a new disease.

I think that there is something similar at work in entertainment. A correction, if you will. It started with Napster. This plucky little peer-to-peer file sharing application was invented by one teenage stoner dude working alone in his dorm room. He only made it so he could trade MP3 music files with his pals. Yet it propagated so quickly that it scared the crap out of every powerful executive at every major record label. Some of them lost their jobs. A lot of them lost their expense accounts. The Universe was trimmin' the fat, though she chose Beavis as her vessel. That is a beautiful thing.

It's a good example of how to make something you do travel the world at viral speed. The world *needed* Napster. Napster didn't require much of an advertising campaign. And if you make movies the world *needs*, the world will do some of the work for you. And that generally entails making movies with some kind of social conscience. Which is why I am trying to instill/encourage/nurture some in you.

Of course, Napster got shut down, but others, like Kazaa, took its place. *The Man* will not be able to keep shutting this stuff out because, as the hackers say, "Information wants to be free."

> **NOTE**
>
> A call to programmers: Basically, the way "they" shut down peer-to-peer services is by serving papers to whoever is running the central database. There are P2P services without a central database (like Gnutella), but they search very slowly, as they have to go out and read actual nodes on the Net, not a central database. How about some sort of *distributed* database? One that would be segmented across several machines, and would move periodically in a sort of shell game of cheese and mouse?

Bandwidth is increasing and compression schemes are improving and soon DVD-quality movies will be able to be shared like this. I watch TV cartoons on my computer all the time, and it doesn't cost the companies a dime. It probably makes them money because I get excited about them and brag to friends, and that helps make the shows more popular.

I've already seen lots of people distribute a whole feature-length movie as a 300-meg file in Windows Media format. You can fit two of those on a single CD, and only takes a few minutes to download on a standard DSL line. And it shows full-screen on the computer and looks and sounds good. Not great, but good.

The Man will keep coming up with encoding algorithms to attempt to protect their crappy movies, and lone-nut teenaged hacker kids in their bedrooms will keep breaking them. The hack for the DVD lock, only four lines of code, was posted on the Internet days after first public use.

See the problem is this: It's all breakable. Even if you can make the disk uncopy-able (and you can't), as soon as it's played on a system, you can copy it. Picture this: If it's coming out of a speaker, you can put a microphone in front of it and record it. Now picture that your sound card and video card in your computer can do the same thing, in better fidelity. It will be in the analog realm for a microsecond, but it will look and sound great.

This is nature's way of leveling the playing field. Information *demands* to be free. You can still disseminate information for a living and make a plumber's wage if you're lucky.

The world *is* changing.

Sooner or later, books will be the only media not worth bootlegging. No one has come up with a portable screen that's comfortable to read on, and it costs more to print one out on your computer printer than to buy one. And they aren't worth counterfeiting in small quantities. You need to print several thousand of them to get the price break to make it worthwhile. And in our illiterate society, that isn't worth doing and risking jail the way it is to some for music, movies, and software.

Actually, my friend Newt just got back from traveling in Southeast Asia, and said he did see bootleg books, in English, being sold by street venders. Mostly just travel guides and best sellers like Tom Clancy so far. They were photocopied, and hand bound by sewing the sides. I guess labor is so cheap over there that they can make a profit.

Bootlegging is cool, in theory, in some situations. You get to steal from the richest men in the world, and get away with it.

Not all software companies are rich. Many I like and mention are not. And I like that they gave me free stuff. (But please know that I would never recommend a bad program.) Not that I couldn't hack most of this stuff myself, but it would be nicer, I think, to have the real version....not that a hacked version screenshot would look different...any more than a girl looks different after she loses her virginity. (Or does she?)

Adding Copy Protection

Okay. Since I'm supposed to be teaching you all aspects of making films, now that I've told you why you shouldn't use copy protection, I'll tell you how to do it if you want to. (Blaine helped with this part. He doesn't like copy protection much, but part of his bread and butter involves putting it on disks.)

There are three basic breeds of copy protection.

1. CSS Digital Copy Protection and Rights Management—tries to prevent people from copying a DVD and also to stop them from playing the MPEG-2/Audio off of the disc.

   Adding CSS to a project in authoring is just a few simple clicks to specify the settings. It's different in every program, check the menus. When the Disc Image is output to DLT it is created at 2054 bytes per block as opposed to the standard 2048, with the extra 6 bytes left empty for the CSS Key to be added later. Then the replication plant is alerted to CSS being used, and when they offload the DLT and before replication, they actually insert the CSS Encryption Keys into your pre-formatted Disc Image. You have to pay a royalty of a few pennies per disc for CSS.

2. Macrovision Analog Copy Protection—this is from the VHS days, and inserts a code in the actual video stream that is read by VCRs and TVs. The result is that copies play back with visual distortion ranging from pulsing colors and chroma to a totally unwatchable image, depending on the level of Macrovision applied (1, 2, or 3) and what generation the copy is. You also pay a few pennies per VHS for Macrovision.

3. DVD-9—Right now, this is sort of the ultimate in copy protection, since you can only burn 4.7GB of data to a DVD-R (=DVD-5) a DVD-9 therefore has too much data to simply dupe to a blank.

Removing Copy Protection

Oh, and since I'm supposed to be teaching you all aspects of making films, now that I've told how to do copy protection, I'll tell you how one could break it, if one were so inclined.

1. CSS: DeCSS and things like DVD X Copy (programs which are illegal to download, but can be downloaded freely on the Internet, along with information on how to use them, strictly for theoretical understanding

only) will defeat it. Of course, I wouldn't advise you to do anything illegal. I mention this only from an academic position.

2. Macrovision. You can beat it with a $50 box from Radio Shack-type stores or online called a CopyMaster.

3. DeCSS can split a DVD-9 into 2 DVD-Rs.

Rights

Any course on creating media should include an explanation of legalities, rights, and violations of rights. A lot of filmmakers don't know the difference between a copyright, a trademark, and a patent. Many writers can't tell slander from libel, or know the difference between fair use, parody, and defamation. This stuff is also related to copy protection, bootlegging, and that whole battle. Here are a few terms that may help you understand this corner of the legal world.

Slander/Libel

Saying or publishing hurtful and/or untrue things about people. Slander is usually spoken, libel printed. Though if it's said on radio or TV, it's considered published, then usually libel. The full legal nature of these is complex and outside of the scope of this book. I'll just point out that they exist. A good place to start is the *United Press International (UPI) Stylebook*, which has a good section on slander and libel. (See also "Fair Use.")

Copyright, Trademark, Service Mark, Patent

Most people get these all confused. Obviously, copyright is the most important to a creator of media. But I will give a brief layman's explanation of all. (This covers only the United States system. Other countries have their own offices, and U.S. protection may or may not be covered by reciprocal agreements.)

Copyrights are registered by the United States Copyright Office, which is a division of the Library of Congress (www.loc.gov/copyright). Copyrights are granted to one's self; the Copyright Office merely registers this in case of dispute. This makes it easier to sue in case of infringement.

You copyright something simply by putting "Copyright" (or the little © symbol), your name, and the year, like:

©2002 Michael W. Dean

or

Copyright 2002 Michael W. Dean

and then publishing it to the public.

It costs very little money, about 30 bucks, to register and is easy to do. Some say you can do a "Poor man's copyright" and just mail it to yourself, and use the post-mark to establish date in a dispute. This is not recommended. It's too easy to alter a letter. A copyright is good for the life of the author plus 70 years. That's a long time.

"Copyright, a form of intellectual property law, protects original works of authorship including literary, dramatic, musical, and artistic works such as poetry, novels, movies, songs, computer software, and architecture. Copyright does not protect facts, ideas, systems, or methods of operation, although it may protect the way these things are expressed."—From the U.S. government copyright site. (www.loc.gov/copyright/)

This excerpt is used as Fair Use, although much government stuff is, by nature, copyright free if credited. (I always check the "legal" or "copyright" link on a site before citing it elsewhere.) It belongs to the People. And that includes you.

I have never registered a copyright. I get a work done, put my notice on it, and then make at least a thousand copies and sell them. This is, for me, proof enough. I've made a lot of good art, albums, books, and movies, and no one has ever claimed my work as their own.

Many people get too hung up on this and spend too much time working on this and not enough on the art itself. Complete or partial works are rarely stolen. (*Ideas*, which are not copyrightable, sometimes are). I know a budding novelist who paid to consult with an attorney on how to copyright that novel she has big plans to write someday.

There is a pay service for common-law copyrights that some people use called ProtectRight (www.protectrite.com). I have used it for screenplays, but only after a year of working on them daily.

TIP

Regarding use rights as it relates to your writing: When writing scripts, it is a good idea not to specify particular popular songs, as the rights may not be available. Don't put, "Music: Tainted Love by Soft Cell," put "Music: 80s new wave dance hit." This is a moot point if you are just making films to show in your bedroom, but once you get past that stage, you should think in terms of rights and permissions. Work small, but think big.

Patents and **trademarks** are issued by the United States Patent and Trademark Office (www.uspto.gov). They are harder to get and cost a lot more money. A search has to be done to prove that an existing patent or trademark is not being violated. Done without a lawyer (it is recommended to use a lawyer) a trademark costs $375. A patent can cost over $10,000 with legal expenses. (You can register a provisional or temporary patent for 75 bucks, but it's only good for a year and you have to get a real one or it's gone.) A patent lasts between 14 and 20 years, and they are rarely renewable. A trademark lasts 15 years, but can easily be renewed forever if the product is actually being sold. You cannot "park" a trademark for a non-existent product the way you can park a domain name.

Trademarks cover company names or names of services, and the marks associated with them. Patents cover "*any new and useful process, machine, manufacture, or composition of matter,*" and they also cover designs….the shape of soda bottles can be covered by a design patent.

The connection between domain name registrations and copyrights is so complicated that there are whole law firms devoted exclusively to this aspect of intellectual property law.

Servicemarks are trademarks for services rather than for things. Like an online music community or a DVD mastering company or a talent agency.

Fair use is the legal term for referencing small amounts of someone else's copyrighted or trademarked work in your own work, without permission or payment, for parody, criticism, educational use, homage, or cultural reference. It is protected by the U.S. Supreme Court, but is open to endless interpretation. Contrary to popular rumor, there is no set amount of a work that can be used. (Some used to say "seven notes of music is okay," but sampling in hip-hop changed this.) It's up to the lawyers. And lawyers cost a lot of money.

In the end, cover your ass, don't steal, and don't let the lawyers win. I avoid them at all costs, because they cost all. Sometimes you have to use them, but you can also choose not to buy into the whole system:

The above "Don't Steal" advice may seem like a contradiction in a book advocating peer-to-peer file sharing, but it isn't. I'm all for honorable use. It's okay and not a moral crime when it's a victimless act. I guess it would be more accurate to say, "Don't steal from humans." I think it's okay to steal from heartless conglomerates that care about profits but not individuals. In fact, I consider it self-defense. They want to crush you and use and abuse you. Fight back. And "If you do steal, don't get caught." Publishing the work of another without permission and credit is a real moral crime, and also one likely to get you caught. Copying a friend's software program or album or movie for personal use ain't gonna anger the universe, and you are also unlikely to get busted.

Some people are pretty dumb about what constitutes fair use. If you clearly violate trademark in a title, name, work, or especially a company (including a band name), of course they're gonna come after you. If you call your band "Malibu Barbie," of course you're gonna get a cease-and-desist letter from a law firm.

The general punk rock ethic that I have always heard goes something like this: "Dude…they can go ahead and sue us! We don't have any money and we could use the free publicity." But generally the reality of it is that they just crush you with legal action until you give up. They can certainly make it so those thousand CDs you pressed with your own money are illegal to sell in stores, and you'll end up bulldozing them into a landfill to keep out of jail.

If you're truly creative, it's totally easy to come up with your own names for stuff, so why bother glomming onto the name of some crappy company you don't even like anyway?

Basically the test for infringement is "Could a consumer versed in that field of trade be confused?" (The term is "dilution of trademark"—where the violator is diluting the strength of the brand name the name owner has spent a lot of money making strong and recognizable.) Sometimes, however, people will come after any and all uses. Huge corporations generally will. They have hundreds of lawyers that they pay full time anyway, so it doesn't cost them extra to pursue *every* case. That's part of how they become huge corporations.

I understand the protection of intellectual property, in theory. But I don't think one has to be piggy about it. For instance, Dischord Records does not copyright their materials. The individual bands sometimes copyright the songs, but the label does not own the copyright, nor do they add a notice on the records if the band doesn't. And they still make a living. See?

Bootleg, Counterfeit, and Pirate

These are often used interchangeably, but are a bit different. A **bootleg** is copyrighted material being released without trying to make it resemble any existing product. An illegally released recording of a live concert would be an example. A **pirated** version is a copy of an existing work without attempting to make it look passable. A cassette tape of a record, a burned CD of software, or a hand-labeled VHS or home-burned DVD of a movie would be pirated. A **counterfeit** tries to look like the real thing. A record, software disk, or movie that attempts to duplicate the commercial packaging to pass for the original would be an example. So would a fake Rolex watch.

Ratings

This isn't really an issue of rights, but it seemed to fit here more than anywhere else because it is a matter of a private board appointing themselves to determine where you have the *right* to present or sell your art.

Ratings seem like a scam to me. You have to pay the MPAA to get them to rate your movie. The ratings (G, PG, R, NC-17) are trademarked and you can't rate your own movie. Movies that come from studios that tend to play ball with the MPAA tend to get milder ratings than similar movies from a different studio that is more defiant.

The ratings reflect a system of morals that I don't subscribe to. Sex is out, violence is in, etc. It's extremely conservative and doesn't have anything to do with reality or protecting children in any realistic way. So I didn't rate my movie. However, if you don't have a rating on your movie, a lot of places (like Blockbuster) won't consider taking your movie. They also won't take an NC-17 movie. I say just put movies out unrated and let the world deal with it.

Conclusion

The locks are off the door, the cow's out of the barn, and nothing's going to put her back in at this point. Do your part to dismantle the vast faceless monolithic multinational conglomerates that tyrannize individuals, discourage originality, and elevate mediocrity.

Superior information wants to be free. Help it be free. Know your rights and the rights of others, but in the end, do what *you* know is right.

Chapter 15

Closing Arguments

Ah, Grasshopper....you have done well in *$30 Film School*. But before you go out into the world and kick some serious artistic back, we've got a few last things to run by you.

No technique here, you've already mastered that. This is the part where you think about what you're about to do, and why you're gonna do it, before you go do it. That will train you to be able to do it without having to think about it while you do it. (Still with us?)

Also, we'll have a little on the people you'll run up against who *don't* want you doing it....

Integrity

Doing the right thing is its own reward, but sometimes it has instant and obvious rewards in the real world. Contrary to common opinion, people who do the right thing don't get crushed; they get appreciated. Here's an example:

I had *D.I.Y. or DIE* booked into the Echo Park Film Center in Los Angeles. This is a tiny non-profit organization set in a storefront where the owner, Paulo, teaches poor kids from the neighborhood to make films. He doesn't charge for this. And they do a lot more—they show films, do cheap movie camera repairs, sell parts cheaply, provide a film and book library, and act as a community drop-in center. They're all about doing the right thing. It's a few blocks away from my house, and I often attend their $5 Thursday night screenings of films made mostly by filmmakers from the neighborhood. The screening room holds about 40 people, tops.

I got an offer to show my film in one of the larger independent film fests in Los Angeles, one that has a good bit of cachet among the industry, one that is often a stepping stone to distribution. But they didn't want me to show at Echo Park Film Center until after they showed it. I called up Paulo and asked him if we could change the showing to two months later. He said, "It's already in the schedule.

Let's just do it." I e-mailed the bigger film fest and told them, "I am gonna have to decline your festival. Sorry. I need to keep my word with Paulo. I can't screw over the little guy for the bigger guy."

The film festival lady surprised me by sending back an e-mail that said, "All right. You're a good man, and I like the film a lot so I'm going to break my rules and still play it."

See? The Universe was watching out for me.

Dealing with Criticism

My novel came out two years ago and got some great reviews. It also got some horrible ones. It is said that you should read the bad ones once and the good ones twice and not think much about either.

My famous cinematographer friend told me that critics are often only telling you what you should have done differently because they are telling you to make the movie they would have made. And that they should just go make their own movie. That's the *reason* that at the end of my movie, it says, "NOW GO MAKE YOUR OWN MOVIE."

Everyone who sees my movie has an opinion about something I should have done differently. Usually they want me to add more of one person and delete another person. If I removed everyone that I've been told to remove, the movie would have been about three minutes long….just the intro and the credits.

Critics do their job: They criticize. They write reviews. And sometimes they're lazy. It's a lot easier to destroy than it is to create. It's easier to write a bad review. I know. I've written them.

With reviews, don't believe your hype. You know what you are. Some guy bitching into his word processor doesn't really know what you are.

You can even use adversity as a marketing strategy—get people to cheer for the underdog. I didn't set out to do this, but when newspapers looking for an angle started doing it, I began to let them. (They *always* need an angle or they won't write about you.) Soon, the worse things were for me, the better it looked to the press.

The *D.I.Y. or DIE* Hollywood premiere was at the Knitting Factory a block from Grauman's Chinese Theater where *Star Wars Episode Two* was premiering. I liked it...the world's biggest movie and the world's smallest were debuting on the same night a hundred yards apart. The papers liked that too.

Some papers ran with this stuff and exaggerated it. They also exaggerated my non-industry stance as an anti-industry and anti-establishment stance. An article in a paper in Maine made it sound like I was gonna pull into town for my showing blasting Minor Threat, flipping off the citizens out the window of a stolen police car with my arm around the mayor's teenage daughter.

Whatever. I just wanna make art.

Dealing with Resentment

If you get nasty e-mails or phone calls from people, don't reply. If you get *any* success, the envious will come out to feast on you. Some will even be people you thought were friends.

It's hard not to reply, but don't. Save the e-mails in a folder if they're threatening (you may need them later as evidence), but don't respond. And don't make the mistake I did of writing to reviewers and complaining. There's always that thing of "Bad press is better than no press," and "It's not bad press as long as they spell your name right."

And when you resent someone, you are admitting that, in some way, he is better than you.

If you end up consumed with anger over this junk (like I have been at times), try wishing that your foes have the good things you want. Write your resentment down and burn it. Meditate. Take your mind off it by listening to someone else talk about her problems. Better yet, help someone else solve a problem. Do anything but give into it. Just keep making art and know that the more commercially successful you are, the more people you are seen by. Some of these people are insane. Famous people living righteous lives still get mentally unstable folks stalking them. I've even heard that having a stalker is considered a badge of success. Regardless, when someone's trying to get inside your head, don't believe the lie. Ignore them and they really will go away, most of the time.

Hollywood: Ignoring the Call

Like the Karate master who teaches the student to fill his head with wisdom before using his head to break bricks, we will give your soul a tune-up before you go out into battle. You are David going up against the Goliath of the entertainment industry. You'd better damn well be pure of heart first. We offer examples and encouragement on how to keep your soul clean while doing business with heartless bloodsucking devils, or how to simply sidestep that entire system:

> Los Angeles, an endless sprawl of suburban subdivisions spread out in a massive grid encircling Hollywood, the fraudulent Mecca of egotistical schemers. Everyone's got a grift in Hollywood, or working hard on devising one. The city is paved with broken hearts, shattered dreams, dashed hopes. Everyone expects their fifteen minutes, not realizing their minor brush with greatness will pollute the rest of their tortured lives, creating an almost unbearable torment whose mantra cries out for what could have been, what should have been, what will never be.
>
> —Lydia Lunch was used with permission
> From her book *Paradoxia*

There used to be a punk band from Texas called The Big Boys. They would end their set with the singer yelling into the microphone, "NOW GO START YOUR OWN BAND!". This was my *inspiration* for putting "NOW GO MAKE YOUR OWN MOVIE," at the end of *D.I.Y. or DIE*. (One reviewer even said that putting that in made the film "Critic-proof." I loved that.)

As far as being happy with making art on a small D.I.Y. level, I am. I think that the problem many people have, everywhere (but *especially* here in Los Angeles) is thinking that the world owes them a living for their talents. And they are willing to do *anything* to get into The Machine in order to have a million-to-one shot at big stardom.

I think that many folks believe that a fairy godmother, in the form of some corporation, is gonna wave her funded-debt magic wand and whisk them upwards in a tornado of easy money, acceptance, fame, happiness and love.

If that's your game, know that the odds against you are astronomical. You should buy lottery tickets instead. But if you do art just for the fun of doing it, you will be successful no matter what. And who knows…The Universe might surprise you.

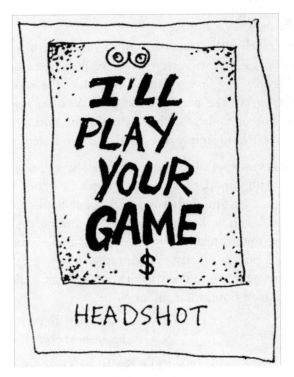

Figure 15.1 *Sticker by Lisa Freedom.*

Only do art full time if it's what you *have* to do. Don't do it to make money. You'll fail. If you want money, go into advertising. If you want security, join the Army. (When asked for his advice to young musicians, Frank Zappa said, "Get a real estate license instead.")

We don't do art for money. And that's its own reward. Our day-to-day connection with the infinite is deeper than it would be otherwise.

In *$30 Film School*, there are no overnight successes. I think that an honest art career involves a lifetime of small triumphs and daily hardships. It gets better as things go on, but there is no point where you "make it." You're making it all along. And projects lead into projects. There is no point (until you die of old age) that you can really say, "I'm done, I've succeeded."

The band Nirvana toured eight years in a van before you ever heard of them. (But not before I heard them.) And they were friggin' *great*.

If anyone thinks I had overnight success because I got some attention on my first film, consider what I do; that attention was the culmination of a lifetime of making all kinds of art. Making movies uses all the skills I'd already developed: writing, photography, music, editing sound, and much more.

People always ask me, "What's next for you as a filmmaker?" But I may not make another film. I didn't set out to be a filmmaker. I don't define myself as a filmmaker. I just learned filmmaking because I needed to make one particular film.

Art is a process, a means—not an end. And I like the little level I'm operating at because I don't have to compromise.

A friend of mine has a Hollywood-level distribution deal and gets into the stores and is shown in big theaters. But she has little control over how her movies are marketed, what's on the DVD cover and the poster, and can't pick the movies that play before her film when it shows. I have total control and always show my friends' short features before my film.

I would seriously rather earn ten grand making something great[1] than selling it for ten times that much and having it optioned but not produced at all, or worse yet, ruined, by a big studio.

I like small-but-good scenarios better. The band Fugazi intentionally charges about half the national average for their shows. The label they run, Dischord Records, sells their records cheap, and they still make a good living. And they are rewarded with a fierce faithfulness amongst fans. I think this is a good business model.

Pearl Jam even tried to replicate this on a huge level, combating the monopoly that Ticketmaster had. Pearl Jam lost a lot of money, but in my mind, did the right thing.

I think the Fugazi/Dischord business model should be studied in Harvard Business School.[2] Seriously. It is American Free Enterprise in the true meaning of the phrase—the Jeffersonian sense—the *old*-school sense.

---

1. By the way, sm(art) girls know. *They know that a guy who makes $20,000 a year making cool art is about a thousand times sexier than a suit who makes $200,000 a year marketing other people's art.*

2. Must be something in the air. I wrote this sentence and two months later came across an interview with MacKaye in Salon.com where he says someone he knows told him he should go speak at Harvard Business School.

I feel that encouraging people to copy my movie is my duty as an American, to encourage people to get back to how America used to be—ideas and people before profits.

If someone (a person, not a company) wants to make a few copies of my film, I'll get by somehow. They're not taking bread off my table: They're probably actually putting bread *on* my table by saving me the cost of making and distributing copies.

What's good for art is good for America.

And I *love* America. That's why I complain.

I also feel that the message of my movie is more important than I am. It's certainly more important than my making a big profit.

Hollywood will never adopt this. It's so expensive to make their movies that they can't. Heck, their movies cost so much that even the artists who make them have little control over the art they create.

Don't Hustle People

Have hustle, but don't be a hustler. Just do your thing. Help anyone for free; volunteer on other shoots. Do lights, sound, camera, acting, editing, whatever needs doing. Don't think, "What can I get from this?" Just help people out. It's art karma, and it will come back, if in no other way, as knowledge. The more you know, the better you will be as a director.

I live in L.A. and see the hustle every day—in the industry; at low-key "indie" parties, even in line at the supermarket. It's ugly and obvious. A lot of people here just look at everyone as potential steppingstones, not actual humans. They will only be nice to people they can get something from. This place is surreal—They even sell *Billboard*, *Variety*, *Cashbox*, *The Hollywood Reporter*, and *Hollywood Scriptwriter* magazines at the 7-Elevens.

I've been to slick Hollywood parties too, but I was out of place. It was the "beautiful people," and I ain't really one of them. Some seemed really cool; some seemed to have nothing but a big hustle going on. Hustle, as in "con." Maybe they'd even conned themselves. That's the first step in being able to con others. Lots of business cards trading hands, in a sick desperation disguised as a calm and stylish, "We don't need the work" demeanor. The first question out of everyone's mouth is "What do you do?" which basically means, "What can you do for me."

Sometimes I don't get this town.

I *hate* that Hollywood thing of pretending people you met once or twice are your friends. It's very common. And it's BS.

Films and rock & roll are magic and make you think you know the stars. But you don't. Like I said, my test is "Did they/would they invite you to their wedding? Did they help you when you moved?"

If a star didn't invite you to his wedding, don't tell people that you are friends him.

Work Versus Selling Out

The hacker thriller movie *Swordfish* begins with John Travolta's character giving an amazingly eloquent speech about what's wrong with Hollywood films. Then the rest of the film is all downhill, being the exact type of film against which the opening salvo rages.

I love some art that is administered by large corporations: *The Simpsons, Beavis and Butthead, Southpark,* and *King of the Hill* help make my life worthwhile. I love the films of Robert Altman and they are *big* budget with *tons* of huge stars. I love Led Zeppelin and Nirvana.

I am not D.I.Y. to be cool. I'm D.I.Y. because it's the best way for me. If a huge corporation wanted to get behind me and give me total artistic control, I would consider it. (And they wouldn't have to be politically correct by mission statement, but I wouldn't work with someone who would melt puppies or third-world children into DVDs.) And I would only do it on a project-by-project basis. I won't sign my life over to anyone.

I would accept **work** from almost anyone if it paid enough. Working is different than selling your own art. I wouldn't sell *D.I.Y. or DIE* to a big corporation and have it all out of my control. I couldn't do that to myself or the people in it. But I would do editing or score a soundtrack for some big dumb commercial I didn't believe in (as long as they weren't something I was *against*) if you paid me enough. This is not selling out. It's working.

Huh?

You may wonder what all this non-film stuff has to do with making films. First, I want you to have something to make films about. There are enough films that are really about nothing, and that's what most film schools prepare you for. Having something significant to shoot is as important, if not more important, than anything beyond the basics of the technical stuff. You wanna be able to shoot, get good sound and image, and edit the result? Well, that takes a week to learn. You wanna make art that *matters*? That takes months!

Second, I want to get you excited not only about film but also about being alive. Film is just a symptom. I jump out of bed every day wanting to go go go. Sometimes I don't sleep enough…I sort of have reverse insomnia. I never have trouble falling asleep, but I get up too early and start working because I'm too excited about life to sleep any longer. This is why I have to nap each afternoon.

When I nail down another booking of one of my films, I get really happy. Even though it may only be for $50 or $100 or $200 in the end, I am elated. I used to work for a software company as a salesman and make sales for $3,000, and my commission would be 500 bucks. I didn't get excited about that. I would rather spread art and work for the Universe and kick ass in the world and change lives and fall asleep happy than just make a lot of money.

I Answer to No One

Would you rather wait for your tiny minuscule insignificant infinitesimal baby kitty chance of getting juice in the Hollywood jungle on a huge level, or would you rather make good movies on a smaller, sweeter level *now*?

I know tons of people in L.A. who have a good pitch and nothing more. They live on coffee-shop blather. They think I'm a loser because I'm operating down here near Earth and they dream of commanding casts of thousands. But I have an actual movie out, and all they have is a business card.

At the moment, as I'm writing this, I make a McDonald's wage at art, but I have to work an 80-hour week to do it. It always takes a lot of work to make a little bit of money doing what you love. But all of my work is rewarding, and most of it is very enjoyable. And I answer to no one. And sometimes part of my work is watching a movie, surfing the Web, or hanging out drinking coffee with a friend.

I'm out to spread ideas more than I am out to make money. Money is good, but ideas mean more to me. I self-published the first pressing of my novel, 1,000 copies. It took me two years to get rid of them. I probably sold half and gave the rest away. Some would look at that as a failure—"Gosh, you had to give away half of them?" To me, it was a success—I *got* to give away half of them. And not only broke even, but made a tiny profit.

I have taken a vow of poverty for my art. I got this idea from my friend who is a priest who ministers to runaway kids. He told me he took a vow of poverty, but his house is full of nice stuff: computer, cell phone, Palm Pilot and he drives a relatively new mini-van. I asked him, "How can you have all this nice stuff and say you're living in poverty?" He told me that he only has things that help with his ministry, and has nothing for luxury. He isn't living wretchedly, only simply. I am the same way. No matter how much I make, I'm gonna only need stuff that allows me to make and spread art easier.

An even more real example of my vow of poverty (and I know I might get in trouble for this) but I believe that if you take a vow of poverty for art, no matter how much you make, you won't owe any taxes.

If you only spend money on your craft, and keep receipts for *everything*, then everything should be deductible.

There. I said it.

My lawyer implores me at this point to state that this "is theoretical opinion only and does not constitute tax advice or legal counsel."

The Universe is insulted at the idea of individual humans making a hundred million dollars a year. Be honored to make twenty grand or a hundred grand a year, and you might survive. You can even make a million and keep your soul, if you spread it around and let it flow through you.

This is not communism; this is compassionate capitalism. Or rather, free enterprise, kick-ass, small-business ideology with heart.

The Universe resents big business. It doesn't resent money; it resents conspicuous expenditure and squandered resources. It resents too many cars, global warming, and population pollution. It hates billionaires ruining lives at the click of a mouse.

I have a contract with the Universe. I do art full time and I don't starve, and don't end up on the street. It's our agreement. Art is my employer.

Thanks, Art.

Join the light side. Leave the dark side. Fight mammon. Make art, support art, give love, and The Universe will regard you and reward you a thousand-fold.

Sell What You Love

I think part of what's wrong with the world is that people in business sell things that make the most money. Which means a lot of people are being tricked into buying stuff they don't want or need. And when you sell what you love, you're a better salesman.

If you're into music, sell music. If you're into guns, heck, sell guns. I think it's disgusting that people spend four years in college learning to sell and then shill *anything* they're hired to. I think that's distinctly un-American somehow, although it is what a lot of Americans do.

I can't get excited about selling cheese, so when I try, I fail. Nothing is gonna get me up in the morning without wanting to kill myself and my coworkers except working for me.

Art is more fun than business. Business school graduates and other blank corporate food tubes my age have to pay to get laid, in one way or another. I don't. Sexy people love art and artists. And sex and love are art food. It all works.

In school, they even showed us the world honestly for one second, in second-grade history class. They told us about the gleaming kings with unlimited power, who always got killed by the oppressed. Then the oppressed took over and became the new kings, only to be killed, ad nauseam.

Then they showed us the alternative: the wandering poets and minstrels who lived off the crumbs of the rich, traveled from city to city, seduced fair maidens with their words and songs, and enjoyed a direct connection to the infinite.

Who would you rather be?

More Ignoring the Call

Hollywood works like Kentucky Fried Chicken or like Project Mayhem. There is a heavy division of labor, so that not many folks know what's in the secret sauce. They don't want you to be able to make a film on your own, or people might actually see how easy it is to do it. People might actually *make* their own movies, and do it better and cheaper.

There are lots of very cool, incredibly talented creative people working in Hollywood. Film and TV at that level are well-oiled monsters that get amazing things done. But I would like to see it done a little differently. So I stay down here where the air's better.[3]

Much of what passes for "independent" is actually either made through the Big Studios or made on the cheap for the purpose of later farming out to them. (Many of the movies that win at Sundance are faux-independents made with 5- to 10-million-dollar budgets laundered off the big boys somehow. And they have bona fide *stars* slumming in the lead roles. Independent, my ass....)

What to do? Make real independent films. And keep up on the world. Explore alternative media, as well as reading the mainstream financial pages. (All the smart people do. And not just the millionaires, but the people who want to keep the millionaires honest.) Support other independent art. Go see it. Buy it. Talk it up.

Don't offer to sell out your vision to the first suit who offers to buy you lunch. And keep in mind that not all suits wear suits. Some look "hip" or "street" or "edgy." But they're still suits. And *never* trust anyone with a "power pony"—a tiny, easily hideable pony tail on an otherwise conservative-looking, over-40 male. And never *ever* trust anyone who uses the term "edgy" and believes it.

When you deal with companies, check 'em out. Search 'em online. Ask around. Ask them directly. Ask 'em where their funding comes from. Contact people who've done business with them. If someone is on the up and up, they will not mind this. Big companies do it all the time. They're even required to by law. It's called *due diligence*.

Do your research, and follow your heart.

It may seem hard to avoid giving into the machine, but you'll feel better staying pure. You can make something even cooler, and not sell it out to the Beast. Make art for the sake of art, and never compromise your vision. Keep *all* the money, and control *every* aspect of your career yourself.

It's the Thirty Dollar way.

---

3. Figuratively. If you've ever been to L.A., you know what a joke this is. And the air is ghastly in L.A. because of corporations. A long time ago, L.A. had a great light rail system. The car companies, oil companies, and tire companies got together, bought it out, and dug up the tracks.

Humility

There is a false modesty in the independent film and music worlds…that it's wrong to take credit for what you do. I think that's crap. I think if everyone took credit for what they did, the world would be a better place. I would love it if, when I opened up the hood of my car, there were a bunch of stickers with the actual names of the people who worked on it (rather than "Inspected By # 7" or "Made in the U.S.A."). I would think that true American Pride actually existed again. (As opposed to the blind "follow the leader" variety that is so popular right now.)

I think that instead of having a system with a few huge stars being admired by a bunch of nobodies, that we need a lot more little stars. Everybody. Starting with you and me. I'd rather be in support of 1,000 interesting women each selling 20,000 records than one Britney selling 20 million records.

Just be humble and confident but not cocky. People can sense motives, and if yours are pure, you will attract great helpers and, eventually, an audience.

I have to remember: people rallying around my film ain't all about me. They're rallying around the film.

Focus

A great rock guitar solo, while you're hearing it, sounds like it's the exact best thing any guitar could *ever* play. It feels like the electric guitar was only invented to play *that* particular solo.

If you work out your skills in any medium, and follow your he(art), and are honest, you can't help but create with this much spirit.

Make art like it is all. Because it is.

I always work. Every day. I at least write. Writing is free. When you have nothing else, you can still do it. I've never seen a homeless guy authoring a DVD, but I have seen a lot of them scribbling novels on paper bags and notebooks in alleyways.

Writing is an important part of making films, even documentaries. Learn to organize and edit your thoughts on paper. Take a class. Ask questions, But mainly practice. It's like anything: it's a connection to the heart that grows stronger with application and time.

Writing is pulling lightning out of the air. Pound the keys with the force of a hundred tons of dynamite, etching each stroke into the ten million layers of papyrus that will eventually comprise the totality of all copies sold.

Apply this passion to all that you do.

Art is basically a lifetime of putting things in their right place, and intuitively knowing where that right place is. And even knowing that such a process and project should exist to even need to put those things in their right places.

You *envision* all art into being. The rest is just work. Production and promo are seamlessly integrated—multiple windows open on the world. Multitasking. True artists work seven days a week, every day of the year. "Slow and steady wins the race."

Do what you love and you'll *want* to work every day.

Don't be greedy. Live simply. Hone your talents and structure your life to be prepared and skilled enough to move on something very quickly when needed. When you are ready, the opportunities will arise.

And screw dreams. Dreams alone are overrated and useless. Action is *all*.

This film school is 99% inspiration and 99% perspiration.

Don't forget to take breaks, relax for a minute and look at the sky. That's where all the inspiration comes from anyway.

Keep moving forward. Don't rest on what you've already done. And don't just replicate your successes. That's not art, it's just facilitating. It's industrial manufacturing.

Priorities

I have very dark-colored teeth. My teeth are perfectly healthy. Strong. They are discolored because a doctor gave me a drug called tetracycline for a lung infection when I was six. (I am asthmatic and had life-threatening asthma attacks sometimes as a child, and frequent infections. I still get sick a lot.)

Having black teeth is a detriment. An employer once told me he wouldn't hire me because the job involved dealing with the public. Women have told me they won't date me because of it. I've noticed people talking to me and being friendly until I smile. Then they get weird and walk away.

Tetracycline was a new drug, and they didn't know that you can't give it to children because it discolors their teeth before they grow in. For adults it's fine.

A lot of people around my age have yellow teeth from tetracycline; mine is an advanced case, and they got darker as I got older.

Normal teeth whitening will not fix them; that would require a veneer, which would cost about $10,000. I'd never had $10,000 at one time in my life.

But when my mother died, I inherited $15,000. I thought about getting my teeth fixed. Instead, I made *D.I.Y. or DIE*, and went on tour to promote it. I feel I made a great decision. My film is done, and my teeth are still black. I don't care.

This is not suffering for art. It's caring about art. In 100 years, my black teeth are going to be in a box underground in my skull turning to dust. My film, in some form, will still be out in the world. And even if it's not, its effect will still be felt somehow.

I'm far more concerned with the eternal than the external.

Chapter 16

Interviews and Advice from Cool Film Folk

f you plan to make independent films on very little money, it might help you to see what your new peers have to say. Here are interviews with a lot of influential people who make great stuff regardless of a continuous paycheck. Some of what they say even contradicts what others say here. I have included them all to foster an open discussion, not to pound home a certain point of view.

The interviews were mostly conducted via e-mail, as not all of the people live in my town.

The opinions here belong solely to the people being interviewed and do not represent Muska & Lipman or Michael Dean.

Joshua Leonard	Burke Roberts
Jon Moritsugu	Danny Plotnick
Kevin Epps	Jill Morley
Rusty Nails	Becky Goldberg
Nicole Panter	Scott Beibin
Daryl Haney	Esther Bell

Not all these folks work in digital video. Some work in film exclusively or in both. A few are not even filmmakers, per se. They are, however, a well-rounded group of people whose opinions and experience add to the material in the rest of this book.

Before you complain to me that it's too many boys and not enough girls, I asked an equal number of both. More boys got back to me than girls. Sorry. That's just what happened. Two other women actually turned in really good interviews and then decided they hadn't said brilliant enough stuff and asked me to pull them. Maybe this speaks to the reason there are way more male directors than female: Many women don't have enough confidence in themselves. Judging from all the crappy movies I've seen many boys make, I think most boys have too much confidence.

In order to even the score a little, I highly recommend *Girl Director* by Andrea Richards. It interviews only female directors, and it rocks.

*Photo by
Michael Dean.*

JOSHUA LEONARD is a filmmaker/photographer/actor living in Los Angeles. He did freelance photography and documentary filmmaking for Mystic Fire Video in New York City. He worked with Judith Malina and the Living Theater in an anti-death penalty guerrilla theater piece called "Not in My Name."

Joshua was one of the three principal actors and one of two main camera people on *Blair Witch Project*, the biggest grossing independent film of all time. It was an unusual situation: He was an actor playing a cameraman, but he was actually running the camera too. His character, who is named Josh Leonard, dies at the end.

He is currently very much alive, and co-directing a documentary on street artists, called *Beautiful Losers*. It is being shot on DV, Super-8, and 16 mm. He recently directed a music video for The Campfire Girls. Since *BWP*, Joshua has acted in about 15 films, ranging from very small and obscure to super mainstream. He just finished playing, of all things, a cameraman, in the HBO movie *Live from Baghdad*.

MD: Did you go to film school? Did you go to college? How did you learn your craft?

JL: College never really worked out for me, and film school was always too expensive. I did have several jobs working in equipment rooms at the New School and at the Film Academy in New York. For me, this worked out better because I was able to borrow gear on weekends and still pay my rent. Some great actors and filmmakers have come out of the ranks of higher education, and as I don't pretend to be either, I guess I should probably keep my opinions to myself. But in my experience, it is better to make mistakes outside of the safe zone of a classroom. There is more at stake, and that very fact pushes me to suck less.

MD: What's wrong with the Hollywood system, and what is right with it?

In general, I don't believe the Hollywood system has any interest in making art or taking chances. There are exceptions to this rule, of course, but I think any true maverick ethos kind of died out with the 70s. As an actor, I get a chance to see all kinds of mediocre scripts….and they come in waves. One month I'll get three heist movies, the next month will be war movies or romantic comedies. It's like this multimillion-dollar game of keeping up with the Joneses.

Not that I think there's anything wrong with popcorn movies, I just believe that within that world there is still a place for some kind of definitive vision. It's become art by committee, and I think that's a dangerous place to come from.

From an anthropological standpoint, I do find it interesting to see what films the majority of the population is going to see. The way that Shakespeare was the art of the masses (timely and self-referential), I think the blockbusters of today tell a lot more about the state of public taste than the more obscure art films. I just wish they were better.

MD: Do you work in DV? What do you think of DV?

I've done several films in DV.

There are going to be a lot of lousy films out. But Francis Ford Coppola said that his dream is that some little fat girl in Ohio is going to make the next Citizen Kane on her home movie camera. And now's really a time where that can happen, where the equipment's available for people to just go out and do something.

Sometimes I think you trade social skills out for a unique vision of the planet. I think that a lot of the guys and gals that have really different perceptions of the world aren't necessarily going to be the best people to go in and convince Eisner that they need $20 million to do a film. They are more interested in the art than the money. So having a medium where they can go out and just create without having to ask somebody's permission is changing and will change what gets made.

MD: What advantages do you see to making films without relying on backing from others?

JL: I know so many people who are sitting around waiting for agencies to get back to them to tell them how their stars responded to their material, which they can then take to a finance company to get money based on said stars' attachment. And people spend *years* doing that.

And as far as I'm concerned, there's just no time to do that. I don't know if it's fair to call yourself a filmmaker when you're sitting around for three years waiting to get permission to make your film. If you're a painter, you don't spend three years waiting for the paint company to mix the right color.

The vanity aspect plays in pretty heavily with a lot of the guys who say that they're independent filmmakers but have never really done anything. I find that it's really about the way that they like to perceive themselves, as opposed to something that they really wake up and live and eat and breathe to do.

And then there are those guys that are always working on something. You make a documentary, you shoot it when you can. You make a feature, you shoot it on weekends. You do what you can to roll film to communicate yourself through the medium that you've chosen.

MD: Los Angeles seems like a town of people waiting.

JL: It certainly does. And I've fallen prey to that too. Los Angeles is a place where everybody is ready for their life to change at any moment. So few people really commit to the journey of knowing themselves creatively because they're waiting to be ready to jump from the precipice.

I spent my first year-and-a-half out here in temporary apartments and hotels and not knowing if I was going back to New York, not knowing if I was going to get a big job and

Figure 16.1 *Cartoon by Keith Knight.*

be able to afford to buy a house or not going to get any work and have to get that $300 apartment in Hollywood. Since I couldn't commit to anything, to just being where I was, everything suffered. My creativity suffered, my relationships suffered. It's such an underwhelming way to live.

MD: What do you think is the lowest budget possible for a good feature-length film? Why?

JL: I haven't been involved with the finance end from inception to completion on many projects, but I know that we got *Blair Witch* in the can for 30 thousand and it was certainly watchable. Not much changed…the film that went to Sundance was 30,000 dollars plus the 35 mm blowup, but we didn't have the blowup when we submitted it. I think that by the time they put it in theaters, they did do a more professional sound mix and do a couple other things to it, but not much. It wasn't like *El Mariachi* where it was unwatchable and then they spent hundreds of thousands of dollars reconstructing it; it wasn't a full reconstruction. It was just a fine-tuning that they did after it was picked up when it was getting ready to go out to theaters.

MD: What would you do with $1.2 million?

JL: Move to Montana and make a film about pig farmers. I don't know. If I had a story at that point, I'd find a way to tell it.

MD: How does the Hollywood system hurt the environment, the economy, and our national pride?

JL: I've really been waiting and listening because of the current political climate and the way that extremism seems to be bigger than ever…I don't think that in my lifetime the planet has ever felt so polarized, which seems like the ripest environment for the true insurgents to come to the forefront and create lasting works. Historically, times of political upheaval have been so rich creatively. And years later, so much of what you remember is the art that came out of that period. And yet so little of what's accessible at your local multiplex or Virgin Megastore is really weighted with any kind of consciousness at all. It's almost like we've gone the other way and embraced the pastels: The boy bands and the blockbusters as a form of social catharsis, as opposed to being active members of our country or active humans on our planet. It feels like we're all just taking our lithium and listening to cheese and just kind of napping away our lives. That's what I find unfortunate about Hollywood: At a time when there's a statement to be made (and I wouldn't pretend to know what that statement is), at a time where there's room to do something revolutionary, that nobody's stepping to the plate and doing it. We haven't had anybody rise out of the ashes of 9/11 and respond to it in a historical manner.

MD: What did you think of the movie *Fight Club*?

JL: I didn't love *Fight Club*…I thought it "missed" a little bit, but I thought it tried. I think it was one of a handful of movies that really tried to do something more than it had to. Because it already had Brad Pitt and Ed Norton, that's really all you need to make a movie these days. I really appreciated that Fincher went in and tried to do something important.

MD: I don't think it would have gotten made post-9/11.

JL: For sure.

MD: Do you play music?

JL: Not well. (Laughs).

MD: What is wrong with the independent film, and what is right with it?

JL: I feel like all the possible answers to this are cliché at this point because people much smarter than me have already answered them. But I think that what's great about independent film is that it allows a place for unique and sometimes off-putting visions to make their way to the screen. Smaller stories get told. There's a lot of ways to look at the world. Sometimes the broad strokes are interesting, but sometimes the minutia is more interesting. I always find *why* people do things much more interesting than *what* people are doing. The personal and cultural motivations for one's actions are kinda fascinating because they are unique, yet human.

That being said, calling a lot of the Angelica fare and Sunset Five fare "independent" really isn't too accurate anymore. And I've certainly been involved in "independent" productions that were completely predicated on getting star names involved.

The difference between working in independent film, or any film, in Los Angeles, and working anywhere else in the country is you very rarely have a conversation about film in Los Angeles that money doesn't enter into somehow. And that just gets boring. At the same time, film is certainly a medium that you don't want to screw off too much. It's so cost prohibitive and time-consuming, that you are ultimately going to want to try to make something that people are going to see.

The reason that I was interested in *Blair Witch*, and independent film in general, is that there's a creative collaboration involved. You don't get that when you work on bigger stuff—stuff where you're pretty much there to do the job you were hired to do. And whether you can make it better or not doesn't matter. And that's a shame. If that were different, I might be more interested in acting.

In Hollywood, all the decisions have been made before you even show up on set. What they're trying to do is stick to whatever corporate demographic they've chosen. They've already decided their aesthetic and know how they're gonna market the thing. They've got marketing guys involved before their script's done sometimes, which is kinda ludicrous to me—a script is coming out of how it's going to be sold.

A friend of mine who worked in the music business in the 80s said that one of the major labels had essentially five marketing plans, and would not sign any band that didn't fit one of those plans: You were either the heavy metal band, or the chick band, or the hair band or whatever…if you didn't fit into one of those categories, you weren't getting signed.

This is more and more how films on a studio level are getting made. Everything's become so derivative that they know how to do these six things with these 20 stars, and if it doesn't fit into that….. There's not a lot of room anymore to take risks and do something unprecedented because there's so much money at stake these days.

I'm proud of *Blair Witch*. I think we made the best film that we could within the constraints that we had. I'm certainly proud of it from a creative standpoint. Did we expect the film to do as much as it did? Of course not. It was a fluke. We were making a film for $30,000 on high-8 video and 16 mm film that was never meant to be a cultural phenomena. The video was just shot on a camcorder from Wal-Mart.

It's like Dennis Hopper said about *Easy Rider*….if he hadn't made that movie, someone else would have made that movie. It wasn't necessarily that it was the most original thing, it was just the perfect thing for the social climate, and what people were looking for at the time. I feel very much the same about *Blair Witch*, that if we hadn't done it, someone else would have.

MD: Have you seen *The Last Broadcast*?

JL: No, and I have to because people keep making the comparisons.

MD: Other than improvising your lines and doing the filming, how much did you have to do with *Blair Witch*?

The concept itself? Very little…Ed and Dan, the directors, and to some extent Greg Hale, who was kind of the main creative producer, came up with the concept in a stoned conversation in their dorm rooms 10 years previous. All we did was show up, learn how to use the cameras, try not to sound too contrived when we were talking, and respond to the situations that they set up as naturally as we could.

MD: Weren't you already a filmmaker, and used to the cameras?

JL: I'd never used the CP-16 before, but I had used other cameras and had fixed Bolexes and Arriflexes and had worked on documentaries for a while.

MD: Were you treated equitably with money in the way things have worked out after the movie? (Asked three years after the release of the film.)

JL: We'll see (laughs).

MD: What would you like to see done differently in the American film system?

JL: I'd just like to see more chances taken. I'd like to see the freaks get more of the money and the businessmen keep their mouths shut.

Photo courtesy of Apathy Productions.

JON MORITSUGU was born in Hawaii and went to college in Rhode Island. His senior thesis film, DER ELVIS (23 mins, 1987), was a hit on the film festival circuit and was chosen as one of the Top 50 Films of the 1980s by the *Village Voice*. Moritsugu made a few more shorts, then an industrial accident nearly severed his right arm. After rehabilitation and a move to the West, he continued his filmmaking activities and has made six features: My Degeneration, Hippy Porn, Terminal USA, Fame Whore, and Scumrock (shot on analog Hi8). These films have received numerous awards, critical acclaim, and screenings including: Cannes, Berlin, Sundance, Rotterdam, Toronto, Singapore, Venice, NY Underground, Chicago Underground Film Festival, and the Guggenheim, MOMA, Whitney, Museum of Modern Art-Paris, and more.

MD: Did you go to film school? Did you go to college? How did you learn your craft?

No, I didn't go to film school. I went to an artsy-fartsy liberal arts college with a small film department (5 Bolexes and 1 flatbed)…learned some basic stuff but learned **everything** else out in the world.

MD: What's your favorite movie from Hollywood and your favorite indie film? Why?

JM: Fave Hollywood movie: *Back To The Future II.*

Fave indie film: *Aguirre Wrath Of God.*

MD: What is wrong with the Hollywood system?

JM: Most movies are made by committee/test screenings and lack any singular vision. This is lame and they should just be called marketing surveys or commercials.

MD: What is right with it?

JM: Chopper ride to the premiere!

MD: What is wrong with independent film?

JM: Often, people in the scene assume that lack of studio/mainstream backing ensures a great film. No way!

MD: What is right with it?

JM: More room to go crazy (in every way).

MD: What advantages do you see to making films without relying on backing from others?

JM: Freedom, brothers and sister, freedom!

MD: What do you think is the lowest budget possible for a good feature-length film? Why?

JM: I dunno, I think you can make a really good feature film for practically nothing. Of course, film costs money, but I don't believe you need tons of gear, highly paid actors, huge crews, etc. in order to make something engaging and entertaining.

MD: Do you think the films shown at Sundance are really independent? Why or why not?

JM: It's hard to say. I mean, Sundance still shows some weird cheap lo-fi stuff that no distributor will touch, but they're also the launching pad for these almost-major-label $30 million movies.

MD: What advice do you have for people starting out in independent film?

JM: Follow your vision and be prepared to bleed for it.

MD: What would you do with $1.2 million?

JM: Cocaine and tequila block party!!! No actually, I'd use some of the money to make a period piece flick shot in cinemascope, then I'd throw the party.

MD: How does the Hollywood system hurt the environment, the economy, and our national pride?

JM: The people are exploited, other people are overpaid, tons of resources are used, and THE MAN holds onto his power. Dude, the Hollywood system is highly problematic.

MD: What would you like to see done differently in the American film system?

JM: Less advertising and less corporate tie-ins with movies. The destruction of the Hollywood "star system." "Free-movie" Fridays.

KEVIN EPPS is the San Francisco guerrilla filmmaker who made *Straight Outta Hunter's Point*, a compelling look at life in the ghetto. With it he showed the horror of his friends being gunned down, sprinkled with his hope for redemption.

MD: Did you go to film school?

KE: Nope.

MD: Did you go to college?

KE: A little bit. Didn't graduate.

MD: How did you learn your craft?

Kevin Epps with Mister T. Photo by "Li'l" Mike Martzke: lilmike@ eventmagic.com.

KE: Learned from classes at Film Arts Foundation and by volunteering at local cable access.

MD: What's your favorite movie from Hollywood and your favorite indie film? Why?

KE: Hollywood film: *Scarface*. It was futuristic. It was the epitome of what was to come, with the ghettos and crack and everything. It was deep.

Also liked *Romancing the Stone* for its energy, pace, and beauty.

Indie: I liked *Straight Outta Brooklyn*. Made me want to make films.

I like any Spike Lee. They are all inspirational because they deal with racial stuff honestly. I especially liked *Bamboozled*. I think it took a layer of skin off everyone who saw it.

MD: What's wrong with the Hollywood system, and what is right with it?

KE: Honestly, I'm infatuated with Hollywood. It's the best of film and it's the worst. But it's such a machine that's already in place, and it's brought so many wonderful experiences.

MD: What is wrong with the independent film, and what is right with it?

KE: It's great in terms of what it adds to the art. It constantly fuses the art because you have so many innovations. The camera work and sound is often before its time.

MD: What advantages do you see to making films without relying on backing from others?

KE: Creative control is amazing. If you don't have that you have nothing. If I worked with bakers, that would be the first point I would have to clear. I have to be omnipotent and omniscient in the direction of my films.

MD: What do you think is the lowest budget possible for a good feature-length film? Why?

KE: I don't even know what I spent. I'm in the hole. Sometimes I spend Gs without even thinking. And I'm always broke. To do a good feature on film I think you need six figures. On DV, ten G's.

MD: Do you think the films shown at Sundance are really independent? Why or why not?

KE: I'm inclined to believe that sort of speak because a lot of films that come out of there are independent. But being in that festival doesn't necessarily mean that you've got a ticket to the top.

MD: What advice do you have for people starting out in independent film?

KE: It has to be something that you really love and have a passion to do. Because there's going to be a lot of sacrifices on your relationships and everything.

Be prepared to ride a Greyhound bus and sleep on some floors. Be willing to get grimy, go to the soup kitchen, borrowing here and there. Using Peter to pay Paul.

MD: What would you do with $1.2 million?

KE: We would start a digital production house. We have a whole collective…an unbelievable collection of talent in filmmaking, hip hop music, documentaries, and dramas. We would sell our friends' talent over the Web. We're already working on this, but would just do it bigger with money.

MD: How does the Hollywood system hurt the environment, the economy, and our national pride?

KE: Well, when you know kids starving in your own neighborhood, do we really need $100-million movies?

MD: What would you like to see done differently in the American film system?

KE: They are too exclusive and should focus more on diversity.

MD: Essay, extra credit: Can you think of anything else you'd like to add?

KE: If you're inspired to go out and make a film, take flight. Do it. It's taken me pretty far. Go for it. Anything is possible. And that applies to anything in life.

Photo of Ozzy Osbourne with Rusty by P. Kimé Lê.

RUSTY NAILS: Director/Writer/Producer—www.neweyefilms.com *Acne* (feature), *Highway Robbery* (documentary feature), *God is Dad* (Arab on Radar Film), *Blood Drinkers* (Goblins Film), "Three" (short), *Santiago Vs. Wigface*, *Animated Corpse*, (Tilt Film), "The Ramones & I" (short).

He is also the curator of the Undershorts Film Festival & Movieside (www.undershortsfilmfestival.com).

MD: Did you go to film school? Did you go to college? How did you learn your craft?

RN: I went to Columbia College in Chicago. Everything I do in some way influences the way I make films—when I walk into a beautiful building/nature area, I take in the surroundings, and it inspires me both as a person and as a filmmaker.

MD: What's your favorite movie from Hollywood and your favorite indie film? Why?

RN: I have many favorite films of both types: Hollywood: *40 Guns* (Sam Fuller*)*, *Kiss Me Stupid* (Billy Wilder), *The Big Clock* (John Farrow), *The Third Man* (Carol Reed), *Man of the West* (Anthony Mann).

Independent: *Mad Max* (George Miller), *Shakes the Clown* (Bobcat Goldthwait), *Polyester* (John Waters), *Repo Man* (Alex Cox), *Down by Law* (Jim Jarmusch), *Band of Outsiders* (Jean-Luc Godard).

MD: Why?

RN: Because I like them. Great stories, inventive, sexy, entertaining, beautiful to look at.

MD: What's wrong with the Hollywood system, and what is right with it?

RN: What's wrong with them? Sexism, Racism, Classism, waste.

What's right with them? When a good film is made.

MD: What is wrong with the independent film, and what is right with it?

RN: What's wrong with them? Sexism, Racism, Classism, waste.

What's right? When a good film is made.

MD: What advantages do you see to making films without relying on backing from others?

RN: The ability to do any and every single thing I want to do without having anyone tell me that it's wrong or right.

MD: What do you think is the lowest budget possible for a good feature-length film? Why?

RN: Someone could take a six-dollar 90-mini-DV tape and edit the entire thing in the camera as they shoot—could everyone do it and do it well? No, but I'm sure there lives a person who could.

MD: Do you think the films shown at Sundance are really independent? Why or why not?

RN: Many of them are. I've really enjoyed some of the films I've seen at Sundance: *The Virgin Suicides*, *Dark Days*, *Rejected*, *By Hook or By Crook*, and others. I do feel it's not exactly fair when a film that costs $20 million, like *Enigma*, plays there, and I think that should be the exception, not the norm, but I like Sundance.

MD: What advice do you have for people starting out in independent film?

RN: Love it. It will break your heart and make you cry and make you laugh from losing your mind at three o'clock in the morning. Get an office job, join a bowling league, fix your house, but don't make films.

MD: What would you do with $1.2 million?

RN: I currently have a script I would like to make for $2 million, but I might be able to do it for $1.2 million. I would try to make the best picture possible for that amount and thankfully get to pay people for their excellent work!

MD: How does the Hollywood system hurt the environment, the economy, and our national pride?

RN: I assume the environment is hurt when film crews go to pristine areas to blow things up for action pictures. I don't know how Hollywood hurts the economy, but I feel stars could make a lot less money and that extra money could be given to other people within the cast and crew. I've been an extra (a person that stands in the background) in big films, and the pay is slave wages. I'm not interested in national pride. I believe people should be proud of the whole world and the universe, if anything.

MD: What would you like to see done differently in the American film system?

RN: Better films, better stories, a lot less macho-man films, a wider variety of ethnic types, sexualities, and human forms.

MD: Essay, extra credit: Can you think of anything else you'd like to add?

RN: Don't spend all of your time watching movies. You have to live a good life in order to make good films.

Photo by Charlotte Beldner.

NICOLE PANTER's first show business job was working on a Mattel Commercial when she was five. In the late 70s, she managed the notorious Los Angeles punk band, The Germs, and was interviewed in *Decline of Western Civilization*. She worked on the original *Pee Wee Herman Show* and later created a short film for London Channel 4 called "Dream Date." She wrote a book of short stories, *Mr. Right On & Other Stories* (1994, Incommunicado) and edited an anthology of California writing, *Unnatural Disasters: Recent Writings from the Golden State* (1996, Incommunicado). Her newest novel, *Swap Meet*, will be out soon. She lives near the ocean in Southern Cali with a vicious dog and an attitudinal cat and teaches screenwriting and a class called FTW/D.I.Y. at Cal Arts.

MD: Did you go to film school?

NP: No, I was very young when I was in college and didn't know what I really wanted to do, other than live an adventurous, glamorous life, so I did a major that had the lightest math requirement and got the hell out of Dodge.

MD: Where did you go to college?

NP: UCLA degree in Sociology w/a secondary anthropology concentration.

MD: How did you learn your craft?

NP: By going out into the world and living a life and traveling to exotic places for huge blocks of time, seeing how other people live. And then coming back to L.A. and working in the film industry.

MD: What's your favorite movie from Hollywood and your favorite indie film?

NP: I could give you a list that goes on for pages—I love movies passionately, but I'll use restraint and pick just one: *Lawrence of Arabia*. The story is an epic adventure, yet the characters are wonderfully drawn, they are not lost in all that epic grandeur. It's just so big and gorgeous and enthralling—all the things a Hollywood movie should be because they have such obscenely huge budgets available to work with.

Well, I can't not mention *Chinatown*—I've seen it dozens of times and it just gets better with each viewing. How many other films can you say that about?

Midnight Cowboy is my favorite Hollywood Indie. That movie was so ahead of its time. It is heavily character-driven, genuinely edgy, and they experimented with a number of film mediums—super 8 and video, and the characters just draw you in without being sappy and cheap about it.

Hollywood does begrudgingly support a few visionary filmmakers—Paul Schrader always makes compelling work, so does Todd Haynes. Todd Solondz has moved into the mainstream, but I'm sure they find his work difficult to market. I don't think any of these guys walk into Mr. Big's office and are showered with money to make their movies, but they each seem to come up with films on a regular basis.

As for truly indie films, well, my favorites change all the time and many of the best independent low budget films I see are documentaries. I love the bodies of work of Naomi Uman and Tom Andersen.

MD: What's wrong with the Hollywood system, and what is right with it?

NP: They *love* tinkering with the script. Too many people have a say in the final product, and they don't have the vaguest idea of what makes a script work, but they have too much ego involvement to just back off. I guess people's bureaucratic film jobs depend on them putting their two cents in and everybody loses sight of the fact that it actually affects the quality of the final product.

What's right with it is that a good mainstream movie can float my boat just as much as anything else in the Universe—a friend and I just went and saw the new Clint Eastwood film, *Blood Work*, and we both had a complete, fully satisfying movie-going experience.

MD: What is wrong with the independent film, and what is right with it?

NP: Well, truly independent film, like the ones I mentioned above—and thousands of others neither of us have any knowledge of—have no real distribution system beyond festivals so it's hard to see them.

What's right with independent film is that good stuff is coming out of strange little corners of the Universe, now that digital technology is widely available. The "No, you can't do that" obstacle has been alleviated to a certain extent. I mean, I learned to write prose by reading it, nobody taught me, so why can't a kid with a solid film vocabulary pick up a camera and make a movie? I do think the challenge with DV is making it look good. Video always looks thin and in contrast, the look of film is so beautiful, so textured and sensual, it's hard to compete with that.

MD: What advantages do you see to making films without relying on backing from others?

NP: Backing from others equals some kind of deal with some kind of devil. You lose complete control and if that is important to you, don't go there. I've heard so many horrible stories from people who worked for years to get their film made, finally got it done, and then lost control in the editing room to the rich Texan who financed it and really wanted to direct it, but didn't have the balls/insight/imagination to and Boom! It becomes something that no longer even remotely resembles what it was they had in mind and they're locked out of the editing room and that old devil, capital, is on the inside making the cuts.

MD: What do you think is the lowest budget possible for a good feature-length film? Why?

NP: In the right hands, good films can be made for the price of equipment, tape, and transfer to film these days. The means of production are available; it depends on whether the filmmaker has the imagination and know-how to use the tools to his/her best advantage.

MD: Do you think the films shown at Sundance are really independent? Why or why not?

NP: Not anymore. The fame and fortune stakes at Sundance have become way, way too high for it to be truly independent. Some purists think that because Robert Redford started Sundance all those years ago that it never was truly indie, but I don't agree with that at all. I think there was a time when Sundance serviced an independent American cinema and perhaps even kept it alive during the years when, if you weren't making a lowest-common-denominator blockbuster, you couldn't get your film made. Sundance nurtured film during those years, and the workshops and labs, which have a lower profile than the Festival are still invaluable, but like most good things, the Festival has come to a corporatized end—it's been globalized, so to speak. On the upside, it's spawned a million little "screw-you Sundance" Slamdance type festivals.

MD: What advice do you have for people starting out in independent film?

NP: Live life, get some miles on you, create some stories to tell about your life, learn how to trust your instincts and edit those stories. Take a vow of poverty for a while. Be of service. Join the Peace Corps. Sit in an old-growth tree for two years to save it from being cut down. Travel in a poor country, but really travel in it—living yourself among the people who live there—without the advantages of the over-privileged. Pick fruit or drive a truck for a living. Learn to become truly self-sufficient and able to move through the world with compassion, keeping your eyes and ears open to the stories of those around you. Learn how to tell a story through the characters who experience that story. Learn what works in cinema in terms of storytelling and what doesn't. Read film editing god Walter Murch's book, *In the Blink of an Eye*. Learn the rules; then, of course, break them. Always, always be scrupulous in maintaining the emotional honesty of your characters and your story.

MD: What would you do with $1.2 million?

NP: I'd split it up and give it to 12 narrative and 12 documentary micro-independent filmmakers ($50,000 each) whose work I like under the condition they make a completed film (with no running time constraints) and see what they come up with.

MD: What would you like to see done differently in the American film system?

NP: One: Don't reward filmmakers who have made small, wonderful, meaningful films with big-budget high-stakes extravaganzas. Reward them by giving them the means to keep doing what they do so beautifully rather than forcing them to walk some lowest-common-denominator commercial high-wire.

Two: Go back to making smaller, intelligent adult films like they did during that brief, but shining time in the 70s. When I say adult films, I mean films that are aimed at grownups, movies like *Midnight Cowboy, Dog Day Afternoon, Chinatown, Raging Bull, Mean Streets, The Godfather 1 & II, Cutter's Way, The Long Goodbye, Bonnie & Clyde, Lenny, Badlands, Days of Heaven, Rancho Deluxe*. These were products of the old studio system, which is different from the corporate parent system that exists now, in which most movie-producing entities are owned by huge multi-national corporations that demand huge profits. In the old studio system, which died in the 70s, the studios were run by visionary studio heads, not CEOs concerned about stock prices.

Three: Get rid of product placement! Outlaw it! It is evil! We don't need subliminal advertising, not here in the U.S. where most of us already have too much stuff and certainly not in places where people are making three cents a day making the tennis shoes that sell for a hundred and fifty bucks that are shown up there onscreen, logo prominently displayed on the Greatest Action Hero's feet. It's an old argument, but I mean, is it really necessary for every last human on the planet to have tasted Coca Cola?

Photo by Phedon Papamichael.

DARYL HANEY is an actor and writer with many produced screenplays to his credit, including *Mockingbird Don't Sing, Crime Zone, Masque of the Red Death, Life Among the Cannibals,* and *Erasable You.* He appeared in major roles in the latter three films: he also appeared in *Sketch Artist,* did numerous roles for legendary king of the Bs, Roger Corman, and, most recently, starred in *War Live,* inspired by 1999's NATO bombing of Serbia. He now divides his time between Belgrade and Los Angeles, where he's putting the finishing touches on a novel. He alternates, like a good many film people, between lean times and fat times. At this writing, he's in one of the former, because he's turning down work to finish his novel.

MD: Did you go to film school? Did you go to college? How did you learn your craft?

DH: No, I never went to college. I'm an autodidact all the way. Talk about your D.I.Y. ethos! I've always felt the film program at Columbia University should give me an honorary degree, as much work as I did up there at one point acting in student productions.

A lot of my grammar and high school English teachers would always tell me I was a naturally gifted writer and I just kind of shrugged it off because I had no interest in writing at the time. Too boring! But, then, somehow, it found me.

I was living in NYC and got a chance to act in a Roger Corman movie and flew out here and within hours had taken over the writing because we had no one else to do it.

One thing about film school: from what I've seen, it's an enormous waste of money. You're basically paying people to allow you the chance to make a few shorts, which would be far cheaper to make on your own. In terms of staff, usually these programs are run by second-raters so it's not like you're getting advice from the masters or anything. I suppose it could be helpful for opening a few doors but that's the career angle. It's got nothing to do with what you're actually learning.

MD: What's your favorite movie from Hollywood and your favorite indie film? Why?

DH: Do you mean all-time favorite movies or more recently? My all-time favorite Hollywood, that is, big studio movie, would either be *Apocalypse Now* or *The Deer Hunter.* The fact that they're both about Viet Nam is coincidental. Both have a lot to do with courage, however, which is one of my favorite themes.

In terms of indie movies, my all-time favorites would be John Cassavetes' *A Woman Under the Influence* or *The Killing of a Chinese Bookie*—like the milieu a great deal in that one. Also, *Mean Streets,* which is probably at the top of the list. In more recent years I'd have to call out *Requiem for Dream.* I just liked the style, found it very moving, although the film itself is a bit moralistic, seen from a certain point of view. There's more than a touch of *Reefer Madness* there. Interestingly, didn't care for *Pi* so much.

MD: What's wrong with the Hollywood system, and what is right with it?

DH: I'd really have to struggle to think of something that's right with Hollywood. What's wrong with it—where do you begin?—but maybe the main thing is the way it promotes this kind of psychic pollution. You know, you see a Hollywood film and learn nothing from it. I've got no problems with the Hollywood emphasis on sex or violence: I'm a big fan of both! My problem is the complete lack of insight into either of them.

And I don't know why anyone would envy today's celebrities. To me, they're a bunch of androids. I used to think it would be a big tragedy when everything, including performers, went CGI. Now I don't think it'll make much difference one way or the other.

MD: What is wrong with the independent film, and what is right with it?

DH: Well, I often have trouble distinguishing between "indie" and "Hollywood." If you make a film independently and sell it to a major, then which is it? I think "independent" has come to mean anything not a franchise movie, anything costing under, say, $20 million and, typically, emphasizing emotion. Fine, but that doesn't really make it independent. I think, in a way, my problem with the indie world is the same as my problem with Hollywood: a fundamental lack of talent.

And that, in turn, is caused by the state of American education. I think reading and being exposed to great music and great art stimulates the imagination in ways pop culture can't.

I notice what a lot of filmmakers do, by way of compensating for this lack of interest, and, also, as a way of demonstrating how "seriously" they should be taken, is they focus on topical political issues which, once again, they treat in a very hackneyed way. You see this in both the mainstream and in the independent world—Spielberg and *The Color Purple* is a great example but, then, so is anything he ever did regarding the second world war. He's demonstrating, time and time again, the evil of Nazism. Uh, isn't that a given already? So whenever I see an American moviemaker purporting to wrestle with sexism or racism or any other hot button issue, I know already, going in, there's not really going to be any real play involved. It's all worked out in advance. You're given some neat little Aesop's moral to cart home, something you can just as easily get off any substandard sitcom.

MD: What advantages do you see to making films without relying on backing from others?

DH: The obvious advantage would be complete artistic control, although, sometimes, that's not such a good idea. You'd better know what to do with it once you get it! But, beyond that, who can really make a film without relying on the backing of others? You'd have to be rich. In fact, the one person I know who has consistently paid for all his own work by borrowing against his own assets is now in the poorhouse. Almost all the independent films during the boom beginning in the late 80s were financed by the director's relatives who, in most cases, never earned a dime back—usually because the movie sucked!

That would certainly be an advantage of making a film *relying* on the backing of others: If it bombs, you aren't the one who goes belly up!

MD: What do you think is the lowest budget possible for a good feature-length film? Why?

DH: Well, digital video will rewrite the figures on this, I'm sure. It's like hitting averages in baseball before aluminum takes over, which they keep saying it will: All the old numbers will be nullified. At the moment, though, based on my personal experience, I can't imagine making a film—that is, using celluloid—for less than, oh, $200,000. There've been people who've claimed less but I think that's publicity BS. The lab costs alone are astronomical.

MD: Do you think the films shown at Sundance are really independent? Why or why not?

DH: Some are; some aren't. What they'll all tend to have in common, though, are those Stalinist Birkenstock politics I mentioned earlier. Just about the entire festival circuit in this country is run by people with an extremely PC mentality. I forget the name of it, but there was a documentary about fat swingers in the suburbs that came out a few years ago, very good, and it was turned down by almost every major festival in the country. They're really puritans, those people, as are, oddly enough, Hollywood people, too. They don't have the stuff to process anything truly challenging. In the end, Sundance has a very Muzak mentality.

MD: What advice do you have for people starting out in independent film?

DH: Well, first of all, I wouldn't necessarily push anyone to become an "independent" filmmaker—having trouble with that distinction again. But I would advocate a good education. That doesn't necessarily mean going to Harvard—in fact, having met a lot of Harvard graduates, I'd probably tell them to avoid it!—But education as an ongoing way of life. I'd say read the classics and, certainly, in terms of film, familiarize yourself with all the greats, which I don't think kids are doing anymore. Also, it really pains me to see American acting in the doldrums it's in. We used to have really terrific actors in this country, I don't care what anyone says, beginning with Brando and continuing up to, probably, the Brat Pack years, when Pacino and DeNiro were still in their prime. That things are now otherwise owes to three things: airhead audiences, airhead casting directors, and the airheads who now call themselves actors. But if acting is ever to be resurrected, a director's going to have to know something about it and, from personal experience, less than zero, I'd say, do.

MD: What would you do with $1.2 million?

DH: I wouldn't necessarily spend it on a film. I think I might use it to invest in my future, for that time when I become completely unemployable. You get a very limited amount of time in which to work in the film business and, after that, nobody cares if you live or die. They'd just as soon run you over as stop and give you a lift to the homeless shelter. So I think I might buy myself a house in Spain or someplace and, from there, write and plan films using other people's money!

MD: What would you like to see done differently in the American film system?

DH: The moguls went out and in came a bunch of Harvard Business School graduates which, to me, is 50 times more horrifying! And, of course, we've seen it in many other ways, too. Revolutions inevitably sour and, often, the ones who paved the way are the first to face the firing squad. So, as much as I dislike what we have now, I'm afraid to think of what might come next. Meantime, in order for any changes to be effective, we'd need massive, massive reform in American culture generally. People would have to abandon the escapist mentality, this whole love of spectacle. Apparently, there was a period in the 50s and 60s where it was actually chic for sophisticated urbanites to see films by Kurosawa and Fellini, but that was a matter of fashion. Possibly, the fashions could swing back again, but I don't see it happening and I don't think it will. Americans have long since determined they want to be fat, lazy, and stupid, and that's what they're going to stick with. So they're going to get just the films they deserve and everyone else, this tiny, dissenting minority, is going to be left out in the cold.

Photo by Michael Dean.

BURKE ROBERTS made his first film at the age of 20. It was a 48-minute mixed-media piece called *JESUS RIDES SHOT-GUN.* Funded by unemployment checks, it cost $4,000 and found its way to Cannes. After being shelved, it somehow became a rare cult film, screened for drunken audiences in basements around America.

This was the birth of BIZZURKE ARMY GUERILLA FILM MALITIA—Burke's own metaphor for the revolutionary stance his films take against "the studio dictatorship" (www.handicapcity.com).

MD: How did you make a cool film on 35 mm on a pizza boy's paycheck?

BR: What I have found is lots of talented, resourceful people who will put effort into helping me realize my projects. This is not easy. You have to have something impressive. My way of alluring people of talent or skill is to present something that reminds them of why the got into this stuff to begin with. A major factor was our D.P. I knew I had to find a seriously experienced cat. One of my closest friends on the planet is Jennifer Lynch. She called up Frank Buyers, the D.P. who had shot her film, *Boxing Helena*, and had also shot her father's series *Twin Peaks*.

Frank had a look at the production sketches (which were dope) and was into it. Here is an example of why your @$$ better be tight! Being a 30-year veteran who works a lot, he has relationships with a lotta folks. Panavision donated use of a camera package (including lenses). That was the big one. But then when you're dealing with a camera that is worth more than a Ferrari, other bull$#!& comes with it. Can't have it without insurance... can't have insurance without a permit...can't have a permit without a cop on set, etc. We nickeled and dimed it: $50 from this friend, $1,500 from that friend, and so on. A couple of kids came through with a lot out of pocket (well, a lot by the standards of my pizza-delivering butt).

MD: What is wrong with the independent film, and what is right with it?

BR: The worst thing about the new indie filmmakers is they have no understanding or respect for the craft of acting. Hollywood is killing it as fast as they can anyway; indies shouldn't be helping.

MD: What advantages do you see to making films without relying on backing from others?

BR: You would think it is creative control, but that ain't the case. (Unless you're rich.) Because without much to work with there are just as many compromises. I can't really answer this because I've not yet had any battles with backers...or even had backers really. I'll tell you this though; it's not even an option for me to compromise my body of work for someone else's commerce.

MD: What do you think is the lowest budget possible for a good feature-length film?

BR: $0.00

MD: Why?

BR: Money just pays for resources and people. In theory all of this could be acquired without money...in theory. Don't get me wrong, I would overpay the people who deserve it, if I could.

MD: What would you do with $1.2 million?

BR: Purchase all the grip, lighting, and camera equipment I could to knock those costs off all my future films. Or use it to wipe my ass because it's possible I won't see money like that until after the promise of "promissory notes" is over.

MD: What would you like to see done differently in the American film system?

BR: The main thing is unions have changed the process of filmmaking into a factory. If a bunch of lighting equipment is sitting outside and it begins to rain and there is a set builder or a P.A. standing there and not a gaffer in sight, they would sooner let the lights get destroyed than do somebody else's job and move it. Even if they wanted to (which is unlikely), they aren't allowed to. I would like to see more efficient all-purpose crews.

And—like any art form, the making of a film should be an intense, improvisational, passionate process. American films rarely are.

MD: Did you go to film school? Did you go to college? How did you learn your craft?

BR: No and no. I'm learning my craft by doing. Hopefully will continue to learn until I die.

Film schools, at least in America, have nothing to offer except technical knowledge. That is valuable. But they cannot teach you vision and will, in fact, try to stifle your vision. You are trained to be a cog in the Hollywood machine, and most become exactly that. Working somewhere low on the totem pole in someone else's film with the film school-conditioned belief that they can climb it. Poor bastards.

MD: Essay, extra credit: Can you think of anything else you'd like to add?

BR: Just know this: Studio executives and their minions are coming from the exact same moral center as dirty drug dealers. They are selling escapism. They've got everyone hooked... and they just keep cutting their $#!& with more and more baking soda.

Photo by Danny Plotnick.

DANNY PLOTNICK is a cool dude. He helped inspire the author of this book to make films, and was making films back when the author was still mucking about in rock bands.

Danny has won so many film festivals that eventually they just make him a judge. He has made many wonderful films including *Steel Belted Romeos* and "Tour Tips" (a short included on the Extras section of Michael Dean's *D.I.Y. or DIE: Burn this DVD*). Danny works as the Director of Education at Film Arts Foundation in San Francisco.

MD: Did you go to film school? Did you go to College?

DP: I did my undergrad at University of Michigan. I did graduate at San Francisco State. Was there a point to either of these endeavors? Maybe. U of M had a terrible film program from a tech perspective. We made super 8 films, but there wasn't a super 8 sound projector to view the films on. I cut my first film on a splicer that didn't have any registration pins. They had worn off. So I was making tape splices with Kodak presstapes with no registration pins. That sums up that experience. But I saw lots of good films that inspired me. In the pre-home video days, one didn't have a tremendous amount of movie-going options. So film school could really open you up to a lot of different things. I bought a super 8 camera from a friend for $80. Rolls of film cost $12 at Kmart. Processing was $2. I just went out and shot a lot of film. Also, the Masters degree has given me the ability to teach, which is how I fund most of my films.

MD: What's your favorite movie from Hollywood and your favorite indie film? Why?

DP: Of recent Hollywood films, I'm gonna pick *Showgirls* or *Starship Troopers* by Verhoven. Both are pretty amazing. On the one hand, they are these overblown, big budget extravaganzas. Yet, at their core they have the vibe of an out-of-control John Waters film. High melodrama, over-the-top dialogue, hyper-real plot developments. In their own way, I think they're a bit of a critique of Hollywood movies, which strive to be heady, yet are hopelessly riddled with clichés and oversimplifications.

Indie Films: You can't really argue with Linklater, Sayles, Jarmusch, or Waters. They always deliver. For the sake of having to pick something, I'm gonna pick *Hairspray* by John Waters. Now there's a movie with an issue, but it doesn't beat you over the head with it like an Ollie Stone movie. It's about something, it's hysterical, and it's got one of the best soundtracks ever.

To go farther beneath the radar, I'd go with Jon Moritsugu's *Terminal USA*. Supremely twisted take on the ideal Japanese-American family. It also managed to tweak the beaks of the folks at PBS, so it gets bonus points for that.

And of course, I assume when you asked this question you were talking about features, so I'm not even gonna get into the shorts rant. You know there are a lot of great films that clock in at about five minutes.

MD: What advantages do you see to making films without relying on backing from others?

DP: You can just focus on making the film you want to make and not have to worry about watering down or changing your vision to please someone signing a check.

MD: Do you think the films shown at Sundance are really independent? Why or why not?

DP: I think this is a pointless question. We should all just be concerned with whether a film is passionate and brilliant and not be so hung up on the means and methods of production.

MD: What advice do you have for people starting out in independent film?

DP: Due to the DV thang, everybody is making films. You, your brother, your mother, a bunch of stoned freshmen at the University of Wisconsin. The competition is gonna be stiff, so spend some time making sure it's good. That sounds pretty obvious, but you'd be surprised (or maybe you wouldn't) at how many half-baked, underdone films I've had to sit through in the last five years. Shooting DV is easy and, that said, people don't spend time thinking before they shoot. Spend time in pre-production. Make sure you have the script, make sure you know how to make stuff look and sound good (or look and sound the way you want it to). Get some nice sets and costumes.

MD: What would you do with $1.2 million?

DP: Is the best response to this question rewarded with a $1.2 million cash prize?

MD: How does the Hollywood system hurt the environment, the economy, and our national pride?

DP: What I do know about film and the environment is the rumor about the reasoning behind Super 8 sound film being discontinued by Kodak was environmental. The film was manufactured at a plant in France. The process that adhered the magnetic stripe to the film caused environmental problems. Apparently, modifications to the plant would have been necessary, and allegedly Kodak couldn't justify the cost.

Photo by Greg Reynolds.

JILL MORLEY is a writer/filmmaker. Her critically acclaimed documentary, *STRIPPED*, about NY Strippers, has been released theatrically in New York and L.A. and is distributed through Vanguard Cinema on VHS and DVD. Jill has written for *The Village Voice, The NY Press, Gear Magazine,* and *Shout Magazine,* and her play *True Confessions of a Go-Go Girl* was published in *Women Playwrights: The Best Women's Plays of 1998.* She has also directed a video production of her play, a music video for Debra DeSalvo's *Take It Off,* and has produced radio documentaries for NPR.

MD: Did you go to film school?

JM: No.

MD: Did you go to college?

JM: Yes, I got a BA in Theater/Communications from Villanova University.

MD: How did you learn your craft?

JM: When I was an actress, I did some production work on the side to pay the bills. Then, when I started to make my film, *STRIPPED*, I really learned technical stuff, step by step. Guess you could say "on-the-job training."

MD: What's your favorite movie from Hollywood and your favorite indie film? Why?

JM: Hollywood....*Midnight Cowboy*. It has the feel of an indie film. Great story, incredible characters, amazing acting, interesting filmmaking, and challenging for its time, *Midnight Cowboy* really sticks with you and has an edge, unlike contemporary Hollywood films.

MD: What's wrong with the Hollywood system, and what is right with it?

JM: What is right is that they have the big money it takes to make films! Many things about it don't seem fair. The best actors are not usually the movie stars, some may not even get work because of the way they look or because it is just too hard for them to break in. The best screenplays certainly don't get made, because Hollywood bigwigs sometimes don't give the general public credit that they may enjoy something a little more intellectual or surreal than usual. Studios don't want to take risks, so many times the filmmaker is forced to make his/her film independently. This is more liberating for the filmmaker as far as creative choices go, but binding in the budget area.

MD: What is wrong with the independent film, and what is right with it?

JM: The independent film world, in the beginning, was so great and supportive. Now, it has a lot of the trappings of Hollywood. So many indies are being made now that there is still snobbery, favoritism, and hypocrisy. For example, certain independent distributors still won't see a film for its merit because they want to focus on the money-making aspect.

There is nothing wrong with that, but we cannot pretend that all independent films are artful creations! Or that the ones that get distributed are the "best" ones. It is almost a mini-Hollywood system in that respect. However, there is still freedom for individual expression and probably much more than a big budget blockbuster studio film. By making a film independently, you are most likely going to have more artistic freedom as a producer/director and perhaps more respect from your peers since you are busting your ass to make the film!

MD: What advantages do you see to making films without relying on backing from others?

JM: Once again, there is the artistic freedom. No one tells you how to shoot, how to edit what to write, or if something seems too edgy. You make all the decisions.

MD: What do you think is the lowest budget possible for a good feature-length film? Why?

JM: This is a difficult question to come up with a number. I guess with the advent of Final Cut Pro, one can just invest in a digital camera, a Final Cut Pro package, digital stock, and take off. That is, of course, if you are making a documentary. If you are making a feature, you have to think about actors, whether to use union, non-union, if you pay them or if you don't pay them, but you at least have to feed them! I would imagine a feature would cost a lot more. Also, if you shot scenes with actors outside you'd need to invest in body mikes, etc.

MD: Do you think the films shown at Sundance are really independent? Why or why not?

JM: The films are independent-ish. By this, I mean that they are usually made by the Hollywood-ized production companies and somehow have a leg up on getting into the Big S. Many seem to have gone through some sort of system that Sundance favors rather than just completely being made independently, being submitted, and getting in.

MD: What advice do you have for people starting out in independent film?

JM: For your first film, be totally committed to getting it made by any means necessary. Believe in your subject/screenplay and that your voice desperately needs to be heard. Once you have that, nothing will get in your way that you can't conquer.

MD: What would you do with $1.2 million?

JM: Buy a house on the beach and rest. I just finished producing, directing, and distributing an independent documentary!

MD: What would you like to see done differently in the American film system?

JM: I would like to see more grants for independent filmmakers by the government and other sources. I would like the grants to be made available for everyone who has a worthwhile project. And to not have to go through a lot of red tape to receive the money!

Drawing by Becky Goldberg.

BECKY GOLDBERG is a documentary filmmaker in New York, originally from Omaha, Nebraska. She recently completed her first documentary, *Hot and Bothered: Feminist Pornography* and is now working on her second documentary.

MD: What's your favorite movie from Hollywood and your favorite indie film? Why?

BG: My favorite Hollywood film is *Ghostbusters*. The effects are cheesy, and it is funny as hell. I am laughing just thinking about it.

My favorite indie film is *Fat Girl*. I guess, in contrast to *Ghostbusters,* it seems odd but I don't care. One's about ghosts; the other is about the sex lives of adolescents. Catherine Breillat is French and an amazing director who makes no excuses for her work, which really rings true to me.

MD: What's wrong with the Hollywood system, and what is right with it?

BG: What's wrong with the Hollywood system is what's wrong in a lot of systems, be it governmental, social, etc. This is an industry based on money, profiting from consumers, which is excusable because this is capitalism. But on top of that, the Hollywood filmmaking machine cares nothing about its audience and, in fact, treats them like idiots.

What's right with the Hollywood system is that if it wasn't for Hollywood Jim Carrey wouldn't be making $20 million a year, would be homeless, and *Ace Ventura: Pet Detective* would have never graced the screens and made the huge social impact that it did.

MD: What is wrong with the independent film, and what is right with it?

BG: Define indie. Indie means different things to different people. Indie can mean Miramax, or indie can mean touring with a projector strapped to your back. Because it can be defined differently, it's harder to say what's wrong with it. From experience being involved in the D.I.Y film scene, I can say that there is too much debate on "Are you D.I.Y/aren't you D.I.Y? Either you're in or you're out." If you get too wrapped up in logistics you have missed the point completely.

MD: What advantages do you see to making films without relying on backing from others?

BG: Because I don't rely on backing from other sources, I have a lot more freedom in terms of my subject matter. (I have a tendency to want to make documentaries that would be considered hard to digest by the mainstream public.) That being said and having made a film "D.I.Y style," I would love HBO to give me money to make a documentary. Filmmaking is hard and expensive, and there is nothing I would rather do, but having the funds to do what I want to do would make it easier.

MD: What do you think is the lowest budget possible for a good feature-length film? Why?

BG: This is a rhetorical question. A good feature length film is *not* determined by budget, it is determined by talent, vision, and drive.

MD: Do you think the films shown at Sundance are really independent? Why or why not?

BG: Who cares?

MD: What advice do you have for people starting out in independent film?

BG: Know what you're getting into. Do your research. If you don't love what you're doing, and I mean *love* it, then it isn't worth it. Realize that it takes time and patience, more than you're willing to give. But if you love it, it's worth it. Lastly, realize the power and influence you have when making a film. Don't make an inconsequential piece of crap. Make a difference in some way.

MD: What would you do with $1.2 million?

BG: Pay my parents back and buy a new CD player.

MD: What would you like to see done differently in the American film system?

BG: I would love to see more films that make you think and are challenging in some way. Also, the "distribute or die" idea, that if you don't get release in theaters worldwide then you haven't made it, is ridiculous.

MD: Extra credit. Anything to add?

BG: If you want to contact me email me at feministporn@yahoo.com.

Photo by Jessica Griffin/Philadelphia Weekly

SCOTT BEIBIN is the Festival Director and co-founder of the West Philadelphia-based *Lost Film Festival.* www.lostfilmfest.com. Beibin also runs the punk label Bloodlink Records ("An Albatross," "Atom & his Package," "Chokehold," "Groundwork," "Frail," etc.), and is a co-producer of the film *Godass* (director, Esther Bell). A jackass of all trades, Scott is a puppeteer, skater, band manager, activist, vegan chef, and vandal. His mischief-making includes an appearance on the Jerry Springer show with Justin Pearson of The Locust, as well as prank phone calls to the stars. Usually he can be found Dumpster-diving for tape stock and props.

MD: Did you go to film school? Did you go to college? How did you learn your craft?

SB: I went to school for Anthropology, and dropped out after five years. It felt as if I were preparing for an *exciting* career as either a professor or a waiter, which are, in essence, the same thing. I wasn't pleased with either option. I wanted to be in complete control of my own life, and feel fulfilled by my work. After touring with bands and writing zines, I started the independent record label, Bloodlink. In the process, I met a lot of folks who were ideologically similar to myself, some of whom were filmmakers or actors. One of my friends recommended that I try my hand at doing locations managing or producing or some such crap, so I tried both. I managed to get a job doing locations for a small digital feature in Philly.

I probably would have done the work for free and been happy to have the experience. Instead it taught me early on that wanna-be-Hollywood-but-morally-broke-indie (read: Indiewood) weasels offer the promise of *deferred payment* (aka "You will never be paid"), while real indie filmmakers on no budget will be totally honest and tell you that you will be paid with a Tofurky sandwich and nothing more. I much preferred the latter…I worked on a few films as an actor and crew member, but I generally felt most of the folks on the set were being treated like subhumans. I knew this needed to change, but I bit my lip in order to get to a place where I could have some influence.

Eventually though, I did become a producer (one of several) for the DV feature *Godass*. By producer I mean the person who gets garbage done (99% of the time for free). Armed with anecdotal knowledge, a hastily learned film biz lexicon, and lots of friends, I was pretty familiar with how and where to get stuff for dirt cheap, or better yet, free.

Fortunately no one figured out that I had absolutely no clue what I was doing. Eventually I realized this is the case with every "Producer."

Since then I've worked for several dot.coms finagling money out of them in order to fund my trips to cover political demonstrations, concerts, and skate demos. This basically means I have been armed with camera, plane tickets, and a skeleton crew to go and shoot footage for companies that folded as neatly as the paper-thin ethos they were built on. "Good riddance" I say.

MD: What is wrong with the independent film, and what is right with it?

SB: Unfortunately, a lot of indie filmmakers are convinced that their work is not valid unless a distributor picks it up, much in the same way self-publishing is taboo in the book world.

MD: What advantages do you see to making films without relying on backing from others?

SB: You get to keep complete control over your ideas and the content you produce. You also don't have to cater to the whims of your sponsors by sticking inappropriate product placements all over your movie, thus ruining the aesthetic. Other benefits, of course, include avoiding censorship of political ideas/ideals, and not restricting what you want to say. Self-censorship is just as evil as state-sanctioned censorship if it is based on fears. The excuse that one needs validation from corporate institutions is nothing short of a copout. If you really believe in your project you can make it happen without having to stoop down a level, while scratching for crumbs. DV, non-linear editing, the Web, and small press allow one to live a comfortable life self-producing movies without selling out. It's all about trying out new ideas and being brave.

MD: What do you think is the lowest budget possible for a good feature-length film? Why?

SB: $0. Anything you need can be either borrowed, Dumpster-dived, or donated. The return policy at major chain stores is a mediamaker's best friend.

MD: Do you think the films shown at Sundance are really independent? Why or why not?

SB: Real independent film festivals don't accept sponsorships from sweatshop companies like The Gap, major polluters like Kodak, or cigarette companies that market their products to children. The other thing that really bugs the skin off of me about Sundance is that it happens in an exclusive mountain ski town resort that is barely affordable to anyone.

MD: What advice do you have for people starting out in independent film?

SB: Don't expect to make money. If you have an idea, get it out there. If you make a film, self-release it. Don't sell out. Build lines of communication with other filmmakers. Build a network.

MD: What would you do with $1.2 million?

SB: Create a grant for organizations to build their own land-trusted non-profit all-ages theater/music venues that run entirely on solar energy and are heated by vegetable oil fuel. This, of course, would include video equipment to be used for free by members of the community. I would probably save $5,000 of that money and produce four DV features, and two shorts.

MD: How does the Hollywood system hurt the environment, the economy, and our national pride?

SB: I'm actually skeptical about the use of film. Generally, nowadays when I say filming, filmmaking, or watching a film, I'm talking about video. The amount of pollution that is created in order to produce a movie on film is not worth the environmental impact. As good as film may look, the best alternative is DV. (Not to mention that film uses gelatin, and is not vegetarian in any sense of the word.)

Photo by Scott Irvine.

ESTHER BELL is a South Carolina transplant who has been living in New York City since paying her way through City College in Harlem. After working on all aspects of film for other people, she formed her own production company named Hells Bells. One of her first films, *Mark Of An Amateur,* won best documentary in a contest for young filmmakers run by The Learning Channel.

She made "Ashley," which documented her friend's relapse into heroin abuse. She cut the interview into a 60-second spot, which was later picked up by *Partners For a Drug-Free America.* The piece was recognized in an honor ceremony, where Esther was invited to meet President Clinton. The spot initiated a national campaign and was featured on *ABC World News* and *Oprah*. Currently, Ms. Bell is finishing her second feature film, *Exist*, and is planning to shoot her third feature, *Flaming Heterosexual Female* with Fairuza Balk.

She has been profiled by *Filmmaker Magazine, Venus, Cosmopolitan, Flair, Film Comment* and *Silicon Alley Reporter*. She appeared on the Oxygen Network and is featured in the book *Girl Director* by Andrea Richards. Esther is also one of the founders of the Golden Trailer Awards (www.goldentrailer.com)—the first award show that rewards movie trailer editors and writers. A full filmology can be seen on her Web site at www.estherbell.com.

MD: Did you go to film school? Did you go to college? How did you learn your craft?

EB: Sort of. I was a history major at City College of New York with a film minor. I had to pay my way through college, so I worked on commercial shoots or any paying gig I could get where I didn't miss too many classes. I also worked on any indie film I could. I did grip work, assistant camera, camera, sound. Whatever they needed. My advice to gals: don't do the typical girl roles for free. Sure, cater a commercial that pays you $250 a day but on indie film don't get trapped as a make-up/stylist person or script supervisor, unless that's what you really want to do. It still amazes me how people still tend to assume that girls can't shoot, do lighting, or whatever. My "extra" advice to girls: Gals are less likely to be given a second chance if they mess up. Remember, guys mess up, and you will too. So learn what you did wrong and make sure you get another chance on another film or the one you're working on.

MD: What is wrong with the independent film, and what is right with it?

EB: What's right is: digital technology. It put the power back into the hands of anyone who is insane enough or, rather, has the initiative to make films.

MD: Wrong?

EB: The problem is that now everyone can make a film. So, getting your film noticed becomes more challenging. Just like a band, you have to build a fan base or an audience. I know that the popularity of *Godass* helped get it sold to Showtime.

MD: What advantages do you see to making films without relying on backing from others?

EB: It's the no-excuse plan to filmmaking. If you save some cash, you can make a film and not have to play the "in development" game. I got trapped in that game for a while with *Godass*. I started shooting *Godass*, and then funds dried up. I made a trailer to fundraise. Suddenly, I was talking to big production companies and doing "development meetings." It's really intoxicating when people say you're talented and start talking about doing your movie on a real budget. I believed the lie for awhile. I got really dependent on the idea that the only way to finish *Godass* was on a big budget. I also got really depressed because people kept making promises that never happened. Finally, I remembered who I was. I was the kid that started a punk magazine at the age of 15. I had always been business savvy and a self-starter. To make my other films, I put on benefit shows and worked weird jobs. Eventually, I realized that I was depressed because I lost my self-determination or my D.I.Y. attitude. So I wrote letters to friends about making small investments in *Godass* to finish it. Soon as I got my first check I started shooting again.

MD: What do you think is the lowest budget possible for a good feature-length film?

EB: Whatever you can beg, borrow, or steal. I don't think that to make a good film you need a lot of money.

MD: What advice do you have for people starting out in independent film?

EB: Keep in mind that you will have to live with your subject matter for no less than five years. So you'd better like your script or at least have a subject that sustains your interest for a long time. For me, *Godass* wasn't just a story about a girl and her magazine. *Godass* was my attempt to "write about what I know." But I avoided making the film "too specific to my life" because I didn't think anyone would give a damn about a "my life" story and watching a film that feels like an inside joke that only the director understands. That isn't rewarding.

EB: For the most part, film production isn't done in a way that is environmentally conscious.

Also, most storylines do little to challenge the status quo or enlighten people. The only way to change anything is do it differently for yourself and usually others will follow. For example: Because people demanded it, you can now find soy products and organic foods in almost every major chain grocery store. More and more people want food made by farmers that don't use GMO (genetically altered foods) or pesticides. Corporate farming is being questioned because the food it produces isn't healthy. The same thing can be said about most studio films. Not all people are willing to watch the same crap. The more people spend their money on other films made and distributed outside the "Hollywood system," the better.

MD: What would you like to see done differently in the American film system?

EB: *More diversity!* Once again, I'm trying to change things by doing it differently with my own films and hope that other people feel the same way.

Also, I wish Americans would get over the double-standard puritan crap. I think there should be more male frontal nudity.

Appendix A
Recommended Reading, Surfing, Viewing, and Listening

Here's a bunch of movies, books, Web sites, and music I like. I think there might be something here that would be helpful to someone starting out.

This may not show you how to get from Point A to Point B (hopefully the rest of the book did that), but at least it might show you a few stops on the map of how *I* did it.

Recommended Reading

How Movies Work; Bruce F. Kawin, University of California Press, Berkeley. 1992.

The whole history of film and filmmaking; very detailed technical stuff, mainly about big-budget filmmaking. More than you need to know to make cool digital films, but surely some useful stuff here.

The Artist's Way; Julia Cameron, J. P. Tarcher. 1995

Ignore the cult of personality. Ignore the wimpy New-Age tone. Ignore the writing assignments. (For my "Morning Pages," I actually write. Stuff like writing this book. I don't need practice, I need *action*.) But read it. This book rocks.

Zen Guitar; by my friend, Phil Sudo (R.I.P.) Fireside. 1998

A martial arts-practicing Japanese-American-Hawaiian rock guitarist gently teaches that music is non-competitive, and he helps you feel this and know it.

Phil Sudo was my friend and helped inspire *D.I.Y. or DIE* as well as *$30 Film School*. He died of cancer in summer of 2002 and was very centered and wise right up to the end. There is a very inspiring interview with him done three weeks before his death on the Extras section of the *D.I.Y. or DIE* DVD.

Screenwriting for Film and Television; William Miller, Allyn & Bacon. 1997

Serious nuts and bolts guide to writing movies. Describes and discusses all the attributes and ingredients in classic storytelling form. This book and a pen (and imagination, drive, and intelligence) are all you need.

Hitting Your Mark: What Every Actor Really Needs to Know on a Hollywood Set; Steve Carlson, Michael Wiese Productions, 1999

Cool stuff. I read it to be able to direct better. But thinking of it, I'll bet I could act...maybe play a short, drunk Irish thug. Wouldn't be much of a stretch.

Days of War, Nights of Love (Crimethink for Beginners); Crimethink Collective, CrimethInc. Workers' Collective 2001

Preachy-but-excellent anarchist manifesto makes you question why you'd even make media at all.

People all wanna be on TV without wondering why they'd want to be on TV. Folks ain't better just because someone pointed a camera at them. Ya know? The media is a pipeline that constantly needs filling. You ain't a god just because they pump you through the sludge hole for fifteen minutes. Once you've questioned it all though, you're more ready to make *pure* art.

Sex, Stupidity and Greed: Inside the American Movie Industry; Ian Grey, Juno Press, 1997

Dead-on insider info of what's wrong with Hollywood.

Girl Director; Andrea Richards, Girlpress.com, 2001

"A how-to guide for the first-time, flat-broke filmmaker." Quite empowering Super-8 stuff, hip, and aimed at teens. Makes me wish I were a girl. I got a copy for my daughter.

It's a great book, and not just for girls, by the way. Would recommend it to anyone interested in making films, and in understanding the history of Hollywood from a female point of view. (Many great female directors go under-noticed.) Andrea's hubby Norwood Cheek helps run www.flicker.org.

It's a great how-to resource site and national network for showing movies shot on film (8 and 16 mm). Get their $3.50 paperback Flicker Super-8 guide. It's smart, groovy and small enough to fit in your pocket. Young cute hipster husband and wife filmmaker/writer couple. How cool is that?

iMovie 2 Fast & Easy; Kevin Harreld, Prima Press

Great quick-start manual written by my editor at Muska & Lipman. Covers the very basic basics of digital film very clearly.

DV Magazine

Existed even before Digital Video, as some analog video magazine. These cats really know their stuff. Kind of like *Guitar Player* magazine for filmmakers.

The manual for all the hardware and software you use

Not the title of a book, stupid, just read the friggin' manual. I'm a total nerd and read technical manuals the way lonely housewives read romance novels. Dig it.

Unrelated, but Maybe Not

Future Shock; Alvin Tofler, Random House, 1970

70s bestseller told us then everything that is happening now, and how to not be destroyed by it.

The Sovereign Individual; James Dale Davidson and Lord William Rees-Mogg, Simon & Schuster, 1997

Computer encryption technology will eliminate taxation and governments and here's how to benefit from it.

The Age of Spiritual Machines; Ray Kurzweil, Penguin, 2000

Technology will make the world an amazing place and the author is helping to create a lot of it.

Tesla: Man Out of Time; Margaret Cheney, 1981, Barnes and Noble

Nikola Tesla invented everything that Thomas Edison stole. Maybe even movies. When Tesla died, the U.S. Army confiscated all his notes. Wanna really think differently? Start here.

The Gift: Imagination and the Erotic Life of Property; Louis Hyde, Vintage Books, (Random House), 1979

An interesting study on the difference, and the connection between, selling things and giving them away. The conclusion is that a combination of the two is the best way to do things. Art is a gift; you can give it away and make a living. That's the theory behind the business model for my "Burn this DVD" idea.

D.I.Y. or DIE: BURN THIS DVD was an attempt to combine the functionality and practicality of selling with the karma of giving. I call this, "Keepin' it Real *and* Getting' Paid."

We use the hacker mentality. Information wants to be free. But you can still make money on it. Find a way to do what the dot com millionaires only tried to do. "Give everything away and still get rich." Just be smarter and think a little harder rather than just slapping ads on everything. And don't sell your database! It's sleazy, and it's the best thing you have. It's priceless, and so is the trust of having that information.

Dear Mr. Mackin; Rich Mackin, Gorsky Press, 2001

Letters to corporation with their ridiculous responses. A punk "The Lazslo Letters" for the millennium. Shows us just how double-plus-dumb corporate-think is.

Fight Club; Chuck Palahniuk, Owl Books, 1996

Like *Doctor Jekyll and Mister Hyde* meets *The Anarchist's Cookbook.* Somehow a fitting parable for where big dumb corporations are taking us.

Also recommended: the script, the shooting script, and movie of the same name. An interesting progression of an amazing adaptation. (The movie, by the way, is the most genuinely subversive piece of art ever put out by a major media concern. And there's absolutely *no way* it would have gotten made post-Sept 11.) The "extras" part of the DVD (disk two) of the movie is a crash course in genius film-making shown in a way that is usually hidden in Hollywood. Also kinda revealing about the "making-of" segments: There sure seem to be a lot of paunchy 40-year-old white males in Hollywood. And little else.

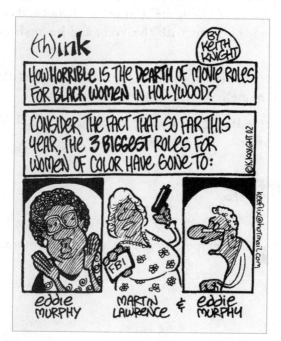

Figure A.1 *Cartoon by Keith Knight.*

Office Space

Sort of a kinder, gentler, funnier *Fight Club*. Look for the cameo of writer/director Mike Judge as the cranky and anal manager of Chotchkie's.

Adbusters Magazine

Glossy magazine making fun of glossy magazines. Done sometimes anonymously by people who make a lot of money by day creating ads for big dumb corporations. They use their skills and money by night to deride the same corporations.

If you can find it, check out *Processed World*: www.processedworld.com.

Similar to *Adbusters*, but written by temps on company time and resources.

Computer Lib (& Dream Machines); Ted Nelson, 1974

Pre-World Wide Web book by hippie visionary talks about why computers must/should/will be available to everyone to help realize their dreams. (This book was written when computers cost millions of dollars, took teams of scientists to run them, were very slow and complicated to use, and were only owned by the government, corporations, and large universities.)

An interesting subnote, even though *Computer Lib* has been reprinted by Web-lovers, Microsoft Press, Nelson's personal "Web site" (http://ted.hyperland.com) complains that we totally missed the point with the Web, and he envisioned something much cooler.

Starving in the Company of Beautiful Women; Michael W. Dean, Kittyfeet Press, 2000 (order from Amazon or from me).

Soon to be a minor motion picture. It's all about sex, cats, and rock 'n' roll. Why should you buy it? Because I wrote it.

Recommended Surfing

www.craigslist.com

Find a crew, camera, interns, home, lover, pet, friend, car, sublet, and more. For free.

www.richmackin.com

Site for above mentioned book.

www.lostfilmfest.com

Cool kids from West Philly who run the most independent film fest in the country. And it travels. They are a collective, a chaocracy, and sweet people too.

They also list all the contact info for the stops on their tours. It's where I got a lot of my contacts.

Lost Film Fest: Coming soon to a basement near you!

www.byofl.org

book your own life. A site with many resources and links to places for punk and alternative bands to play. Some of them also show films. TIP: Most of would show a film if it was something they were interested in (i.e. punk rock, D.I.Y ethic, activism, etc.) and you brought your own projector and screen.

www.regenerationtv.net

Cool socially conscious folks in L.A. making nifty infotainment.

www.dischord.com

My favorite label, both for the music *and* for the business model.

Dischord and Facets Multimedia in Chicago, were the first places to wholesale my film.

www.facets.org

Facets Multimedia, wholesale and retail. About a billion cool, fringe, hard-to-find flicks.

www.filmarts.org

Film Arts Foundation in San Francisco. Rentals, classes, and a lot more. Like Triple-A for filmmakers. They rock. And their magazine, *Release Print*, is worth the price of membership by itself.

www.EchoParkFilmCenter.org

Sort of the Southern California version of Film Arts Foundation. *The* place to get cheap cameras (digital and film), get cheap repairs, cheap and free classes, see films on Thursday, rent indie movies, and just stop in and hang out and have pizza and rap with Paulo and Ken, two of the coolest cats in Los Angeles.

www.couchexchange.org

Going on tour? The Artist Couch Exchange is "A network of independent artists and supporters who offer free lodging to other touring independent artists who are also members of the network."

www.publicenemy.com

Let Chuck D and pals drop some mad science on you. Also a good resource for progressive attitudes on file sharing and avoiding the use of copy protection and encryption. These unrelenting cats take matters into their own hands and get the music out in an uncompromised way without relying on a middleman.

Also check out their video *Fight the Power Live*. Grainy analog video images. Crappy camera work. Tired editing techniques (even for 1989). But amazing content from these 24-hour paramilitary party people that makes it more important than a dozen slick blockbusters.

I like that it opens with a dramatization of the group dressed as soldiers taking over a TV station by force. Other rappers got hung up in the girls and the cars and the cash. PE always knew what all the great revolutionaries know: When an army seizes power in a revolution, the first thing they grab is radio, TV, and newspapers. The media is far more important than chickies and money.

www.Mastamind.com

Kevin Epp's site. He's the spiritual son of those folks above. One guy and a camera *can* change the world.

www.billboardliberation.com

Billboard Liberation Front

People who risk life, limb, and jail to "correct" messages on big dumb corporate billboards. There is a quick homage to them in the movie *Fight Club*, by the way (right before Bob gets shot).

www.nologo.org

And get the book *No Logo: Taking Aim at the Brand Bullies* by Naomi Klein. Tells why you shouldn't pay for shirts with advertising on them, and a whole lot more.

www.SpamAssassin.org

This actually works. It gets rid of 90 percent of your Spam. Or more. But you have to get your system administrator to install it on his end. Then it uses a complex set of rules to instantly analyze incoming mail, and it adds to word *******SPAM******* to the subject line of anything it finds suspect. In two weeks of running it, I've had over 1,000 e-mails labeled as Spam, with no false positives. I just set up a filter to send them straight to the trash. I'm working on getting the SysAdmin to just send them to the trash on his end so I don't even get the notification noise when they show up.

www.allexperts.com

Excellent resource. Get free answers within 24 hours on anything. Editing. Photoshop. Audio. DV cameras. Fixing the transmission on a 1966 Plymouth Barracuda. Who the one true God is. What to do if your cat won't eat. EVERY-THING. I'm serious.

www.kittyfeet.com/dktrial.htm

"Dead Kennedys Trial"

An article I wrote after sitting in court and witnessing first-hand my favorite band suing each other. A non-partisan account, and a good cautionary example. It shows why you have to walk your talk and *still* get everything in writing, even with, or especially with, your friends.

www.lafco.tv

ANGELES FILMMAKERS' CO-OP

Cool folks with a school bus fitted with a production studio to bring digital technology to the peoples!

www.kittyfeet.com/wouldhe.htm

My friend, Michael Woody. Too cheap for his own URL even though he invented the Internet. Well, he didn't, but he's not much older than me and has been making D.I.Y. films and video about 20 years longer than me. He has many interesting ideas, not for everyone.

www.jonmoritsugu.com

Cool no-budget director. Gets big Hollywood movie stars to work for free. Not scale, but *free*. He's *that* cool. Usually works on 16 mm film, but took a step backwards and shot his latest, *Scumrock*, on a consumer hi8 analog video camera and edited linear using just a VHS VCR! And it looks *great*.

www.jpkvideo.com

Very talented San Francisco video dude who taught me a lot of what I know. Hire him for your next shoot.

www.jpkvideo.net

JP's cheap and reliable Web hosting service for artists. Tell him Kittyfeet sent ya.

www.yourbandsucks.com

A hilarious deflating of everything wrong with rock by a guy who actually loves everything that's wrong with rock. And everything that's right with it. A good cautionary example against the dude-we're-totally-gonna-get-signed mentality prevalent in rock and film. And peruse the *whole* site before ever getting a promo photo of yourself taken for any purpose.

I can happily ignore deadlines clicking away for *days* at yourbandsucks.com. (By the way, I came up with the URL for that site.)

www.drooker.com

Eric Drooker. Artist/activist. Sweet, funny, smart guy. Done art for almost every protest poster I've ever seen. And the cover of the *New Yorker*. And *Rage Against The McMachine*. Dig. Check him out.

His newer color stuff is even better than his older monochromatic stuff, which I've loved since I first saw it 15 years ago. He's sort of a part of the collective background of my world view. Buy his books.

www.mole.com

Mole Richardson. HUGE sprawling airline-hanger sized movie lighting sales and rental place in Hollywood. They let us go in and spend three hours like kids in a candy store picking up everything in the place and taking pictures of it.

They have tiny, relatively inexpensive lighting kits that can do a great job with most DV shoots, on up to Klieg lights for your premiere that can pick out an airplane in flight at night, and *everything* in between.

www.pussinbootz.com

Very cool art by Jillian Suzanne, a very cool chick who modeled for photos in Chapter 5.

http://www.attrition.org/news/content/00-04-29.001.html

Article I wrote in 1999 about how I thought technology was going kill the entertainment conglomerates.

http://www.wired.com/wired/archive/11.02/dirge.html

2003 article in *Wired Magazine* with more updates on the death knell for the record industry. As a guy who was kicked off of Warner Brothers, I just say "good." Who's with me?

www.insecto.org

My friend Newt's band, Insecto, and his movie, *PropStars L.A.* (trailer is on the *D.I.Y.* DVD). He was the first graduate of *$30 Film School*—the first person I taught to make a film. Also, Newt took a lot of the photos in this book, under the name *Newtron Foto*.

www.DecimalMedia.com

My friend London May's site for his documentary in progress, *Even the Devil is Scared to Live Here*. It's about the unexplained murders in Juarez, Mexico. London was the second graduate of *$30 Film School*.

Recommended Viewing

Ed Wood

Better than Ed Wood's movies, actually. I like the idea of Ed Wood, and this film does a great job with that idea.

Cecil B. Demented

Inspirational hyperbole, Waters' autobiography, or well-crafted how-to lesson? You be the judge (or "It works on so many levels").

The Player

Swimming With Sharks

Sunset Blvd

Rent these three, draw the blinds, fry up some popcorn, and have an anti-Hollywood mini-film fest, courtesy of Hollywood.

Kern and Zedd's CD retrospectives

I especially like the Zedd thing with Lydia Lunch on "Steal this Video." It's beautiful, and her voiceover says a lot about how it's possible to be well known and broke at the same time. Also nice is Kern filming Zedd playing a woman. Fooled me, but Zedd's hot. I used to date a girl in New Orleans who looked like him.

Be sure to read Cinema of Transgression manifesto. It's Loquaciously erudite. Piquantly pedantic. Repetitively redundant, yet righteously relevant. Yet oh-so apropos. It helped inspire this book. I'll list it even though Zedd's mad at me right now. I don't care. It's still good stuff.

I named the DVD for *D.I.Y. or DIE D.I.Y. OR DIE: Burn this DVD* as a partial homage to Zedd (he has a "product" called "Steal this Video"). Obviously, we were both also nodding to Abbie Hoffman's "Steal this Book"[1] When I was 12, I stole "Steal This Book" (from a guy who stole it) and almost got kicked out of school for Xeroxing selections into a zine and handing them out.

Somebody please hire Zedd, Okay? He deserves it and needs it. Don't just rip off his style like everyone else does. Kern and Zedd influenced most everything you see on MTV, TV, commercials, and in the cinema. And never made a dime. If you were truly cool, you'd already have both of their DVDs and their books. But you don't.

Instrument; Jem Cohen and Fugazi.

Best non-rock video rock video ever.

State and Maine

Frighteningly accurate.

Living in Oblivion

Frighteningly accurate. I especially like all the hustling on the part of the crew members to give the script to the star.

Love and the Monster.

And anything else by my very talented friend, Miles Montalbano (who also did the wonderful editing on *D.I.Y. or DIE*).

---

1. And I did name my DVD before the System of a Down album Steal This Album *came out. And before I heard of that album.*

www.imntv.org

Independent Media Network. Miles Montalbano's activist site. Organizes show-ings nationwide through a loose network of cable access shows.

Anything by Michael Moore

Big cuddly bear protecting the little guy with the tenacity of a bulldog and a sense of humor. His *Roger and Me* is why I started making films.

Standing in the Shadows of Motown

Great documentary on the unsung sidemen who played on all those hits. Also, excellent cautionary example on dealing with media corporations. Imagine play-ing for little money and no credit for years on scores of number-one hits, showing up for work in Michigan and finding a sign on the door, "Sorry, we've moved to California." No warning, just the sign.

Jesus, that part sounds like a Michael Moore movie!

I'm the One That I Want; Margaret Cho

Excellent amazing Frisko comedy. Makes me homesick. Great long funny part on why Hollywood sucks, and why you shouldn't compromise. Damn. This lady is High-larious, smart, strong, foxy, *and* sober. Anyone have her number?

Homeless Movies

Cool PXL and VHS movie by my buddy named "Tentatively a Convenience" ("Tent" for short).

Sean Connery Golf Project; http://www.fyi.net/~anon/WdmUHome.html

Two kids sneak into a major film studio, steal a script, improve it, and take it back. Apparently, they might be facing jail time, so you might not be able to see this one. It was supposed to show with my film at the Silver Lake Film Fest, but they were told by their lawyer to pull it.

Pirates of Silicon Valley

Big Hollywood dramatization of the history and rivalry concerning the popular-ization of personal computing. Reads like an after-grad school special for nerds. Paints Apple founder Steve Jobs as a sexy, radical, acid-gobbling Berkeley hacker who basically channeled computing ideas from alien intelligence and stole fire from the gods (and subsequently went a little mad). It paints Bill Gates as a clumsy, Harvard pocket-protector dork who can't get laid and steals computing ideas from Steve Jobs.

Can either description be far behind? Remember, Apple invented FireWire and Final Cut Pro, sold the first affordable supercomputer, and is one of the main reasons that desktop video editing exists.

Recommended Listening

Jesus, where to start…I love so much music and dislike so much.

Everything I need to know I learned from listening to Minor Threat and that Bob Dylan song *It's Alright, Ma (I'm Only Bleeding)*. And I'd throw in the *Animals* album by Pink Floyd too. Bleating bleak and beautiful. And everyone, in business at least, sometimes *is* either a pig, dog, or sheep. (Though I'm a cat.)

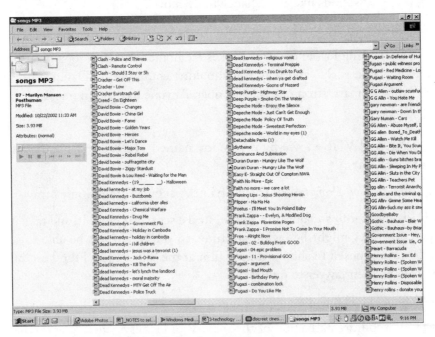

Figure A.2 *Some of the music that inspires me…*

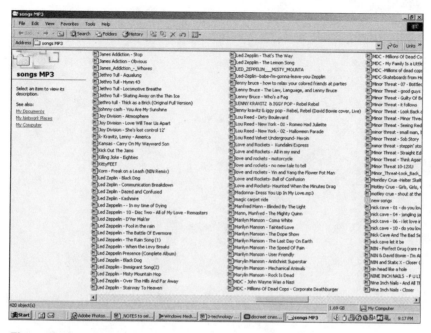

Figure A.3 *...more...*

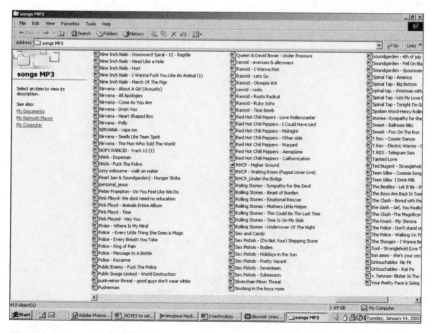

Figure A.4 *...and still more.*

Appendix B

Stops on Michael Dean's D.I.Y. or DIE Movie Tours

These are included to demonstrate what you can do if you follow the suggestions in the book. Also, some of these places do regular showings, and you might want to consider contacting them to show your film. Most of them are easy to find online.

2002 Showings

September, somewhere between Dayton & Cincinnati Ohio, Zero Budget Film Fest.

Cristian Bowie showed the flick in squats in Europe through the summer.

January 19, 2002. Showed Rough cut at Lost Film Fest at Sundance, Park City, Utah.

Thursday, February 4, at 7 p.m. Toledo, Ohio. IWW infospace at 2223 LaGrange.

Saturday, April 13, Other cinema at ATA. San Francisco at A.T.A. Gallery, 992 Valencia St.

Sunday, April 14, 3 p.m. Berkeley. Gilman St. Project. 924 Gilman St.

Wednesday, April 17, Muskogee, Oklahoma BARE BONES FILM FEST.

Sunday, April 21. Chicago at Azone.

May 2-5. Nowhere X Nowhere Festival in Chico, California. Films, a parade, cheap beer, and pretty girls and boyz were the RULE!

May 6. SUNY college, Purchase in New York.

May 9 Tulsa, Oklahoma. The Nightingale Theater.

Sunday, May 12 (Mother's Day). Hollywood, California. Knitting Factory Hollywood.

With: Insecto (my band), Comedienne Alicia B. Dattner, and (D.I.Y. editor) Miles Montalbano's short film "Love and the Monster."

Wednesday, May 15. Portland, Maine, The Skinny.

Thursday, May 16 7:00 p.m. Boston X-Haus.

Saturday, May 18. Providence, Rhode Island, White Electric Coffee.

Sunday, May 19. New York City. The Knitting Factory—AlterKnit Theater.

Monday May 20. Two shows, 9/11 p.m. Washington, D.C. Chief Ike's Mambo Room.

Saturday, June 1. Albuquerque, New Mexico @ Bow Wow Records.

June 15. Bellingham, Washington. Fairhaven College Auditorium.

Wednesday, June 19. San Francisco, California. Yerba Buena Center for the Arts Screening Room Film Arts Foundation True Stories series.

Sunday, June 23. Milwaukee. Hi Hat Garage.

June 23 Sunday also. Bowling Green, Ohio. 4p.m. 111 Olscamp Hall on the campus of Bowling Green State University. Underground Publishing Conference

Monday, June 24. Also Milwaukee. Hi Hat Garage, 1701 N. Arlington Pl. (Arlington and Brady) 8p.m.

Monday, June 24. Champaign, Illinois. The Highdive.

Tuesday, June 25. Indianapolis, Indiana at Solidarity Books.

Wednesday, June 26. Detroit, Michigan. Trumbullplex.

Thursday, June 27. Chicago. The Empty Bottle.

June 28 Urbana-Champaign Indie Media Center 218 West Main Street, Urbana, Illinois.

June 9 at North American Anarchist Gathering - Lawrence, Kansas, at the traveling Lost Film Fest.

Wednesday, June 26. Milwaukee, Wisconsin. Darling Hall, at the traveling Lost Film Fest.

Friday through Sunday, July 5-7. (Dangerous Media) Columbus, Ohio at More than Music Fest at the Rhodes Center-the traveling Lost Film Fest.

Friday, July 5 and Saturday, July 6. Vancouver, British Columbia, Canada The Blinding Light! Cinema.

Tuesday, July 9, Noon. Bellingham, Washington, The Pickford Cinema.

Wednesday, July 10. Seattle, Washington, 911 Media Arts Center.

Thursday July 11. Portland, Oregon. 2 shows. 7:00 & 9:00 p.m. Clinton Street Theater.

Friday, July 12. Portland, Oregon. Portland Zine Fest.

Saturday, July 13. Eugene, Oregon at "My House."

Sunday, July 14. Olympia, Washington. Capitol Theater.

Figure B.2 *Marquee at Capitol Theater.* Photo by Michael Dean.

Tuesday, July 16. Phoenix, Arizona. Modified – an artspace.

Thursday, July 18. Los Angeles, California at Echo Park Film Center.

Friday, August 2. Reno Nevada. Bruka Theater.

Saturday, August 3. Atlanta, Georgia. The Independent Georgia D.I.Y. Festival.

Saturday, August 10. Ypsilanti, Mich. Dreamland Theater, with a puppet show.

Thursday, August 15. Minneapolis, Minnesota. Red Eye Theater.

Saturday, August 17. Ypsilanti, Michigan. (SECOND SHOWING) Dreamland Theater.

Tuesday, August 20. Jacksonville, Florida at the Pit.

Friday, August 30, 8 p.m. Long Island, New York. Long Island Revolt—Freespace Convergence Anarchist meeting and dance party.

Tuesday Sept. 17, 7:00 p.m. Los Angeles, California. SILVER LAKE FILM FESTIVAL, upstairs at Zen Sushi.

September 20. Trenton, Ohio. Lowest Budget Film Fest.

Saturday, September 28. San Diego, California. Che Cafe UCSD campus.

Tuesday, October 1. On the campus of the University of Arizona.

Tuesday and Wednesday, November 5 and 6. Bristol, United Kingdom. Cube Cinema 4 Princess Row. Kingsdown.

Thursday, December 5. Ypsilanti, Michigan. 44 E. Cross Street. Dreamland Theater.

2003 Showings

Tuesday, Feb. 11, 8 p.m. DVD Release Party in a bar in Washington, D.C. Chief Ike's Mambo Room 1725 Columbia Rd. (between 17th &18th streets).

March 13. Los Angeles Museum of Contemporary Art. Invited to show film and lecture to teen apprentice group from the museum.

Thursday, March 13, 8 p.m. Second Showing at 10 p.m. DVD Release Party. in L.A. at SplitId theater with PropStars LA film 6470 Santa Monica Blvd.

2003 *Springtime in Texas* tour

(Texas Tour Sponsor: San Antonio Underground Film Festival www.safilm.com)

Thursday, March 20, 9:30 p.m. New Orleans, Louisiana. Zeitgeist Theater in 1724 ORETHA. www.zeitgeistinc.org.

Friday, March 21, 8 p.m. Baton Rouge, Louisiana. Baton Rouge Gallery 1442 City Park Ave.

Saturday, March 22, 6 p.m. San Antonio. The Mix. On the corner of St. Mary's and Ashby. Two-dollar donation.

Sunday, March 23, 7:30 p.m. Houston at the Proletariat, 903 Richmond Houston, Texas.

Wednesday, March 26, 7 p.m. Austin, Texas. Alamo Drafthouse Cinema, 409 Colorado St.

Thursday, March 27. Houston Radio Interview. 10 p.m. on Mutant Hardcore Flower Hour. On KTRU 91.7 FM.

Friday, March 28, 4 p.m. Houston. Cactus Records in store by director Michael Dean, also Michael playing live music. 2930 S. Shepherd.

Friday March 28, 8 p.m. Houston, Texas. Fitzgerald's 2706 White Oak.

May 22, 7 p.m. Denver, Colorado. The Rock n' Roll Picture Show. The Soiled Dove 1949 Market St.

Television

Every week, it seems, on Channel 29 Cable Access in San Francisco.

Akaku, Hawaii Community Television Air Dates: Sunday, June, 23rd 10p.m. Monday, June 24th 9pm, Sat, June 29th, 10p.m., July 5, Midnight, July 9, 10p.m.

Drexel Public TV dutv@drexel.edu http://www.dutv.org/ Philadelphia area Sept 3 and Oct 8.

9 p.m. and 1 a.m., Channel 54.

Los Angeles on Adelphi Cable Channel 6, Friday, July 12 at 8 p.m.

Los Angeles, M Factor Cable Show (cool interview with Michael Dean done by Sugar Pie Jones).

Part 1 of the interview and film will first air in the LAX area, Westchester, Playa Del Rey, Ladera Heights, Windsor Hills, View Park, and portions of Lennox and Hawthorne. It airs on AT&T Broadband Channel 43 Saturday August 10 at 11:30 p.m.

It aired 8/5/02 at 1:30 a.m. on Channel 57 Manhattan and 8/12/02 1:30 a.m. Channel 57 Manhattan on Team Spider TV.

Part one on Adelphia Cable Ch 77 on Tues Aug. 27th at 11:30 p.m.

Part two on Adelphia Cable Ch 77 on Tues Sept. 3rd at 11:30 p.m.

Adelphia covers Santa Monica, Brentwood, Century City, Bel Air, Boyle Heights, Westwood, West Hills, Eagle Rock, Los Feliz, Silver Lake, Pacific palisades, Highland Park, Hancock Park, Hidden Hills, Glassell Park, West Los Angeles, El Sereno. Also covers parts of the valley up to the Ventura Freeway in Woodland Hills, Sherman Oaks, Van Nuys, Studio City, Encino, and Tarzana. In Beverly Hills, it will air on Channel 37. In Marina Del Rey and West Hollywood on Channel 3.

Tuesday, Oct 1 at 11:00 p.m. on Adelphia Cable Channel 77 (Santa Monica - Eagle Rock) and AT&T Broadband Channel 43 in the LAX (airport) area.

Go Kustom TV- Seattle Channel 29/77. December 12 and 19, 2002 at 10 p.m.

T.V. in Seattle: January 27, 2003 at 10 p.m. on Channel 29/77 on GoKustom TV.

Appendix C

What's on the CD-ROM

I Left My Pants in San Diego

A movie shot on Mini-DV and edited on a computer, illustrating exactly how to shoot a movie on Mini-DV and edit it on a computer. It's me with my friends demonstrating shooting, lighting, sound, editing, examples of film look and filters, promotion, etc. Shot on a trip down to San Diego to show my film at the university.[1]

—Trailer from one of the author's films: *D.I.Y. or Die: How to Survive As An Independent Artist*

Both of these MPEG-format (playable on Mac or PC) movies are included to show what can be done with the information provided in the book.

D.I.Y or DIE was edited on a G4 with Final Cut Pro. *I Left My Pants* and the *D.I.Y.* trailer were edited on a very fast $850 PC in CineStream and compressed using Cleaner 5. (See Figures C.1 and C.2.)

Software Demos

Script Writing Utilities

Final Draft

Final Draft AV

Video Editing and Compositing

Vegas video

Premiere

DigiEffects Plug-ins w/ CopBlur and CineLook and more

---

1. *As I said, there exists a ten-minute version of it, but it cut out a lot of the "how-to" stuff as well as lot of the funny stuff. I left the long version here. Since it's reference material to be viewed in the comfort of the home rather than something to be projected to an audience, you aren't really held captive by it. You can stop and start it as you please. I could have offered a snappier, shorter edit of it, but it would be at the expense of information.*

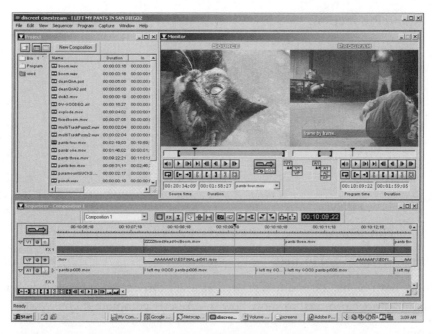

Figure C.1 *Working on* I Left My Pants *in CineStream.*

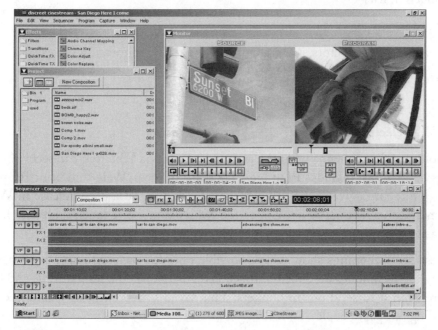

Figure C.2 *More of* I Left My Pants *editing in CineStream.*

Sound Production

Acid

Sound Forge

Sound Forge Noise-Reduction Plug-In

Encoding

TMPGEnc

Cleaner

DVD Player

CinePlayer

—Forms in MS Word format.

Includes both blank for end use, as well as a version of each one already filled in from the author's projects, to show how to properly complete them:

Proposals

Production lists

Script formats

Release forms for: actors, cameramen, music license, editors, interviewees

Letters requesting various services and/or funding

Budgets (in Excel format, with formulas embedded)

—EPK (electronic press kit)

A folder of files showing what the author sent out (via Web links) to secure bookings of his films. Includes PDF high-rez scans of press, Web- and print-rez photos of director as well as stills from the film, a bio and a press release in Word format. It was sent out as one zipped file (which didn't save much space, but made it easier to send). It is shown unzipped here.

These press clippings show what's possible on one's own without a press agent, using the techniques described in this book. Also shows the resultant file and how I prepared it to send out to bookers. This saved time and money compared to sending out paper copies.

I only sent this out to people who were already interested, not to people I was contacting for the first time. Three megs is a big file to send out to people who aren't expecting something. It would probably make them mad.

MouseCount

A small P.C. utility that I designed and a friend programmed for counting and displaying mouse clicks. Counts clicks by session, day, week, month, year, and total. See just how insane you are about computers. I also use it for promo…it has a little ad and link for my movie. Feel free to e-mail it to others or post on your Web site. (I also do custom versions for a fee.)

—**Some noises you can use in your films**

—**Some songs I wrote and sing that you can use in your films**

—**Printable diploma for completing *$30 Film School***

—**Printable ID card for attending *$30 Film School***

These images (Figures C.3 and C.4) are two of about ten quickly and sloppily scanned four-up color prints I posted low-rez in an unlinked folder on my Web site for a few folks to see (the models, the photographer, and a few friends whose opinions I trust). I was trying to decide which single photo to use, and wanted feedback.

Mike Kelley saw the first batch and instantly envisioned the cover, pretty much as it is (sort of an homage to Warhol), and told me over the phone to make it. I did. This is a good example of synchronistic collaboration over the Internet. I do things like that with people all the time.

It's kind of a spoof on film school catalog covers and bus stop ads (that I'd seen everywhere in San Francisco and New York City). Bink said something like, "Discerning, proud young videographer with the most professional gear propped on her shoulder…obviously employed and knowledgeable…with that little mischievous smirk and a glint in her eye…head up with confidence…."

That's the first three frames. The last one is intentionally goofy to block that stream of crap.

When I made the final image, I loved it. It was so that good I couldn't stop looking at it. And it was an equal organic effort between Jen, Lydia, Mike, and myself, without us having to be in the same room. (And Mike never even met Lydia or Jen.)

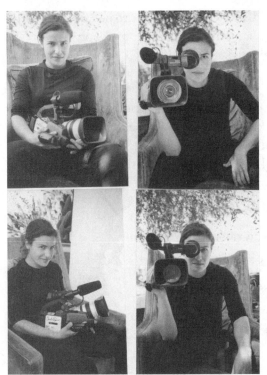

Figure C.3 *Photos of my mellow cool pal, Jennifer Berkowitz by Lydia Lunch. (I was just off-camera to Jen's left, using a piece of typing paper as a bounce card.)*

Figure C.4 *Photos of Jennifer Berkowitz, Adra Andrews, Aaron Jacobs, and Michael Dean by Lydia Lunch*

The publisher came up with different art that they felt was stronger, so this ended up not being the on the jacket, but I like my design. I did include it here because I don't like wasting art, and included it to describe the process, and the fact that not everything ends up getting used as originally envisioned.

NOW GO WRITE YOUR OWN BOOK!

Index

License Agreement/Notice of Limited Warranty